Come Up Higher

RANDALL J. BREWER

COME UP HIGHER

CONTENTS

INTRODUCTION

There is a divine invitation echoing throughout Scripture - an invitation not merely to believe, but to ascend; not merely to survive, but to thrive; not merely to know about God, but to walk closely with Him. It is the call to come up higher. From the opening pages of Genesis to the final vision in Revelation, God reveals His heart for relationship. He does not call His people to distant obedience but to intimate fellowship. He does not form humanity for mediocrity or failure but for purpose, fruitfulness, dominion, and success.

When God created man in His own image, He breathed into him not only life, but the ability to reflect heaven on earth, to partner with God, and to live in alignment with divine design. Yet for many believers, life feels far beneath what scripture promises. Instead of abundance, they experience limitation. Instead of victory, they endure cycles of frustration. Instead of intimacy with God, they settle for information about Him. The tragedy is not that God withholds abundance, but that many never rise to the place where abundance flows. This book is written to awaken hearts to that higher place.

When Jesus spoke of life "more abundantly" in John 10:10, He was revealing the nature of life that flows from union with God. Abundant life is not defined by possessions alone, nor is it limited to eternal life after death. It is the overflow of heaven's life into the present, expressed through peace, wisdom, authority, purpose, fruitfulness, and divine success. Throughout scripture, God repeatedly calls His people upward. He calls us from fear to faith, from bondage to freedom, from survival to stewardship, from distance to intimacy.

To come up higher is to respond to God's invitation to see as He sees, to live as He designed, and to walk in step with His Spirit. It is not an escape from the world, but an elevation above its limitations. At the heart of abundant living is relationship, not performance. The Triune God - the Father, the Son, and the Holy Spirit - invites believers into a shared life with Him. Christianity is not a religion of rules but a relationship of union. The Father's love establishes our identity, the Son's finished work secures our redemption, and the Holy Spirit empowers our daily walk.

When relationship is neglected, success becomes striving. When intimacy is restored, success becomes the natural fruit of alignment. Many attempt to live victorious lives without cultivating closeness with God. They pursue principles without presence, outcomes without obedience, and blessings without communion. But abundance flows from abiding, not effort. Jesus Himself declared that fruitfulness is impossible apart from remaining in Him. To come up higher is to return to that place of abiding - to dwell where heaven and earth meet in the life of the believer.

God did not create humanity with failure in mind. From the beginning, His design was clear: "Be fruitful and multiply, fill the earth and subdue it." These are not commands of pressure, but declarations of capacity. God never assigns responsibility without providing ability. Success, as defined by scripture, is not arrogance or self-exaltation. It is the ability to fulfill God's purpose in every sphere of life. It is living in harmony with God's will, bearing fruit that glorifies Him, and stewarding what He has entrusted to us.

True success flows from knowing who we are in Christ, walking in step with the Spirit, and living under God's authority rather than human limitation. When believers understand that they were created to succeed with God, not apart from Him, life takes on new clarity. Obstacles become opportunities for growth. Challenges become invitations to trust. Seasons of pressure become pathways to promotion. No one ascends alone. The Holy Spirit is the divine guide who leads believers upward into truth, into power, and into maturity. He reveals the heart of the Father, applies the finished work of the Son, and empowers believers to live beyond natural limitations.

To come up higher requires sensitivity to His voice, obedience to His leading, and dependence on His strength. The Spirit does not merely comfort; He transforms. He does not merely inform; He empowers. Life in the Spirit is the gateway to sustained abundance. This book is not a self-help manual, nor is it a formula for instant success. It is an invitation to intimacy, alignment, and elevation. It calls believers to leave behind small thinking, limited expectations, and shallow faith, and to step into a deeper walk with the Triune God.

To come up higher is to embrace the life God intended from the beginning - a life marked by purpose, peace, power, and fruitfulness. It is to live not beneath circumstances, but above them; not driven by fear but anchored in faith; not striving for worth, but secure in identity. The call still stands. God is inviting His people upward into deeper relationship, greater clarity, and fuller expression of the abundant life found in Him. This book exists to help you hear that call, respond in faith, and step into the success for which you were created.

Come up higher.

| 1 |

"PRECIOUS IN HIS SIGHT"

Most people wake up each morning not knowing how valuable they are to the Heavenly Father. They lay there thinking what a horrible sinner they are and that they'll never be good enough to make it into heaven. There is some truth in these thoughts for Ps. 49:7,8 (NIV) says, "No one can redeem the life of another or give to God a ransom for them. The ransom for a life is costly, no payment is ever enough." This verse is saying that there is not enough money in all the world to buy the soul of one person, to pay for it and redeem it. There is, however, one thing and one thing only in all the universe valuable enough to redeem the souls of men. 1 Peter 1:18,19 (NCV) tells you what that one thing is, "You know that in the past you were living in a worthless way, a way passed down from the people who lived before you. But you were saved from that useless life. You were bought, not with something that ruins like gold or silver, but with the precious blood of Christ, who was like a pure and perfect lamb."

The blood of Jesus is extremely valuable; it is precious and has value that exceeds known price. The life of Jesus was in His blood and it was completely pure and perfect in every way. He was like a spotless lamb without blemish and imperfection and the Father accepted His blood as payment for you. You've been "bought with a price" (1 Cor. 6:20) and the value of something is determined by the price somebody is willing to pay for it. The enormity of the price Jesus paid for you should tell you just how valuable you truly are. You can't shout and celebrate how precious His blood is without realizing how important and valuable what He bought with it is. God loves you and He wants you so much that He went to great lengths to get you. He was willing to pay a price that had never been paid before, and this is why you need to come up higher in what you think about yourself. You have eternal value and are precious in His sight.

Never place your value on how successful your career is or who you're married to. These things don't last forever and if you base your value and sense of identity on anything you can lose then it's in the wrong thing. God thinks you're valuable, so much so that He condemns people who say you're not. Jesus said in Matt. 5:22 (NLT), "If you call someone an idiot, you are in danger of being brought before the court. And if you curse someone, you are in danger of the fires of hell." The NASB says, "Whoever says to his brother, 'You good for nothing,' shall be guilty before the supreme court; and whoever says, 'You fool,' shall be guilty enough to go into the fiery hell." The body of Christ has yet to grasp how serious this verse actually is. Anybody who uses degrading words to cut down another person is being used by the enemy to take away their sense of value, worth, and identity which can lead to their destruction if they believe what's being said.

It affects every aspect of their life, and many have even committed suicide because their sense of self-worth was destroyed by the words of another. Name calling and back biting is personally offensive to God because He thinks all people are valuable enough to send His Son to shed His blood and die for. If God says you're valuable, then what right does somebody have to say you're not? You are valuable to God and He even calls you the apple of His eye (Ps. 17:8). You are very precious to Him, greatly cherished and highly treasured, so don't let anybody tell you different. In fact, you're so special that Jesus said "the very hairs of your head are all numbered" (Matt. 10:30). He knew you before you were even born and, when sin entered the world, He was willing to pay the ultimate price to snatch you from the hands of the enemy. Jesus died for you so when somebody says you're worthless then raise your head up high and say you're worth dying for.

If you are born again then you are in Him and He is in you. Col. 3:3 says, "For you died, and your life is hidden with Christ in God." This means that you are just as valuable as He is. Paul said in 1 Cor. 15:10, "But by the grace of God I am what I am." He then said in Gal. 2:20, "I have been crucified with Christ; it is no longer I who live, but Christ lives in me; and the life which I now live in the flesh I live by faith in the Son of God, who loved me and gave Himself for me." Jesus said in Matt. 10:29, "Are not two sparrows sold for a copper coin? And not one of them falls to the ground apart from your Father's will." Jesus is saying that as cheap as these birds are, God notices them and He values them. He then said in vs. 31, "Do not fear therefore; you are of more value than many sparrows." God notices the sparrows and, even greater than the sparrow, He is intimately aware of you. You are God's highest priority, you are greatly valued by Him, so never again do you have to walk in fear.

He said in Luke 12:6, "Are not five sparrows sold for two copper coins? And not one of them is forgotten before God." God doesn't forget these cheap birds. The Amplified Bible says, "Are not five sparrows sold for pennies? And yet not one of them is forgotten or uncared for in the presence of God." If God cares for the sparrow, you can walk in confidence that He will never forget to care for you. Never are you to question God's love for you. You are loved by Him, and you are accepted by Him, not because of anything you've done but because of what Jesus did for you. The apostle John had a revelation of this love and in John 20:2 he called himself the "disciple whom Jesus loved." This also is who you are. You are the one greatly loved and accepted by God. Remember that when the accuser of the brethren shows up at your door, when people say you're worthless and no good. God loves you greatly, it is unconditional, and His favor is on you. Knowing this is the foundation on which you build your life.

You don't fear when bad things happen because you know God loves you. A trial loses its power to harm you when you live every day knowing that you are accepted in the Beloved (Eph. 1:6). God cares for the sparrow, but He cares for you more. Matt. 6:26 says, "Look at the birds of the air, for they neither sow nor reap nor gather into barns; yet your heavenly Father feeds them. Are you not of more value than they?" People only fear and worry when they don't believe they're valued by God and loved by Him. The next time fear tries to come on you do what Jesus told you to do. Go outside and look at all the birds flying around in the air. Then tell yourself that if God cares for them, He will much more care for you also. Don't allow yourself to be burdened down with the challenges of life. You can have total confidence when hard times come because God is totally committed to your success. Nothing can take away God's unfailing love for you.

You are God's top priority and, when He becomes yours, no good thing will He withhold from you. Matt. 6:33 says, "But seek first the kingdom of God and His righteousness, and all these things shall be added to you." When God is first then everything else falls in line. Something great happens when God becomes your top priority. How much do you value God in your life? Your answer is based on what your priorities are. Do you walk with God daily or only on Sunday? Do you talk with Him all the time or only when you need something? How much of your life have you submitted to Him? The answer to these questions are important because whatever you value is what you will invest in. You can tell what's in a person's heart based on their willingness to make an investment in what they say is valuable to them. God loves you and you are very valuable to Him. Consider the investment He made in your life and on your behalf. His top priority is blessing you exceedingly, abundantly above all you could ask or think (Eph. 3:20).

All He asks is that you value Him as much as He values you. Your worth to God is so great that He thinks about you all the time. Ps. 139:17,18 says, "How precious also are Your thoughts to me, O God! How great is the sum of them! If I should count them, they would be more in number than the sand; When I awake, I am still with you." God thinks about you so much that before you were born He made a plan for your life. Vs. 16 (NLT) says, "You saw me before I was born. Every day of my life was recorded in Your book. Every moment was laid out before a single day passed." God's thoughts about you out-number the sand on the seashore and this is why you should never contemplate suicide or waste your life on sex, alcohol, or drugs. God has a plan for your life and this gives you a reason to live. God said in Is. 49:15,16 (NLT), "Can a mother forget her nursing child? Can she feel no love for the child she has borne? But even if that were possible, I would not forget you! See, I have written your name on the palms of My hands."

Not a second goes by that God is not thinking about you. He thinks good thoughts about you and this is why His thoughts need to become your thoughts. You need to see yourself the same way God sees you, to see why He considers you precious and valuable. When you see in yourself what God sees, you will be set free from insecurity and con-demnation, from fear and doubt. You were made in God's image and this is how you need to see yourself. In Him you have unfading beauty and your "inner man is being renewed day by day" (2 Cor. 4:16). It matters not what you look like on the outside but rather what you look like on the inside. This will cause you not to be taken aback when you find a new wrinkle the next time you look in the mirror. 1 Peter 3:3,4 (CEV) says, "Don't depend on things like fancy hairdos or gold jewelry or expensive clothes to make you look beautiful. Be beautiful in your heart by being gentle and quiet. This kind of beauty will last, and God considers it very special."

The BBE says "the ever-shining ornament of a gentle and quiet spirit, which is of great price in the eyes of God." Being rebellious is being ugly and so is being stubborn with an unwillingness to obey God. Being proud and arrogant is also ugly, so much so that it will change the countenance of your face. Don't be that way but instead be like Jesus. He is beautiful beyond description and He said in Matt. 11:29, "Take My yoke upon you and learn from Me, for I am gentle and lowly in heart, and you will find rest for your souls." Humility means to be honest before God and He says that is beautiful. What He finds beautiful is an expression of who He is and who He always will be. Rom. 11:29 says, "For the gifts and the calling of God are irrevocable." When your identity is in what God gave you and the person He made you to be, then your sense of who you are is secure for all eternity.

Knowing who you are in Christ is what makes you feel valuable yet many people are miserable and living worthless lives. Why is this happening? Maybe it's because they're doing miserable and worthless things. How you feel is in accordance with who you identify with and what you're doing with your life. God did not put you here so you could work all your life, retire, and then go fish and play golf all day. These things are okay in and of themselves but they'll never bring value to your life. God planned for His people to have a useful life, a life with meaning and purpose. If you're doing good and meaningful things because of your identity with Christ then you'll feel good about yourself. Those who only focus on themselves and do useless things will be miserable and tormented all the days of their life. Jesus died to save you from living a useless life. He died so you could identify with Him. You must see yourself as He sees you.

When your heart is engaged with His heart, your view of life and the purpose for which you were born will take you to new heights. God's perception and appraisal of you is what should fill your thoughts day and night. You are valuable to Him and are precious in His sight. You are accepted in the Beloved and this makes you His beloved child. You have the full and complete attention of the Heavenly Father. The joy and intention of His heart is to lavish upon you everything your heart desires. This is why He made you, to receive all that He has to give. He made you so He could give Himself to you. His love for you is not based on your performance but that you identify with His Son. When He sees you, He sees Jesus and when He sees Jesus, He sees you. All the love He has for Jesus, He has for you. He has set aside a place for you in Jesus for you to enjoy and know His fullest and complete affection. In Christ He gives you all the things you lack in yourself.

Because you are His beloved child, you inherit all that Jesus is and all that He can do. This means you will never live a worthless life. You have been sanctified and are fit for the Master's use (2 Tim. 2:21) so run into the arms of your Lord for He is the Father you've been look-ing for all your life. Never place your identity in things that can be here today and gone tomorrow. Your identity should not be in your place of employment or where you're going to school or in the per-son you're married to. Neither should it be in how pretty you think you are or how much money you have in the bank. Jesus said in Luke 12:15, "Take heed and beware of covetousness, for one's life does not consist in the abundance of the things he possesses." The Message Bible says, "Life is not defined by what you have, even when you have a lot." God is not against people being rich and having nice things. He is against people placing their identity in these things for their iden-tity should be in Christ and Him alone.

He is against people loving money more than they love Him and other people. God wants His priorities to be your priorities. So many people who are rich and famous go to bed insecure not knowing who they are. They spend their whole life searching for the answer to the ques-tion "Who am I?" and some have even left their family so they can go "find" themselves. How pitiful is that? The only way children of God can find themselves is to find out who Jesus is. If you are a born again believer then you are in Him and He is in you. You are who He says you are. In Christ you are His child and His workmanship. You are His friend and a co-laborer with Him. You're the head and not the tail, above and not beneath. You are His ambassador, His chosen one, His beloved. You've been redeemed by His blood and set free from sin. You were chosen before the foundation of the world and been predestined to be like Jesus. You've been given a sound mind and have been justified freely by His grace.

You've been given great and precious promises and all things pertaining to life and godliness. You've been given the ministry of reconciliation and authority over the enemy. In Christ you are not condemned and have been quickened by His mighty power. You are the light in a dark world, a city on a hill, the salt of the earth. You are secure in Christ, and your foundation is set on a rock. In Christ you have access to the Father, a home in heaven, an anchor to your soul. The Bible also says that in Christ you've been born again, healed by His stripes, and sheltered by His wings. You have faith like a mustard seed and a hope that is sure and steadfast. You can quench all the fiery darts of the enemy and tread on him like a serpent. In Christ you can declare liberty to the captives and put a thousand demons to flight. You cannot perish or be lost, you cannot be moved, and never can you be taken out of your Father's hand. This is who you are in Christ.

How you identify yourself determines how you will approach life. If your identity is in your own accomplishments, then you'll always need to do more and achieve more to find some false sense of value. Also, if you place your worth in what other people think about you then you'll spend all your life trying to please them and not your Heavenly Father. But if you'll listen to who God says you are, if you'll embrace His identity of you in your heart, you will find the freedom to live out all His plans for your life. When you see yourself the way God sees you, when your identity is in Christ and Him alone, you will have confidence because you trust the Heavenly Father who is the only one qualified to answer the question, "Who am I?" Not knowing who you are in Christ will make you insecure, fearful, and unstable. You'll spend your entire life going place to place trying to find something solid to hold onto.

But when the truth of how precious you are in the eyes of God penetrate into your innermost being, you will be established on a solid rock that cannot be moved. You'll wake up in the morning knowing you're somebody special and are of great worth to the Heavenly Father. This alone gives your life meaning and purpose for it allows you to have a close, personal relationship with Him. 1 Peter 2:9 says, "But you are a chosen generation, a royal priesthood, a holy nation, His own special people, that you may proclaim the praises of Him who called you out of darkness into His marvelous light." This makes life worth living. Ps. 91:9,10 says, "Because you have made the Lord, who is my refuge, even the Most High, your habitation, no evil shall befall you, nor shall any plague come near your dwelling." In eternity past Jesus delighted in the knowledge that one day you would grow up to become His habitation, that He would come and dwell in your heart and abide with you forever.

He said in John 15:15, "I have called you friends, for all things that I have heard of My Father I have made known to you." He anticipated the time when He would show you things that nobody else saw or heard, things that matter to Him deep down in His heart. Prov. 3:32 says, "His secret counsel is with the upright." The Lord offers His friendship to the godly and takes the upright into His confidence. He anticipated the love relationship with you so intimately that He rejoiced knowing you would take delight in hearing what He wants to tell you. You know who you are in Christ and this makes you want to walk before Him with a pure heart and have sweet fellowship with Him every moment of every day. Jer. 29:13 says, "And you will seek Me and find Me, when you search for Me with all your heart." God must be sought after to be found for He will not abide in the hearts of those who ignore and neglect Him. He anticipates coming to His habitation but first He must be invited in.

He anticipated this long ago, and this was His delight before the world was created. He looked forward to spending personal time with His children, but many would rather play golf instead. They have time for shopping and gardening and everything else, yet they have no time for Him. These people have fallen short of all the great things God had planned for their life. He wanted them to be so in love with Him that they couldn't endure a day without being in His presence. He wanted to take away their weaknesses, fears, and every sense of inadequacy and rejection. He wanted to teach them how to know and hear His voice. All the anticipation He had, all the great plans and desires He had for their lives, have all been aborted because they made gods out of other things. 2 Chron. 15:2 says, "The Lord is with you while you are with Him. If you seek Him, He will be found by you; but if you forsake Him, He will forsake you."

Right now, set your heart to seek God with all your heart, all your soul, and all your strength. Seek Him with all that is within you. Examine your heart right now and remove all those things that stand before you and God. Seek Him daily and spend quality time with Him. Pray that He would give you a fresh revelation of who He is and how precious you are in His sight. To Him you are a rare treasure that He bought at a price so high it's never been duplicated before or since. You are one of a kind and in all eternity there will never be another you. You are God's own personal creation and He made you in His own image and likeness. He then sent Jesus to die for you. Since Jesus had no earthly father, the blood He shed for you had in it the very life of God Himself. This was the price He paid for you. This is what makes you so precious indeed.

1 Peter 2:10 (CEV) says, "Once you were nobody. Now you are God's people. At one time no one had pity on you. Now God has treated you with kindness." The Message Bible says God took you "from nothing

to something, from rejected to accepted." Through the blood of Jesus, the Father has turned you from a nobody into a somebody, from a zero to a hero. The worst thing you could do is belittle yourself and think you're no good. Never hang your head in shame but meditate on Ps. 3:3 that says, "But You, O Lord, are a shield for me, my glory and the One who lifts up my head." You're worth dying for and this shows how valuable you truly are. Jesus was willing to pay the ultimate price for you because of His desire to have you as His own. You don't determine your own worth, that is determined by the person willing to pay the highest price to get you. Silver and gold couldn't buy you and this makes you more valuable than all the money in the world.

God paid for you with the blood of His Son and in His eyes you are more precious than that. Ps. 49:8,9 (TLB) says, "For a soul is far too precious to be ransomed by mere earthly wealth. There is not enough of it in all the earth to buy eternal life for just one soul, to keep it out of hell." Most of the world does not believe this and there are some people who would kill you for the few coins you have in your pocket. They do not have the same value system as God for to Him people are precious. Their souls are of such high value that there is no earthly wealth to equal it. When you believe that about yourself, your thoughts of who you are in Christ will come up higher than they were before. God's favor and His good will toward you should bring abundant comfort to your soul. He said in Is. 43:1, "Fear not, for I have redeemed you; I have called you by your name; You are mine."

You've been redeemed with the blood of Jesus and God has set you apart for Himself. You are precious in God's sight, so much so that Zeph. 3:17 says, "He will rejoice over you with gladness, He will quiet you in His love, He will rejoice over you with singing." Right now, at this very moment, God is in heaven singing a song of joy because you are His. In Hebrew this phrase can be translated literally as "He rejoices over you with a shout of joy." God is a God who is full of emotion and just as a loving parent cradles a child and sings over it with love, so does your Heavenly Father sing over you. You are precious in His sight and He loves you so much. If you ever go through a hard time, He will dry your tears, comfort your heart, and hold you close to His bosom. He will then begin to sing to you and give you the assurance that everything will work out for your good. He wants you to know that He is on your side and there is nothing that can pull you out of His loving arms.

A rush of exuberant gladness will overtake you when you realize that God will never leave you or forsake you. In moments of uncertainty or fear, His presence remains constant, steady, and unshakable. This assurance fills the heart with peace, courage, and an unbreakable hope for every step ahead. The words God is singing to you rise like a melody of hope, each note alive with purpose and love. They dance with joy across your heart, reminding you that heaven celebrates your steps of faith. In every gentle refrain, He is declaring delight over you and calling you forward with gladness. You are basking in peace and comfort, wrapped in a calm that settles every thought and feeling. There is nothing to worry about, nothing to chase, and nothing pulling at your heart. In this moment, your soul rests fully, secure and content, with not a care in the world. You are in the arms of your Heavenly Father, and this is where you will always be.

| 2 |

"IF GOD BE FOR US"

It is sad that a lot of people don't know God loves them nor have they experienced that love. They see Him as a God of judgment, yet it was because of His great love for them that He sent Jesus to die on the cross. He is a God of love and it was His idea to save mankind from sin and destruction. Jesus came to reveal to the world the Father's love. He is "Abba, Father" (Rom. 8:15) and this is the most intimate way you can address a father. If you don't see Him as "Daddy" then you won't draw near to Him as He'd like you to. You'll fear Him like they did in the Old testament and this will bring you into bondage. Jesus prayed in John 17:11, "Holy Father, keep through Your name those whom You have given Me, that they may be one as We are one." In Greek the word "keep" means 'protect' and Jesus is saying that the Father will protect you when He becomes your Daddy. In the four gospels there is no record of the Lord's disciples ever getting sick or having a need.

Jesus said in vs. 12, "While I was with them in the world, I kept them in Your name." Never forget what true love really is. 1 John 4:10 says, "In this is love, not that we loved God, but that He loved us and sent His Son to be the propitiation for our sins." True love is not defined by how much you love God but rather how much He loves you. Allow His grace to open your eyes to this vital truth. God loves you and He is for you and not against you. John then writes in vs. 19, "We love

Him because He first loved us." Your love for God gives you the assurance that God first loved you. The more you believe He loves you, the more you will love Him back. Stand amazed that He would invite you to partake of those salvation promises and become part of His holy family. Stand in awe that you are the disciple whom Jesus loved. Take your eyes off of your works and how much you love God and place them on how much He loves you. You are precious in His sight and nothing can take His great love away from you.

Never be afraid to boast of God's great love for you. At the last supper Peter boasted of how much he loved Jesus (Matt. 26:35) whereas John leaned on the bosom of Jesus and by doing so was boasting of the Lord's love for him. Scripture goes on to say that Peter denied Jesus three times but John was the only disciple who was at the cross when Jesus died. When you lean on Jesus and boast of His love for you instead of your love for Him, you will hear the heartbeat of God. He will tell you things that He tells no one else. You will see things that nobody else can see. Never see yourself as just a face in a big crowd, see yourself as the Lord's beloved, the one whom He deeply loves. Ps. 34:8 says, "Oh, taste and see that the Lord is good; Blessed is the man who trusts in Him." Feed on His goodness, the very fact that His light is shining on you. Feel special because you are special. Hear your Daddy saying to you the same thing He said to Jesus at His baptism, "This is My beloved Son, in whom I am well pleased" (Matt. 3:17).

Immediately after the Lord's baptism He went into the wilderness where He was tempted by the devil three times. Twice the devil began his temptation by saying, "If you are the Son of God" (Matt. 4:3,6). Notice that the Father called Jesus "My beloved Son" but the devil called Him "the Son of God." Why didn't the devil say, "If you are God's beloved Son, command that these stones become bread"? The devil left out the word "beloved" because he knows temptation against a child of God cannot succeed if they realize they are God's beloved. God wraps His arms around those who are His beloved and the devil can't touch them. When you are God's beloved the opinions of other people don't matter. The reason people give away their virtue and morality is because they've forgotten how precious and beloved they are. They think God is angry at them for falling into sin but there is no verse in the New Testament that says God is mad at a believer. Jesus took upon Himself all of God's anger on the cross and because of that you can be sure that your Daddy will never be mad at you.

You will never know how much God loves you until you know how much He loves Jesus. The Father called Jesus His beloved Son, yet it was this same Son that He gave up for you. Open up your heart and receive God's love for you. When you do that, Paul says you will be "more than conquerors through Him who loved us" (Rom. 8:37). Say farewell to poverty and lack, sickness and disease, fear and doubt. Song of Solomon 6:3 says, "I am my beloved's, and my beloved is mine. He feeds his flock among the lilies." God takes care of His beloved, He delights in His beloved, and He spends time with His beloved. Declaring that you are God's beloved declares the greatness and strength of your faith, it's the glory and excellence of the very thing God has called you to do. Faith works through love (Gal. 5:6). It works through the revelation of God's love for you and this is what allows you to love others as you love yourself. 1 John 4:17 says, "As He is, so are we in this world." Jesus is the Father's beloved and so are you.

Your Daddy loves you and forever wants what's best for you. In fact, He was for you even when you were against Him. Rom. 5:8 (NLT) says, "But God showed His great love for us by sending Christ to die for us while we were still sinners." God has set His heart on you and He has mercies you never dreamed of. Day by day He is pouring His Spirit out on all flesh in hopes of drawing people to His bosom so they can live a life filled with meaning and purpose. He wants your life to be founded on truth and power and on the authority of the Word of God. Jesus said in Luke 10:19, "Behold, I give you the authority to trample on serpents and scorpions, and over all the power of the enemy, and nothing shall by any means hurt you." God is on your side and daily He is directing your steps. When difficulties come you can have confidence knowing that God is for you. You know that what the enemy meant for evil, God can turn around for your good. Why" Because no weapon formed against you will prosper.

God has a wonderful plan and purpose for your life. He is thinking about you all the time with "thoughts of peace and not of evil, to give you a future and a hope" (Jer. 29:11). Setbacks may come but God can use those trials to light a fire on the inside of you that can't be put out. Times of adversity will cause you to pray bold prayers and to openly declare that God's favor is on your life. With reckless abandon you will rise up and confess out loud Ps. 118:6, "The Lord is on my side; I will not fear. What can man do to me?" Don't get mad at people who do you wrong. Trust God and allow Him to help you show the devil he picked the wrong person to mess with. If the devil had known what he was doing when he crucified Jesus on the cross, he never would have done it (1 Cor. 2:8). He thought the crucifixion was his greatest victory but three days later it became his biggest defeat. When the devil attacks you he thinks he is doing some terrible thing that will finish you off. Little does he know that God has another plan entirely.

Trust God and never doubt His great love for you. He would never let something happen to you if He didn't know it would help lead you to your destiny. He never allows one door to close unless He is ready and willing to open another. Jesus died on the cross but His resurrection was only three days away. Ps. 30:5 says, "Weeping may endure for a night, but joy comes in the morning." The simple fact that weeping only endures for a night is a good reason to praise God. The Hebrew word for "endure" is 'loon' which means 'to lodge or stop over.' When you travel you will lodge in a hotel room but it's not your permanent home. So it is with your weeping. It lodges or stops for only a night.

The good news is that when the sun sets and darkness takes over the sky, it's only a few short hours before the sun starts to rise again. The sunshine erases the darkness from the sky and David uses this to show that weeping is only temporary. Because God is on your side, you can have the assurance that the trial you're now facing is not going to last very long.

A believer should never say, "Nobody ever did anything for me." Who are they trying to fool? Jesus took their infirmities and bore their sicknesses. He went to hell for them so they wouldn't have to and today He forever lives to make intercession for them. Whoever said a thing as foolish as that needs to get on their knees and apologize to the Lord. Their heavenly Daddy loves them and is forever ready to bless them with a good life. These people need to come up higher in how they view God's love for them and His plan for their future. Know with certainty that God is on your side and He is helping you more than you may know. He's already blessed you with every spiritual blessing in heavenly places because you've been united with Christ (Eph. 1:3). He has given you all things that pertain to life and godliness, everything you'll need to live a godly life (2 Peter 1:3). God knows the end from the beginning and has predetermined that you would be conformed into the image of His Son (Rom. 8:29).

He's with you every step of the way and nothing shall by any means hurt you. Because you are in your Daddy's arms you'll be able to run your race and finish your course. You'll run through a troop and leap over a wall. Nothing can stop you from fulfilling your destiny. Rom. 8:31 (NLT) says, "What shall we say about such wonderful things as these? If God is for us, who can ever be against us?" God is your never-failing, everlasting Daddy and He is actively engaged in your life. None of your enemies, whether visible or invisible, can stop you from enjoying the blessings that come from being a child of God. Vs. 32 says, "He who did not spare His own Son, but delivered Him up for us all, how shall He not with Him also freely give us all things?" Jesus is God's free gift to you and everything else you need or desire will be given to you in a similar manner. It is not by your own merit that these things are given but rather by the divine mercy of God, your Daddy and your friend.

Jesus is a well of abundance out of which pours all manner of blessing and provision. Everything is given to you when you make Jesus the Lord of your life. He is the heir of all things, and you possess all you need in Him. Since God is for you, for somebody to be successfully against you they'd have to be bigger than Him. Take comfort that God is your protective Daddy and there is nobody bigger than Him. Jesus said in John 10:27-30 (NLT), "My sheep listen to My voice; I know them, and they follow Me. I give them eternal life, and they will never perish. No one can snatch them away from Me, for My Father has given them to Me, and He is more powerful than anyone else. No one can snatch them from the Father's hand. The Father and I are one." If you stay close to God nothing can be successfully against you. The danger comes if you walk away from Him. People who rebel against God because they'd rather go off and do their own thing open themselves up to the devil who roams about like a roaring lion seeking whom he can devour.

Don't pull away from God but draw near to Him. Be like David who said in Ps. 63:8, "My soul follows close behind You; Your right hand upholds me." In your Daddy's arms is the safest place in all the universe. God is for you and to live a good life you've got to let God be God. Settle in your mind right now that there will be questions in life that won't get answered, things that can never be explained. There will be things you can never change and things you cannot control. To be successful you've got to know what your limitations are. If you believe you are more than you are, the Bible says you are not wise. Gal. 6:3 says, "For if anyone thinks himself to be something, when he is nothing, he deceives himself." Knowing your limitations will keep you peaceful because you won't struggle trying to do something you can't do. Settle in your mind that there are some things that only God can do. People who try to do such things are trying to be like God in a wrong way. They're trying to be God instead of letting God be God.

There are things that only God knows and understands so stop trying to change those things you can't control. Let God be God and go to bed and have a peaceful sleep. You're in good hands and you know your Daddy will never let you down. Ps. 54:4,5 says, "Behold, God is my helper; The Lord is with those who uphold my life. He will repay my enemies for their evil. Cut them off in Your truth." People who walk in fear are not fully persuaded that God is on their side. On the other hand, the absence of fear shows the presence of faith, a faith that believes God is real and He is here to help in whatever situation you may find yourself in. Ps. 118:7 (NLT) says, "Yes, the Lord is for me; He will help me. I will look in triumph at those who hate me." Every answer to your prayers is evidence that God is on your side and this is why you need not fear what man can do to you. Paul asked, "If God be for us, who can be against us?"

Be aware of the enemy but never fear him. Neither should you give him the opportunity to harm you by pulling away from your close relationship with the Lord. Many in the world are living as if there is no God and no devil, no heaven and no hell. These people are deceived, not knowing that the whole design of the devil is to destroy their life and bring about their eternal ruin. The gold mines of all spiritual comfort and protection are God's alone and when you cast your cares on Him all that you need will be provided. Your responsibility is to be sober and vigilant (1 Peter 5:8), to be watchful and diligent to prevent the devil's schemes from coming to pass. Resist the devil and be steadfast in your faith (vs. 9). You cannot fight the good fight of faith on sand that is wet and soft. There is no standing without firm ground to tread upon and it is only faith that provides this solid foundation for you. Use your faith to believe that God is on your side and be willing to do whatever He tells you to do.

Cooperate with Him so He can bless you and keep you protected at all times. Those who rebel are the ones who get destroyed, the ones who say God never does anything for them. They have no one to blame but themselves for it's the people who love God who will do what He says and it's this obedience that gives Him access to their life. It is foolish to blame God when calamity comes and wreaks havoc in your life. Instead of blaming God, go look in the mirror and ask yourself if you've been doing what God told you to do. It's the knowing that God is on your side that sets you free from dread and fear which, by the way, is a foretaste of hell itself. 1 John 4:8 says, "There is no fear in love; but perfect love casts out fear, because fear involves torment." The word "torment" is the same word used in Rev. 20:10 to describe hell, and this is what happens to those who don't believe God is for them and not against them. It is a life of freedom to know and believe that God will take care of you all the days of your life.

God said in Ex. 23:22, "But if you indeed obey His voice and do all that I speak, then I will be an enemy to your enemies and an adversary to your adversaries." God is faithful to take care of His own children and, if you'll do what He tells you to do, you can relax when hard times come. When you trust God, you will never fear or worry. These things irritate Him and Jesus often reprimanded His disciples when they were this way (Matt. 8:26). Faith is what pleases God and you must trust God and use your faith when things aren't going in your life as they should. In the eyes of God, there is no excuse for not trusting Him. Faith is a choice you make, a choice that must be made every day of your life. Ps. 56:9 says, "When I cry out to You, then my enemies will turn back; This I know, because God is for me." Faith has confidence and never wavers for it knows that God is on your side.

Faith begins where the will of God is known so when you have full assurance that God is for you, the enemy has no choice but to back off and cease from his efforts to pull you down. If God be for you, who can successfully be against you? The answer is nobody. Ps. 91:15 says,

"He shall call upon Me, and I will answer him; I will be with him in trouble; I will deliver him and honor him." God has ordained you to use your faith as a sword to cut off the powers of darkness from your life. When you do that, Ps. 91:3 says, "Surely He shall deliver you from the snare of the fowler, and from the perilous pestilence." Vs. 7, "A thousand may fall at your side, and ten thousand at your right hand; But it shall not come near you." If God be for you, who cares who is against you? God said in Josh. 1:5, "No man shall be able to stand before you all the days of your life; as I was with Moses, so I will be with you. I will not leave you nor forsake you."

Encourage yourself with the promise and presence of God, knowing that He is all-sufficient and well able to take good care of you. He is watching over you and He is working in your life. Rom. 8:28 says, "And we know that all things work together for good to those who love God, to those who are called according to His purpose." With glorious assurance you can know that in a variety of unexpected ways and unthought of means God can turn your situation around in a moment of time. The Message Bible says, "That's why we can be so sure that every detail in our lives of love for God is worked into something good." This is a promise that the sinners of the world know nothing about. Paul says "we know" this promise, referring to those who are saved and born again. This is a family secret that gives all believers an advantage over the rest of the sinful world. Those who are beloved of God need not be overwhelmed with the sorrows of this present age.

More than others, they can find rest in their souls when the rest of the world is in a chaotic uproar. Is. 26:3 says, "You will keep him in perfect peace, whose mind is stayed on You, because he trusts in You." Trust in the Lord for that peace which passes all understanding. Trust that you will receive from Him the peace and strength that will cause you to come up higher to a level of blessedness that will last forever. Acknowledge Him in all your ways and rely on Him in all your trials. Jesus said in John 14:1, "Let not your heart be troubled; you believe in God, believe also in Me." Here is the remedy for a troubled mind. Comfort is gained when you believe that God is on your side. If an unexpected crisis were to arise in your life you would quickly go to the Lord for help and here is what He would say to you, "I am on your side. Let not your heart be troubled." The question is, how would you respond to that?

There is power in the Word of God and the very fact that Jesus told you to "let not your heart be troubled" means you are well able to do it. The Lord knows what you can and cannot do and He would never tell you to do something if He knew you couldn't do it. In other words, His Word empowers you to let not your heart be troubled. Him telling you to do it is what gives you the power to do it. You can do this if you will come up higher and believe you can. Jesus then said in John 14:27, "Peace I leave with you, My peace I give to you. Let not your heart be troubled, neither let it be afraid." This is the same peace Jesus walked in when He was on the earth. This peace cannot be found in any religion or psychology class or illegal drug. It can only be found in Jesus. It's His own personal peace and He is giving it to you. Therefore, if your heart is troubled, regardless of the cause, it's because you let it get that way. Choose instead to believe that you can go through life without a troubled heart. After all, Jesus said you could.

Ps. 23:4 says, "Yea, though I walk through the valley of the shadow of death, I will fear no evil; For You are with me; Your rod and Your staff, they comfort me." As an act of his will, David made the choice to let not his heart be troubled and to fear no evil. He did this because he knew God was on his side. Do not allow the devil to convince you that you are a helpless victim to your circumstances, thoughts, and feelings. You are in the world but are not of the world. You once were lost but now am found. You are in Jesus and He is in you. This gives you the power and ability to not be troubled and to refuse to fear even when hard times come your way. Your confidence is high because you're not alone in the valley. The Lord is with you every step of the way. Your life is affected by what you believe, and this is why you must always believe that God is on your side. Don't be afraid when you get word that your place of employment is closing down or when the calendar tells you it's the flu season. Believe that God is for you and nothing can be against you.

There is much trouble on the earth today but the God who made all the planets is on your side. This alone gives you reason to be not concerned about what's going on. David said the Lord's rod and staff will comfort you. This refers to His protection and provision. With this staff a shepherd rules and guides the flock to green pastures and defends them from their enemies. With it he also corrects them when disobedient and brings them back when they wander away. Knowing the Lord will never leave you and will always be there to defend you is how you overcome the temptation to have a troubled heart when trials come your way. You can't control everything that's going on around you, but you can control how you respond to it. Say out loud, "Fear, I resist you! God is on my side and my heart will not be troubled." Your words of faith give God access to your life and with it the promise that nothing by any means can harm you. You walk by faith and not by sight and are not moved by what you see and feel.

Don't ask yourself how you feel, tell yourself how you feel. Yes, feelings are real, but they don't have to determine the outcome of your life. Do not give permission to the devil and those fickle feelings to hinder your life any longer. Allow the protection and provision of God to comfort you every day of your life. 1 John 4:4 says, "You are of God, little children, and have overcome them, because He who is in you is greater than he who is in the world." Because God is on your side, you are well able to escape the snares and delusions of the enemy. It is through His strength and grace that you are able to achieve this victory. God is still on the throne, He is your heavenly Daddy, and He will never leave you or forsake you. He loves you with an everlasting love and will cause everything to work out for your good and His glory. Stop crying and feeling sorry for yourself but always keep your eyes on Him. He is the creator of the heavens and the earth, and He is on your side. He is good and He is all powerful. Who can fear with a Daddy like that?

| 3 |

"THE RICHES OF HIS GOODNESS"

The holy scriptures were written to reveal to man the goodness of God. Why wouldn't they be? He is a good God and His goodness remains the central theme and content of these inspired writings. Rom. 2:4 (NLT) says, "Don't you see how wonderfully kind, tolerant, and patient God is with you? Does this mean nothing to you? Can't you see that His kindness is intended to turn you from your sin?" More people come to Christ when they hear how good He is than hearing about their eternal destruction if they don't. The NKJV says, "Or do you despise the riches of His goodness, forbearance, and long-suffering, not knowing that the goodness of God leads you to repentance?" People don't want to hear about a God who is mean and judgmental and forever ready to send them to a fiery grave. No, they want to hear about a God who is kind and gracious, a God who is willing to bless their lives abundantly.

This is why Paul said in Rom. 1:1 (MB), "Paul, passionately engaged by Jesus Christ, identified in Him to represent Him. My mandate is to announce the goodness of God to mankind." God is a God of love, and goodness is the only thing that's on His mind. It was your Daddy's goodness that motivated Him to send Jesus to the earth to pay the ultimate price for the sins of man. The angels announced the Lord's birth to some shepherds living in the fields by saying, "Do not be afraid, for behold, I bring you good tidings of great joy which will be to all people" (Luke 2:10). Moments later a multitude of angelic host began praising God with these words, "Glory to God in the highest, and on earth peace, good will toward men!" (vs. 14). God wants His children to live a far better life than most people realize. He wants to pour His goodness into you every day of your life. If it's not received then for you Jesus died in vain.

David had a revelation of God's love for him and wrote in Ps. 23:6, "Surely goodness and mercy shall follow me all the days of my life; And I will dwell in the house of the Lord forever." God is good all the time, therefore, if something that's happening in your life is not good, it's not from God. James 1:17 (NLT) says, "Whatever is good and perfect comes down to us from God our Father, who created all the lights in the heavens." In the book of Genesis, whenever God created something, He saw that it was good. Why? Because everything He does is good. That's all He knows and this is why you have to use your faith to tap into His goodness. Rom. 5:2 (AMP) says, "Through Him we also have access by faith into this remarkable state of grace in which we firmly and safely and securely stand. Let us rejoice in our hope and the confident assurance of experiencing and enjoying the glory of our great God, the manifestation of His excellence and power."

Paul is saying you can live in a continual state of God's grace and favor and enjoy the glory and goodness of your Daddy continually. It needs to be deeply rooted in your heart that God is on your side and He wants to be good to you. Rom. 5:9 (MB) says, "If God could love us that much when we were ungodly and guilty, how much more are we free to realize His love now that we are declared innocent by His blood." To experience this grace and favor you've got to know that God's nature is to be good all the time. Jesus prayed, "And this is eternal life, that they may know You, the only true God" (John 17:3). The greatest expression of the nature and character of God is found in 1 John 4:8 where it says, "God is love." He is a God of love and the message of the entire Bible is that He is ready and willing to pour all His goodness out on you. Every verse of scripture points to the ultimate conclusion that God is for you and not against you.

He held nothing back when He sent Jesus to die on the cross for you and this is the undeniable evidence of His great love for all of mankind. Don't allow religious tradition to convince you that God always has a tendency to judge harshly but rather let the revelation of His goodness shape your thoughts. Once you realize that your Daddy in heaven loves you just as much as He loves Jesus, it should be normal for you to expect His goodness to continually be manifested in your life. God is for you and nothing can separate you from His great love. This means daily you can experience His grace and favor which will bring an abundance of blessings your way. Never again will you consider failure and defeat because the revelation of the goodness of God has reshaped your thoughts. Paul wrote in Eph. 1:18 (MB), "And I pray that your thoughts will be flooded with light and inspired insight so that you may know how precious you are to Him."

Nothing good is held back when somebody is precious to you. How much more will God bless you because you are precious to Him? Ps. 84:11 says, "No good thing will He withhold from those who walk uprightly." Paul said in 1 Tim. 6:17 that God "gives us richly all things to enjoy." The grace of God can be described as His overwhelming desire to treat you as if sin never happened. He planned to bless you long before the foundations of the world were created. The blessing of God will empower you to prosper, and favor produces the opportunity to make it happen. That's the goodness of God which you can experience all the days of your life. When God is good to you, your life will never be the same. Nothing can stop you from declaring to others how good God is. David wrote in Ps. 145:6,7, "Men shall speak of the might of your awesome acts, and I will declare Your greatness. They shall utter the memory of your great goodness and shall sing of Your righteousness."

David continued in Ps. 145:8,9, "The Lord is gracious and full of compassion, slow to anger and great in mercy. The Lord is good to all, and His tender mercies are over all His works." Being good is what God is all about and it's His goodness that is the foundation for your faith and expectation. It will cause you to come up higher as you dream new dreams and get a fresh revelation concerning all the great things you can accomplish in and for the kingdom of God. It's the knowledge that God is on your side that will cause you to strive and be more consistent as you seek to fulfill your destiny. Once you know this in your heart, be sure to speak it out of your mouth every single day. David said in Ps. 35:27,28, "Let them shout for joy and be glad, who favor my righteous cause, and let them say continually, 'Let the Lord be magnified, Who has pleasure in the prosperity of His servant.' And my tongue shall speak of Your righteousness and of Your praise all the day long."

What you believe is what you'll talk about the most and this is why you should proclaim daily, "God is good to me." Never stop celebrating the goodness of God in your life. Wake up each morning and thank Him for all the good things He's already done for you. After you've done that, you can then expect Him to do even better and greater things and it will come to pass just as you have believed. Because God is your heavenly Daddy, you can enjoy His goodness for you have obtained the right to live in a continual state of His divine favor. This will cause your life to get better and better with each passing day. Doors that were closed in the past will suddenly open for you. God will make a way where in the past there seemed to be no way. What once was lost has now been found. You'll be at the right place at the right time. As you go through your daily routine there will be people who will go out of their way to be good to you. You'll receive preferential treatment wherever you go.

You'll get that promotion at work when another person was more qualified than you. God is being good to you and He is taking you to a higher level of living. 2 Cor. 1:20 says, "For all the promises of God in Him are Yes, and in Him Amen, to the glory of God through us." The Message Bible says, "Whatever God has promised gets stamped with the Yes of Jesus. In Him, this is what we preach and pray, and great Amen, God's Yes and our Yes together, gloriously evident." God has already set the date for when your dreams will come to pass, it's on His divine calendar. Still, in order for this to happen, you will have to use your faith and get in agreement with Him. Destinies get fulfilled when your "Yes" gets coupled together with God's "Yes." God's desire to be good to you is not enough. He works through faith and this is why you need to get in agreement with Him as quickly as you can. Ps. 65:11 says, "You crown the year with Your goodness, and your paths drip with abundance."

In faith believe that this will be a blessed and prosperous year for you. Believe that all things will work out for your good, that you'll come behind in no good thing. God said yes, you said yes, now step back and watch the blessings flow. You have a destiny to fulfill and you need to know that God's dream for your life is bigger than your own. He wants to take you farther in life than you ever dreamed possible. Eph. 3:20 says, "Now to Him who is able to do exceedingly, abundantly above all that we ask or think." The Message Bible says God can do "far more than you could ever imagine or guess or request in your wildest dreams." Don't limit God with small thinking for as a man "thinks in his heart, so is he" (Prov. 23:7). You need to come up higher and think big thoughts and dream big dreams. God is able to take those dreams and make them bigger and more rewarding than you've ever imagined. Blessings will chase after you instead of you chasing after them.

When you give your life away, when you seek to fulfill your God-given destiny, God will step in and pour His favor into your life. You'll receive blessings that are unheard of with human thinking and reasoning. They'll be "pressed down, shaken together, and running over"

(Luke 6:38). Your life will be running over with prosperity, good health, and influence in the world in which you live. God wants you to live a normal life, but what most people accept as being normal is not God's viewpoint of normal. To walk in the goodness of God you've got to set your sights higher than where they're now at. You've got to conform to God's standard of life, to what He says is normal. Rom. 12:2 (NLT) says, "Don't copy the behavior and customs of this world, but let God transform you into a new person by changing the way you think. Then you will learn to know God's will for you, which is good and pleasing and perfect." Many people go to church but they're still living by the standard set by the world.

Paul is saying that if you'll start thinking differently, if you'll think like God thinks, you will live a higher quality of life. The Message Bible says, "Don't become so well-adjusted to your culture that you fit into it without even thinking." Don't accept the world's standard as being the only way in which a person can live. No, renew your mind to God's standard. The Message Bible continues, "Instead, fix your attention on God. You'll be changed from the inside out." The world's standard will always drag you down to the level of immaturity. Don't think how the world thinks but renew your mind and begin to think like God. If you want God's best to be manifested in your life, determine today that conforming to what God calls normal will become the top priority of your life. Allow God to take your life to a higher level. 2 Sam. 22:31 says, "As for God, His way is perfect; The word of the Lord is proven; He is a shield to all who trust in Him."

Why settle for what is average and normal when you can live a life that is above and beyond what you could ever ask or think? Renew your mind and break free from what the world calls normal. Come up higher and surpass what is common and ordinary by worldly standards. Now is the time to break free from those things that will hinder you from fulfilling your destiny. Don't let anything hold you back from reaching the top of your mountain, from becoming the person

God said you can become and from doing the things God said you can do. Allow what God says is normal to become your standard of living today. You renew your mind by reading the Bible for it is the model of what normal living is from God's viewpoint. Gen. 1:27 says, "So God created man in His own image; in the image of God He created him; male and female He created them." To be like God is what He calls normal.

To reign in life, according to vs. 26, is living a normal lifestyle. The word "reign" means 'to possess royal authority, to exercise sovereign power, to rule, to have dominion, and to have influence.' This is how Jesus lived when He walked on the earth and you are to be just like Him. 1 John 4:17 says "as He is, so are we in this world." The people of His day were dumbfounded by what Jesus said and did and even His own disciples asked, "What manner of man is this, that even the winds and the sea obey Him?" (Matt. 8:27). People today should be asking the same thing about you. Jesus lived a normal life and this is what you should be doing as well. Reigning in life is normal living according to God. This was God's divine purpose for man back in the Garden of Eden, and this is how it should be in your life today. Gen. 1:28 says, "Then God blessed them." In the mind of God, you being blessed is normal. To be blessed means 'to enjoy the bliss of heaven' which implies total and complete happiness.

It's hard to be happy if you're sick all the time and can't pay your bills when they're due. Jesus came to restore back to mankind what was lost when sin entered the world. Jesus said in John 10:10, "I have come that they may have life, and that they may have it more abundantly." The Amplified Bible says, "That they may have and enjoy life, have it in abundance to the full and until it overflows." The Message Bible calls it a "Better life than they ever imagined or ever dreamed." This is what Jesus came to do. He came to restore to mankind the ability to reign and to live blessed, to enjoy total and complete happiness. Job 36:11 says, "If they obey and serve Him, they shall spend their days in prosperity, and their years in pleasures." This is the goodness of God, what He calls normal. Never allow the world to tell you what's normal. Without a doubt, God's normal is far better.

Deut. 28:2 says, "And all these blessings shall come upon you and overtake you, because you obey the voice of the Lord your God." Normal living in the mind of God is blessings coming on you and overtaking you all the time. Get up every morning expecting blessings to come on you and overtake you. This is normal living for a child of God who's experiencing His goodness. Vs. 3 says, "Blessed shall you be in the city and blessed shall you be in the field." You're blessed wherever you go. Vs. 8, "The Lord will command the blessing on you in your storehouses and in all to which you set your hand." Put your hand in front of you and say, "These are blessed hands. Everything they touch is blessed by God." Vs. 10, "And all the people of the earth shall stand in awe of you. They'll see that you're called by the name of the Lord." Vs. 11, "And the Lord will grant you plenty of goods, in the fruit of your body, in the increase of your livestock, and in the produce of your ground."

Come up higher and expect to be blessed with great abundance. After all, having plenty is just normal in the eyes of God. Vs. 12, "The Lord will open to you His good treasure." God never promised that this lifestyle of being abundantly blessed would happen overnight. However, if you will keep renewing your mind to His standard, you will progressively get to the place where you'll be blessed more consistently than you've ever been before. God is on your side, and He wants to bless you with His goodness every single day of your life. Deut. 28:13 says, "And the Lord will make you the head and not the tail; you shall be above only, and not be beneath, if you heed the commandment of the Lord your God, which I command you today, and are careful to observe them." This means you will excel in everything you do. No more will you win a few and lose a few, you'll win every time. Determine that from this day forward you are going to enjoy normal living as God sees it.

Your days of bondage are over. God has a plan for your life that is second to none, a plan that at one time you never imagined was possible. Begin to spend quality time in the Word of God both day and night. If you don't start that process of renewing your mind, you're only going to know the world's standard of what is normal. Let the Word show you a better way of living, a way of life that is normal in the eyes of God. Grasp the fact that you are qualified to receive God's goodness. You've been justified by faith (Rom. 5:1) and it's through this faith that you gain access to the grace and blessings of God (vs. 2). Confess out loud that you are blessed by Him. Ps. 107:2 says, "Let the redeemed of the Lord say so." Start talking about all the good things your Daddy has already done for you. He has called you into His eternal family and has made it possible for you to live in a state of His divine favor. Believe it and speak it out your mouth. 2 Cor. 4:13 says, "I believed and therefore have I spoken."

You are now walking in faith so start expecting good things to happen and begin to thank God for all the wonderful things He's about to do in your life. Have a close encounter with God and give Him praise and honor and glory. This will open the doors of His goodness in your life like you've never experienced before. Surely goodness and mercy shall follow you all the days of your life. Believe that the blessings of God will chase you down and then talk and act like it is so. Believe you can become like Jacob who said in Gen. 33:11 (MSG), "God has been good to me and I have more than enough." God's best for your life is that you have more than enough so that you can be a blessing to others. This is what fulfilling your destiny is all about. God told Abraham in Gen. 12:2, "I will make you a great nation; I will bless you and make your name great; And you shall be a blessing." When this happens, you will be experiencing life at its best, life as it is supposed to be lived.

You've come up higher and now God is using you to be a positive influence to others. Take what God has given you and pour it out into the lives of other people. Allow God to use you to be the answer to another person's prayer. All it takes is a willingness to be blessed and a willingness to be a blessing. Be like Isaiah who said, "Here I am. Send me" (Is. 6:8). Expect to be used by God and thank Him in advance for what He is about to do. When you do that, your faith will rise to a higher level, and nothing will be impossible to you. Gone are the days of mediocre living. Gone are the days of just barely getting by. Gone are the days of never having enough for you and your family and those around you. God is good and His plans for your life are also good. He has plans to bless you and prosper you and to give you a good future. He has plans to make your name great so that you can be a great blessing to many people.

He is thinking about you for you are always on His mind. What is He thinking? Ps. 115:12 says, "The Lord has been mindful of us; He will bless us." God is in heaven right now thinking of ways that He can bless your life. He is thinking of ways to prosper you beyond measure and to give you a future that is exceedingly, abundantly above all that you could ask or think. This is what God thinks about all the time and if that don't put a bounce in your step then nothing will. God wants to bless you more and more and manifest His goodness in your life. This in turn will give you unspeakable joy and peace that passes all understanding. These are manifestations of the goodness of God. Don't let religious tradition or the unbelief of others tell you differently. God says He wants to bless you, and this should settle in your mind as to what His perfect will is.

You need a divine revelation of just how good God actually is. Head knowledge is not enough for this revelation cannot be grasped with the intellect. It takes a supernatural revelation to activate these promises that will bless your life and help you to fulfill your destiny. His goodness is phenomenal according to most people but it's normal according to the Bible. What you know about God changes who you are and defines your purpose and destiny. It shapes how you live your life and your perspective on what life is all about. This divine revelation is an open invitation from God for you to taste and see that He is good. Taste is an experience but to see something is perception. You'll perceive more clearly what you can experience, and the Lord is inviting you to come up higher and partake of His goodness on a whole new level. God's goodness is the foundation on which the Christian life is built on. Everything comes down from the goodness of God. He is love and is as good as He is holy.

When this truth becomes real to you, it will bring a rest to your heart that will cause you to trust Him no matter what the enemy may bring your way. The answer to every question is that God is good. Your knowledge may not always increase but the answer you need is that your heavenly Daddy is a perfect Father and He is always good. This was the revelation Jesus came to unveil when He walked the earth. Questions may abound but the answer is always the same. God is good and He is forever on your side. Never fear what the enemy can do to you. Believe that God is good and be like David who picked up five smooth stones and ran toward Goliath. If God be for you, who can be against you (Rom. 8:31)? You must perceive reality according to how God sees things. The facts may say something is wrong in your life, but the truth of God's Word says you're blessed coming in and going out. Truth is life and this is what you confront the enemy with.

If the devil can get you to believe God is not good, then he has injured your capacity to live a blessed life and to share with others how good God actually is. Do not allow him to rob you of your destiny by getting you to question the goodness of God. If you question His goodness, you'll question His promises to you. If you do that, you'll undermine your destiny. Real faith doesn't deny the existence of a problem, but it does deny its ability to influence your life. If you know and believe that God is good then no weapon formed against you will prosper (Is. 54:17). Through the eyes of faith you can see a favorable outcome to your situation through the intentions and purposes of a loving and caring Father. When you taste His goodness and see that He is good, then everything else in your life becomes redefined by that goodness. Your life will never be the same again. Believe that God will bless you in such a way that nobody will be able to deny the greatness of the Lord above.

The time has come for you to be blessed abundantly, to experience the goodness of God. Ps. 102:13 says, "You will arise and have mercy on Zion; For the time to favor her, yes, the set time, has come." The word "arise" means 'to spring up and go into action.' Ps. 68:1 says, "Let God arise, let His enemies be scattered." The psalmist is saying that when God arises, He takes action. The Message Bible says, "Up with God! Down with His enemies! Adversaries, run for the hills!" Vs. 2 says, "So let the wicked perish at the presence of God." Come up higher and let God arise in your life. When this happens, what needs to be done will be done. God will take action and His favor and goodness will flow into your life. In Ex. 3:8 God said, "So I have come down to deliver them out of the hand of the Egyptians, and to bring them up from that land to a good and large land, to a land flowing with milk and honey."

He then said in vs. 21, "And I will give this people favor in the sight of the Egyptians; and it shall be, when you go, that you shall not go empty-handed." Shout for joy because the favor of God is about to profusely abound in your life. You will be abundantly blessed, and this will allow you to bless those around you. Not only will you be able to pay off the mortgage of your house, you'll be able to pay off your neighbor's house as well. You will be a vessel of honor through which the goodness of God will flow. God will be so good to you that His blessings will overflow beyond what you can contain. He will place you in a position where abundance is not just for you but flows through you. You will take what He has poured into your life and release it into the lives of others, becoming a vessel of blessing and purpose. This is what the Christ life is all about. This is what He is all about and, hopefully, this is what you will be about as well.

| 4 |

"MAKE YOUR LIFE COUNT"

You were born to be a blessing and, to help you fulfill this heavenly call, God will bless you so that you can be an even bigger blessing. Don't settle for a limited lifestyle especially since God wants to pour His goodness out on you. You can't give away what you don't have so be open to receive what God says is rightfully yours. Don't live your life based on how you think it should go but come up higher and think how God thinks. He said in Is. 55:9, "For as the heavens are higher than the earth, so are My ways higher than your ways, and My thoughts than your thoughts." Live the rest of your life based on how God thinks. You were made to experience more of the goodness of God and He wants to take you higher and farther than you've ever been before. God wanted Abraham to become the father of a great nation but first he had to leave behind his family and those things that put a limit on his life.

Abraham obeyed and not long after that God showed him the stars and said, "So shall your descendants be" (Gen. 15:5). Abraham took the limits off his life and so should you. This will happen when you renew your mind and think the thoughts of God. There is a destiny inside of you that's waiting to be released. You've been called to do more with your life than you've already done. You were born to make your life count and, as long as there is breath inside of you, there will always be more for you to do. God wanted Abraham to do more with his life and Gen. 15:6 says, "And he believed in the Lord, and He accounted it to him for righteousness." Your faith has everything to do with you stepping into the call God has for your life, the call to have more and become more and to bless more. Jabez prayed, "Oh, that you would bless me and enlarge my territory" (1 Chron. 4:10).

To have more you've got to get rid of small thinking and of having a limited view of what God can do for you. Joshua and Caleb saw that the land of Canaan was a large, bountiful place but the rest of the people shrunk back and stayed small. Joshua and Caleb wanted more and believed they could overcome the giants in the land. The others were afraid to even try and wandered in the wilderness for forty years. Both reward and wisdom comes when you begin to think like God and use your faith to receive all He has for you. Is. 54:2 says, "Enlarge the place of your tent, and let them stretch out the curtains of your habitations; Do not spare; Lengthen your cords, and strengthen your stakes." Your limitations determine the size of your tent. To enlarge the place of your tent means you've got to think bigger than you've ever thought before. Your tent is not to stay the same size.

You've got to expand your thinking about what God wants to do in your life and the role He will play in the fulfillment of your destiny. You've got to enlarge your capacity to receive what God wants to do in your life. Go beyond thinking about getting your own needs met and allow God to use you to meet the needs of other people. Expand your tent by knowing that God wants to bless you for the purpose of being a blessing to those around you. Spare not when it comes to showing the world how good your Daddy is. Prepare to receive more and prepare to give more. This is why you're here, this is why you were born. You were born to be blessed, and you were born to be a blessing. This is the destiny you were called to fulfill. David said in Ps. 23:5, "My cup runs over." This means he had more than enough. When Jesus fed the multitude there were twelve baskets left over. Likewise, they had more than enough.

Don't pray to just get by, pray that you'll have more than enough so others can feed off of God's goodness toward you. Be willing to ask big, for those things God already said you could have. This is how you enlarge your tent and take the limits off what God can do for you. Ask Him for those abundant blessings that will propel you to your destiny and purpose. Ask Him to help you come up higher so that you "may be complete, thoroughly equipped for every good work" (2 Tim. 3:17). God can make happen what you can't make happen on your own. Your future is already planned out and what you need to fulfill your destiny is waiting for you to come take possession of it. Ask God for big things and use your faith to believe He will direct your steps (Prov. 16:9). No longer are you to have a survival mentality but trust in God who is more than enough. Ask big and receive big. This is how God will enlarge your territory.

God created the entire universe so why would you go to Him asking for little things? A big God needs to be asked for big things. Some people think cancer is bigger than God so they don't ask Him to be instantly healed of this dreaded disease. At best they ask Him to help them endure the treatments they must go through. No, God is a God of more than enough and has the Name that is above every name, including cancer. Ask Him for big things. Believe He can heal all your sickness and disease and take away poverty and lack. Believe that He will cause you to break free from whatever is holding you back. When you enlarge your tents, your faith will rise to a higher level and your expectations will begin to increase. It's the releasing of your faith that gives God permission to do great things in your life. When the odds seem to be against you, always remember that God is on your side. Be like Jabez and pray bold prayers and expect big things to happen.

God said in Ps. 2:8 (NLT), "Only ask, and I will give you the nations as your inheritance, the whole earth as your possessions." What could be bigger than that? Don't limit God by asking Him for only five loaves of bread and two fish (Matt. 14:19). No, ask Him for the twelve baskets that were left over (vs. 20). Ask big and receive big. Don't be shy and don't hold back. Come up higher and ask God for what you really want. Always remember that with Him the sky is the limit. You won't offend your Daddy if you ask for big things. He'll be honored that you believed He's big enough to give it to you. If you will do your part and enlarge your tent, God will step in and move heaven and earth to get for you that which you asked for. That's the kind of Daddy He is. Jesus said in Luke 12:32 that "it is your Father's good pleasure to give you the kingdom." He'll give you the kingdom and everything else you ask for.

He wants you to be blessed beyond measure and He wants you to fulfill your destiny. That's what He planned for your life long ago so don't disappoint Him. Rise up and ask Him for big things. Nothing will make Him happier than for you to step up and become the person He created you to be and to do what He called you to do. Gal. 5:13 (MSG) says, "It is absolutely clear that God has called you to a free life. Just make sure that you don't use this freedom as an excuse to do whatever you want to do and destroy your freedom. Rather, use your freedom to serve one another in love; that's how freedom grows." God wants to use you as a channel through which His blessings flow into the lives of other people. For this reason, He has set you free from all the consequences of sin that is in the world. He didn't heal your sore back so you could play golf without pain. No, He did it so you could be physically ready and able to do what He has called you to do.

Financial blessings are not so you can indulge yourself in worldly pleasures, they come so you won't have to work yourself into an early grave plus have enough resources to help others if and when the need arises. God wants to bless you so you can be a blessing to others. When this becomes your motive as well, your tents will be enlarged and so will be your bank account. There will be no limit as to how much God will bless your life. Time is quickly passing by so daily look for opportunities to be a blessing to somebody. Surely they are there.

Seek for them and you will find them. Believe God and ask Him to make you more beneficial to those around you, to help you pour into others what He has poured into you. Choose to make decisions that will put you in a position to do this. Decide to put the needs of others above your own knowing that what you make happen for others, God will make happen for you.

Don't be like those people who only live for themselves, those who believe that the person who dies with the most toys wins. This is foolishness to the highest degree. 1 Cor. 15:19 (NLT) says, "And if our hope in Christ is only for this life, we are more to be pitied than anyone in the world." Life only has meaning when you are used by God to help make somebody else's life better. The joy of getting a new toy lasts but a moment but the excitement of blessing another person will give you a joyous memory that will last a lifetime. In fact, it will bless you so much that you'll want to do it again and again. Jesus spoke about this in John 12:25,26, "He who loves his life will lose it, and he who hates his life in this world will keep it for eternal life. If anyone serves Me, let him follow Me; and where I am, there My servant will be also. If anyone serves Me, him My Father will honor."

There are not enough pleasures in this world to give your life purpose, meaning, and satisfaction. You are a spiritual being created in the image of God and true meaning in life comes from the inside of you. The more you grow in Christ and get used by Him, the less you'll desire the lustful pleasures of this world. Live with the awareness that there is a better life to live than what the world offers. Come up higher and step into the plan God has for your life. Paul said in 1 Cor. 15:10, "But by the grace of God I am what I am." Having grace does not mean you can do whatever you want to do, it's the empowerment to continually go in the right direction. With grace you can do what He tells you to do and go where He tells you to go. It will cause you to raise your hand and say, "Here I am! Send me" (Is. 6:8). People who do this are the ones blessed by God.

Being a servant of the Lord is not without its rewards. God said in Joel 2:26, "You shall eat plenty and be satisfied, and praise the name of the Lord your God, who has dealt wondrously with you; and My people shall never be put to shame." This is what happens when you fulfill the purpose for which God made you. Sad to say, most people don't know what their purpose is. A nationwide survey was taken where people were asked if they could ask God one question, what would it be? The answer most people gave was, "Why am I here?" People don't know why they're here and instead of trying to find out they take on the attitude of "whatever will be, will be." They just take whatever life throws at them instead of taking charge of their destiny and finding out what God wants them to do. These are the people who leave this planet and have nothing to show for their lives. Not long after they're gone the world will forget they were even here.

It is a sad commentary for a person to get to the end of their life and find out they lived it in vain; a life lived with no meaning and no purpose. A lot of believers don't realize this but there are two narrow roads mentioned in the Bible. Most people are familiar with the one Jesus talked about in Matt. 7:13,14, "Enter by the narrow gate; for wide is the gate and broad is the way that leads to destruction, and there are many who go into it. Because narrow is the gate and difficult is the way which leads to life, and there are few who find it." Those who not saved are on this broad path and Jesus is telling them to get born-again and take the narrow road. Why did He say there are few who take this path? Because difficult is the way which leads to life. Most people take the easy way out but if you are born again then you have chosen this difficult path and the Lord will honor you for doing so.

As a believer you have chosen to travel on this narrow path and as you journey down the road of life you will look ahead and see another narrow path looming in front of you. This path is described in Matt. 20:16, "So the last shall be first, and the first last. For many are called, but few are chosen." The first narrow path was called "the road to eternal life" and this second narrow path is called "the road of the chosen few" which is the road of fulfilling your God-given destiny. Notice that both these paths are narrow and both are difficult and, yes, there are few who find each path. They say that ten percent of all believers do ninety percent of the work. Unfortunately, this is a true statement, but the time will soon be here when each and every child of God will proudly stand before the Lord Jesus and receive eternal rewards for works of service done here on planet earth.

For sure, the rewards in heaven will be great but you do the things you do because of the deep love you have for your Daddy. As one of the chosen few you want to make a difference in this sinful world and this is why you pray every day that the Lord will expand your territory and enlarge your tents, thus giving you the opportunity to do so. This gives you a reason to live, a reason to get up each and every morning. 2 Tim. 1:9 says God "has saved us and called us with a holy calling, not according to our works, but according to His own purpose and grace which was given to us in Christ Jesus before time began." The call on your life is a holy call. It is divine in nature and divine in purpose and should be taken very seriously. The dream that is down in your heart is not something you came up with on your own but was put there by God Himself. Remember, you don't decide your calling, you discover it.

God sees what is special about you. He sees your potential and what you're capable of doing. He doesn't see where you're at today, He always sees what you can become. He called Abraham the father of many nations when the patriarch was an old man and childless. He also called David a king when he was still a lad tending to his father's sheep out in some field. God is also calling you and to become all you were meant to be, to be promoted from a nobody to a somebody, you must listen to God and discover the divine calling on your life. Get alone with your heavenly Father and He will reveal to you specifically that work He wants you to perform. You have a destiny, you were born for such a time as this, and you know true success is not how high you climb the corporate ladder but only comes when you fulfill the purpose for which God made you. Celebrate the fact that God made you unique and different from anybody else who has ever been born.

There is no other person alive quite like you. In the eyes of God, you are special. You are truly one of a kind and this means that there are certain things you can do for the kingdom of God that nobody else can do. Even in your mother's womb you were given special talents and abilities by God that only a person with your personality can develop and perform to the degree God wants them done. Paul encouraged Timothy to "not neglect the gift that is in you" (1 Tim. 4:14). Develop your gift and the skills that go with it and then turn yourself over to God to be used by Him to fulfill His purpose on planet earth. A lifestyle of reaching out to others will come as a result of your willingness to be used by God. Prov. 3:27 says, "Withhold not good from them to whom it is due, when it is in the power of your hand to do it." Everything God has made is a solution to a problem and your worth and significance is determined by the kinds of problems you are solving for someone.

There is something in you and about you that someone else needs. Realize that you may be God's answer to somebody's prayer. Daily be diligent and look for problems to solve. Think and look for extra ways to benefit others. Go the extra mile. Jesus said, "And whoever compels you to go one mile, go with him two" (Matt. 5:41). Believe that God will cause you to cross paths with someone in need. When that happens do whatever it takes to get that person on the straight and narrow path to victory. It is only when you turn your eyes off of yourself and begin to focus on others that you will be able to experience the true, genuine God-given joy that being a blessing to other people bring. People everywhere are craving for a reason to live, and this is why God wants to give you a future and a hope. God has a specific plan for your life that is consistent with your talents and God-given desires.

A lot of people, however, don't understand how to get their assignment from God. They think all believers line up in front of the throne of God and He passes out lifetime callings and assignments to each person as He pleases. People believe that God decides what you're supposed to do and it's their responsibility to adapt to those plans whether they like it or not. Thankfully, this is not how heavenly callings are bestowed on committed servants. God's will and your desire work hand-in-hand. When you surrender your plans to God, His will and your desire begin to move in harmony, shaping a life that fulfills both His purpose and your deepest calling. What you enjoy doing the most is a clue to what God wants you to do with your life. God wants you happy and whatever brings you the most fulfillment can be used for the kingdom of God. Eccl. 3:22 says, "Wherefore I perceive that there is nothing better than that a man should rejoice in his own works, for that is his heritage."

The last days are here, and the urgency of the hour has never been greater. Now more than ever, the Kingdom of God needs faithful laborers willing to rise, serve, and answer the call. Laboring for God is not a burden as some would think. Yes, you do enter into a war zone but at the same time it will be the most joyful thing you do with your life. Eccl. 5:20 gives you the assurance that "God keeps every man busy with the joy of his heart." God will use you in whatever area brings you the most joy. Take your gifts, talents, and desires and place them in the hands of God to be used according to His perfect will. There is power in desire, and this is why God will give you the desires of your heart. If you don't want to go to Africa to be a jungle missionary, then that is a sign that God probably doesn't want you to go to Africa. If you instead have a heart for children, He will then bless you and give you the anointing to be a children's minister.

So many people sit around and do nothing as they wait for God to tell them what to do. This is not how it works. Instead, they should look within their own heart and see what their desires are. This is what will give them direction for their life. It is God's will that there should be nobody working for Him who doesn't want to do what they're doing. If you're not having fun what you're doing, you are in the wrong call. Why? Because there is power in desire. Desire breeds excitement and excitement produces energy. Your desire will stir up your passion and the anointing to fulfill your call. The harvest is plentiful, but the laborers are few. Many are called but few are chosen because people lack desire. If you want to serve God, then you're on your way to an exciting life. Know what your desires are and dream about them all the time. God will give you the desires of your heart, but you must know what those desires are. And don't forget, the call of God and your desires go hand-in-hand.

Eccl. 9:1 says, "For I considered all this in my heart, so that I could declare it all that the righteous and the wise and their works are in the hand of God." When you go to work for God don't go at it half-heartedly. In the kingdom of God being a servant is a promotion, and you must give it everything you've got and then some. Paul says in Rom. 12:11 to be "not lagging in diligence, fervent in spirit, serving the Lord." To be "fervent in spirit" means to be aglow and burning with the Spirit of God in your heart. You are to maintain that spiritual glow in your work for the Lord and have the attitude that "whatever your hand finds to do, do it with all your might" (Eccl. 9:10). Paul says, "I press toward the goal for the prize of the upward call of God in Christ Jesus" (Phil. 3:14). If you will do that then you are promised in Rom. 8:28 a victorious life, "And we know that all things work together for good to those who love God, to those who are called according to His purpose."

When you give your all to God, God will give His all to you. Paul said to "press toward the goal." Your vision and its fulfillment won't just come running up to you and jump in your lap. No, you've got to go after it. Press on toward your call and run to it the same way David ran toward the giant. Dispel all gloom, sorrow and fear and cast down evil imaginations. Infuse life into yourself and shout unto God with a voice of triumph. In the book of Job, you will read that he was a very blessed man. He then entered a season of his life where he lost everything he had. He suffered hardship after devastating hardship and then afterward he miraculously experienced a turnaround. His life was going in one direction and then the path he was on shifted and he began going in another direction. Eventually he received twice as much as he had before and Job 42:12 says, "God blessed the latter days of Job more than at the beginning."

Job died old and full of days and this all came about because the "Lord of the breakthrough" gave him a turnaround. What is a turnaround? Ps. 30:5 says, "Weeping may endure for the night, but joy comes in the morning." That's a turnaround. God will give you beauty for ashes. The father of the prodigal son said, "for this my son was dead and is alive again; he was lost and is found." That is what it means to have a turnaround. It's a condition of the heart and our circumstances have absolutely nothing to do with it. Life is not always peaches and cream, but you can still cling to your call and do what the Lord has anointed you to do. Remember, change comes from the inside out. When you change on the inside, God steps in and will change your circumstances on the outside. This is the key to having a turnaround in your life. Job 42:12 did not say Job blessed himself. No, Job changed his attitude and God blessed him. Job had a turnaround and his life got twice as good as it was before.

It's time for everybody in the kingdom of God to wake up and smell the roses. Yes, all roses have thorns but so what? Winners focus on the beauty of the flower whereas losers focus on the thorns. You need to look at life from God's perspective. The Bible says in Prov. 23:7, "For as he thinks in his heart, so is he." Get up every morning and picture yourself succeeding in everything you set out to do. If you'll keep the right image in front of you and always submit yourself to the Lord through prayer and thanksgiving, God promises that nothing will be impossible to you. Sometimes the circumstances of life can make you feel like you're in a dead-end situation but keep going forward anyway and never give up. What may look like a dead-end situation may in reality be the beginning of a fresh, supernatural flow of God's divine power and favor into your life. This is why you need to learn to not trust in yourself but in the God who raises the dead.

Think about it. When your hopes seem buried and you've got nowhere to turn, isn't that when God's power begins to operate in your life to the greatest measure? As long as you've got a loving Father you can call on, a word from the Lord to stand on, and faith to activate all His promises, you have got reason to rejoice. You can have a turnaround that will give you a gloriously bright future. Call on your Heavenly Father today and do it in faith. Expect Him to release His power on your behalf and watch Him begin to turn your dead-end situation around. Know that God did not take you this far to leave you stranded. What He started, He is going to finish (Phil. 1:6). Helen Keller said the one thing worse than being blind was having no vision. Those who are successful in life are motivated by vision. It is imperative for you to understand that you can spend your life any way you want to, but you can only spend it once.

Too many people walk away from the call of God on their life and end up settling for too little too soon. They take the path of least resistance and don't realize that it's not what happens to them that matters, it's how they respond to what happens that really matters. It is Satan's plan that you be defeated but you have God's personal guarantee that you will win through Him. You draw your life and strength from Him and He draws His fulfillment from you. It's true, you only live once but if you do it right once is enough. In order to fulfill the call of God on your life you must rise up above the tests and trials that come your way. As long as you live you will never outgrow fighting the enemy, so you better learn to lean on Jesus and fight the good fight of faith. The enemy's goal is to frustrate God's purpose in your life because you can't be a blessing to others if you're bogged down with your own problems.

You are the subject of this warfare because the enemy knows you're only as big as your dreams or as small as your fears. The choice is yours as to whether or not you will stand your ground in the face of adversity. To go forward and fulfill your holy calling you must face your giant, cut his stupid head off, and then go forward and be a blessing to somebody else. This is what the Christian life is all about. The result of doing this on a daily basis is a blessed life. No, it's not about how much money you have or how many toys you accumulate. It's about making your life count. It's about making a positive difference in the lives of other people. Life is what you make it and in order for it to count you must step forward and be all that you can be. You can't let trials and hardship stop you and get you down. You must be bigger than that! Take your mind off your problems and look at the big picture.

God is a big God and He's still in control. In a million years your problems won't mean a thing but, rest assured, God will still be on the throne. Don't give your problems credit for being bigger than they are. There is no problem too big or dream too great to stop you from fulfilling your destiny. God is not limited by your age or income or background. He is all powerful and when He speaks stars get flung into the outer darkness and worlds come into existence. He would not have given you your call if He was not willing to bring it to pass. God is bigger than your problems and so are you. Come up higher and cast all your cares on Jesus. Instead of focusing on all your problems go and do something nice for somebody else. Make their lives better just by them being around you but for a few moments. Their victory will be your victory. Their joy will be your joy. So press on. Look beyond yourself and be a blessing to others. Let your light shine. Make your life count. Make a difference in the life of someone else. You only live once but, if you do it right, once is enough.

| 5 |

"FLAWED BUT MIGHTY"

God has a specific plan for your life, a divine call that is so big and so special that it should set your heart racing at the mere thought of it. He is on your side and this means there is nothing you can't accomplish as you seek the fulfillment of your destiny. As you walk in faith, He will direct your steps and give you the strength and wisdom to bring to pass all He has called you to do. Inside of you is an endless supply of potential and talent put there by God that will allow you to run your race and finish your course. The seeds of greatness God planted in you are taking root and will soon break forth and take you to the top of the mountain you've been ordained to climb. When you live with this much expectancy there is nothing the enemy can do to pull you back or hold you down. The sky is the limit in the things you can do in and for the kingdom of God. The possibilities are endless because you serve a big God whose blessings know no limits.

Jesus said in Luke 18:27 (NLT), "What is impossible with people is possible with God." Come up higher and allow God to turn your dreams into a reality. 2 Tim. 1:9 says God "has saved us and called us with a holy calling, not according to our works, but according to His own purpose and grace which was given to us in Christ Jesus before time began." Sandwiched between God's salvation and His grace being poured into your life is calling and purpose. Your calling is what you have in your hand, that which you're qualified to do, and your purpose is what you have in your heart, the things you love and the reason you do what you do. To fulfill your destiny, you've got to combine your calling with your purpose to serve God. Ultimately, it's all about God and what He wants you to do. Col. 1:17 says, "And He is before all things, and in Him all things consist." This means you were saved for His purpose, you are called for His purpose, and you are graced for His purpose. It's all about Him and His purpose.

Your gifts and talents, your time and energy, your marriage and family, and your finances and resources are all to be used to fulfill His divine purpose on planet Earth. When God's purpose is deep down in your heart, when His will becomes your will, it will eliminate some of the struggle and tension that is there when natural needs and desires try to push God off into a corner somewhere. When you understand that everything in life is all about God and His purpose, then all those roadblocks will disappear from your life. Eccl. 3:11 says, "He has made everything beautiful in its time. Also, He has put eternity in their hearts." The Amplified Bible says, "He has made everything beautiful and appropriate in its time. He has also planted eternity [a sense of divine purpose] in the human heart [a mysterious longing which nothing under the sun can satisfy, except God] - yet man cannot find out (comprehend, grasp) what God has done (His overall plan) from the beginning to the end."

God will put His purpose down in your heart and this is what gives you a reason to get up in the morning, a reason to come up higher in your thoughts and actions during the day. You're no longer living for what you want to do but rather that God would use you to fulfill His plan and divine purpose. God implanted His purpose inside of you and this tells you that you are here for something bigger than yourself. Having a sense that your life is about something more than just you and what you want is what fulfilling His purpose and your destiny is all about. God called Moses to go to Egypt to deliver His people from bondage. When Moses began to make excuses as to why he shouldn't go God asked him, "What is that in your hand?" (Ex. 4:2). God is going to use what is in your hand to fulfill the purpose He put in your heart. The best way to fulfill your destiny, to fulfill what is in your heart, is to be fruitful and a good steward over what He has put in your hand.

Some people spend their entire life trying to find out what their calling is and ultimately never do what they've been called to do. The word "call" in Greek means 'to shout' so ask yourself what's shouting out to you. What are you gifted at? What is it you like to do? What is it you're passionate about? The answer is so obvious that some people try to make finding their call more difficult than it actually is. James 1:17 says, "Every good gift and every perfect gift is from above, and comes down from the Father of lights, with whom there is no variation or shadow of turning." The Message Bible says, "Every desirable and beneficial gift comes out of heaven. The gifts are rivers of light cascading down from the Father of Light." God will not change His mind concerning what He wants you to do. He won't make you one way and then use you another way. You are fearfully and wonderfully made and God created you with His purpose in mind.

You need to understand that what's in your hand is just as noble and precious as what's in your heart. Serving God is being faithful to what's in your hand for this is what God uses to fulfill the purpose He put in your heart. Don't despise what's in your hand because of the responsibility and the challenges of day-to-day life that come with it. It is never easy to fulfill a heavenly call but the love and purpose that's in your heart makes it all worth it. What's in your hand brings with it the weight of expectation but, if you'll come up higher and focus on what's in your heart, you'll rise up and meet every challenge. There is potential in the dream God puts in your heart for in your dreams lies your destiny. Your dream from above will keep you on course and will give you the motivation to count the cost and make the sacrifices necessary to bring about its fulfillment. Dreams are necessary for Prov.

29:18 (KJV) says, "Where there is no vision, the people perish." The NLT says "they run wild."

People cast off restraint and run wild when they lose their ability to see the dream God placed in their heart. Never underestimate the potential of a dream for when you lose your capacity to dream, you will lose your vision for the future. Don't allow the devil or anybody else to rob you of your God-given dream which has the potential to gain new territory for the kingdom of God. Your dream gives your life a future and a hope and it will fill you up with a sense of purpose. You must have the will to succeed because God will never give you a mediocre dream. His dreams are always big dreams, and you must have the will and tenacity to overcome every obstacle that stands in your way. Many dreams don't get fulfilled because people run away when the going gets tough. James 1:12 (MSG) says, "Anyone who meets a testing challenge head-on and manages to stick it out is mighty fortunate."

Success is born out of adversity, and you need to view your tests and trials as steppingstones on your journey to becoming Christlike and to fulfilling the call of God on your life. Heb. 12:1 says to "run with endurance the race that is set before us." The word "endurance" means 'to hold up consistently under fire.' When you get knocked down, get back up for "greater is He that is in you than he that is in the world" (1 John 4:4). A test or trial does not give you a reason to quit and run. No, it gives you an opportunity to put on the armor of God and stand up and fight. Tests and trials are an open invitation for you to use your faith against whatever the enemy brings your way. You also need to understand that if your dream wasn't important then the devil wouldn't try to hinder its fulfillment like he does. View your trial as a sign that you're making progress, that the kingdom of darkness is being torn down and the kingdom of God is being built up.

Rejoice that God has considered you worthy to be a part of what's happening in His kingdom on the earth today. This is what having a

God-given dream is all about. If the fulfillment of your dream seems a long way off, don't get discouraged and never lose hope. Behind the scenes God is working everything out on your behalf. Rom. 8:28 says "all things work together for good to those who love God, to those who are the called according to His purpose." Have the will to keep going forward no matter what obstacles may lay in your path. Have the will to live a wholesome life and to make a positive difference in the world today. You live to succeed and you succeed to serve. Most people want to live but they don't succeed because they don't want to make those sacrifices that are necessary to succeed and are quick to run away when opposition comes knocking on their door. This is why Jesus said in Matt. 22:14, "For many are called, but few are chosen."

God's call is shouting out to you. It's your dream so never stop pursuing it until it is completely and totally fulfilled. It should be the goal of every believer to be continually used by God to make a positive difference in the world in spite of their ever-present shortcomings. You can be flawed in and of yourself but in Christ be mighty in terms of spiritual power and influence. Accept by faith that God has a glorious, good plan for your life. Everybody who has ever been born has been called to serve God. They've been given an assignment from on high and this is what gives people a reason to live. Still, excuses abound as to why these individual calls are not fulfilled. When called upon to save Israel from the hand of the Midianites Gideon said, "O my Lord, how can I save Israel? Indeed my clan is the weakest in Manasseh, and I am least in my father's house" (Judges 6:15).

Gideon was indeed flawed but for some reason he did not grasp what the Angel of the Lord said to him in vs. 12, "The Lord is with you, you mighty man of valor." Consider what Moses said to God at the burning bush, "Who am I that I should go to Pharaoh, and that I should bring the children of Israel out of Egypt?" (Ex. 3:11). What all people need to understand is that God is in the business of making champions out of failures. He will take a person who is flawed and make them mighty. He'll give you beauty for ashes (Is. 61:3). He'll turn a nobody into a somebody, a zero into a hero. God has hand-picked every person for a special work to do and He is fully expecting them to fulfill that call. It's what they've been born for. God can use anybody, including you! You are not too old to serve God. Moses was eighty years old when God called him to deliver His people out of Egypt. Neither are you too young. Jesus fed the multitude with the loaves and fishes of a young boy.

God used murderers, adulterers, prostitutes, and smelly fishermen to do His work on planet Earth. Consider the lustful Samson and the ever-impulsive Peter. Who was more flawed than they? Saul of Tarsus, Moses, Gideon, Elijah, and David all made mistakes, but God used each one of them in a powerful way. They were flawed but mighty. If you think you are not qualified to be used by God, then you are right where God wants you to be. 1 Cor. 1:26-29 says, "For you see your calling, brethren, that not many wise according to the flesh, not many mighty, not many noble are called. But God has chosen the foolish things of the world to put to shame the things that are mighty; and the base things of the world and the things which are despised God has chosen, and the things which are not to bring to nothing the things that are, that no flesh should glory in His presence."

The New Berkley translation says, "God has chosen the world's insignificant, and despised, and nobodies, in order to bring to nothing those who amount to something so that nobody may boast in the presence of God." People who are important in their own eyes are in for a letdown when they want to be used by God. God uses people who do not think too highly of themselves (Rom. 12:3). God uses nobodies, people who are flawed. When God finds a somebody, He first turns them into a nobody. Moses was raised as the son of Pharaoh's daughter but before he could be used by God he was sent to the backside of the desert for forty years where he became a nobody. Saul of

Tarsus was a somebody but after being struck down on the road to Damascus he was sent to Arabia for several years away from the view of all the people. He became a nobody and God raised him up to write most of the New Testament.

One of the greatest prophets in Old Testament scripture was Elijah but the time came when he became too important in his own eyes. After his miracle on Mt. Carmel the wicked Queen Jezebel sought to kill him and Elijah ran away. Self-pity grabbed hold of his soul and he told the Lord, "I have been very zealous for the Lord God of hosts; for the children of Israel have forsaken Your covenant, torn down Your altars, and killed Your prophets with the sword. I alone am left; and they seek to take my life" (1 Kings 19:10). In other words, Elijah was saying, "God, no one is serving You except me! What will you do without me?" Elijah had become too important in his own eyes and had forgotten that he was a nobody when God found him. Because Elijah would not stop complaining God decided to replace him with a nobody farmer named Elisha.

Faithfulness is the key to being used mightily by God. 1 Cor. 4:2 says, "Moreover it is required in stewards that one be found faithful." Elisha wasn't in school studying to be a prophet. No, he was faithfully working in his father's field. Later he was just as faithful to Elijah as he had been to his own father. Elijah made things difficult for Elisha but he never left the prophet's side and for a number of years followed Elijah without question. You can be flawed but if you prove yourself faithful God will use you in a mighty way. The "nobody" Elisha received double the spirit that was on the "somebody" Elijah and performed fourteen miracles compared to Elijah's seven. You can teach a person skills to make them qualified, but you can never teach faithfulness. You're either faithful or you're not. Paul says in 1 Tim. 1:12, "And I thank Christ Jesus our Lord Who has enabled me, because He counted me faithful, putting me in the ministry."

God is not looking for a person with colossal qualifications or somebody with great skills in a certain area. Above all else, He is looking for faithfulness. Jesus said, "He who is faithful in what is least is faithful also in much" (Luke 16:10). God will grant spiritual blessings and favor upon you according to your faithfulness and integrity. Faithfulness in life will be the foundation for all your eternal rewards. Daily you should long for Jesus to one day say to you, "Well done, good and faithful servant; you were faithful over a few things, I will make you ruler over many things. Enter into the joy of the Lord" (Matt. 25:21). God speaks to those who are faithfully doing something. Elisha was plowing a field, Gideon was thrashing wheat, David was taking care of his father's sheep, and Peter was fishing when the Lord spoke to them of their upcoming ministries. It is time for you to begin doing faithfully whatever your hand finds to do. You will then begin to live a good life.

People need to stop making excuses for why they are not serving the Lord. Too many people are waiting for God to do something when in fact it is He who is waiting on them to do something. God will move in your life but, more times than not, you must move first. Stop telling God how flawed and unworthy you are and begin to put your hand to the plow and do the job that is available to you now. God does not look for the many, He looks for the few. He is looking for "a few good men" who will love Him above all others and have hearts to serve Him no matter the cost. Always remember, the door of tomorrow will not open until you do something today. To those who are flawed in character but mighty in Spirit the Lord gives a powerful command in Luke 17:32, "Remember Lot's wife." When God delivered Lot and his family out of Sodom and Gomorrah, He told them in Gen. 19:17, "Do not look behind you."

God was telling them that everything they needed to live a good life was ahead of them. Lot's wife ignored this command, looked back, and instantly was turned into a pillar of salt. Lot's wife lost her future because she looked back. There is a reason the windshield of your car is bigger than the rear-view mirror. God wants you focused so much on what's ahead of you that you don't even notice what's going on behind you. Is. 43:18,19 says, "Do not remember the former things, nor consider the things of old. Behold, I will do a new thing, now it shall spring forth, shall you not know it?" You cannot pursue your future if there is something still tying you to your past. Satan is a thief and he is after your dream. He wants you stuck in the past so you'll never move forward. He's hoping that you will lose your future by looking back. The good news is that God sees you as a world overcomer (1 John 5:4). Your faith will overcome every attack from the enemy, including negative thoughts and memories from your past.

Remember Lot's wife. Don't look back, always look forward. The deciding factor in having a bright future where you live a good life and do great things in and for the kingdom of God is based on whether or not you step forward and do that which you were born to do. Jesus said in Mark 10:46, "Even the Son of Man did not come to be served, but to serve, and to give His life as a ransom for many." Since Jesus gave His life to serve others, you also should devote your life to doing the same thing. In order to serve others, Jesus gives His people special gifts and abilities with which they may fulfill their heavenly call. The best way to discover your spiritual gift is to sit back and reflect on those things you really enjoy doing, activities which repeatedly bring you joy and satisfaction. Think about your desires and inclinations. God does not want you miserable and won't make you go places you don't want to go or make you do things you don't want to do.

He has given you your likes and dislikes, your desires and preferences, for a purpose. By looking to the desires that are most basic to your personality, you can gain vital insight into where God is leading you in your service to Him. Now that you know what your spiritual gifts are, it is time to make a quality decision to step forward and do that which you were born to do. Decisions are like earthquakes, they have tremors and they last on and on and affect the lives of other people around you. Your destiny is calling out to you and it's time to step out of your comfort zone and into the unknown. Stepping out definitely requires overcoming fear and insecurities, doing what may not come natural to you, and flat-out trusting God with everything in you. Serving God is one big, exciting adventure and it begins right here. Many people don't hear the call on their lives because they've ignored it for so long. Other people may see the gifts you possess and the potential in you, but you don't see it anymore.

Pick up the call and put one foot in front of the other. Your days are numbered and your life is fleeing away. James 4:14 says, "For what is your life? It is even a vapor that appears for a little time and then vanishes away." It's time to pursue God's calling with everything you've got and it's time to prioritize your life. Don't prioritize your schedule, schedule your priorities. Make time with God your number one priority. When you pursue God, you are pursuing your dream. Spending time with God will cause you to get closer to Him, more comfortable with Him, and more sensitive to His voice. Divine direction will come because very rarely will God allow you to see beyond the horizon that is looming ahead of you. Bobby Knight once said, "The will to succeed is important, but what's even more important is the will to prepare." You have to invest in your future. Preparation takes effort and you must make time to learn, to grow, and to expand your thinking.

Expose yourself to new things, new people, new books, new places. Your calling won't just happen by itself; you have to go after it. Remember the words of John Wooden, "When opportunity comes, it is too late to prepare." You need to make up your mind that you are going on with God no matter what. You are here to please God, not man. Col. 3:22 says, "Servants, obey in all things your masters according to the flesh, not with eye service, as men-pleasers, but in sincerity of heart, fearing God." Your life is precious. Every single day of your life is recorded in history. Be so determined to go after God's plan for your life that turning back is not an option. Decide today that you will answer and fulfill God's calling on your life. Your decision today will affect your tomorrow. Always remember that you will get whatever it is you pursue, whether good or bad.

James 1:8 says a double-minded man is "unstable in all his ways." Vs. 11 says "the rich man also will fade away in his pursuits" and vs. 14 says, "But each one is tempted when he is drawn away by his own desires and enticed." James makes it clear that your ways, your pursuits, and your dreams are not going to produce the purpose of God in your life. What are you going for? What are you actively pursuing? Are you living your life to get what you want all the time or are you seeking to fulfill your God-given purpose? Like bait on a fisherman's hook, your own selfish desires will draw you away from the things of God. You need to know that there will always be consequences that come with making wrong choices. Don't allow the devil to entice you and pull you away from all the wonderful things God has planned for your life. Understand that you're not going to see God's will fulfilled your way, it gets fulfilled His way.

You need to always pursue God's will and purpose for your life knowing you'll never come in second when you put God first. He has so many astounding things planned for your life. James 1:5 says He is a God "who gives liberally and without reproach." He will give you gifts and talents and the resources you need to do what He has called you to do. Your life will have a storybook ending when you make the things of God the primary pursuit of your life. Solomon writes in Eccl. 5:3, "For a dream comes through much activity." It has been said that success is the willingness to bear pain. You better learn to fight for your dream because all your plans will not fall into place automatically. There is an enemy out there who comes to kill, steal, and destroy and perseverance is needed for all dreams to be fulfilled. Rejoice knowing that the trials you face is an indicator that much progress is being made in your life.

Determine to never give up and keep going on the path you're currently on. Go on the offensive and use your faith and the words you speak to prophecy your future. Prov. 18:21 says, "Life and death are in the power of the tongue." What's coming out of your mouth has everything to do with what happens in your future. 1 Sam. 17:44 says, "And the Philistine said to David." The devil talks to you. What should you do when he does? Vs. 45 tells us, "Then David said to the Philistine." Talk back to the devil and do it out loud! You need to declare openly what you are believing for. That's exactly how God spoke the entire world into existence. You must do the same. Finally, procrastinate no more! You now know what your spiritual gifts are and you've come to realize that you can be flawed in character but mighty in Spirit. You are strong in the Lord and the power of His might (Eph. 6:10). Nothing can stop you now. You can do all things through Christ which strengthens you. You are more than a conqueror.

The past is behind you. Learn from it, release it, and refuse to live there any longer. The future stands ever before you, full of purpose, possibility, and the promise of what you can still become. Don't let another day slip by without taking a step toward the calling God has placed on your life. Every small act of obedience moves you closer to the purpose He designed specifically for you. Start today, because delay steals momentum and quietly robs you of progress. Every moment you wait is energy leaking away from the purpose placed inside you. Action, even imperfect action, awakens clarity, confidence, and direction. When you move forward now, you unlock the destiny that hesitation keeps hidden. Time is flying by. You don't have to be great to start but you have to start to be great. What are you waiting for? Get started today and fulfill your God-given call.

| 6 |

"A HIGHER ANOINTING"

What would you ask for if God appeared to you and said He would grant you one wish? If He stood before you and promised to fulfill one request, what would your heart choose? If only a single desire could be granted, what would be the foremost thing on your mind? It happened to Solomon. 1 Kings 3:5 says, "At Gibeon the Lord appeared to Solomon in a dream by night; and God said, 'Ask! What shall I give you?'" The truth is, God asks each of us that very same question every day of our lives. Jesus said in John 15:16, "Whatever you ask the Father in My Name He will give you." Again He said in John 16:23,24, "And in that day you will ask Me nothing. Most assuredly, I say to you, whatever you ask the Father in My Name, He will give you. Until now you have asked nothing in My Name. Ask, and you will receive, that your joy may be full." Isn't that amazing? When you ask with faith and expectation, when you ask in alignment with God's will, you will receive what you ask for and your joy will be complete.

So, what would you ask for? Solomon's answer to this offer establishes the pattern for how we also should respond if the same question were asked of us. He said in 1 Kings 3:9, "Therefore give to Your servant an understanding heart to judge Your people, that I may discern between good and evil. For who is able to judge this great people of Yours?" This great man, the son of David, asked God for the wisdom and the anointing to better serve God and His people. He sought first the kingdom of God and not his own interests. His answer shows that when God offers blessing, wisdom must be valued above power, wealth, or personal gain. His response sets the pattern for us to seek God's heart and purposes first, trusting that everything else will be added in His perfect way. And because of his unselfishness, God also blessed him with riches and honor. To this day Solomon is known as the wisest and richest man who ever lived.

In 1 Chron. 4:9,10 an otherwise unknown man named Jabez steps out of obscurity and prayed a daring faith-filled prayer that contains the pathway to a life of extraordinary favor with God. Jabez doesn't stand out like a Moses or a David in the Old Testament or light up the book of Acts like those early Christians who turned the world upside down. The fact is you'll find him hiding in the least read section of one of the least read books of the Bible. The first nine chapters of 1 Chron. gives us a boring history of the Hebrew tribes and from this long list of unfamiliar and difficult names a story of great importance suddenly breaks through. "Now Jabez was more honorable than his brothers, and his mother called his name Jabez, saying, 'Because I bore him in pain.' And Jabez called on the God of Israel saying, 'Oh, that You would bless me indeed, and enlarge my territory, that Your hand would be with me, and that You would keep me from evil, that I may not cause pain!' So God granted him what he requested."

Though his name was associated with pain, Jabez refused to let his beginning define his destiny. Instead, he boldly cried out to God, asking for blessing, expansion, divine presence, and protection from harm. His prayer was an audacious appeal rooted in trust in God's goodness and power. Jabez's prayer stands as a timeless reminder that when a person aligns their desires with God's purposes and calls on Him with bold expectation, God delights in releasing uncommon favor and transforming ordinary lives into testimonies of His grace. Scripture records that God granted his request, showing that heaven responds to faith that dares to ask beyond circumstances. Notice where he asked God to "enlarge my territory." This was not a request for more real estate. In essence, what he was saying was this, "O God and King, please expand my opportunities and my influence in such a way that I touch more lives for Your glory. Let me do more for You." Because his heart was right, God granted him his request.

One more story that should be of special interest to all who seek to fulfill their destiny is that of Elijah and Elisha. The great prophet Elijah was about to be taken to heaven in a fiery chariot and God had chosen a farmer named Elisha to carry on the role of prophet in the land. Before his departure Elijah said to Elisha, "Ask! What may I do for you, before I am taken away from you?" (2 Kings 2:9). Once again, this very important question is asked. And Elisha responded, "Please let a double portion of your spirit be upon me." Elisha, along with Solomon and Jabez, longed for both the opportunity and the anointing to serve God at a greater measure, refusing to settle for less than God's best. In the same way, you must cultivate a holy hunger to grow deeper, reach higher, and walk more fully in God's will and purpose. God desires to lift you into a new and higher level in Him, where you step into your full potential and experience the fullness of what He has prepared for you.

Hungry believers who refuse to settle for shallow encounters can step into a higher dimension of the anointing, where intimacy with God produces extraordinary power. In this realm, all who walk in it are saturated with His glory, carrying the unmistakable presence and authority of God wherever they go. Jesus said in Matt. 5:6, "Blessed are those who hunger and thirst for righteousness, for they shall be filled." Hunger and thirst is a sign that you are about to be filled. Your cup is about to overflow with the anointing of God. Elisha wanted a double portion of Elijah's anointing but first his mentor led him on a journey to four destinations that shows us what must happen first if this special anointing is to become a reality in our lives. There are no meaningless details in the Word of God. Scriptures are not put in the Word just to fill up space. No, each and every verse of scripture has great significance to our lives and so it is with Elisha's journey to a new anointing.

2 Kings 2:1 tells us that Elijah first took Elisha to Gilgal. Josh. 4:19,20 tells us that Gilgal was the first camp of Israel after crossing the Jordan River into the Promised Land. It was here at Gilgal where the manna stopped falling from heaven to feed the people. Now they had to walk by faith and not by sight. For forty years they saw the manna on the ground outside their tents but all that stopped at Gilgal. Elijah brought Elisha to Gilgal to show him that living by faith is the first step that will lead you to your full potential. When you walk by faith life gets a little more difficult. The Israelites now had to plow the ground and plant seeds if they were going to have food to eat. Faith demands work on your part because faith without works is dead. God wants to strengthen your spiritual muscles, and this is what walking by faith does for you. Also, in the wilderness Moses was their mediator with God but at Gilgal you stop depending on others to tell you what God is saying. By faith you hear from God yourself.

Next, Elijah took Elisha to Bethel (2 Kings 2:2). At Gilgal you lose what you can see and at Bethel you lose what you can feel. On your journey to a higher anointing you come to a place where the presence of God is no longer felt and you enter into a season of silence. It was at Bethel that Jacob met God and wrestled with Him all during the night. Often God tried to pull away but Jacob held on even tighter. What was God doing? He was trying to find out how badly Jacob wanted his blessing. God said "No!" but Jacob said "Yes!" Over and over again this happened and Gen. 32:28 tells us that Jacob struggled with God and prevailed. At Bethel, you learn that if you don't wrestle with God you'll wrestle with man. Saul didn't wrestle with God, so he wrestled with Samuel. If Jacob had not wrestled with God he would have wrestled with Esau who came with an army of 400 men to kill him. Likewise, if you also want to prevail in life and come out on top then you also have to enter into a struggle with God.

Like Jacob you need to grab hold onto God and not let go until you receive the full manifestation of what has been promised. There is, however, one aspect of this story that often gets overlooked but has great significance to your walk with God. After a long night of struggling with God the heavenly agent whom Jacob held on so tightly to touched his hip and threw it out of joint. For the rest of his life Jacob walked with a limp because of his wrestling match with God. Why did this happen? Was Jacob getting the best of his visitor so God had to do this in order to get the advantage? Of course not! The ole boy had wrestled all night and was near exhaustion as it was. So what was the reason for Jacob's limp? First of all, we know Jacob wanted to get blessed. He said with bold determination, "I will not let You go until You bless me!" What happened next? The blessing? No, the limp! Jacob received his limp before he received his blessing.

Let's analyze what it means to have a limp. It means that you will always need someone or something to lean on and you will also have to struggle doing what you want to do. The meaning of Jacob's limp is that if you want to walk in the blessings of God and have a higher anointing then you will have to learn to lean on Him because many struggles will come your way. Forget the idea that being blessed by God means you're on a beach somewhere drinking pineapple juice as you swing on a hammock between two palm trees. This is not reality. We are in a war and being saved and anointed does not mean that you will live on "Easy Street." Jesus said to "count the cost" and He told Peter you could have a hundredfold return on your giving "with persecutions." There always has been and there always will be a struggle to walk in the perfect will of God. The decision we all must make is whether or not we want to confront these struggles in order to fulfill the call of God on our lives.

Contrary to what the misinformed may believe, receiving a higher anointing is not a joy ride in the park. It's a journey into a war zone where strength and endurance will be needed with each step you take. Every morning Jacob had to lean on a cane when he got out of bed. It was a struggle to get from one place to the next. But the man was blessed! Experience teaches us that the rewards of getting blessed by God far exceed whatever struggle you may go through if, that is, you are willing to pay the price. And what price is that? You must learn to lean on God rather than trusting in the arm of the flesh because human strength will always fall short. When you place your full confidence in Him, you discover a power, wisdom, and peace that no earthly support can provide. Success is not free nor is it cheap. Indeed, there is a price to pay for success. You need to realize that success is forged in adversity where pressure refines purpose, trials build strength, and perseverance turns obstacles into triumph.

Tests, trials, and oftentimes failure come to all who believe. When they do, a decision must be made as to what your attitude will be in the midst of these afflictions? Do roadblocks signal the end of your journey or are they steppingstones that lead to a place that is "exceedingly abundantly above all that we ask or think" (Eph. 3:20)? Success that is birthed as a result of tests and trials can be compared to a farmer putting manure in a cornfield before the planting season begins. As manure is used to fertilize the soil so the seeds can grow, so do tests and trials help develop within you that special character trait that causes you to never give up and press on in the good fight of faith. It will also help to realize that adversity is the devil's response to your progress, and this is why James 1:2-4 instructs us to "count it all joy" when tests and trials come our way. Paul gives us the assurance that "if God be for us, who can be against us?" In Christ we always win if we don't quit.

As wonderful as the blessings of God are, it is a certainty that these blessings are not for the faint-hearted. They require courage to steward, faith to endure opposition, and obedience to walk worthy of what God has entrusted to you. God said in Ps. 89:19, "I have given help to one who is mighty: and the book of James tells us that the unstable and double-minded man should not "suppose that he will receive anything from the Lord." When a struggle comes your way, rise up in faith and remember that you never face it alone. With God by your side, you are stronger than anything the enemy could ever throw against you. Remember, Jacob's limp came before his blessing. Likewise, the cross came before the empty tomb. Any struggle can rightfully be called a prelude to a blessing because pressure is often the place where purpose is formed and faith is refined. What feels like resistance today may be God's preparation for the strength, clarity, and breakthrough you will walk in tomorrow.

It's always darkest just before the dawn. If you are in a struggle, then hold on tight like Jacob did because a blessing is on the way. Every time something goes wrong use your faith and focus on the blessing that is about to follow. The difference between losers and winners is that losers focus on the limp whereas winners always focus on the blessing. This is the key to having a higher anointing and living a victorious life. Rejoice over the fact that your cup is half full instead of complaining that it's half empty. With this attitude you'll breeze through anything the devil throws your way. Anything! Just don't lose your focus. Yes, the struggles will be there. They will always be there. Jacob's limp never went away and Paul had his "thorn in the flesh." But thank God, His grace is sufficient for all of us. It is true, the more you focus on something the bigger it gets. Little molehills turn into giant mountains when all you do is focus on them. The same applies to the blessings of God.

Wimps focus on limps whereas overcomers focus on the blessings. Jacob was tired and exhausted, but when he spoke, he focused on the blessing. He said, "I will not let you go until you bless me." Also, nowhere in scripture does it say he ever spoke one word about his limp. Wimps with limps always gripe and complain about their problems. They say, "Woe is me!" and by doing so their struggle gets bigger. But winners are different. They see the light at the end of the tunnel, and they focus on the prize at the end of the race. Winners focus on the blessing and if you will do the same then the blessings will flow into your life on the crest of every wave. In life circumstances rarely go as we'd like but in Jesus, you can rise up above those roadblocks that hinder your walk with Him. Being blessed with a higher anointing does not mean you will have no more struggles. Jacob still had his limp. Being blessed does mean you can rise up above your trials and live on a higher plane than where your problems are.

The good news is that once the blessing is manifested the pains of your struggle are quickly forgotten. What once felt overwhelming fades in the light of fulfillment, replaced by gratitude and renewed strength. In the end, the victory speaks louder than the suffering that brought you there. Jesus said in John 16:21, "A woman, when she is in labor, has sorrow because her hour has come; but as soon as she has given birth to the child, she no longer remembers the anguish, for joy that a human being has been born into the world." The key is to focus on the blessing and not the struggle. Many Christians fail to grow because they never see the connection between their problems and their future dreams and victories. A crisis is a signal for you to learn and grow, not lose. Your problem is your promotion. A problem will introduce you to yourself and cause you to find out what you're made of. Every obstacle will bring change into your life. You'll either be stronger because of it or you'll be weaker.

Great leaders are those who refuse to quit and rise above their problems. All born-again believers should view the tests and trials that come their way as opportunities for their lives to be built up and molded until they become mature in the Lord. This is how holiness comes and God Himself said, "Be holy, for I am holy" (1 Peter 1:16). Do not let your head hang low and confess that you're walking through the valley. In Christ there are no valley experiences. Some mountains are just higher than others. At Bethel you learn to lean on God even though His presence is not felt. It is so vital that you learn this lesson because the next city Elijah took Elisha to was Jericho (2 Kings 2:4). Historians tell us that it was near Jericho that Jesus spent 40 days fasting in the wilderness. Jesus went to Jericho alone and waiting for Him there was the devil himself. At Jericho you face your toughest battle, your biggest obstacle. The devil always shows up when the presence of God is gone from your life.

At Gilgal you don't see anything. At Bethel you don't feel anything. At Jericho you experience the darkest moment of your life. Jesus met the devil in the wilderness of Jericho and so will you. The temptation will be there to cry out in anguished frustration, "My God, My God, why have You forsaken Me? Why are You so far from helping Me, and from the words of My groaning? O My God, I cry in the daytime, but You do not hear; And in the night season, and am not silent" (Ps. 22:1,2). Every demon in hell will show up at Jericho and nobody will be there to help you. Like Jesus you also will be all alone, but we learn from our Savior that at this critical point in our lives all we can do is follow His example and say, "It is written..." During Job's Jericho experience he confessed, "Though He slay me, yet will I trust Him" (Job 13:15). This is how you defeat the enemy at Jericho. David wrote in Ps. 34:17, "The righteous cry out, and the Lord hears, and delivers them out of all their troubles."

Great battles bring great victories. After going to Jericho Elijah then brought Elisha a short five miles to the Jordan River. It was at the Jordan that Elijah asked his protégé, "What do you want?" God also will ask you this question but not until after you have passed through Jericho. The Jordan River was a place of new beginnings. It bordered the land that was flowing with milk and honey, and it was here that Joshua and Caleb began their quest to conquer the Promised Land. Jesus was baptized in the Jordan River and immediately the Holy Spirit came down like a dove and filled Him with anointed power and majesty. And it was here that Elisha asked for and received a double portion of the spirit that was upon Elijah. His request was answered but first he had to go to Gilgal, Bethel, and Jericho and so also must you if you want to walk in a higher anointing. As you make this journey never take your eyes off of what awaits you at Jordan. It's the place where your destiny begins.

"THE CHARACTER TO SUCCEED"

Every person who has ever been born has been given a dream from God and a destiny to fulfill. What's so exciting about this is that His dream for your life is always bigger than any dream you could ever come up on your own, just like His destiny is bigger than your destiny. The dream He gives you is your calling and His purpose is your destiny. Understand that the fulfillment of a heavenly call is not for the faint-hearted. There is an enemy out there who comes to kill, steal, and destroy. He roams about like a roaring lion seeking whom he can devour and you are in his crosshairs. What all this means is that there will be obstacles you must face and tests you must pass before the fulfillment of your dream becomes a reality. Yes, God is on your side but that does not mean you forget about the devil. You need to know who he is and how he works and the destruction he wants to bring to your life. Paul said in 2 Cor. 2:11, "Lest Satan should take advantage of us; for we are not ignorant of his devices."

One of the first things you'll learn about the devil is that he is very prideful. Ezek. 28:17 says, "Your heart was lifted up because of your beauty; You corrupted your wisdom for the sake of your splendor; I cast you to the ground, I laid you before kings, that they may gaze at you." Pride brought about the devil's downfall and he will use it to try to bring about yours as well. This is why you never want to become arrogant and brag about the dream God gives you. Don't become high minded if God uses you to reach millions of people for the kingdom of God whereas some little ole grandmother is never seen in the public eye because she's off in her prayer closet for several hours a day. Don't brag, just be faithful in all He has called you to do. There is nothing wrong with giving God glory for what He has done but people who brag are giving themselves the credit and the honor for what is happening in their lives.

James was adamant when he said, "Do not be deceived, my beloved brethren. Every good gift and every perfect gift is from above and comes down from the Father of lights" (James 1:16,17). People brag as the result of pride being in their heart. Matt. 12:34 says, "For out of the abundance of the heart the mouth speaks." Pride always has to have a voice, it always wants to be heard, and it always interrupts other people. People with pride think their opinion is more important than the other person's opinion so they're always cutting into the conversation to make sure their voice if heard. Prov. 10:19 says, "In the multitude of words sin is not lacking, but he who restrains his lips is wise." The Message Bible says, "The more talk, the less truth; the wise measure their words. The speech of a good person is worth waiting for; the blabber of the wicked is worthless. The talk of a good person is rich fare for many, but chatterboxes die of an empty heart" (vs. 19-21).

Yes, you may have a dream that will make you well known to many, but this is not the purpose of the dream. God's purpose for your life is that He can use you as a means of blessing other people. Your influence in the lives of those around you is for the glory of God, not your own. James 4:10 says, "Humble yourselves in the sight of the Lord, and He will lift you up." It takes maturity to fulfill a God-given dream and humility is what helps make you mature. If you become prideful when God gives you the dream then you'll never have the maturity to handle the destiny. In fact, pride will cause the destiny to never come to pass. God gives you a dream that will put you on the path to maturity so you'll be able to handle the destiny when it arrives. As you grow and mature you will begin to see yourself through the eyes of God. Gone will be the insecurities you once had, and this is how you defeat pride. All pride is rooted in insecurity. If pride is in your heart, then insecurity is in your soul.

You need to know who you are in Christ and trust Him completely because with every new challenge comes new insecurities. It takes maturity to handle the new levels of responsibility that are coming your way. The closer you get to the fulfillment of your destiny the more confident you must become in the Lord. If you know who you are in Christ and who your heavenly Daddy is, you'll defeat pride and the insecurity that goes with it. It takes strength of character to fulfill a heavenly call and this is why most people live with their dreams but never step into their destiny. God will not allow these people to fulfill the destiny He has for their lives because they're not ready to handle the responsibility that goes along with it. Daily the cry of your heart should be, "Search me, O God, and know my heart; Try me, and know my anxieties; And see if there is any wicked way in me, and lead me in the way everlasting" (Ps. 139:23,24).

Stop blaming other people for the rough times you've had in the past and grow up and take responsibility for the one life God has given you. Allow God to search your heart and He'll show you how to walk in integrity and develop an inward character that is both godly and transforming. He will deliver you from everything that holds you in bondage and will bring you into an even closer relationship with Him. The Message Bible says, "Investigate my life, O God, find out everything about me; Cross examine and test me, get a clear picture of what I'm about; See for Yourself whether I've done anything wrong - then guide me on the road to eternal life." Success comes as the result of being close to God. Gen. 39:2 says, "The Lord was with Joseph, and he was a successful man." Vs. 23 says "whatever he did, the Lord made it prosper." The Message Bible says, "Whatever he did God made sure it worked out for the best."

The key to prospering in life and to fulfilling your heavenly call is to forever be in the presence of the Lord. God wants to prosper you and make you successful in your life, your marriage, your health, and in the dream He gives you to fulfill. He wants to prosper you so you can help prosper others. In Hebrew the word "prosperity" means 'to push forward' and this is what God will do when you draw near to Him. He'll push you forward so you'll be able to accomplish all He set aside for you to do with your life. God never fails so, if you'll walk with Him, you'll prosper and will develop the character to succeed in whatever you set out to do. Deut. 29:9 says, "Therefore keep the words of this covenant, and do them, that you may prosper in all that you do." God wants to push you forward in all that you put your hand to do but first you must be in His presence at all times.

Some people view success differently than how God views success. Joseph was a slave in Egypt yet scripture says he was a successful man. He had no goods or property of his own and had no money in the bank. These are the things the world says you need in order to be successful but Joseph had none of these. He was successful and prosperous because the Lord was with him. Likewise, the sum total of all the success you'll ever have in your life will be based on the presence of God being manifested wherever you go. The measure to which you allow yourself to be led by the Spirit of God is what determines if you'll deal wisely with the affairs of life. Gen. 39:3 says, "And his master saw that the Lord was with him and that the Lord made all he did to prosper in his hand." When the Lord is with you, success will come with little or no self-effort. Vs. 4, "So Joseph found favor in his sight, and served him. Then he made him overseer of his house, and all that he had put in his hand."

This was the kind of success that caused people to know that God's hand was in on it. There is worldly success and there is success that can only be accredited to the presence of God in your life. You will be able to do things that other people on their own cannot do, things that are above the norm of everyday living. The Lord was with Joseph and the blessing that was on his life allowed him to be a blessing to someone else. Vs. 5 says, "So it was, from the time that he had made him overseer of his house and all that he had, that the Lord blessed the Egyptian's house for Joseph's sake; and the blessing of the Lord was on all that he had in the house and in the field." The favor that was on Joseph was distributed to those around him. He was blessed to be a blessing. The last thing you want to do is store up and hoard the blessings God gives you. No, they are meant to be shared with others. This is why there is an overflow of all the good things the Lord gives you.

The abundance of the blessings in your life will cause you to become a funnel through which the favor of God can flow into the lives of other people. Never forget that this is why you're being blessed. You're blessed to be a blessing. God is not going to bless you so you can sit around and brag about all the nice things you have. When God blesses you, start looking around to see who you can be a blessing to. Allow God to use you to bless someone else all because they've been in your presence for a little while. Notice that Joseph was successful because the Lord was with him but the Egyptian was blessed because he was with Joseph. Prosperity and success is always based on who you're with and this is why you need the presence of the Lord in your life morning, noon, and night. When you're with Him daily His presence will be wherever you go. When you go to work, the presence of the Lord will be there. When you go to the store, the presence of the Lord will be there as well.

In the presence of the Lord are blessings galore and this is why you need to leave a trail of blessings wherever you go. Do something that will cause people to say, "The Lord is in this place." And when you show favor to those around you, God will cause people to show favor to you. This is why Joseph was promoted and found success in whatever situation he found himself in. If you want to succeed in life and fulfill your destiny, you've got to come up higher and obey God. This does not mean you won't have any trials but, if you'll obey your Daddy, He will take you through those storms that come your way. It is not hard to obey God if you trust Him and are daily walking in faith. You need to believe that there are rewards if you obey God and serious consequences if you don't. Heb. 3:18,19 says, "And to whom did He swear that they would not enter His rest, but to those who did not obey? So we see that they could not enter in because of unbelief."

Faith produces obedience and this verse is saying that people don't obey because they don't believe. It takes faith to obey God. If these people had believed that God would reward them, they would have obeyed. Rom. 10:17 says, "So then faith comes by hearing, and hearing by the word of God." Read your Bible daily and confess out loud those promises you're believing will come to pass in your life. Listen to as many sermons as you can that teach the Word accurately. Do this for in the Word is the power to change your life. It will produce in you the character to succeed. Your character affects your entire life. Don't be like those who think they can sin and get away with it because those thoughts are delusional. Gal. 6:7 says, "Do not be deceived, God is not mocked; for whatever a man sows, that he will also reap." It is foolish to ignore the consequences that come with every decision you make. To ensure a long and successful life you need to decide to obey God at all costs, at all times.

Obedience is one of the greatest character builders there is, so much so that the prophet Samuel once said, "To obey is better than sacrifice" (1 Sam. 15:22). Determine today to obey God at all times and leave all the consequences to Him. He'll open doors you can't open and take you places you could never go on your own. Obedience may not always be easy, but you can do it when you realize that God is the sovereign ruler of the universe, and He knows what He's doing and what's best for your life. Ps. 103:19 says, "The Lord has established His throne in heaven, and His kingdom rules over all." Success comes when you allow your Daddy to be the absolute and final authority in your life. It was through obedience that Joseph ran away when Potiphar's wife tried to seduce him. God had the final authority in his life and he said to her, "How then can I do this great wickedness and sin against God?" (Gen. 39:9). Joseph did the right thing, yet he was thrown into prison anyway.

Even so, God was with him and vs. 21 says, "But the Lord was with Joseph and showed him mercy, and He gave him favor in the sight of the keeper of the prison." The character to succeed was being developed in his life through these trials and, because the Lord was with him, he was able to persevere through each and every one of them. Rom. 5:3,4 (NLT) says, "We can rejoice, too, when we run into problems and trials, for we know that they help us develop endurance. And endurance develops strength of character, and character strengthens our confident hope of salvation." It takes a person with spiritual insight to rejoice and be happy when something bad happens but this is what Paul is telling you to do. You can do this if you'll trust God and believe that at the end of every storm is a beautiful multi-colored rainbow. You don't rejoice because the trial has come, you rejoice in the midst of it because you know something good will come as the result of it.

James 1:2-4 says, "My brethren, count it all joy when you fall into various trials, knowing that the resting of your faith produces patience. But let patience have its perfect work, that you may be perfect and complete, lacking nothing." Trials produce patience and tribulations produce perseverance. Patience is the ability to wait on God with contentment, to do the right thing and display a godly character while you wait. Perseverance is the battle you fight while you wait. A trial is brief but tribulations are long and difficult yet this is the only thing the Bible says will produce in your life the character to succeed. It is so important that this character get developed in you for it is your response to the trial that oftentimes determines how long the trial lasts. A trial in the life of a mature believer does not last as long as the trials in the lives of carnal, lukewarm believers. They have developed perseverance in their life and now have the character to obey God and trust Him to deliver them out of whatever they're going through.

One of the worst things that can happen is for you to get delivered out of a trial that God is using to build character in your life. No trial means no character. David said in Ps. 23:4 that he was walking through the valley of the shadow of death. He didn't say he was delivered out of this valley. No, he was walking through it with the Lord forever by his side. In prison Joseph interpreted the dreams of the chef and butler and then said to the butler, "Make mention of me to Pharaoh, and get me out of this house" (Gen. 40:14). The butler then forgot about Joseph and the Lord did not give Pharaoh his dream until two years later. Why so long? Because Joseph tried to manipulate his way out of prison and God never rewards this type of behavior. At that time Joseph's character was not quite ready to support his destiny and if he was released right then he wouldn't have been successful in what God called him to do.

God never promotes people until they have first developed within themselves the character to succeed. It took Joseph two more years in prison to get to the point where God could use him successfully. Character is not only based on how you act in certain situations, it's also based on how you react when things don't go the way they should. Many times in life you will do the right thing and be persecuted for it. How you react in those situations reveal whether or not you have the character to succeed. Rom. 5:4 says that character produces hope and vs.5 says, "Now hope does not disappoint, because the love of God has been poured out in our hearts by the Holy Spirit who was given to us." Hope is not given to help you believe that God will deliver you from all your trials, it's given to help you believe that He will be with you as you walk through your circumstances. As David walked through his valley he said in Ps. 23:4, "I will fear no evil; For You are with me."

This hope in God is needed because your heart can grow weary if your trial is not resolved in a timely manner. When your hope is in the living God, you can believe that this hope will produce for you a divine appointment that will allow you to step into your destiny. It takes a certain type of character to fulfill a God-given dream and, to prove you've got what it takes to do so, you can know with certainty that your character will be tested. Ps. 105:19 (NLT) says, "Until the time came to fulfill his dreams, the Lord tested Joseph's character." There are many people who will not fulfill their destiny because their lives don't line up with the Word of God. James 1:22 says, "But be doers of the word, and not hearers only, deceiving yourselves." You need to read your Bible and do what it tells you to do. Paul wrote to Timothy about "having faith and a good conscience" (1 Tim. 1;19). You receive faith by hearing the Word (Rom. 10:17) but you have a good conscience by doing the Word.

You can't fulfill your destiny if you don't have the character to do the Word of God. It's the Word that will mold you and shape you into the type of person who will run the race with endurance and stand strong when trials come your way. When you show God that you will always be a doer of the Word, then and only then, will He allow you to step into your destiny. Tests come to all believers and where your destiny is concerned many of these tests come through the avenue of success. A lot of people dream of success but when it comes they fail the test that comes with it. They're fine being under authority but for some reason they step out of character when power and authority is handed to them. Promotions can sometimes come very quickly. Joseph went from the prison to the palace in a single day. This is why prior to promotion you need to develop inside yourself the character that is needed to properly handle success when it comes and the power that goes with it.

It will help to know that you have no power of your own but that all power comes from God. Ps. 62:11 says, "God has spoken once, twice I heard this: That power belongs to God." Pilate told Jesus that he had the power to either crucify Him or release Him to which the Lord responded, "You could have no power at all against Me unless it had been given you from above." You can work as hard as you want to fulfill your destiny but without the blessing and power of God in your life it won't happen. You need to recognize that God's blessing and His power will come on you when you respond to the call on your life and do the right thing. It is not wrong to desire this power if you have the character and humility to use it in the proper way. This power is not to be used selfishly for your own good but rather to be used to bless other people. Joseph was given authority over all of Egypt, and he used this power to prepare for a seven-year drought that was soon coming upon the land.

He understood what the authority was for and he used his power correctly and was able to feed multitudes of people. It is not wrong to want to be great and powerful in God's kingdom as long as you have the right motive for doing so. Jesus said in Mark 10:43-45 that "whoever desires to become great among you shall be your servant. And whoever of you desires to be first shall be slave of all. For even the Son of Man did not come to be served, but to serve, and to give His life a ransom for many." Serving others is what power and authority is all about. It is a good thing to desire power for the right reason. If you humble yourself, God will lift you up by giving you power and authority with which you'll be able to fulfill your destiny. The formula for spiritual success is less of you and more of God. He gives grace and power to the humble for the purpose of being a blessing to others. This is what happened with Jesus and you are made in His image.

Acts 10:38 says "God anointed Jesus of Nazareth with the Holy Spirit and with power, who went about doing good and healing all who were oppressed by the devil, for God was with Him." God is looking for humble stewards through whom He can channel His power and His resources through to other people. Deut. 8:17,18 says don't "say in your heart, 'My power and the might of my hand have gained me this wealth.' And you shall remember the Lord your God, for it is He who gives you power to get wealth, that He may establish His covenant which He swore to your fathers, as it is this day." God does not bless you just so you can get a new car, He gives you the power to get wealth so that His covenant of blessing can be manifested throughout the world. Showing the world how good God is should be your main motive in life, the reason you get up each and every morning. God has a purpose for everybody, yet most people wander aimlessly through life not knowing if they're coming or going.

In order to fulfill your destiny, you've got to first believe that there is a purpose for your life. Eccl. 3:1 says, "To everything there is a season, a time for every purpose under heaven." Everything God created has a purpose. He created the sun and moon for a purpose and He created trees and rivers for a purpose. To find out what the purpose is for these things you've got to discover how God created them. For instance, He made the sun big, bright, and very hot. This tells you that the purpose of the sun is to give the earth warmth and light. God also created you for a purpose and to discover what that purpose is you've got to look how God made you. You are unique and there are special qualities in you that are different from anybody else in the world. This means there is a specific purpose that only you can do to the degree that God wants it done. Inventors design things with a specific purpose in mind and this is what happened when God designed you.

He created you with a divine purpose in mind and it is your responsibility to discover what that purpose is. You don't decide what your assignment is, you discover it and then you spend the rest of your life fulfilling it. Never desire to die early just so you can go to heaven sooner than it was intended that you should go. That's selfishness. People need you down here and you can't help them if you're in heaven. Rest assured, heaven will be there waiting for you when you've fulfilled your destiny and it's the proper time for you to go. In the meantime, discover how God created you and then go out and do what God designed you to do. While you were yet in your mother's womb He knew you and spoke His word over you. Is. 55:11 (MMSG) says, "So will the words that come out of My mouth not come back empty-handed. They'll do the work I sent them to do, they'll complete the assignment I gave them." God's word has the power to produce the purpose for which He sent it.

God has spoken a word over your life and, if you will develop within yourself the character to succeed, you can have the full assurance that His word will not return until it accomplishes the purpose for which He sent it. God is telling you here that He is on your side and that no weapon formed against you will prosper (Is. 54:17). Once you realize this, you next need to understand that the gifts and purpose God gives you has to do with serving other people. Equally important is that you start today. Don't wait until you get some kind of promotion to start serving other people. If this is your attitude then you'll never come up higher and get that promotion. Start today. Actively look for ways to bless those around you. When you do this consistently, before long bigger doors will be opened to you and greater opportunities to serve will come your way. Setbacks will come but you must remain faithful at all costs. Don't serve God half-heartedly but press forward and give it everything you've got.

Eccl. 9:10 says, "Whatever your hand finds to do, do it with all your might." The Message Bible says, "Whatever turns up, grab it and do it. And heartily!" No matter what it is you're going through, always be conscious of the needs of those around you. Take your eyes off of yourself and help other people knowing that what you make happen for others, God will make happen for you (Eph. 6:8). Doing this is what causes you to step into your destiny. Remain faithful and keep moving in the direction you know you're supposed to go. As you do this, you can have the confidence that God will direct your steps. Ps. 119:105 says, "Your word is a lamp to my feet and a light to my path." You may not always see a bright light at the end of the tunnel but for sure God will give you enough light to take the next step. And when you take that step, more light will be given and eventually you will be put in a position to influence thousands of people. Rejoice for God has taken you from your dream to your destiny. Hallelujah!

| 8 |

"RISE UP AND SOAR"

God wants you to fulfill your destiny and to live a long and prosperous good life. For that to happen the Bible says you must take on the characteristics of a mighty eagle. Is. 40:31 says, "But those who wait on the Lord shall renew their strength; they shall mount up with wings like eagles, they shall run and not be weary, they shall walk and not be faint." To "wait on the Lord" means to be 'braided together' or 'twisted together' with the great God of the universe. It means that the character you display is so much like God that you've become an example of what He is like. The world gets changed one person at a time and it happens when a light shines in a dark place. The world is waiting for somebody to turn the light on and that somebody is you. Jesus said in Matt. 5:14-16, "You are the light of the world. A city that is set on a hill cannot be hidden. Nor do they light a lamp and put it under a basket, but on a lampstand, and it gives light to all who are in the house. Let your light so shine before men, that they may see your good works and glorify your Father in heaven."

The Message Bible says, "By opening up to others, you'll prompt people to open up with God, this generous Father in heaven." The world is watching and the character you display in front of them may be the determining factor as to whether or not they receive Jesus into their heart. You won't motivate people to change if you go around acting like a buzzard or a crow or a chicken who flaps its wings all day but doesn't go anywhere. What gets their attention is a strong majestic eagle who spreads its wings and soars high above the storm clouds of test and trial. You have been called to be God's own personal representative and you need to have and display a God-kind of character in your life. It means that you will respond to situations that come up in a certain way without even thinking about it. It's been built into you to do the right thing because you've been walking in the light and have taken on the character of God. When you do something long enough it becomes a part of who you are.

People can't see what's in your heart, they can only see what you do. They're looking for someone to show them what being a true Christian is all about. If they surrender their heart to Jesus will they live in the low places of life or will they live in a glamorous penthouse on top of the tallest building in the city? This is what happens when you repent. God takes you from the pit of sackcloth and ashes and returns you to the high places in Him. It's up here in the penthouse of life that you soar like an eagle. God has put inside of you the desire to be adventurous, the need to do something you've never done before. Eagles want to fly to new heights and soar over the tallest mountains. Never think you can't do what you've been called to do. All it takes is the right motive, a heart full of faith, and the willingness to say, "Here I am, Lord. Send me." An eagle is not afraid of the storms of life. They see the storm coming before it arrives and uses the thermal currents to lift it up where it soars high above the clouds.

What type of bird are you? Chickens seldom fly and rarely reach their full potential in life. All they do is flap their wings aimlessly and hang out with other chickens. When storms come they run and hide in the chicken house. They refuse to face their trials but run away instead. They are lazy and they stay enclosed inside a fence all the days of their life. A magpie is a bully and drives people away from God. They are selfish and arrogant and causes other people to disrespect the true followers of God. The cockatoo bird never takes life seriously and wants to party all the time. He's like a court jester who tells jokes continually and is never sensitive to the needs of others. The Bible says you need to be sober-minded and pay attention to what's going on around you. The vulture enjoys the filth of life, things that are corrupt and no good. They have to criticize other people and tear them apart. He spreads rumors that destroy the reputation of others. The smell of death is round about him.

Parrots are the talkers in the kingdom. They talk the talk but don't walk the walk. They mimic other people and make a lot of noise but have no action to back up what they say. They're copycats and never have an original thought of their own. Then there's the cuckoo bird and for sure there are a lot of cuckoo Christians in the world. The Bible says when you come to Christ you get your mind renewed but cuckoo Christians think it says you get your mind removed. A cuckoo bird does not like to work and is content to sponge off of someone else. It's so lazy it won't even build its own nest. It lays its eggs in the nest of another bird and then flies away and leaves the care of its babies to the care of the bird who built the nest in the first place. There are cuckoo birds in the church today who only want to live on the handouts and the goodness of other people. They wouldn't think of getting a job of their own. These are the people who have a form of godliness but lack the power thereof.

Peacock Christians are flashy and deeply in love with themselves. They feel like they're superior to everyone else and love to show off how glamorous they think they are. They wear the best clothes and the finest jewelry and think they're too good to consider the needs of others. The pelicans are the eaters and are always looking for things to chew on. These are the pot-bellied believers who sit around with a beer in one hand and a cigarette in the other. They're content to sit back and let their wives take their children to Sunday school while they stay home and watch a ballgame on TV. A crow is a self-centered bird who only looks out for himself. Nothing else matters except the fulfillment of his own selfish desires. He cuts people down who don't think and believe like he does. He is a cunning and dangerous bird and thinks nothing of destroying the reputation of a good pastor and bringing division to a local church. These are the people who poke at and pester those trying to live a good, wholesome Christian lifestyle.

A canary is a beautiful bird with great potential but remains content to be in a cage all its life. They feel inferior and insecure and won't do anything about it. They stay locked up in religious tradition and a dead church and never fulfills its destiny. They live behind the bars of an unhappy childhood and believe this is how the rest of their life is supposed to be. And then there's the eagle. They're bold, strong, and they soar on the wind currents of the Holy Spirit effortlessly. They are committed and devoted and is the bird God has chosen to compare the strong Christian to in hopes of getting them to rise up and become all they were predestined to become. An eagle is confident to stand alone in life as it spreads its wings and soars above the clouds of destruction. This bird dwells on the rocks of the high places on the earth. They spend time alone with God while others are out playing golf or going to a party somewhere. Chickens always flock together but eagles soar alone.

Who are you spending time with? Who has the most input in your life? It's your responsibility to guard your heart with all diligence for out of it spring the issues of life (Prov. 4:23). You become like the people you hang around so you must be careful who you let influence you. Eagles don't spend time with chickens and neither should you. You should desire to be challenged by those on a higher level than you so that you can come up higher in life and become as they are. Their behavior alone will convict you to press on to the high calling in Christ. What kind of Christian are you and what type are you willing to become? There are so many phony Christians today who are only going through the motions of godly living. They go to church on Sunday but live like the devil the rest of the week. They put on a show outwardly but inside they are unclean and their righteousness is like filthy rags (Is. 64:6). The Message Bible says in 2 Tim. 3:5, "They'll make a show of religion, but behind the scenes they're animals. Stay clear of these people."

The Bible says in Prov. 23:7, "For as he thinks in his heart, so is he." What do you think of yourself? If you think you're a chicken, you'll act like a chicken. You need to value yourself and who you are in Christ. If you don't, you'll never rise up and soar like an eagle. You're special, so much so that God thinks you're worth dying for. There are seeds of greatness inside of you waiting to sprout out and grow into a mighty oak tree. You won't reach your full potential and fulfill your destiny if you stay cooped up in the chicken yard all your life. Something inside of you is calling out for greatness to be achieved. For that to happen you must rise up and soar as eagles soar. You won't reach prominence in life if all you do is sit around and flap your wings all day. Stop being lazy and get up and do something. God is waiting on you to move because He won't do anything until you take the first step. You move and then He moves. You move some more and He'll move some more. This is how greatness is achieved in the kingdom of God.

Wings are for flying, not sitting. Right now there is something stirring on the inside of you prompting you to spread those wings and fly away. It's okay to be adventurous and the only person who gets out of the boat and walks on the water. Chickens stay in the boat with other chickens but an eagle soars majestically alone. People may think you're strange and different because you're not one of them but deep down you really don't care what they think. You're soaring and they're not. Their approval or lack of approval means nothing to you because you live to please God, not man. Paul said in Gal.1:10, "For do I now persuade me, or God? Or do I seek to please men? For if I still pleased men, I would not be a servant of Christ." The devil will steal your destiny and you'll never reach your full potential if all you do is live for the approval of others. John 12:42,43 says, "Nevertheless even among the rulers many believed in Him, but because of the Pharisees they did not confess Him, lest they should be put out of the synagogue; for they loved the praise of men more than the praise of God."

It's okay to be alone as long as the Lord is by your side. After all, that is what eagles do. Chickens flock together but eagles soar alone. Jesus was alone in the Garden of Gethsemane but the Father was with Him. He said in John 16:32, "Indeed the hour is coming, yes, has now come, that you will be scattered, each to his own, and will leave Me alone. And yet I am not alone, because the Father is with Me." Keep your eyes on Jesus and never let the opinions of others distract you from doing what you've been called to do. The devil is the author of distraction. If he can't kill you he'll do everything he can to distract you and one of his biggest weapons is the opinions of other people. Don't let what other people think derail you from the course you're on. Rise above it all and soar like an eagle. The truth is, these people want what you have but they don't have the character and the tenacity to come up higher and get it. So they decide to sit around and gossip with other chickens all the while on the inside they're craving what you have.

Deep inside of you are the qualities of a mighty eagle and you must decide how far you're willing to go to turn this truth into a living reality. How committed are you and what sacrifices are you willing to make? God will lead you and guide you but there comes a point where you have to decide what you want to make happen in your life. It's not all up to God because the person you become depends more on the decisions you make than on the things He is willing to do for you. This is why Paul said in Col. 3:2, "Set your mind on things above, not on things on the earth." Make your mind up that you will do whatever it takes to become the person God designed you to be and to have everything He says you can have. Don't back down when the storms of life blow your way but rise up and soar on the wind currents of the

Spirit of God. Allow Him to take you to new heights in the kingdom of heaven. Dream big dreams and never back down when opposition comes your way. Come up higher and soar as eagles soar.

The best things in life don't happen overnight. A weed can grow almost immediately bit a mighty oak tree takes years to reach its full height and potential. Also, the higher quality a thing is, the more it will cost you to get it. It takes time and sacrifice to soar above the clouds and if hard work scares you then there is always room for you in the chicken yard. It takes greatness to fulfill a heavenly call and for that to happen you've got to allow God to change you into His image. He's the potter, you're the clay. This means He knows what you need more than you do. Allow Him to mold you and shape you into the person you need to be. Be willing to submit to His direction and guidance and, if need be, His chastening and correction. Job 5:17 says, "Behold, happy is the man whom God corrects; Therefore do not despise the chastening of the Almighty." As the greatness of your character begins to unfold before your very eyes, you'll be able to see things others don't see. An eagle can see a rabbit on the ground from two miles up in the air. As you grow in the Lord you'll also be able to see all the great things He has in store for you even if they appear a long way off.

How hungry are you for the things of God? Are you hungry enough that you're willing to get out of the chicken yard so you can learn how to fly? Is there a desire inside of you to get to know God better so you'll be able to obtain greatness in His kingdom? If you will believe that one touch from God can change your life forever, you'll walk away from those other chickens and the things that hold you back and will do whatever it takes to get that one touch. The more of God you get, the more you'll want. Jesus said in Matt. 5:6, "Blessed are those who hunger and thirst for righteousness, for they shall be filled." Never settle for second best. Why give up a close relationship with God just so you can please somebody who won't be there when you need them anyway? No, get out of the chicken yard and soar like an eagle. Believe that God will restore back to you more than you're willing to give up for Him. He'll give you new friends who soar like you do and together you'll fly to the top of the highest mountain and do things for God that chickens only dream about.

You will never fulfill your destiny and gain prominence in the kingdom of God unless you develop inside yourself the same commitment an eagle has when it comes time to mate with a female eagle. At age four the male eagle leaves the nest in search of a mate. When he finds her they play a game where she flies in a figure eight pattern and he follows her. He's no longer in charge of where he's going but is following somebody who's going in a different direction. There comes a time when the female dives to the ground and picks up a small twig. She then flies to ten thousand feet and drops the twig where the male eagle dives after it at two hundred miles an hour. He catches the twig in mid-air and when he returns to the female she ignores him. It's at this point that the male eagle has to decide how committed he actually is. Will he see this through to the end or should he fly off and find something easier to do with his time? It is never easy to fulfill a heavenly call and this is a decision every Christian has to make.

The female repeats this process over and over and each time the twig gets a little larger and she flies to a lower altitude. This means the twig is going to hit the ground faster and the male eagle has to work harder to keep this from happening. In like manner, the Lord is going to test you to see how committed you really are, to see if you've got what it takes to go the distance with Him. This game the female is playing can literally go on for days until finally she picks up a branch that weighs more than her male follower. This time she only flies to five hundred feet and drops it. She is giving the male eagle the ultimate challenge, a task that seems impossible by normal standards. If he catches it they mate for life and, if not, she flies off and looks for another male eagle with the tenacity and strength of character to be her mate. It takes commitment to win the devotion of the female eagle and for the male eagle it is worth doing whatever it takes to obtain this valuable prize.

How committed are you? What is your dream and how committed are you to fulfill your destiny? God is looking for a person who will come up higher and stay committed to their call even when the going gets tough. It is to these people that the Lord gives the bigger and more prominent tasks to fulfill. John was so committed to Jesus that he was the only disciple who was at the cross when Jesus was crucified and it was to him that the Lord gave the task of taking care of His mother (John 19:26,27). This was a huge responsibility and John had shown that he had the commitment to take on this very important assignment. People who live for ease and comfort all their life will not go far in the kingdom of God. Serving the Lord is not for the weak-kneed individual who panics when a little adversity comes their way. It's through test and trial where the real you is revealed. Will you quit and run or will you press forward and finish the task you've been assigned to do? Do you have the commitment of an eagle or don't you?

One of the main characteristics of an eagle that all believers need to imitate is that there is a youthful mentality in all of them. There is a spark inside of them and they are full of life and energy. Ps. 103:5 says to bless the Lord at all times for it is He "who satisfies your mouth with good things so that your youth is renewed like the eagle's." In today's society there are many young people who act older than those who are three and four times older than they are. Your behavior is not based on how old your body is but rather on what's going on inside of you. If your spirit is active and strong it will affect both your body and your mind. You've got to know God intimately and have a close, personal relationship with Him. Anybody can go to church on Sunday but it's those committed believers who hunger and thirst to be in the Lord's presence day in and day out who get their youth renewed like the eagle's. This relationship with God will strengthen you and get you through that valley standing tall with your head held high because you know the Lord is by your side.

Everything you need to live a good life is on the inside of you. He gives you the ability to do what needs to be done in any given situation. He'll enable you to overcome disappointment for in Him you know a better future awaits you. Staying close to God keeps you young at heart and this is one of the greatest blessings there is. Never again do you have to feel old or act old because your youth is being renewed day by day. Live on the edge of life and go out and do something you've never done before. Get rid of that mindset that thinks the only thing you can do when you get older is sit on the porch and watch the grass grow. No, you've got a lot of living to do and you've got to believe that your best days are ahead of you. There is a call on your life that you never retire from so each and every day you've got a reason to get out of bed in the morning. The Message Bible says, "He wraps you in goodness - beauty eternal. He renews your youth - you're always young in His presence. God makes everything come out right; He puts victims back on their feet" (Ps. 103:5,6).

Never have the mentality of a victim and don't let what happened in your past dictate what takes place in your future. 2 Cor. 5:17 says, "Therefore, if anyone is in Christ, he is a new creation; old things have passed away; behold, all things have become new." You need to decide once and for all that you're going to enjoy life and have fun doing it. It doesn't matter how old you are for your life is being renewed like the eagle's. You can rise up and soar because on the inside of you you're like a child again. God has some awesome plans for your life and your future has never looked brighter. If you will keep the right attitude then there will be nothing you won't be able to do with your life. You'll be blessed many times over and you'll do great exploits in the kingdom of God. You'll do more in your latter years than all the years of your youth combined. You're wiser now and you've learned what's important in life and what isn't. You know it's better to please God rather than man and, if necessary, you're willing to soar alone.

The word "renew" means 'to go back to the starting place.' It's okay to begin your childhood in the latter years of your life. It's appropriate to do this because this is how God planned it. Jesus said in Matt. 11:28, "Come to Me, all you who labor and are heavy laden, and I will give you rest." The Message Bible says, "Are you tired? Worn out? Burned out on religion? Come to Me. Get away with Me and you'll recover your life. I'll show you how to take a real rest." In Christ you can have a fresh start each and every morning. You wake up and the first thing you do is spend time with your Daddy. You thank Him for His goodness and you praise His holy Name. As you wait on Him your strength is renewed and you rise up ready to take on the world. You're soaring like an eagle and there is nothing you can't do and no place you can't go. The winds of opportunity are blowing and you're rising higher and higher. All those mountains you've been trying to climb with your own strength are now below you. Nothing can stop you now.

There is truly nothing as majestic as watching a mighty eagle as it soars high above the clouds. By watching him you can never tell what he went through to get his strength renewed. There was a time when that eagle began to feel old and he wasn't as quick as he once was. His feathers were worn and gave off a whistling sound thus giving his prey notice that he was coming. His talons were not as sharp as they once were and neither was his beak. It was time for a fresh start. That eagle then flew to a rocky place high up on the mountain as close to the sun as he can get. He then began to pluck out his old feathers one by one, and for a big eagle this could be as many as seven thousand feathers. He's not as concerned with the pain of doing this as he is in the progress that is being made. He then finds a stream to cool off in. Refreshed and naked he now stands before the sun and waits for up to forty days for his feathers to regrow. His talons and beak get sharpened by rubbing them continually against a rock. Slowly but surely his strength is being renewed.

The Bible says Jesus is the Rock of your salvation (Ps. 89:26) and the Sun of righteousness (Mal. 4:2) and like that eagle you need to come up higher and get as close to the Son as you possibly can. There may be times when you feel worn out and defeated. Discouragement may set in because life isn't going the way you think it should. It is times like this when you need to do whatever it takes to get alone with God. Turn the television off and let your relatives watch your children for a few days. If need be, go out of town where nobody knows you and rent a motel room so you won't be disturbed as you go through the process of waiting on God and getting your strength renewed. If you'll do that, you'll become a new person. Old things have passed away, behold, all things become new. This will happen if you're willing to pay the price to make it so. You can get as close to God as you want and live a good life if you'll make the effort and take the time to make it happen. And as you watch that eagle soar high above your head you can have the assurance that whatever you have to go through will be well worth the effort.

| 9 |

"GOD'S PLAN FOR YOUR LIFE"

Life is a journey and God has a plan that will help you run your race and finish your course. This plan is for those committed believers who will lay their life down in order to build up the kingdom of God. It is a good plan and answers the question people the world over are asking, "Why am I here?" It's always best to start at the beginning and the first thing God desires is for you to be adopted into His holy family. Eph. 2:19 says, "Now, therefore, you are no longer strangers and foreigners, but fellow citizens with the saints and members of the household of God." You are now a part of God's family and no longer is He "God" to you, He is now your heavenly Daddy. David describes Him as "A father to the fatherless, a defender of widows, is God in His holy habitation. God sets the solitary in families; He brings out those who are bound into prosperity; But the rebellious dwell in a dry land" (Ps. 68:5,6).

Many people see the church as a big religious organization, but this is not what it is. It's a family where everybody knows your faults but love you anyway. Unconditional love is the foundation on which the family of God is built with Jesus being the chief cornerstone (Matt. 21:42). People are commissioned by God to love you unconditionally and you are commissioned to love them the same way. Jesus said in John 13:24, "A new commandment I give to you, that you love one another; as I have loved you, that you also love one another." Another blessing of being part of God's family is that you take on a new identity. No longer are you just the person you see in the mirror. Paul says in Eph. 5:30, "For we are members of His body, of His flesh and of His bones." In the realm of the Spirit you are literally connected to Jesus. He's the head and you are part of His body (Eph. 1:22,23). When the Bible says the church is "the body of Christ" it's talking about the literal, physical body of Jesus.

You and Jesus are connected for you are flesh of His flesh and bone of His bones. The same way you nourish and take care of your own physical body, so will Jesus nourish and take care of you. Be careful how you treat other believers because how you treat them is actually how you're treating Jesus. The Lord said in Matt. 25:40, "Assuredly, I say to you, inasmuch as you did it to one of the least of these My brethren, you did it to Me." It's a great privilege to be in the body of Christ but with it comes a great responsibility. You must treat people the same way you treat Jesus for you are all members of the same family and citizens of the same kingdom. Col. 1:13,14 says, "He has delivered us from the power of darkness and translated us into the kingdom of the Son of His love, in whom we have redemption through His blood, the forgiveness of sins." Because of this transformation you now have the right to be forgiven of your sins and to be loved with a love that is unconditional.

Rom. 14:17 (NLT) says, "For the kingdom of God is not a matter of what we eat or drink, but of living a life of goodness and peace and joy in the Holy Spirit." Paul is saying that you can live a good life and have fun doing it. People who don't have fun as they're growing and developing in Christ rarely advance and go far in the kingdom of God. The Holy Spirit is building the structure that allows the children of God to live in peace and safety. He wants to restore back to the church the authority it has over the devil and his cohorts. Jesus said in Luke 10:19, "Behold, I give you the authority to trample on serpents and scorpions, and over all the power of the enemy, and nothing shall by any means hurt you." Before God's plan can come to pass in your life, you have to understand that there are demonic spirits who are trying to stop you from seeing what that plan is. Willful and habitual sin will blind you from seeing God's plan plus it will rob you of the authority you've been given.

First and foremost, you've got to get sin out of your life. Lay your pride aside and ask God to cleanse you from all unrighteousness. Ask Him to save you and to make you one of His children. Make Him the Lord of your life because if He isn't your Master neither can He be your Savior. It is a horrible thing when people go to church all their life but never make it into heaven. They may do many mighty works for the kingdom but because their heart wasn't right the Lord will say to them, "I never knew you; depart from Me" (Matt. 7:21-23). David wrote in Ps. 23:1, "The Lord is my shepherd; I shall not want" and Ps. 100:3 says, "We are His people and the sheep of His pasture." Shepherds are for leading and sheep are for following and this theme is seen all through the Bible. God has put shepherds in the church, people who are like Him who will love you, protect you, feed you and, if necessary, lay down their life for you.

Once you get born again it is God's plan for you to be under the care of a loving shepherd and you must allow Him to lead you to the flock that He wants you to be a part of. This direction is necessary because like false prophets and teachers who are in the land, so also are there false shepherds. Jer. 23:1,2 says, "'Woe to the shepherds who destroy and scatter the sheep of My pasture!' says the Lord. Therefore thus says the Lord God of Israel against the shepherds who feed My people: 'You have scattered My flock, driven them away, and not attended to them. Behold, I will attend to you for the evil of your doings.' says the Lord." The Message Bible says, "Doom to the shepherd - leaders who butcher and scatter My sheep!" The Bible warns us to stay alert to false shepherds, for they surely exist and seek to lead the flock astray.

A true and good shepherd protects, guides, and gathers the sheep together rather than scattering them.

The Lord said in Jer. 23:3,4, "'But I will gather the remnant of My flock out of all countries where I have driven them, and bring them back to their folds; and they shall be fruitful and increase. I will set up shepherds over them who will feed them; and they shall fear no more, not be dismayed, nor shall they be lacking,' says the Lord." Shepherds are called to help people, to serve them and minister to their needs. A good shepherd cares more about the sheep than he does his own life. David faced a vicious lion and a powerful bear who tried to eat the sheep who were under his care. Good shepherds are precious indeed and Jer. 3:15 says, "And I will give you shepherds according to My heart, who will feed you with knowledge and understanding." A good pastor is one who is called and gifted by God (Eph. 4:11) and it is your responsibility to discern in your heart who is a good shepherd and who isn't based on the holy scriptures. This is why you need godly direction before you join any church.

All good shepherds pattern their lives and ministry after Jesus because He is the Great Shepherd (Heb. 13:20). Mark 6:34 says, "And Jesus, when He came out, saw a great multitude and was moved with compassion for them, because they were like sheep not having a shepherd. So He began to teach them many things." A good shepherd is always feeding his flock by teaching them great spiritual truths right out of the Bible. Jesus then said in John 10:27,28, "My sheep hear My voice, and I know them, and they follow Me. And I give them eternal life, and they shall never perish; neither shall anyone snatch them out of My hand." There are four privileges that come with being in the flock of the Lord. You get to hear God, know God, follow God, and live forever. A good pastor will feed you once or twice a week but Jesus feeds you every day of your life. Read your Bible every day and you will be changed from the inside out. You will become an entirely different person set aside for the Master's use.

Your heavenly Daddy loves you and cares for you because you are one of His children. At the same time, He has just as much love and care for the lost sinner who is wandering through life without a shepherd to watch over them. This is why when Jesus called His disciples He said to them, "Follow Me, and I will make you fishers of men" (Matt. 4:19). The purpose of sitting under the ministry of a good pastor is that you will be equipped to do the work of the ministry (Eph. 4:12). Everybody has a call on their life and you have to believe that Jesus is talking to you personally when He said in Luke 5:10, "Do not be afraid. From now on you will catch men." There is always some small task you can do but do it with all your heart and soul knowing that you will never do anything big for God unless you first do something small. When you serve Him faithfully you will find that there is no thrill like the thrill of being used by God.

There is nothing that remotely approaches the excitement and satisfaction of being an instrument in the hands of God to help change the life of another person. The only reason you are here is to be used by the Master. This is God's plan for your life and is the very reason you were born. You are here to help change the world and there is no higher calling than that. This, by the way, is the reason Jesus came to the earth. He said in Luke 19:10, "For the Son of Man has come to seek and to save that which was lost." Like Jesus, you also need to do some serious seeking. Look for someone who needs a helping hand or someone who needs to hear the good news about Jesus. If you will set your heart to do this then surely you won't have to look very long. In no time at all God will send someone across your path who needs what you have to give them. Sociologists say that people who are alive today are the most discouraged and most medicated people in all of human history.

This is so because the devil knows his time is short (Rev. 12:12) so he seeks to bring as much misery and destruction to people as he possibly can. Love is what these people are looking for and who can show it to them better than a child of the Daddy of love? Jesus said in John 13:34, "A new commandment I give to you, that you love one another; as I have loved you, that you also love one another." When you understand what Jesus calls "the first and great commandment" of love (Matt. 22:37-40) you will then understand God's plan for your life. True love is when you care for someone more than you care for yourself. It always honors the dignity of others and will even go so far as to love the unlovable. Jesus said in Matt. 5:44, "But I say to you, love your enemies, bless those who curse you, do good to those who hate you, and pray for those who spitefully use you and persecute you." Only God can love a person in such a way and He has chosen to show this love through you.

You are to be His instrument that He can use to show the outcasts of this world how special He thinks they are and how much He truly loves them. A person's dignity is honored when you love them more than they deserve to be loved. These people may not go to church but in you they will see a reflection of who God is and what He is really like. God's love does not have to wait on the acceptable performance of another person before it is shown. He set the example for you to follow in Rom. 5:8, "But God demonstrates His own love toward us, in that while we were still sinners, Christ died for us." Something supernatural takes place on the inside of you when you begin to love like God on the outside. In other words, the more you love, the easier it gets to love. The love of God that's flowing in you and through you will allow you to come up higher and love someone even if they don't first love you.

Jesus said in Matt. 5:46, "For if you love those who love you, what reward have you? Do not even the tax collectors do the same?" Love honors the dignity of other people even if they don't act in dignified ways. It sees the potential in people and all the great things they're capable of doing. This is why love will invest in the destiny of others. Love will help you put their needs above your own needs. It will cause you to go the extra mile to help that other person go as far in life as they can possibly go. Love is the answer to every problem in the world and God's plan for your life is to show and express this love to every person you meet. Hurting people are craving for a love that is real and genuine and God has called you to show it to them. Perfect love casts out the fear that these people may not love you in return. God loves you and that is all that matters. His love fills the need you have to be loved.

When you walk in the love of God you will quickly realize that your need to love is greater than your need to be loved. You will reach a point where each day you're alive you won't rest satisfied until you've shown love to at least one person. Like yourself, these people are made in the image of God, and it is His plan that you treat them as such. The more they learn about how good God is through your kind words and actions, the more they'll be drawn to the wonderful gift of eternal salvation that He is offering to them. Rom. 2:4 says, "The goodness of God leads you to repentance." The Message Bible says, "In kindness He takes us firmly by the hand and leads us into a radical life-change." The love of God will change your life, and this is why love is the central theme of the entire Bible. Believers everywhere need to wipe the dust off their Bible and make a fresh commitment to read it every day.

The Lord said in Jer. 6:16, "Stand in the ways and see, and ask for the old paths, where the good way is, and walk in it; Then you will find rest for your souls." You need to base everything you say and do and every decision you make on the Word of God. 1 Peter 1:25 says, "But the word of the Lord endures forever" and when you put it in your heart it will bear fruit. Is. 40:8 says, "The grass withers, the flower fades, but the word of our God stands forever." Jesus said in Matt. 4:4, "Man shall not live by bread alone, but by every word that proceeds from the mouth of God." The truth be told, many believers are not reading their Bible as they should and this is why they need to go back to the old paths and make reading the Bible their top priority each and every day. This is why Jesus prayed to the Father, "Give us this day out daily bread" (Matt. 6:11). Heb. 4:12 says, "For the word of God is living and powerful, and sharper than any two-edged sword."

When you read your Bible you receive more than just knowledge, you receive the very life of God. Stop thinking of your Bible as just some old book you read once in a great while. It's a book of wisdom and power and it will give direction to your life. 2 Tim. 3:16,17 says, "All scripture is given by inspiration of God, and is profitable for doctrine, for reproof, for correction, for instruction in righteousness, that the man of God may be complete, thoroughly equipped for every good work." The word "inspiration" means 'divinely breathed in' and the NIV says, "All scripture is God-breathed." When you read your Bible, the life and breath of God is coming into you. John 1:4,5 says, "In Him was life, and the life was the light of men. And the light shines in the darkness, and the darkness did not comprehend it." The life of God that is in the Word will give light to the path you're on thus giving you divine direction for your life. This is why you need to continually "walk in the light as he is in the light" (1 John 1:7).

God refers to His Word as a sword and in Eph. 6:12 Paul says to "take the sword of the Spirit, which is the word of God." The phrase "sword of the Spirit" is only found in this passage of scripture and the purpose of this sword is to make you strong and able to withstand the onslaught of the enemy. The Holy Spirit uses the power of the Word to save souls and then to give people spiritual strength to become mature soldiers in the army of the Lord. The more you know and understand the Word of God, the more useful you will be in His kingdom and the more effective you'll be in standing against the wiles of the enemy. You are going to have opposition in your quest to fulfill your destiny, but you can have confidence in the battle of life knowing that victory is part of God's plan for your life. 1 Cor. 15:57 says, "But thanks be to God, who gives us the victory through our Lord Jesus Christ."

If you know the battle is won, then you won't give in to the fear that comes with almost every trial.

Is. 41;10 says, "Fear not, for I am with you; Be not dismayed, for I am your God. I will strengthen you, yes, I will help you." Nehemiah had opposition in his quest to rebuild the walls of Jerusalem and a hireling of the enemy told him to run and hide. His response should be an inspiration to you when the enemy comes looking for you. Nehemiah said, "Should such a man as I flee?" (Neh. 6:11). Your Daddy is the creator of the universe, and you are His beloved child. Should a person such as yourself be afraid and flee when the enemy comes knocking on your door? David didn't flee from the lion and the bear and neither did he run away from Goliath. On the contrary, he ran toward the giant knowing God was on his side and that victory was part of the divine plan for his life. Nehemiah said of the hireling in vs. 13, "For this reason he was hired, that I should be afraid and act that way and sin." The enemy knows that fear opens the door to sin and this is why you should never fear.

The devil is a liar and the father of lies (John 8:44) and he will lie to you and spread false rumors all in an effort to take your eyes off of God and get into fear. When that happens remember what Paul said in Rom. 3:4, "Let God be true but every man a liar." Nehemiah had a mission he was on and when the enemy came against him a plan was made to deal with both issues. Neh. 4:16, 17 says, "So it was, from that time on, that half of my servants worked at construction, while the other half held the spears, the shields, the bows, and wore armor; and the leaders were behind all the house of Judah. Those who built on the wall, and those who carried burdens, loaded themselves so that with one hand they worked at construction, and with the other held a weapon." This is one of the greatest descriptions in all the Bible of the Christian life. In one hand are the tools for building up the kingdom of God and in the other hand is a weapon for tearing down the kingdom of darkness.

To successfully fulfill your destiny, you've got to do both at the same time. The enemy don't care if you oppose him as long as he can get you to stop building for a little while. That's his plan to begin with but God has another plan. Nehemiah's men kept building the walls and the enemy never did attack them. It's the enemy who will flee when he sees he can't stop you and that you're ready to fight. You are not alone in your quest to fulfill your destiny. God is on your side and as you build His kingdom, He will take care of your enemies. Rom. 8:31 says, "If God is for us, who can be against us?" God loves you with an everlasting love and as you trust in Him no enemy or weapon or calamity will be able to overtake you. 2 Cor. 2:14 says, "But thanks be to God, who always puts us on display in Christ and through us spreads the aroma of the knowledge of Him in every place." Nehemiah had a plan and you need one as well. The best plan for your life is the plan God designed for you before you were even born.

By now you should know what that plan is so always stay on the path God has given you to walk on. If you'll follow that plan and not allow yourself to be distracted by the enemy, you will experience victory in your life and you will fulfill your destiny. The devil can try to stop you all he wants but as long as you know God is on your side, nothing he does will succeed. Joseph told his brothers in Gen. 50:20 (NLT), "You intended to harm me, but God intended it all for good." Neh. 13:2 says, "However, our God turned the curse into a blessing." The foremost desire in the Father's heart is to bless you abundantly. At the same time, it is also His desire to instill in your heart a godly character through which He will be able to reward you for all the good things you do. This is why Paul wrote in Gal. 6:9,10, "And let us not grow weary while doing good, for in due season we shall reap if we do not lose heart. Therefore, as we have opportunity, let us do good to all, especially to those who are of the household of faith."

God loves to give and He wants you to be just like Him. This is why He uses the promise of a blessed reward as a means to motivate you to be good to other people. The law of sowing and reaping says, "Whatever a man sows, that he will also reap" (Gal. 6:7). Jesus talked about this in Luke 6:38 when He said, "Give, and it will be given to you: good measure, pressed down, shaken together, and running over will be put into your bosom. For with the same measure that you use, it will be measured back to you." When your heart is on fire for the things of God then the idea of giving yourself and your resources will excite you. You'll go out of your way to be a blessing to somebody else. You are a child of a giving God and His nature has become your nature. People who are selfish scoff at the concept of giving tithes and offerings and then wonder why their life is in the mess it's in. They don't realize that God has promised to bless those who obey Him and become cheerful givers.

God's plan for your life is that you be blessed so you can be a blessing to others. Take a portion of what God gives you and sow it back into the kingdom. If you will do this, God promises that you will be blessed with more than you could ever ask or think. 1 Tim. 6:17 says God "gives us richly all things to enjoy." You'll be blessed abundantly plus you'll have additional resources with which to bless others with. If, by chance, your life is not going the way you'd like it to then maybe it's because you've stepped out of God's plan for you to be a blessing to others. If that be the case, then know that there is no better time to start being a giver than today. If Jesus is in your heart, then by nature you should want to give so this should not be a hard decision to make. It all comes down to how much you trust your Daddy. He said He would bless you when you give. Do you trust Him to do that? If so, then put action to what you believe and get ready for a blessed life.

| 10 |

"CREATED TO BE SUCCESSFUL"

Many years ago a world renowned newscaster would always end his program with these words, "And that's the way it is." When hard times come many believers say the same thing. "That's the way it is. Whatever will be will be." They then go off and have a lousy day and wonder where God is while all this calamity is going on. These same people are a walking testimony of what the Bible says in Hosea 4:6, "My people are destroyed for a lack of knowledge." Surprisingly, the number of people who don't know all the glorious things that's been made available to them is phenomenal. For some reason, they've always seen less than what God intended to show them. They put God in a box and continually struggle when it comes to believing a big God for big things. They can't grasp with their mind what is said in 3 John 2, "I pray that you will prosper and be in health even as your soul prospers."

The Message Bible says, "We're the best of friends, and I pray for good fortune in everything you do, and for your good health - that your everyday affairs prosper, as well as your soul!" Your mind and the way you think is part of your soul and soul prosperity is achieved when you study the Word and fill your mind with the knowledge of God and all that He desires to give you. Most people would be shocked were they to find out that, more times than not, their hardship came as a result of a lack of knowledge more than the trial itself. What's more, Hosea says in the same verse that the people's lack of knowledge came about because they rejected the knowledge that was being offered to them. There is, however, a ray of hope for believers living in the last days. Hab. 2:14 says, "For the earth will be filled with the knowledge of the glory of the Lord, as the waters cover the sea." The Message Bible says, "Meanwhile the earth fills up with awareness of God's glory as the waters cover the sea."

Notice it doesn't say the glory of the Lord will cover the earth; it says the knowledge of the glory of the Lord will cover the earth. How will this prophetic word come into manifestation? The answer is found in Is. 60:1-3, "Arise, shine; for your light has come! And the glory of the Lord is risen upon you. For behold, the darkness shall cover the earth, and deep darkness the people; but the Lord will arise over you, and His glory will be seen upon you. The Gentiles shall come to your light, and kings to the brightness of your rising." The glory of God can be described as the radiant, visible, manifestation of the presence of God. Ezekiel saw the glory of God coming in waves rolling in like a tide (Ezek. 47:1-9). The glory is rolling in like a flood, and a flood can't be stopped. As the world gets darker, the church will get brighter and brighter. Where sin abounds, grace does much more abound (Rom. 5:20). The glory of God will be seen in your life when the world is at its darkest hour.

It will be in such manifestation that the unsaved will see it. They will look at you and see that you're the head and not the tail, above and not beneath. They'll see you living a blessed life and will be compelled to serve the same God you do. 1 Cor. 2:14 says, "But the natural man does not receive the things of the Spirit of God, for they are foolishness to him; nor can he know them, because they are spiritually discerned." The Message Bible puts a little more light on this, "The unspiritual self can't receive the gifts of God's Spirit. There's no capacity for them. They seem like so much silliness. Spirit can be known only by spirit - God's Spirit and our spirits in open communion. Spiritually alive, we have access to everything God's Spirit is doing and can't be judged by unspiritual critics." How can the heathen of the world see the glory of God if only true believers can understand and discern things in the spiritual realm? Simple, they will see God doing good things to those who are His.

The natural world can tell when God has been good to somebody. Daily your life should be a testimony to the goodness of God. Moses requested of God in Ex. 33:18, "Please, show me your glory." God replied in vs. 19, "I will make My goodness pass before you, and I will proclaim the name of the Lord before you. I will be gracious to whom I will be gracious, and I will have compassion on whom I will have compassion." Moses asked to see the glory of God and God showed him His goodness. Therefore, the glory of God equals the goodness of God. So when Isaiah says the glory of God will be seen upon you, he is actually saying that the heathen will see with their natural eyes God being good to you. The good life is the route that takes you to the top of your mountain. Jesus is coming back for a glorious church, a church that is walking in the fullness of the glory of God. You are a part of that generation and will see great manifestations of the glory and goodness of God.

God is calling you to come up higher and to go further than you've ever gone before. God wants you to experience the good life and live in the fullness of all the blessings that have been made available to those who believe. What's more, He wants the world to see it, a world that is forever ready and willing to mock and criticize the church of the living God. The Message Bible records the words of Isaiah this way, "But God rises on you, His sunrise glory breaks over you. Nations will come to your light, kings to your sunburst brightness." The psalmist asks, "Why should the Gentiles say, 'Where now is their God?'" (Ps. 115:2). It is your responsibility and privilege to let the world see the physical manifestations of God's goodness as you enjoy every day of your life. Living the good life is not a series of exciting events and emotions where you feel like your body is being pene-trated by millions of needles. Neither should you only be happy on weekends and vacations.

More times than not, normal everyday life means you get up, go to work, come home, play with the kids, eat, do the dishes, mow the lawn, watch a little television, go to bed. You then get up the next day and repeat the same process all over again. But when you're addicted to Jesus, when you are living the good life, you will be anointed by God to live ordinary lives while at the same time being extraordinar-ily joyful. You'll wake up each morning and boldly declare, "This is the day which the Lord has made; We will rejoice and be glad in it" (Ps. 118:24). You can rejoice because your name is written in the Lamb's book of life and you can be happy because Jesus is alive in your heart. That alone is reason to celebrate. David prayed in Ps. 51:12, "Restore to me the joy of Your salvation, and uphold me with Your generous Spirit." The Message Bible says, "God, make a fresh start in me, shape a Genesis week from the chaos of my life."

With God's generosity comes a joy unspeakable that is overflowing and Neh. 8:10 says "The joy of the Lord is your strength." You can enjoy God so much that you'll have the strength to resist whatever it is the devil brings against you. Yes, you are to take life seriously but in Jesus you can have fun doing it. Ps. 3:3 says the Lord is the glory and the lifter of your head. There is a well of joy inside of you so tap into it. Train yourself to enjoy the normal activities of the day, things like doing the dishes and mowing the lawn. Life is to be enjoyed and not just endured. A bad day is a wasted day so be determined to enjoy every single day you're alive. Don't look at what you don't have but re-joice in what you do have. Yes, the other man's grass may be greener, but he's also got a bigger water bill than you. Think about that the next time you're tempted to get envious of what others have and lose your sense of joy.

Be happy and content with what you have and believe that God is working behind the scenes changing things in your favor. You've got one life to live, and you can only live it once so enjoy the journey. God's definition of the good life is found in Deut. 28:1-14. Vs. 2 says, "And all these blessings shall come upon you and overtake you, because you obey the voice of the Lord your God." The word "overtake" means 'surprise' and this verse is saying that when you live the good life the blessings of God will come on you and He will continually surprise you with things you have not even asked for. Vs. 11 says, "And the Lord will grant you plenty of goods, in the fruit of your body, in the increase of your livestock, and in the produce of your ground, in the land of which the Lord swore to your fathers to give you." In the mind of God, if you are not in the over and above, then you have not yet entered into the good life.

The fullness of the good life is overflow, more than enough, above and beyond what you could ask or think. The Message Bible says in John 10:10, "A thief is only there to steal and kill and destroy. I came so they can have real and eternal life, more and better life than they ever dreamed of." The Amplified Bible says, "I came that they may have and enjoy life, and have it in abundance." The Message Bible also says in 2 Cor. 9:8,9, "God can pour on the blessings in astonishing ways so that you're ready for anything and everything, more than just ready to do what needs to be done. As one psalmist puts it, 'He throws caution to the winds, giving to the needy in reckless abandon. His right-living, right-giving ways never run out, never wear out.'" Like Abraham, you'll be blessed beyond measure so that you can turn around and be a blessing to somebody else.

Vs. 10,11 says, "This most generous God Who gives seed to the farmer that becomes bread for your meals is more than extravagant with you. He gives you something you can give away, which grows into full formed lives, robust in God, wealthy in every way, so that you can be generous in every way, producing with us great praise to God." God is extravagant, so much so that "eye has not seen, nor ear heard, nor have entered into the heart of man the things which God has prepared for those who love Him" (1 Cor. 2:9). Success is the result of steady, forward movement and real success involves helping others. This is the path on which God wants you to travel and once you get on that path, and stay on it, there is no way anybody can stop you from living the good life. Those who are successful never quit. Paul tells the church in 1 Cor. 15:58 to "be steadfast, immovable, always abounding in the work of the Lord, knowing that your labor is not in vain in the Lord."

The Message Bible says, "With all this going for us, my dear, dear friends, stand your ground. And don't hold back. Throw yourselves into the work of the Master, confident that nothing you do for Him is a waste of time or effort." Thomas Edison once said, "I start where other men quit." People are afraid to expect good things in their lives because they've experienced so many disappointments and failures in the past. Thomas Edison failed thousands of times, but he did not quit. In order to live the good life you have to forget about the failures of the past and raise the level of your expectations. Jesus once asked the blind men, "Do you believe that I am able to do this?" (Matt. 9:28). When they said "Yes, Lord" Jesus touched their eyes and said, "According to your faith let it be to you" (vs. 28). Your faith limits and determines the amount of God's power that is manifested in your life. This is why you must think big thoughts because God is able to do far more than you can ask or think.

The Bible says that what you behold, you will become (2 Cor. 3:18). When you behold His glory, His goodness will be manifested in your life. Do not allow yourself to be moved by what's happening around you but instead be moved only by the Word of God and the image of the good life that you have on the inside of you. What you see down in your spirit, that which you behold, will eventually become so real to you that no matter what the circumstances look like on the outside, you will be fully persuaded that the good life is your destiny. You were created to be successful. You were created to live the good life. This always has been and always will be God's plan and purpose for your life. This truth was evident way back in the Garden of Eden. Gen. 1:27,28 says, "So God created man in His image; in the image of God He created him; male and female He created them. Then He blessed them." The first thing God did to Adam and Eve after He created them was He blessed them.

The word "bless" means 'empowered to prosper' and after blessing them God gave the command to "be fruitful and multiply" (vs. 28). To be fruitful means to be successful and this is a direct command from God himself. The time came when sin entered in and God eventually destroyed the earth with a flood and started things all over again with Noah and his sons. This was a new beginning to the human race and again the first thing God did was bless them. Gen. 9:1 says, "So God blessed Noah and his sons, and said to them, 'Be fruitful and multiply, and fill the earth.'" Again the command was given to be successful. The same thing happened to Abraham (Gen. 17:2,6), Isaac (Gen. 26:22), Jacob (Gen. 28:3), and Joseph (Gen. 41:52). In the New Testament Paul prays in Col. 1:10 "that you may have a walk worthy of the Lord, fully pleasing Him, being fruitful in every good work and increasing in the knowledge of God." You also were created to be fruitful and multiply.

Success is a choice, not an accident. Neither is it a one-time event but instead is a continuous journey. You must believe for this to become a reality in your life. There will be times when you will face what appears to be impossible situations but Jesus said in Mark 9:23, "If you can believe, all things are possible to him who believes." Your faith will only rise to the level of your dreams. In other words, if you think small, you'll stay small. Ps. 78:41 tells how after Moses delivered God's people out of Egypt "again and again they tempted God and limited the Holy One of Israel." How did they limit God? Vs. 42 says,

"They did not remember His power." With unbelief they questioned the power of God and His willingness to deliver them. They asked continually, "Can God do this?" and "Can God do that?" They did not comprehend the good life that was waiting for them across the Jordan River in the land of Canaan. They thought small and they stayed small.

With the exception of Joshua and Caleb that entire generation died off in the wilderness and never experienced the good life. The same scenario happened in Matt. 13:54-58. Jesus traveled to His home town of Nazareth but "He did not do many mighty miracles there because of their unbelief." For sure, unbelief limits the ability of God to bless your life. If you think small, you'll stay small. Of course, the solution to all this is to think big thoughts. God wants to remove every limitation that would hinder you from living the good life. He does that by enlarging your thinking capacity. This is why Paul prayed in Eph. 3:14-20 that we would be able to comprehend all that God has planned for us. You can live the good life but comprehension comes first. If you can think it, God can do it. If you can mold it in your thoughts, you'll hold it in your hands. Sad to say, people don't desire the things of God enough.

Mark 11:24 says, "Therefore I say to you, whatever things you desire when you pray, believe that you receive them, and you will have them." Desire comes before possession. Here's how you live the good life. You see a promised blessing in the Word and you desire it in your heart. You then imagine receiving it with your thoughts. Next, you believe you receive it when you pray and in God's perfect timing the blessing will be manifested in your life. Jesus is saying if you can conceive it, you can receive it. Your future is in your hands or, more accurately, in your thoughts. Like an architect you can design for yourself a better future by reshaping your thought life. When you think like God thinks, your future will match His plan for your life. Jer. 29:11 says, "For I know the thoughts that I think toward you, says the Lord, thoughts of peace and not of evil, to give you a future and a hope." Vs. 14 says, "I will bring you back from your captivity."

A person's downfall comes when they can't picture themselves getting out of their present condition. Prov. 23:7 says, "For as he thinks in his heart, so is he." Your life goes in the direction of your most dominate thought. Mentor your thoughts. Be selective about what you think about. Your imagination is a God-given gift and without it you can never receive anything from God. This is why God wants you to think big thoughts. Is. 54:2,3 says, "Enlarge the place of your tent, and let them stretch out the curtains of your habitation; Do not spare; lengthen your cords, and strengthen your stakes. For you shall expand to the right and to the left, and your descendants will inherit the nations, and make the desolate cities inhabited." God is a God of increase so think big thoughts. You'll disappoint Him if you don't. If times of hardship dominate your life you can go to 2 Cor. 4 and Paul will tell you what to do. First, he says in vs.16 to not lose heart. Don't abandon hope and never give up.

Vs. 18 then says, "While we do not look at the things which are seen, but at the things which are not seen. For the things which are seen are temporary, but the things which are not seen are eternal." The Message Bible says, "So we're not giving up. How could we? Even though on the outside it often looks like things are falling apart on us, on the inside, where God is making new life, not a day goes by without His unfolding grace. These hard times are small potatoes compared to the coming good times, the lavish celebration prepared for us. There's far more here than meets the eye. The things we see now are here today, gone tomorrow. But the things we can't see now will last forever." Think like God thinks and your circumstances will change. That's a promise from God. When all is said and done, the bottom line is that you must be thoroughly and completely convinced that God has made the good life available to you.

Paul wrote in Rom. 8:38,39, "For I am persuaded that neither death nor life, nor angels nor principalities nor powers, nor things present nor things to come, nor height nor depth, nor any other created thing, shall be able to separate us from the love of God which is in Christ Jesus our Lord." Paul was convinced that God was willing and able to create for him a good life. He later said in 2 Tim. 1:12, "For I know whom I have believed and am persuaded that He is able to keep what I have committed to Him until that day." People have settled for too less for too long but by renewing your mind (Rom.12:2) you can also be fully persuaded that God wants to take away all your limitations. You must have a fresh mental and spiritual attitude and come up to a higher way of thinking. You must think like God thinks. Is. 55:8 says, "'For My thoughts are not your thoughts, nor are your ways My ways,' says the Lord. 'For as the heavens are higher than the earth, so are My ways higher than your ways.'"

Ps. 45:1 says, "My heart is overflowing with a good theme." Think good thoughts for out of the abundance of the heart the mouth speaks (Matt. 12:34). It's your heart that gives meaning to your words and it's your words that determine your destiny. What you talk about is what's going to come to pass in your life. Words are powerful so take them seriously. This is how you fight the good fight of faith. A promise from God gives you reason for expectation but you must stand your ground and not waver. Living the good life is a fight but too many people are looking for comfortable Christianity. There is no such thing. To live the good life you must stand your ground and think godly thoughts and speak godly words. Heb. 10:23 says, "Let us hold fast the confession of our hope without wavering, for He Who promised is faithful." The Amplified Bible says, "Seize and hold fast, retain without wavering" and the Message Bible says, "Let's keep a firm grip on the promises that keep us going."

Vs. 35 says, "Therefore do not cast away your confidence which has great reward." The great reward the author speaks of is a good life and it's worth fighting for. To experience the good life you must have a "no quit" attitude. Speaking of Abraham Rom. 4:20 says, "He did waver at the promise of God through unbelief, but was strengthened in faith, giving glory to God." A promise from God gives you reason for expectation, a chance to have hope and faith for a better future. Faith believes what it can't see and expectancy reinforces it. Faith always expects so stand your ground and don't waver. Ps. 62:5,6 says, "My soul, wait silently for God alone, for my expectation is from Him. He alone is my rock and my salvation; He is my defense; I shall not be moved." The Message Bible says, "I'll wait as long as He says." You get what you expect and for what you are willing to wait for. Jesus said to the centurion, "Go your way; as you have believed, so let it be done for you" (Matt. 8:13).

He is actually saying "become what you believe." The word "expect" means 'to look for, to fix the eyes upon, to reach for.' It means to be excited and enthusiastic and is founded on the evidence of God's Word and not just wishful thinking. Paul said in Acts 27:25, "Therefore, take heart, men, for I believe God that it will be just as it was told me." The perfect will of God is available to you and it's all based on your ability to comprehend it and your willingness to wait for it to come to pass. The good life is determined by a hunger for God, an unending search for Him and His will for your life. To experience the good life you must do three things. You must see it, say it, and seize it. Prov. 29:18 says, "Where there is no vision, the people perish." You must see in the scriptures the good life God wants you to have. See it with your thoughts and faith imaginations and then decree it. Say out loud what you believe.

In 1 Sam. 17:37 David said that the giant would fall. He said out loud what he believed. 2 Cor. 4:13 says, "But since we have the same spirit of faith, according to what is written, 'I believed and therefore I spoke,' we also believe and therefore speak." Next, you act on what you believe. David ran toward the giant. Placed before him was a

God-given opportunity to experience the good life and with no fear in his heart he ran toward his dream. You, too, must do the same thing. Run to your dream with everything you have. Don't tiptoe toward it, don't wait for permission, and don't let fear slow your stride. Grab hold of the vision God placed in your heart and refuse to let go, even when the path is steep or the voices of doubt grow loud. Dreams worth having demand courage, endurance, and faith, but they also carry the promise of purpose. Hold on through setbacks and press forward through uncertainty. What you chase with faith and determination today can become the testimony you live out tomorrow.

| 11 |

"THE GOOD LIFE"

It is remarkable how simple the gospel message truly is to them that believe. To the unsaved it is a stumbling block and a rock of offense (1 Peter 2:8) but to those who are born again it is the source of life and godliness. In the Old Testament there were 613 commandments that had to be followed and obeyed but Jesus came and said if you would follow what He called "the first and great commandment" (Matt. 22:28) then all the others would be fulfilled. He said in Mark 12:30, "And you shall love the Lord your God with all your heart, with all your soul, with all your mind, and with all your strength." It doesn't get any easier than that yet many people struggle every day in following this command. The reason this is so is because deep down in their hearts they don't know Him and what He is truly like. Ps. 119:68 gives a simple but precise description of the character of the Heavenly Father, "You are good, and do good." The greatest attribute of God is that He is a God of love and is completely good.

God is the complete picture of what being good is all about. In Ex.33:18 Moses said to Him, "Please, show me your glory." People become famous and receive glory for doing something very well. Moses was saying to God, "Show me what You're famous for. Show me what You're good at. Show me what You can do better than anybody else. Show me Your glory." God responded to Moses in vs. 19, "I will make all My goodness pass before you." God wants to be known to all people for His goodness. Ex. 34:6,7 says, "And the Lord passed before him and proclaimed, 'The Lord, the Lord God, merciful and gracious, longsuffering, and abounding in goodness and truth, keeping mercy for thousands, forgiving iniquity and transgressions and sin.'" God is infinite and His goodness cannot be measured. There are no boundaries and no limitations as to how far God will go to be good to you.

The Heavenly Father wants to be famous for doing good things for His children, so much so that the devil will do everything he can to convince you otherwise. Don't let that sly serpent do it. Be convinced in your heart that since God cannot change (Mal. 3:6), neither will His goodness ever change. Your life was designed to give God glory and this happens when you live a good and blessed life. It is the plan of God that you have dominion over all that which tries to pull you down and it's the blessing of God on your life that gives you that dominion. You need to be bold and have the courage to believe for more of God's favor and blessing in your life. God is not limited in what He can do in your life as long as you're not limited in believing that He can do it. If you're limited in your asking, then God is limited in His doing. If you have no boldness in what you're willing to ask Him for, then He will be limited in His ability to give you exceedingly, abundantly above what you can ask or think.

James 4:2 (NLT) says, "You don't have what you want because you don't ask God for it." God desires to give you the things you want and need but you still must walk in faith and ask Him for those things. The blessed life is God's idea and He plants in your heart a spark of desire for all those good things. Your prayer request then fans that spark into a flame and before long all those blessings will be poured into your life. A life that is blessed by God is essential to fulfill His purpose for your life. He would not send you to the front lines of battle without giving you what you need to do what He called you to do. How can you leave your mark on this generation if God doesn't bless you with His wisdom, His goodness, and His ability? If you are not blessed with

His favor and power you will not be able to fulfill your assignment from on high. As a child of God it is your divine right to be blessed by God and to live a good life.

John 1:12 says, "But as many as received Him, to them He gave the right to become children of God. He gave you the power to become His child, the power to be blessed, and the power to fulfill your destiny. All you have to do is ask for it and believe you receive it. Heb. 4:16 says, "Let us therefore come boldly to the throne of grace, that we may obtain mercy and find grace to help in time of need." Being bold doesn't mean you're arrogant, it means you're obedient and confident. You've been washed by the blood of Jesus and, as far as God is concerned, you have the same right to boldly approach Him as Jesus. God is good and He wants you to live a good life, a life where you can daily experience God's best in everything you do. It's life with an exclamation point after it and will cause ordinary people to live extraordinary lives. God has unclaimed blessings waiting for you to claim as your own so allow your desire to reach out for that good life that will bring honor to Him for all time.

How do you grab hold of the good life? The Message Bible says in Matt. 7:7-11, "Don't bargain with God. Be direct. Ask for what you need. This isn't a cat-and-mouse, hide-and-seek game we're in. If your child asks for bread, do you trick him with sawdust? If he asks for fish, do you scare him with a live snake on his plate? As bad as you are, you wouldn't think of such a thing. You're at least decent to your own children. So don't you think the God who conceived you in love will be even better?" Jesus said in vs.7, "Ask, and it will be given to you." God told you to be bold when you ask Him to bless you with a good life. It is the desire of God for you to have so much of His extraordinary goodness in your life that it overflows into the lives of others. No matter what your life has been like in the past, He can give you "beauty for ashes" (Is. 61:3). All He's waiting for is you to ask Him.

Paul wrote in Eph. 2:7,8 (MSG), "Now God has us right where He wants us, with all the time in this world and the next to shower grace and kindness upon us in Christ Jesus. Saving is all His idea, and all His work. All we do is trust Him enough to let Him do it." He then goes on to say in vs. 10 (AMP), "For we are God's own handiwork (His workmanship), recreated in Christ Jesus, born anew that we may do those good works which God predestined (planned beforehand) for us, taking paths which He prepared ahead of time, that we should walk in them, living the good life which He prearranged and made ready for us to live."

There should be something inside of you that wants to go beyond the norm, something that compels you to believe for bigger and better things. Inside of you is the hunger for more of the good things in life because you know that what you currently have is not all there is. Living the good life is a choice you have to make. Deut. 30:19 says, "I call heaven and earth as witnesses today against you, that I have set before you life and death, blessing and cursing; therefore choose life, that both you and your descendants may live." Jesus did His part on the cross and now it's up to you to decide if you want to have all that's been made available to you. Why live in the prison of mediocrity? Come up higher and live a good life, a life that is blessed abundantly by God. Choose today to walk in the fullness of everything God has for you. Dare to believe that with these blessings you'll be able to fulfill God's call on your life. No longer will you be just a pretty face in the crowd but every room you walk into the power and blessing of God enters with you. God is using you to change the world for that is what the blessing is for.

The devil will try to convince you that you're being selfish if you ask God to bless you in a great way. He'll remind you of past failures in an attempt to make you feel guilty and unworthy to receive those blessings. You've got to get over the feeling that's it's wrong to ask God to bless you. You need to know that God deeply wants you to live a blessed life and He has chosen prayer as the vehicle through which these blessings will come. Jabez prayed to be blessed and God granted his request. Jabez wanted to be set apart for success, happiness, and prosperity and so should you. He wanted to be blessed everywhere he went and in everything he did. Ask God to expand your territory. Ask Him to increase your influence in the world in which you live. Ask Him to work in your life. Phil 2:13 (NT) says, "For God is working in you, giving you the desire and the power to do what pleases Him."

The Message Bible says, "Be energetic in your life of salvation, reverent and sensitive before God. That energy is God's energy, an energy deep within you, God himself willing and working at what will give Him the most pleasure." God wants to enlarge your territory so He can enlarge His kingdom. Ask Him to do it and He will. Jabez then prayed "that Your hand would be with me." As the opportunities for your ministry grow and increase you will need God by your side like never before. You will need His divine power and anointing on your life. You will need Him to direct your steps, to tell you where to go and what to do and what to say. Acts 11:21 says, "And the hand of the Lord was with them, and a great number believed and turned to the Lord." As you receive more blessings and along with it more territory, you will need more power so you can do what you've been called to do. When God's hand is on your life you will be more valuable to the kingdom than you could ever imagine.

When that happens, like Jabez you need to pray "that You would keep me from evil." There are temptations that come with having success and influence and some people fall prey to the wiles of the enemy. Pray like Jesus taught in Matt. 6:33, "And do not lead us into temptation, but deliver us from the evil one." Always flee from evil. Run from it and don't look back. Jabez prayed that God would keep him from evil "that I may not cause pain!" Evil always causes pain and never do you want to be an instrument of the enemy to bring pain to another human being. Put a muzzle over your mouth so you won't say bad things that you'll regret a short time later (Ps. 141:3). Flee sexual immorality (1 Cor. 6:18) and never put yourself in a position where you'll be alone with the opposite sex. Walk away from those who gossip and slander other people (James 4:11). All these things cause pain, especially to those you love the most.

Pray that God's hand would be with you, guiding every step you take and strengthening you for what lies ahead. Ask Him to keep you from evil, guarding your heart, mind, and actions from anything that would lead you astray. Trust that as you walk under His protection, He will shape your life so that you bring healing, hope, and blessing rather than pain. Don't get so caught up in getting blessed that you ignore the fact that the devil wants to use you to hurt somebody else. Flee from evil and walk in love at all times. Rom. 13:10 says, "Love does no harm to a neighbor; therefore love is the fulfillment of the law." Get on your knees and pray, surrendering your heart fully to God's will. Ask Him to shape your thoughts, words, and actions so that you become an instrument of good in a broken world. Commit yourself daily to walk in humility, love, and obedience, rejecting every path that leads to evil.

God wants you blessed and He wants you to be happy all the days of your life. Paul told Timothy, "Command those who are rich in this present age not to be haughty, nor to trust in uncertain riches but in the living God, who gives us richly all things to enjoy" (1 Tim. 6:17). The Message Bible says, "Tell them to go after God, who piles on all the riches we could ever manage." God wants to bless the world so much that He sent His only Son to live and die so that everybody could live the good life and reap the benefits of His ultimate sacrifice. Rom. 8:31,32 says, "If God is for us, who can be against us? He who did not spare His own Son, but delivered Him up for us all, how shall He not with Him also freely give us all things?" The Lord Jesus, your precious Savior who loves you so much that He bled and died for your salvation, has made available to you a life of joy, happiness, and victory. It's a life where all your needs are met (Phil. 4:19) and all your desires are fulfilled with glorious splendor (Ps. 37:4).

God has so many wonderful blessings in store for you that if only for a moment you could comprehend it all you'd be overwhelmed with joy beyond measure. Indeed, He is a good God and He wants you to live the good life. David wrote in Ps. 23:6, "Surely Your goodness and love will follow me all the days of my life." Sad to say, many people never really manage to enjoy their lives and obtain from God all that He has made available to them. They spend day after day, year after year, just going through the motions hoping things will get better. They don't realize that the good life won't come to them by chance but instead must be vigorously pursued with all that is within them. Before people can experience the good life they must first "be able to comprehend with all the saints what is the width and length and depth and height - to know the love of Christ which passes knowledge; that you may be filled with all the goodness of God" (Eph. 3:18,19).

The word "comprehend" means 'to seize, to grasp, to take hold of, to completely understand.' The Message Bible says Paul desires that "you'll be able to take in with all Christians the extravagant dimensions of Christ's love. Reach out and experience the breadth! Test it's length! Plumb the depths! Rise to the heights! Live full lives, full in the fullness of God." Living the good life is based on your ability to comprehend it and this happens when you have a thirst and hunger for God that can't be quenched. You need to open up your Bible and pursue with aggressive determination and relentless boldness the abundant life that rightfully belongs to you. God has promised to give those who believe everything they need to live a joy-filled life where they can become the happy, healthy, victorious champions that God by His eternal grace and favor has already made them to be. In order to escape from the shackles of mediocrity you need to stretch your faith and go beyond where you're now at.

God is ready to take you to the next level but first you must get new dreams and set new goals. God said in Deut. 1:6, "You have dwelt long enough at this mountain." There is more God wants you to have but first you have to get off the mountain you are currently on. Christians who desire to live extraordinary lives should refrain from setting ordinary goals such as is common in the ordinary world. When people of the world think of the good life they usually think of material prosperity, of pleasure and popularity. For some it's a comfortable home that's paid for and having sufficient money for a winter vacation in the sun plus a summer home on some sandy beach. The world is after fame and fortune, the latest fashion of designer clothes, fast cars and big houses, diamond rings, and a membership at a high-class country club and golf course. Popular culture today is centered on one's own selfish ambitions and success.

People of the world believe that "he who dies with the most toys wins." The cravings of this world is ever consuming for there is always the next hottest fashion to get or the latest electronic gadget that they must add to their collection. Sad to say, the goals the world sets are goals which many never achieve. Achievement does not ensure happiness and those who fail to achieve their goals are made even more miserable by their failure. Even a casual observer would agree that most wealthy, high-living and famous people are not happy and thus are not living the good life. What good is fame and fortune if you're not happy? Yet these same people continue to seek after these worldly things without realizing that they are on a road that will lead to their eternal doom. The desire to live the good life is not new. It's been the dream of every generation since the dawn of time. It's been the goal of teachers and philosophers, of kings and queens and the common man.

Living the good life is a good desire, a Godly desire, but you must take the first step and learn not to make material possessions, pleasures, and fame your main goal in life. Solomon once wrote, "He who loves silver will not be satisfied with silver; nor he who loves abundance, with increase, this also is vanity" (Eccl. 5:10). Prov. 10:22 says, "The blessing of the Lord makes one rich, and He adds no sorrow with it." God can give what the world cannot give. He offers a peace which things of the world cannot give and a joy that is complete and full. The bottom line is that God wants to be first in your life. Paul writes in Col. 3:2, "Set your mind on things above, not on things on the earth." The Message Bible says, "Pursue the things over which Christ presides. Don't shuffle along, eyes to the ground, absorbed with the things right in front of you. Look up and be alert to what is going on around Christ - that's where the action is. See things from His perspective."

Without a doubt, Jesus is the ultimate and only path to the good life. 1 John 2:15 says, "Do not love the world or the things in the world. If anyone loves the world, the love of the Father is not in him." Without Jesus the world is a very sinful and wicked place. It can be described as a community of sinful humanity that possesses a spirit of rebellion against God. 1 John 5:19 says, "We know that we are of God, and the whole world lies under the sway of the wicked one." Because of its opposition to God, the world values those things that are contrary to God's will. 1 John 2:16 says, "For all that is in the world - the lust of the flesh, the lust of the eyes, and the pride of life - is not of the Father but is of the world." The attraction of the world and its sensual pleasures is amplified by Satan who is head of the world system. He is called the "ruler of this world" (John 12:31) and the whole world is said to be under his power. The solution to the love of the world is to have a greater love for God.

The Christian who seeks daily to please God in everything and who strives for spiritual growth need not fall prey to the seducing temptations of the world. The Message translation of 1 John 2:15-17 says, "Don't love the world's ways. Don't love the world's goods. Love of the world squeezes out love for the Father. It just isolates you from

Him. The world and all it's wanting, wanting, wanting is on the way out - but whoever does what God wants is set for eternity." The pursuit of the good life must originate in the spiritual realm of the heavenly domain regardless of the physical circumstances you might find yourself in. Jesus taught in Luke 12:15 that there is more to life than material possessions. He said, "Take heed and beware of covetousness, for one's life does not consist in the abundance of the things he possesses." The Message Bible says, "Life is not defined by what you have, even when you have a lot."

Jesus warns of the folly of seeking after earthly riches but instead encourages people to "lay up for yourselves treasures in heaven, where neither moth nor rust destroy and where thieves do not break in and steal" (Matt. 6:19,20). The great blessing about living the good life is that once you learn not to make material possessions and worldly pleasures your primary goal in life, God will then step in and bless you with an unexpected and abundant portion of these very things. Matt. 6:33 says, "But seek first the kingdom of God and His righteousness, and all these things will be added to you." You can't sit still and do nothing and expect God to bless your life. You've got to search the scriptures and meditate in the Word day and night (Ps. 1:1-3). When God wanted to get the attention of Moses He set a bush on fire that didn't burn up. When Moses saw the fiery bush he said, "I will now turn aside and see this great sight, why the bush does not burn."

So when the Lord saw that he turned aside to look, God called to him from the midst of the bush (Ex. 3:1-4). If Moses had not turned aside to investigate then God would not have spoken to him. You also need to be alert in your spirit and take the time to investigate what the Bible says about you living a good life. When you do that consistently, God will speak to you, and He'll direct the steps you need to take. Obey what He tells you to do and don't let the devil convince you otherwise. Enforce your will over the enemy for the voice of a stranger you will not follow (John 10:5). Say what God says and do what He tells you to do. Say out loud, "I'm blessed in the city, and I'm blessed in the field. I'm blessed coming in and I'm blessed going out." Imagine what your life would be like if you lived in a realm of love and goodness. Jesus taught you to pray that your life would come up higher so that it would be a reflection of what life is like in heaven (Matt. 6:10).

Embrace this good life that God so adamantly wants you to have. Frame your world by constantly confessing His promises over your life and the lives of your loved ones. Ask Him for the wisdom that will help you make right choices that in turn will create for you a life that is well-pleasing in His eyes. It is His will for you to live under the blessings that get poured out from an open heaven. Deut. 28:12 says, "The Lord will open to you His good treasure, the heavens, to give the rain to your land in its season, and to bless all the work of your hand. You shall lend to many nations, but you shall not borrow." The rain of God's blessing will come down on you so powerfully that everything you put your hand to will prosper and be blessed. The accelerated presence of God will be with you wherever you go causing you to live the good life. The windows of heaven are open and you can live under them every day of your life.

God is on your side and Deut. 28:8 says, "The Lord will command the blessing on you and in your storehouses and in all to which you set your hand, and He will bless you in the land which the Lord your God is giving you." Never doubt that things happen when God commands something to be done. In the beginning He commanded "Let there be light" and there was light (Gen. 1:3). Take a moment and dwell on the fact that God has commanded the blessing of a good life to fall on you. He wants all the world to know that He has blessed your life. Deut. 28:10 says, "Then all people of the earth shall see that you are called by the name of the Lord, and they shall be afraid of you." God wants you to enjoy the best things life has to offer as a testimony to the world showing them how good He truly is. Who wants to draw close to a God who causes His children to be poor and sick all the time? No, it's the goodness of God that leads people to repentance (Rom. 2:4). Help the world get saved by allowing God to be good to you. Live the good life.

| 12 |

"FIRST THINGS FIRST"

It goes without saying that nobody will experience the good life without a close, personal relationship with the Triune God. Don't spend your life seeking things that don't have the power within itself to please you. No, seek God who gives you richly all things to enjoy. Jesus said in John 1:6, "I am the way, the truth, and the life." Since Jesus is good and everything about Him is good, this verse can be rendered, "I am the good way, the good truth, and the good life." The reality of it all is that the "good life" is a person and His name is Jesus. God wants to have an exciting, deep, intimate, and personal relationship with you but first you must crave, pursue, and go after Him with all your strength and might. Unless you invest your time and energy in seeking Him regularly throughout the day you will surely miss out on the good life and all the wonderful blessings He has waiting for you.

God is a good God but He must be sought after to be found. So seek Him on purpose. Seek Him by design. Get up early and spend time with your Heavenly Father and Your savior Jesus Christ. Tell the Holy Spirit how much He means to you. Think about them, talk about them, communicate with them all day long. The danger of not putting God first is constant. Sometimes people get so busy doing things for God that they don't spend the right amount of time with Him. He may have blessed you with a new house but now you spend all your time taking care of it. Or maybe He blessed you with a promotion at your job and now you're required to work more hours each day and most weekends. Then, when you're home, you're too tired to do anything else. You ignore God and your family and before long your life begins to crumble before your very eyes. You cannot let these things come between you and God. If your heart's desire is to spend quality time with God then you will find the time to do it.

For some people it's easier to give money than time but God wants a relationship with you more than He wants your money. Determine to put God first in everything you do and He'll honor whatever effort you make to draw closer to Him. A special promise is given to all serious God seekers in Deut. 4:29, "But from there you will seek the Lord your God, and you will find Him if you seek Him with all your heart and with all your soul." To have a close relationship with God you've got to be more than just a Sunday Christian. You've got to stop seeking Him only during times of need and ignore Him the rest of the time when things are going well. You've got to keep God in the place that rightfully belongs to Him which is first place in your life. If you will give the first portion of your time and seek Him consistently on a regular basis, it will be the answer to every problem you'll ever have. You cannot stay strong in the Lord if you don't spend quality time with Him.

It won't take long to realize that when you truly seek God with all your heart and soul that you won't find some form of God or a false religion. Instead, you will find the one true and living God. You don't have to be educated, famous, or wealthy. It doesn't matter if you are young or old, male or female, married or single, or completely Bible illiterate. When you seek Him with all your heart you will find Him and He will get you through all the roadblocks of life. God promises that while seeking Him you are never on your own. Hosea 10:12 says, "Sow for yourselves righteousness; reap in mercy; break up your fallow ground, for it is time to seek the Lord, till He comes and rains righteousness on you." Now is the time to seek the Lord because He is longing to have fellowship with you. James 4:8 says, "Draw near to God and He will draw near to you." Notice who takes the first step. You do!

David wrote in Ps. 63:1, "O God, You are my God; Early will I seek You; My soul thirsts for You; My flesh longs for You in a dry and thirsty land where there is no water." He says in vs. 6, "When I remember You on my bed, I meditate on You in the night watches." David sought God in the morning when he arose and at night when he went to bed and every minute in between. He sought the Lord nonstop because he was a man after God's own heart. It goes without saying that when your heart is sold out to Jesus, you will do whatever it takes to seek Him out and spend time with Him. Ps. 84:2 says, "My soul longs, yes, even faints for the courts of the Lord; My heart and my flesh cry out for the living God." Ps. 42:1,2 says, "As the deer pants for the water brooks, so pants my soul for You, O God. My soul thirsts for God, for the living God." The very purpose of man's existence is to seek God. "For in Him we live and move and have our being" (Acts 17:28).

Intimacy with God and the fullest possible fellowship and partnership with Him comes as you desire and seek to know Him. Prayer and spending time with God is all about desire and passion. David wrote in Ps. 27:4, "One thing I have desired of the Lord, that will I seek: That I may dwell in the house of the Lord all the days of my life, to behold the beauty of the Lord, and to inquire in His temple." The "beauty of the Lord" can also be translated "the delightfulness of the Lord." Yes, seeking and finding God is a pure delight. Jesus prayed to the Father in John 17:3, "And this is eternal life, that they may know You, the only true God, and Jesus Christ whom You have sent." When you love someone, it is only natural that you want to know them more and more. It takes time and effort and desire and determination to know God. Being fully devoted to God is a lifelong process. The Greek word for "devoted" means to 'latch on to and refuse to let go.' Latch on to Jesus and make knowing Him your main desire in life.

Nothing will please Him more. And the more you know Jesus the more you will love Him and trust Him and delight in Him. It's what the good life is all about. God is seeking for those who will seek Him. Ps. 53:2 says, "God looks down from heaven upon the children of men, to see if there are any who understand, who seek God." The word "seek" means 'to desire; to examine or explore; to seek earnestly; to diligently search for; to crave; to investigate; to pursue.' God is worthy of your praise and the more you know Him the more you will reverence Him and be in awe of Him. The word "praise" means 'to place great value on someone,' so when you praise God you are communicating how much you care for Him and value Him. And when you do this, God will reach down and gently touch your heart, awakening a deep hunger to seek Him and know Him more. As you respond to His touch, He will draw you closer, shaping your desires to align with His will and purpose.

God said in Jer. 24:7, "For I will set My eyes on them for good, and I will bring them back to their land; I will build them and not pull them down, and I will plant them and not pluck them up. Then I will give them a heart to know Me, that I am the Lord; and they shall be My people, and I will be their God, for they shall return to Me with all their heart." You should always be seeking to know Him better, to have a closer, more personal relationship with Him. Your desire should be that you can communicate with God as a child would his or her parent. This is His desire and He is forever ready to draw you into His bosom. He must, however, be sought after to be found. The good news is that you don't seek Him in vain. If you will seek Him with all your heart you will find Him. Deut. 30:6 says, "And the Lord your God will circumcise your heart and the heart of your descendants, to love the Lord your God with all your heart and with all your soul, that you may live."

With the Lord's help you are to seek Him continually (1 Chron. 16:11) and wholeheartedly. Jer. 29:12,13 says, "Then you will call upon Me and go and pray to Me, and I will listen to you. And you will seek Me and find Me, when you search for Me with all your heart." You need to become like those believers in the Old Testament who "entered into a covenant to seek the Lord God of their fathers with all their heart and with all their soul; and whoever would not seek the Lord God of Israel was to be put to death, whether small or great, whether man or woman. Then they took an oath before the Lord with a loud voice, with shouting and trumpets and ram's horns. And all Judah rejoiced at the oath, for they had sworn with all their heart and sought Him with all their soul; and He was found by them, and the Lord gave them rest all around" (2 Chron. 15:12-15). God rewards those who seek Him diligently.

Prov. 8:17,18 says, "I love those who love Me, and those Who seek me diligently will find Me. Riches and honor are with Me, enduring riches and righteousness." Seeking God with all your heart will bring you joy unspeakable. Ps. 70:4 says, "Let all those who seek You rejoice and be glad in You; and let those who love Your salvation say continually, 'Let God be magnified!'" You can also read in Ps. 105:3, "Glory in His holy name; Let the hearts of those rejoice who seek the Lord." Peace and rest will be yours when you seek God above all else. 2 Chron.14:7 says, "We have sought Him, and He has given us rest on every side." Divine revelation will come to you and secrets will be revealed when you seek God. He said in Jer. 33:3, "Call to Me, and I will answer you, and show you great and mighty things, which you do not know." Along with all this will come perception and understanding in all things. Prov. 28:5 says, "Evil men do not understand justice, but those who seek the Lord will understand all."

God has revealed to His people that joy comes when you diligently seek Him and along with that will come strength and maturity. Ps. 105:3,4 says, "Glory in His holy name; Let the hearts of those rejoice who seek the Lord. Seek the Lord and His strength; Seek His face forevermore." The Lord said in Jer. 9:24, "But let him who glories glory in this, that He understands and knows Me." Do not forget what Paul said in Eph. 1:17,18, "That the God of our Lord Jesus Christ, the Father of glory, may give to you the spirit of wisdom and revelation in the knowledge of Him, the eyes of your understanding being enlightened; that you may know what is the hope of His calling, what are the riches of the glory of His inheritance in the saints." The Message Bible says Paul asked God "to make you intelligent and discerning in knowing Him personally, your eyes focused and clean, so that you can see exactly what it is He is calling you to do."

Prosperity and supernatural provision are the byproduct of a life devoted to seeking God first. When we align our hearts with Him, heaven responds with provision that goes beyond human effort and natural limitation. David wrote in Ps. 34:8-10, "Oh, taste and see that the Lord is good; Blessed is the man who trusts in Him! Oh, fear the Lord, you His saints! There is no want to those who fear Him. The young lions lack and suffer hunger; But those who seek the Lord shall not lack any good thing." Uzziah "sought God in the days of Zechariah, who had understanding in the vision of God; and as long as he sought the Lord, God made him to prosper" (2 Chron. 26:5). A sense of security will overcome you as you seek the Lord and become wrapped in His loving embrace. Ps. 31:23,24 says, "Oh, love the Lord, all you His saints! For the Lord preserves the faithful, and fully repays the proud person. Be of good courage, and He shall strengthen your heart, all you who hope in the Lord."

The Message Bible says, "Love God, all you saints; God takes care of all who stay close to Him. But He pays back in full those arrogant enough to go it alone. Be brave. Be strong. Don't give up. Expect God to get here soon." David teaches you to trust in the Lord and be not afraid when he wrote, "For in the time of trouble He shall hide me in His pavilion; In the secret place of His tabernacle He shall hide me;

He shall set me high upon a rock" (Ps. 27: 5). David sought the Lord and trusted Him to take care of him. No wonder he lived the good life. There was one thing that was more important to David than anything else. He was a man after God's own heart (Acts 13:22) and all he wanted was to have a close, personal relationship with the Lord his God. He couldn't live without God being in his life. Many believers spend most of their time seeking what God can do for them thinking it's the same thing as seeking God. It's not. God wants you to seek His face and not His hand.

The good news is that if you'll seek His face, His hand will always be open. Matt. 6:33 says, "But seek first the kingdom of God and His righteousness, and all these things will be added to you." Like David, you need to do whatever it takes to spend personal, quality time alone with God. If you'll do that then God will fight your battles for you and everything in your life will turn out for your good. You'll have a good marriage, your bills will get paid, you'll walk in good health, and you'll fulfill your destiny. The key is that you've got to put first things first. You've got to make your relationship with God the top priority of your life. Being a true Christian and keeping God first in your life is going to take more effort than going to church for an hour on Sunday morning. Most believers know this, yet the distractions of everyday life take them away from what should be their top priority. They try to work God into their schedule when what they should be doing is working their schedule around God.

They think being religious is good enough, but Jesus didn't die so you could have some flaky religion. No, He died so you could have a deep, personal, and intimate relationship with the Heavenly Father through Him. Your Daddy wants to have a vital part in every decision you make and everything you put your hand to do. He knows that the deeper your personal relationship is with Him, the more the devil will be afraid of you and the more victory you'll have in your life. The church is not impressing the world as it should be doing. The body of Christ is to be a light in a dark world, but many have not turned the switch on. People need to get more serious about what's going on in the world today and in their own personal relationship with God. God has to come first in everything you say and do. Don't waste your time and His time by taking up space and bearing no fruit in your life. No, come up higher and get close to God and stay close to Him for the rest of your life.

You must take the time to make this happen for, if you don't, you'll never be whole on the inside and you'll never fulfill your destiny. One of the most tragic things in the world is to be a Christian and be unhappy and miserable. This happens when a person is unwilling to make the necessary sacrifices to draw close to God. There is no real joy and happiness without God being first in your life, without you having a close, intimate relationship with Him. God is good and He's got a good plan for your life but He's not going to do everything for you. You've got to rise up and draw close to Him. You've got to make a wholesome effort to do this and persevere when distractions come your way. Discipline yourself and do the right thing. Heb. 12:11 (NLT) says, "But afterward there will be a peaceful harvest of right living for those who are trained this way." The word "intimate" means 'to be involved; aware of every detail.' This is the type of relationship God wants you and Him to have.

He wants you to know Him and He wants to know you. Passionately love Him the same way He loves you. Intimately draw close to Him and intimately He'll draw close to you. As this happens, you'll develop a deep bond with Him that can't be broken. You'll have a more detailed knowledge of who He is and a deeper understanding of what He's about. His ways will become your ways and His will becomes your will. This is how you turn the switch on that will cause your light to shine. God is light and now His light is shining through you. Love Him without reservation and have Him in your heart at all times. Share every detail of your life with Him the same way two friends talk and share for hours at a time. There is nothing too small in your life that your Daddy does not take an interest in. As you do this, you will receive the power and strength to do what you've been called to do.

Eph. 6:10 (AMP) says, "In conclusion, be strong in the Lord, be empowered through your union with Him; draw your strength from Him, that strength which His boundless might provides." Spending time with God needs to be the foundation your life is built on. Don't wait for things to get desperate before you seek Him out. The truth is, without God in your life desperate times will be all you'll ever have. Scripture and experience will teach you that it is you and not God who determines your level of intimacy with Him. Right now, at this very moment, you are as close to God as you want to be. God and His Word are one and the same (John 1:1) and with all diligence you must strive for and make a conscious effort to obtain a thorough knowledge of God's Word. The more you know the Bible, the more you'll know God. Jesus once told a parable about a man who had a fanatical passion for the Word of God and was willing to make the ultimate sacrifice.

He said, "The kingdom of heaven is like treasure hidden in a field, which a man found and hid; and for the joy over it he goes and sells all that he has and buys the field" (Matt. 13:44). This verse reveals the diligence it takes to get the Word planted within you. Because the Word and the joy it brings was first place in this man's life, he went and sold all that he had in order to obtain It. Nothing should come between you and the time you spend in the Word. Notice also that the treasure is buried in the field. People who do not study the Bible but only skim over it maybe once a week are only looking at the surface of the field. The richest mines are often in grounds that appear most barren. Prov. 15:28 says, "The heart of the righteous studies how to answer." The word "study" means 'to apply the mind in acquiring knowledge, to examine and search into, to memorize, to follow a regular course of instruction.'

The Hebrew word for "study" means 'to make an effort, to labor.' Time and effort will be required in order to obtain the true riches that are buried in God's Word. You'll get out of it what you put into it. God and His blessings must be sought after in order to be found. Therefore, don't just read the Word, study it! Prov. 4:20-22 says, "My son, give attention to my words; Incline your ear to my sayings. Do not let them depart from your eyes; Keep them in the midst of your heart; For they are life to those who find them and health to all their flesh." The Words of God are life to those who find them. Ps. 119:2 says, "Blessed are those who keep His testimonies, who seek Him with the whole heart!" You cannot seek God half-heartedly and expect to receive in return all the blessings that He has prepared for you. No, the verse says to seek Him with your whole heart and when you diligently do that you will develop within yourself a deep, fanatical passion for God and His Word.

Prov. 2:1,4,5 says, "My son, if you receive my words, and treasure my command within you, if you seek her as silver and search for her as hidden treasure; then you will understand the fear of the Lord and find the knowledge of God." You will never know God in an intimate way until you develop a strong passion for His Word. The word "passion is defined as 'intense, extreme, ardent, affection for, strong desire, fanaticism.' Many Christians struggle to know God deeply because they have settled for a casual relationship with His Word. The uncompromised Word of God was never meant to be sampled occasionally but pursued with holy intensity and unwavering devotion. When believers are not fanatical about truth, they unintentionally allow compromise, tradition, and comfort to shape their faith. True intimacy with God is born when His Word becomes the supreme authority, passion, and pursuit of one's life. This is so vital because God and His Word are one and the same.

Luke 10:28-42 tells the story about a young woman who had a fanatical passion for God's Word. These verses tell about a time of refreshing Jesus spent in Bethany at the home of Lazarus and his two sisters, Mary and Martha. This was not a home where Jesus was treated as a stranger but rather as a member of the family. It seems that Martha was the owner of the house and being the older sister was the dominate figure as well. While Martha busied herself with the distracting details of serving her guests, Mary instead chose to sit at the feet of Jesus in the recognized posture of a disciple and listened to every precious word that her Lord had to say. She had a passion for the Word and her actions depict the attitude of an eager learner not wanting one morsel of truth spoken from the mouth of Jesus to slip past her. Troubled by her sister's reluctance to help with the serving, Martha was filled with an inward anxiety thus creating an outward response.

Without thinking she boldly and bluntly confronted Jesus and said, "Lord, do you not care that my sister has left me to serve alone? Therefore, tell her to help me." Jesus answered and said to her, "Martha, Martha, you are worried and troubled about many things." Notice that worry and trouble always go together and that you can never worry about just one thing. It was not Martha's service that Jesus rebuked. Her preoccupation with the preparation of an elaborate meal for Jesus and His disciples was a praiseworthy desire born out of a deep regard for her honored guest. What Jesus rebuked was her over occupation with the material side of her duties which caused her to have anxiety and a nervous distraction which eventually led to her jealous outburst of temper. Jesus continued, "But one thing is needed, and Mary has chosen that good part which will not be taken from her." The lesson that is being taught here is that to be occupied with Jesus is more important than being occupied for Jesus.

To devote oneself to the Word of God is more important than to be busy for Him. Jesus said that one good thing was needed. Not two, one! And that good thing is to receive His words and to treasure them in the deepest caverns of your heart. Millions of people believe in God and go to church faithfully every Sunday morning, yet He is not their top priority. This is so sad because these same people are His top priority. Take comfort knowing that you are on God's mind all the time. His thoughts toward you outnumber the stars in the night sky and the grains of sand on the seashore. The question to be asked is whether or not He is on your mind all the time. Is knowing Him intimately your top priority? Is the lifestyle you're living and the things you do and say truly for God? You need to discern in the secret chambers of your heart if you truly know God and if He truly knows you.

Examine closely the words you say and the thoughts you think. Are they centered around God? Are they bringing glory to His name? What's the first thing you think about in the morning and the last thing you think about at night? Have you made a willful decision to allow His will for your life to become your will? The answer to all these questions will reveal what the top priority of your life really is. Your actions will follow your desires. If you really desire to know God in an intimate way, you will rearrange your daily schedule and act accordingly. You'll spend quality time alone with God and, as a result of drawing close to Him, He will draw close to you. This is what will happen if you're willing to pay the price to get to know God in a personal way. Rise up and take responsibility for your life. Forget about the past and make a serious and decisive dedication to God that you will make Him your top priority all the days of your life.

Put first things first. Rom. 12:1 says, "I beseech you, therefore, brethren, by the mercies of God, that you present your bodies a living sacrifice, holy, acceptable to God, which is your reasonable service." Giving your all to God means surrendering every part of your life to His will, trusting that He knows what is best. Putting Him first is not just a priority - it's a daily commitment to love, obey, and rely on Him above all else. Make a commitment today that nothing will be allowed to stand between you and truly knowing God in an intimate way. Guard your time, your heart, and your priorities so that distractions never replace devotion. Choose daily to pursue His presence, because intimacy with God is the foundation of a transformed life. Time is flying by and there's not much time left before Jesus returns for His people. Make God your top priority before it's too late.

| 13 |

"TO THOSE WHO LOVE GOD"

Contrary to the beliefs of many people, not everything written in the Bible applies to every person on the planet. More times than not, certain conditions have to be met before what was written can be applied to your life and the lives of other people. For example, in the parable of the talents the master told two of his servants, "You have been faithful over a few things, I will make you ruler over many things" (Matt. 25:21,23). This promotion was conditional. The two servants first had to prove themselves faithful before they could be made ruler over many things. Consider also Prov. 3:6, "In all your ways acknowledge Him, and He shall direct your paths." This verse does not say God will direct the paths of every person but only those who acknowledge Him. Even getting born again is conditional. Rom. 10:9 says, "If you confess with your mouth the Lord Jesus and believe in your heart that God has raised Him from the dead, you will be saved."

Everybody has not met these conditions, and this is why not everybody is saved. That being said, there is a popular verse in Paul's letter to the Roman church that all believers like to quote and claim the blessing mentioned therein as their own. Little do these people realize that the promise contained in this verse is also conditional. Rom. 8:28 says, "And we know that all things work together for good to those who love God, to those who are the called according to His purpose."

This verse is not speaking to everybody but to a specific group of people. Paul is writing to those who love God. Considering the condition the world is in today makes it quite clear that not everybody loves God, therefore, this verse does not apply to them. But when you love God, He can take what the enemy meant for your harm and turn it around for your good. You can lose your job one day and get a better job the next day. This is the sort of thing that can happen to you all the time if you will meet the condition of first loving God.

People say they love God, but the condition of their lives prove they don't. People need to stand up and take responsibility for the choices they make. The path they are now on is the result of the choices they've made in the past. When things go wrong they blame God yet it was their poor choices that caused the problem to happen in the first place. The bottom line is you can choose to love God or you can choose to not love God. Just know that whichever choice you make will bring consequences that you will have to live with, sometimes for the rest of your life. If you're smart, you will do what Jesus said and "love the Lord your God will all your heart, with all your soul, and with all your mind" (Matt. 23:37). Choosing to love God is the greatest thing you can ever do yet even then you will come to a place where you can love Him more than you do now. Love can grow and you must seek to love Him more and more with each passing day.

The good news is that the more you love God, the more you will be known by God. 1 Cor. 8:2,3 (NLT) says, "Anyone who claims to know all the answers doesn't really know very much. But the person who loves God is the one whom God recognizes." Does God know you? The answer is based on how much you love Him. Yes, it is a good thing to know your Bible and to have the ability to quote scriptures left and right. This is all well and good but understand that having head knowledge of the Word is not the same as having a deep love for your Heavenly Father. If you're not careful you can get into trouble because Paul says in 1 Cor. 8:1, "Knowledge puffs up, but love edifies."

The Message Bible says, "Sometimes our humble hearts can help us more than our proud minds." You don't have a relationship with God based on how much you know about Him. No, you must have a personal relationship with Him by having a deep intimacy for Him.

You are to have an experience with Him that gets birthed by you loving Him more than you love anybody else, and that includes your spouse and children. A good life is when you know God and He knows you. When you love God with all your heart, soul, and mind then He will reveal and manifest Himself to you in a way that you will experience Him even more than in times past. Those who truly love their Lord are passionate about it while those with only head knowledge are cold and logical. These are the ones who like to debate about theological doctrine to the point that they'll get mad if you don't agree with what they say. These people do not know God and God does not know them for He only reveals Himself to those who love Him. Why would He open His arms and embrace those who wouldn't receive His love anyway? The answer is He wouldn't do that. James 4:8 says, "Draw near to God and He will draw near to you."

If people only knew God for who He is they would run to Him and embrace Him and never let go. One of the greatest tragedies in all of life is love that is not returned. God loves everybody but percentage wise relatively few love Him back. Jesus said in John 15:18, "If the world hates you, you know that it hated Me before it hated you." How can you expect people to love you if they hate the God who created you? Don't concern yourself with what other people think and say but focus instead on your great love for the Master. The average person on the street will tell you they love God but their behavior and the words they speak reveal differently. They say they love God but the truth is they don't even know Him. What about you? Can people see by your lifestyle that you are truly a lover of God? Do you have the characteristics that reveal Him as the most important person in your life? Loving God should be your top priority. Even Jesus calls this "the first and great commandment" (Matt. 22:38).

You should be loving God when you sit down and when you stand up. Love Him when you wake up in the morning and love Him when you go to bed at night. Love Him when you're working and love Him when you're playing. Love Him all day long. The Lord should be foremost in your thinking wherever you go and in whatever you do. When you love God, you are giving yourself totally and completely to Him and this is what brings Him joy. You are giving Him honor and glory when your love for Him causes you to surrender your purpose for living to His purpose. Love is when you say, "Not my will be done but Your will be done." How much of the things you do each day is an expression of a genuine love for God? Are you living each day for His purpose and His glory? Are you allowing Him to dictate what you think and how you feel and what acts of love you perform each day? How you treat other people is an expression of how much you love God.

Jesus said in John 13:35, "By this all will know that you are My disciple, if you have love for one another." As far as Jesus is concerned, it's your actions that reveal whether or not you love Him. It's true, actions speak louder than words. You are loving God when you do something nice for another person. When you forgive somebody who did you wrong, you are loving God. When you help them with a problem they're having, you are loving God. When you help some person with a financial need, you are loving God. This is why fulfilling your destiny is so important. Your assignment from on high centers around helping other people and the fulfillment of this call is a direct manifestation of how much you love God. When you love God with every part of your being you will naturally do what He wants you to do. Jesus said, "He who has My commandments and keeps them, it is he who loves Me. And he who loves Me will be loved by My Father, and I will love him and manifest Myself to him" (John 14:21).

It is God's will for you to have a lasting love for Him, a love that is deeply rooted in Him so that it will stay strong for a lifetime. A person who loves God will long for personal communion with Him. Nothing will be more valuable to you than your time spent alone with your Daddy. When you're in love you just naturally want to spend time with the person you're in love with. When you spend time alone with God you will begin to love the same things He loves. What's important to Him will be important to you. His nature is becoming your nature. God hates sin and so should you. Ps. 97:10 says, "You who love the Lord, hate evil!" God loves people and He wants you to love them also. 1 John 3:14 says, "We know that we have passed from death to life, because we love the brethren. He who does not love his brother abides in death." The proof of your love for God is in the things you say and do. This is why you have to make obeying Him a part of your everyday life.

Jesus said in John 14:15, "If you love Me, keep My commandments." The Lord wants to be number one in your life and He wants you to be faithful to Him by doing those things He tells you to do. You don't have to do these things to be loved by God, you should obey Him because you know you are already loved by Him and now you are loving Him in return. The things you do are a response to His love for you and is the determining factor as to whether or not you live a good life. You need to live your life the way God determined it should be lived. Come up higher and choose to live a life that matters. Corrie ten Boom once said, "The measure of a life is not its duration but its donation." Paul said in Acts 20:24 (NLT), "But my life is worth nothing to me unless I use it for finishing the work assigned to me by the Lord Jesus - the work of telling others the Good News about the wonderful grace of God."

In the game of life you must play to win. 1 Cor. 9:24 (NLT) says, "Don't you realize that in a race everyone runs, but only one person gets the prize. So run to win!" You are to live your life with no regrets and no sorrows. This happens when your primary objective is to love God and obey Him at all times, at all costs. When you do that, the Bible says God will bless you abundantly. Paul wrote in 1 Cor. 2:9, "But as it is written: 'Eye has not seen, nor ear heard, nor have entered into the heart of man the things which God has prepared for those who love Him.'" The blessings of God are given to those who love Him. James 1:12 says, "Blessed is the man who endures temptation; for when he has been proved, he will receive the crown of life which the Lord has promised to those who love Him." It is your deep love for God that will cause you to overcome the evil temptations that come your way. In your heart is the desire to please the Lord more than you want to please your flesh.

Draw close to God and get to know who He is. Fall in love with Him and receive the power to do what millions of people cannot do. Most people dwell on the fact that God loves them which He most certainly does. However, they make little effort in trying to love Him in return. When it comes to love, they leave all the work up to God and make little or no demand on themselves to love Him back. These people are self-centered and will not experience the blessings that are given to those who love God. It's time to get serious when it comes to your relationship with Him. Stop going through the motions by doing things that are socially correct all the time and going to church with a fake smile on your face. Get real! Is. 64:6 (MSG) says, "Our best efforts are grease-stained rags." What matters most is the condition of your heart. The Lord said to Samuel, "For the Lord does not see as man sees; for man looks at the outward appearance, but the Lord looks at the heart" (1 Sam. 16:7).

There are people who have forsaken God yet they go to church every Sunday morning. They are religious hypocrites who don't realize they will one day have to bow before God and give an account for why they didn't love Him as they were commanded to do. This is serious business and you need to start loving Him today. You need to get to the place in your life where all your decisions are based on the love you have for God. Being a Christian means you want to know Him so intimately that you want to be in His presence every second of every day. You love Him so much that you want to serve Him with no reservations and tell others about Him without fail. When you have an overwhelming and consuming affection for your Daddy you'll never allow anything or anyone to come between you and Him. Because of your great love for Him you'll take up your cross and follow Him wherever He may go. His will becomes your will and His life becomes your life.

Love is when you have a passion for God, when you desire Him more that the food you eat and the air you breathe. The sign of a genuine love for God is that you will begin to hate the sin you once loved and love the righteousness you once ignored. Eternal life does not begin when you die and go to heaven. No, eternal life begins when you know God and love Him with all your heart. Jesus said in John 17:3, "And this is eternal life, that they may know You, the only true God and Jesus Christ whom You have sent." Are you willing to lay down your life for Him? Are you willing to lose those who say they're your friends on account of Him? Are you willing to walk away from those family members who don't support you in your walk with the Lord? Jesus said in Luke 14:26 (MSG), "Anyone who comes to Me but refuses to let go of father, mother, spouse, children, brothers, sisters - yes, even one's own self! - can't be My disciple. Anyone who won't shoulder his own cross and follow behind Me can't be My disciple."

It will cost you to love God and follow Him and that cost is everything you hold dear that you place before Him. Jesus said, "So likewise, whoever of you does not forsake all that he has cannot be My disciple" (Luke 14:33). God will not allow Himself to be second place in the life of any person. If God is not your everything then He will be nothing to you. He is pressing you to make a decision today to love Him with all that is in you. He will not be put off and you must tell Him today if you will love Him or not. Know that He is increasing the commitment that He is calling for. You must transfer the ownership of all that you are and all that you have to all that He is. Your life is no longer your life, your time is no longer your time, and your possessions are no longer your possessions. All these things belong to God when you make Him the Lord of your life. To love God there must be a complete surrender of your life to Christ. It's when you come to the end of yourself and completely trust Him to live His life through you.

What's in your heart? Is how you're living today the legacy you want to leave when you're gone? The world is being baptized in filth and many in the church are sliding into the pit of gloom and despair. This is a time of war and there needs to be a spiritual awakening in the church of which you are a part. It is time for the body of Christ to look and act like the body of Christ. It's time to come up higher and live righteous lives and to have the sweet aroma of Jesus fall on you wherever you go. It's time to love God! It's time to do what He is telling you to do. Everything you do needs to be done because it is the will of God and because it brings glory to Him. You must esteem Him infinitely above all things and live in accordance with that estimation. Your purpose in life is to grow in the truth that everything you do is for the glory of God. The call on your life is that you will be controlled by the singular passion of doing the will of God and loving Him with all your heart, soul, and mind.

You were not made to live like the rest of the world. You were made to surrender your life to God and to give of yourself to something that is eternal. Adam was given the command to bring everything in creation into harmony with the will of God and this he did not do. Now we live in a fallen world that lives in darkness yet the will of God remains the same. You are not called to play video games or play golf all day. You are called with the same call God gave to Adam. You are called to advance His kingdom, to live with a passion for Him that is so strong you'd do anything He asks you to do. You don't live for ease and comfort, you live to fight like a warrior in the army of the Lord.

Your love for Him is sacrificial and you are determined to do what He has called you to do. You know that it's going to cost you but you do it anyway. That's what love is all about. Jesus loved you so much that He died for you and now you must be willing to do the same for Him.

What does the world need from you? It needs you to be like Jesus, it needs you to love them and show them what God is really like. This is what you are to strive for every day of your life. Be like Jesus who said, "He who has seen Me has seen the Father" (John 14:9). What you need to know is that you can't love these people as you should until you first love God from the inner chambers of your heart. Your love for Him should be extreme and deliberate. 1 Tim. 4:7 says, "But have nothing to do with worldly fables fit only for old women, on the other hand discipline yourself for the purpose of godliness." Love God on purpose and do it willingly and openly. Be determined to walk through the muck and mire of this sinful generation with the glory of God on your life and His love in your heart. Don't stay home and be lazy but go out into the world and fulfill your destiny. Tell somebody about Jesus and show them how good He is by doing something good for them. Let them see Jesus in the works you do.

Get involved in the work of God. One of the deepest problems the church faces today is that its pews are filled with lazy Christians. These are the people who look forward more to the coffee and donuts they'll get before the service begins than to the message that's being preached. They have no reverence for the things of God and know nothing of what being a true Christian is all about. They don't read their Bible, they have no prayer life, and they shed a boatload of tears when the enemy comes in and brings destruction to their life. Don't be this way. Understand that you are not here to just take up space. You are here for a divine purpose. You are here to love God and to help other people love Him also. You are here to walk in the light as He is in the light. You are here to be a living testimony to the goodness of God, a spiritual force that will have to be reckoned with. One day God is going to look you in the eye and ask you to tell Him what you did with the grace He gave you.

How did you live your life? Did you glorify Him before others? Did you fulfill your destiny? Rev. 2:17 says, "To him who overcomes I will give some of the hidden manna to eat." When you determine in your heart to be a lover of God, He will give you supernatural strength and divine provision to become all that He called you to be. He will take you from glory to glory. He will raise you up and cause you to come up to the high places in Him. He'll show you what the meaning of life is all about. Just rise up and put your hand to the plow and never look back. Stop making excuses for bad behavior but instead do what you know you're supposed to do. James 1:27 (NLT) says, "Pure and genuine religion in the sight of God the Father means caring for orphans and widows in their distress and refusing to let the world corrupt you." The Message Bible says, "Reach out to the homeless and loveless in their plight, and guard against corruption from the godless world."

God will change you into another person and people will see you standing there engulfed in the glory of God. They'll run to you and ask you to tell them how they can get what you have. In John 21:15-17 Jesus asks Peter three times, "Do you love Me?" He is asking you the same question. Do you love Jesus enough to go all the way with Him? Are you willing to live a life of self-denial and abandon your own ambitions in order to follow Him wherever He may lead? Are you willing to submit to His plan and purpose for your life so that through you He can reach a lost and dying world? This is what loving God is all about. It's when you say, "Here I am! Send me" (Is. 6:8). Do you love Jesus? Is He the source of all your joy? Those who love Jesus have their delight in knowing Him. They think about Him all the time and talk about Him morning, noon, and night. They are consumed with Him and all His goodness.

Their heart leaps for joy at the mention of His name and they're grieved when His name is cursed and taken in vain. Does this describe you? Are you a lover of God? If so, then Jesus is saying to you the same thing He told Peter, "Feed My sheep" (vs. 17). In other words, go out and help others to love the same Jesus you love. If you truly love God then you will be a reflection of Him. You'll be like Jesus who said, "Father, the hour has come. Glorify Your Son, that Your Son also may glorify You" (John 17:1). The word "glory" in this verse means 'that which attracts, making the object described significant or prominent.' As you get transformed into His image, you become reflectors of His glory, drawing and attracting many people to Jesus. As you set about to glorify Jesus things around you will begin to change. Families will be converted to Jesus and whole cities and communities will experience a spiritual awakening.

All it takes is one person who loves Jesus and says to Him, "Lord, take me wherever You want me to go and let my life be an expression of who You are." Is this person you? Are you asking Him to be glorified in your life? If so, then get ready to live an exciting life. Get ready to stand before Pharaoh like Moses did and say with boldness, "Let My people go!" Get ready to help an entire generation get down on their knees before the great God of the universe. Get ready! The time has come for you to choose what you will do with the rest of your life. Be like Joshua who said, "Choose for yourselves this day whom you will serve. As for me and my house, we will serve the Lord" (Josh. 24:15). Choose to come up higher and be a light in a dark world. Choose to live your life in such a way that will cause Jesus to say to you, "Well done, good and faithful servant" (Matt. 25;21). There's not much time left. Jesus is coming soon and the people who are lost need you to show them the way to eternal life.

They need you to show them what Jesus is really like and that He loves them in spite of their sinful behavior. Rise up and tell them that the world will only offer them temporary pleasure but in the end will be permanent captivity and suffering. You then tell them that in Jesus is permanent joy and life eternal. As their eyes are fixed on Him they will be changed into His glorious image. His victory over death and the grave will be their victory. Every day they will grow in grace as the world around them steps into darkness. Is God working in your life? Do you love Him enough for this to happen? If so, then you are living a blessed life. If not, be forewarned because Jesus said in John 15:1,2, "I am the vine, and My Father is the vinedresser. Every branch in Me that does not bear fruit He takes away." God takes your destiny very seriously and so should you. There are multitudes of people in churches today that believe themselves right with God but the truth is they don't know Him nor do they love Him.

It is to these people that Jesus will one day say, "Depart from Me. I never knew you" (Matt. 7:23). This is a sobering thought and is the reason Paul said in 2 Cor. 13:5 (NLT), "Examine yourselves to see if your faith is genuine. Test yourselves. Surely you know that Jesus Christ is in you; if not, you have failed the test of genuine faith." What Paul is saying here is that you must humbly choose to change from the inside out. You cannot successfully change your actions and circumstances without first changing the inner condition of your heart. To know God is to love God, and to love God is to do what He tells you to do. Don't ignore what Jesus said in Matt. 7:19-21 just because it rubs you the wrong way, "Every tree that does not bear fruit is cut down and thrown into the fire. Therefore by their fruits you will know them. Not everyone who says to Me, 'Lord, Lord,' shall enter the kingdom of heaven, but he who does the will of My Father in heaven."

Is it possible for a person to verbally acknowledge Christ and still not be saved if there is no evident change in their lifestyle? Yes, it is very possible. Examine yourself and if you sense that your relationship with God is shallow and incomplete then it probably is. Let that awareness drive you deeper, not into guilt, but into genuine repentance, renewed devotion, and a stronger pursuit of His presence. This is why you must invest your time and energy in getting to know Him better. Just as physical exercise strengthens and conditions the body, time intentionally spent with God strengthens and deepens your relationship with Him. The more consistently you seek Him, the stronger your faith, trust, and spiritual endurance will become. A wonderful change will soon happen on the inside of you and with it will be the unquenchable desire to serve Him. After all, this is what loving God is all about.

"EVERYTHING YOU NEED"

Too many people think they know God when the truth is they don't know Him at all. They may know a little bit about Him but that is not the same as knowing Him in a personal way. It cannot be denied that in the eyes of most people God is greatly misunderstood. He gets blamed for things He didn't do and doesn't get the credit for all the good things He does do. People blame God for their problems but take the credit when all is going well in their lives. One of the biggest reasons for this mass confusion concerning who God is centers around the fact that the enemy has convinced people that despicable and abominable behavior is now acceptable in today's world. People don't know right from wrong and this blinds their eyes from knowing who God is. 1 John 1:5,6 says, "This is the message which we have heard from Him and declare to you, that God is light and in Him is no darkness at all. If we say that we have fellowship with Him, and walk in darkness, we lie and do not practice the truth."

Who is God? First of all, He's everything you need to live a good life. David wrote in Ps. 23:1, "The Lord is my shepherd; I shall not want." There are many names for God in the Bible and each one represents something good that He does. When a baby is born, God is there because He is the "giver of life" (Ps. 36:9). If you're having a peaceful day, God is there also because He is the "Prince of Peace" (Is. 9:6). God is everywhere at all times and you need to become more aware of all that He is doing in your everyday life. In the Bible, names have great meaning. They represent who a person is and what they're like. Abram was a man who had no children and, when God called him, his name was changed to Abraham meaning "father of many nations" (Gen. 17:5). You can know God in a more intimate way by studying His names in the Bible that reveal His character and who He is and what He is really like. Knowing God should be the biggest desire of your heart.

Even after writing most of the New Testament, Paul said in Phil. 3:10 (NLT), "I want to know Christ and experience the mighty power that raised Him from the dead." Like Paul, the determined purpose of your life should be to know God and have a daily experience with Him, to recognize and know when He is working in your life. The Amplified Bible expands on the deepest desire in Paul's heart, "And this, so that I may know Him experientially, becoming more thoroughly acquainted with Him, understanding the remarkable wonders of His Person more completely and in that same way experience the power of His resurrection which overflows and is active in believers." There is no greater thrill than to feel His presence and to know that He is working in your life. Stop focusing on your problems all the time but instead aim all your efforts in getting to know Him.

Paul said in Eph. 1:17 (NLT), "I pray for you constantly, asking God, the glorious Father of our Lord Jesus Christ, to give you spiritual wisdom and insight so that you might grow in your knowledge of God." Paul did not pray for all your problems to go away; he prayed that you would have intimate knowledge of God for wrapped up in Him is everything you need. One of the first names of God in the Bible is "Yahweh" and it's first seen in Gen. 2:4. This name means 'Lord and Master' and in the early years the Israelites so revered God they were afraid to speak His name. Therefore, they just wrote four capital letters without any vowels and thus He became known as YHWH. This name is derived from the word for "I AM" and reveals that God always was and forever will be. He is constant for He is the same yesterday, today, and forever (Heb. 13:8). He is who He is, the absolute and extreme standard of truth, goodness, and beauty.

God will do what He will do and when you know who He is then all your fears and problems will crumble like the sand on the seashore. He is all things to all people. He has all power to protect you, all knowledge to guide you, and His presence goes with you wherever you go. Knowing this will allow you to enter into rest having the confidence that your Daddy will take care of any situation you are in. He answers to nobody and is absolutely independent. He does as He pleases, only as He pleases, and always as He pleases. When you understand who God is, it will change your life and your walk with Him. Col. 1:17 (NIV) says, "He is before all things, and in Him all things hold together." The Message Bible says, "Everything got started in Him and finds its purpose in Him. He was there before any of it came into existence and holds it all together right up to this moment." He is a sovereign God possessing supreme and ultimate power.

Dan. 4:34,35 says, "For His dominion is an everlasting dominion, and His kingdom is from generation to generation. All the inhabitants of the earth are reputed as nothing; He does according to His will in the army of heaven and among the inhabitants of the earth. No one can restrain His hand or say to Him, 'What have You done?'" It is this all-powerful God who enables you to have a peace that passes all understanding. It is He who anoints you to be a blessing to somebody else. The harvest that comes in as the result of all the good you've done is what God will use to help solve your problems. It's the power of God that caused Paul to write, "I can do all things through Christ who strengthens me" (Col. 1:17). God is the beginning and the end and everything in between. He said in Rev. 1:8, "I am the Alpha and the Omega, the Beginning and the End, who is and who was and who is to come, the Almighty." Only God could make such a statement and it is He who wants to hold you close to His bosom.

Get to know Him intimately and meditate daily on Ps. 48:14 (NIV), "For this God is our God forever and ever; He will be our guide even to the end." Get personal with God and allow Him to become your God. It is only through an intimate knowledge of Him and knowing what He is like that allows Him to become your Daddy. Paul said in Rom. 8:15 that you can cry out and call Him "Abba, Father." The word "Abba" is an Aramaic word that means "Daddy" and only a child of God has the right to call Him by this name. Having Him as your Daddy is the highest privilege and honor that can be imagined. He wants to be the source of all your hope and the security for your future. Him being your Daddy is what motivates you to "walk worthy of the calling with which you were called" (Eph. 4:1). It's what compels you to come up to a higher standard of living, a different way of life. Your Daddy is a sovereign God possessing supreme and ultimate power. He is Jehovah El Elyon which means "God Most High."

In the midst of a great trial David wrote in Ps. 27:2, "I will cry out to God Most High, to God who performs all things for me." This name for God stresses His highest supremacy in all the universe and can literally be translated as "the Extremely-Exalted, Sovereign, High God." People who truly know who God is are not cowards for knowing Him strips the fear out of their lives. 2 Tim. 1:7 says, "For God has not given us a spirit of fear, but of power and of love and of a sound mind." People who know God as the Most High God are aggressive and never passive. They face their enemies head-on and take immediate action. In Gen. 14 Abram took 318 of his servants and went up against a huge army who had taken his nephew Lot captive. He took back what the enemy had stolen and afterward Melchizedek the high priest blessed him and said, "Blessed be Abram of God Most High, Possessor of heaven and earth; And blessed be God Most High, Who has delivered your enemies into your hand" (Gen. 14:19,20).

God did not create you to be a coward and you need to see yourself as God sees you. An Angel of the Lord appeared to Gideon and said to him, "The Lord is with you, you mighty man of valor!"(Judges 6:12). God saw Gideon as a great warrior but Gideon saw himself as the least of his brethren and unworthy of being called such a name. God saw Gideon totally different from how Gideon saw himself and this is usually the case with most people. God sees your potential and what you're capable of doing and becoming. He said to Gideon in vs. 14, "Go in this might of yours, and you shall save Israel from the hand of the Midianites. Have I not sent you?" God sees you as being more amazing than you think you actually are. Get fear out of your life and boldly declare, "If God be for me, who can be against me? I am who God says I am and I can do what God says I can do!" God is on your side and you need to stand up and act like it. He is in you and He's not going anywhere.

The Most High God goes wherever you go and, because of that, there is no reason to doubt and fear. Stand up in this might of yours and do what God tells you to do. You never have to fear because the Lord your God is El Shaddai, the Lord God Almighty (Gen. 17:1). He has all might, all power, and nothing is impossible for Him. There is no problem too big that He can't solve it. What is so amazing is that this same power that God has is available to you. Jesus said in Luke 10:19, "Behold, I give you the authority to trample on serpents and scorpions, and over all the power of the enemy, and nothing shall by any means hurt you." Paul wrote in Eph. 1:19,20 (NLT), "I also pray that you will understand the incredible greatness of God's power for us who believe Him. This is the same mighty power that raised Christ from the dead and seated Him in the place of honor at God's right hand in the heavenly realms."

Satan is a defeated foe (Col. 2:15) and 1 John 4:4 says, "You are of God, little children, and have overcome them, because He who is in you is greater than he who is in the world." The Message Bible says, "My dear children, you come from God and belong to God. You have already won a big victory over those false teachers, for the Spirit in you is far stronger than anything in the world." God is everything you need. You can be bold as a lion knowing that the strength and power you need to live a victorious life comes from Him. Paul wrote in 2 Cor. 3:5, "Not that we are sufficient of ourselves to think of anything as being from ourselves, but our sufficiency is from God." God is the source of all power and you need to stay plugged into Him every moment of every day. Samson was a man anointed to be very strong and his connection to God was his long hair (Judges 13:5).

He later got involved with Delilah and when she cut his hair off he got unplugged from the power source and lost all his strength and might. Stay close to God and be quick to repent when you've done something wrong. If you'll do that you won't lose your connection to God. You'll be strong and with boldness you'll be able to stand up and confront the enemy. The power of God is available to you and you've got to have faith in that power. David said in 1 Chron. 29:12, "Both riches and honor come from You, and You reign over all. In Your hand is power and might; In Your hand it is to make great and to give strength to all." The power of God is yours for the asking. You can have faith in that power because the one who gives it to you is the one, true God. He is Jehovah Elohim. Deut. 4:35 says, "To you it was shown, that you might know that the Lord Himself is God; there is none other besides Him."

Vs. 39 says, "Therefore know this day, and consider it in your heart, that the Lord Himself is God in heaven above and on the earth beneath; there is no other." The first word translated as God in the Bible is found in Gen. 1:1, "In the beginning God created the heavens and the earth." The word for God here is the Hebrew word "Elohim" and is the most often used word translated as God in the Old Testament. Elohim is a plural word showing that there is more than one member of the Godhead. There is the Father, the Son, and the Holy Spirit and the word Elohim refers to all of them. You may not understand with your mind the Three-In-One nature of God but with your spirit you can know that together as one the Triune God is Elohim, the one true God. In order to experience all of God's goodness in your life you must first understand who He is. Another significant name by which God reveals Himself to His people is Jehovah Shalom and this name is only found in Judges 6:24.

During the time of Gideon the people of God were living under the oppression of the Midianites. The enemy took all their food and livestock and the people were forced to live in caves. It was during this time of bondage that Israel cried out for deliverance. God called Gideon to deliver them and by faith he built an altar to God in Ophrah where the Angel of the Lord appeared to him. He called the altar Jehovah-Shalom in expectation of victory and peace. The word "shalom" means 'peace, the absence of strife, to be complete and sound.' The great God whom you love and serve is called by the name which means "The Lord Is Peace." When it seems like the whole world is against you or that you are completely unable to deal with whatever problem is in front of you, turn to the God of peace to find comfort and strength. Ps. 29:11 says, "The Lord will give strength to His people; The Lord will bless His people with peace."

Peace expresses the deepest desire and need of the human heart. It represents the greatest measure of contentment and satisfaction in life and God has a desire to give you His peace. Jer. 29:11 says, "For I know the thoughts that I think toward you, says the Lord, thoughts of peace and not of evil, to give you a future and a hope." God wants you to know and experience the fullness of His perfect peace which passes all understanding and will sustain you in difficult times. Daily you need to be walking in the light because the peace of God is with those who continually abide in Him. Is. 57:20,21 says, "But the wicked are like the troubled sea when it cannot rest, whose waters cast up mire and dirt. 'There is no peace,' says my God, 'for the wicked.'" Paul wrote in Rom. 8:6, "For to be carnally minded is death, but to be spiritually minded is life and peace." The more you allow God to govern your life, when His will becomes your will, the more peace you will have.

Jesus said, "These things I have spoken to you, that in Me you may have peace. In the world you will have tribulation, but be of good cheer, I have overcome the world" (John 16:33). Ps. 136:1 says, "Oh, give thanks to the Lord, for He is good! For His mercy endures forever." God's mercy will never stop and it never decreases. It goes on and on and on. It endures forever and compels God to do something good because of the great love He has for you. God is many things to many people but there is no greater attribute given to describe who God is than to say He is a God of love. In fact, 1 John 4:7,8 says that "God is love." Because of this love God will give you everything you need to live a victorious life. He is Jehovah Jireh which means "The Lord Will Provide" (Gen. 22:14). God told Abraham to offer up his son Isaac as a burnt offering. He demonstrated his faith and obedience by rising early the next morning and traveled to Mt. Moriah where he built an altar, bound his son, and placed him on the wood.

Before Abraham could finish the offering a voice called to him from heaven and Isaac's life was spared. He then looked up and saw in a thicket a ram caught by its horns which he took and offered to God instead. He called that place Jehovah Jireh because of God's gracious provision of a substitute for Isaac. The name Jehovah Jireh is not "The Lord Did Provide" but "The Lord Will Provide." In other words, the name does not memorialize a past event but rather it anticipates a future action. Paul spoke of this in Phil. 4:19, "And my God shall supply all your need according to His riches in glory by Christ Jesus." Not only did God give you provision in times past, He will also provide for your needs today and tomorrow. The disciples of Jesus were worried about their future and the Lord said to them, "Look at the birds of the air, for they neither sow nor reap nor gather into barns, yet your heavenly Father feeds them. Are you not of more value than they?" (Matt. 6:26).

In the world today there is a lot of uncertainty about the economy, the educational system, and one's upcoming retirement. God wants you to know that He is Jehovah Jireh, that He is faithful and will provide everything you need. Thank God every day for meeting your needs even if you don't see it yet. You know the provision is coming because His very name says He is the Lord who will provide. As you learn to be a generous giver, you can have the faith and confidence that God will give back to you. There is no greater way to know God than for you to become how He is. He is love and so are you. His nature has become your nature. He has supplied all your needs and now you are allowing Him to use you to help meet the needs of others. Don't get so busy and self-consumed with your own life that you forget there are people all around you who have needs and challenges also. This is why Heb. 10:24 says, "And let us consider one another in order to stir up love and good works."

The family of God is to be a loving community where people are vitally concerned about the welfare of one another. You must go out of your way and consider the needs of those around you. Be determined to know and understand them and what you can do to help them along. This won't happen on its own but will take a determined effort on your part. You need to observe those you're in contact with so you'll know how best to help them. A person who is walking in love will stand by the side of others no matter what they're going through and will look for ways to assist them when they are experiencing challenging times. One of the best things you can ever do for yourself is become a generous giver. Always do more than what's being asked of you. Love is unselfish and always gives toward the advancement of others. This is how God is. John 3:16 says, "For God so loved the world that He gave His only begotten Son." Love is all about giving for it never seeks its own (1 Cor. 13:5).

Paul said in Rom. 12:3 that you are to be "distributing to the needs of the saints, given to hospitality." In Greek the word "given" means 'to aggressively pursue something; to ardently follow after something; to hotly pursue something until you finally catch it." This verse can then be translated, "Hotly pursue and never stop pursuing the goal of becoming hospitable until you have caught on to the idea of hospitality and have genuinely become a hospitable person." Make a decision today that you will develop in your life the trait of being aggressive in your pursuit to bless other people. When you put your whole heart into doing this you will experience what God is like and will get to know Him in a more intimate way. Ps. 34:8 says, "Oh, taste and see that the Lord is good. Blessed is the man who trusts in Him!" Everything that is good comes from God. He is a Daddy who always takes care of His children.

Heb. 13:5,6 (AMP) says, "For He has said, 'I will never under any circumstances desert you nor give you up nor leave you without support, nor will I in any degree leave you helpless, nor will I forsake or let you down or relax My hold on you, assuredly not!' So we take comfort and are encouraged and confidently say, 'The Lord is my Helper in time of need, I will not be afraid. What can man do to me?'" Take comfort knowing that God will not fail to support and take care of you. He is Jehovah Rapha (EX. 15:26), The Lord Who Heals You. He is the Great Physician who heals His people. This applies equally to emotional, psychological, and physical healing as well as to entire nations and individuals alike. God alone provides the remedy for mankind's brokenness. He is the physical, moral, and spiritual remedy for all people. He'll heal your body, your relationships, your financial needs, and the spiritual disease called sin.

God is so amazing. He's your provider and healer. He gives you strength, wisdom, and peace. He is the God of all hope, your comfort in the midst of the storm. He is your hiding place, your refuge and strength, an ever-present help in trouble. He is Jehovah Tsebaoth, The Lord Of Hosts. This is a military term and refers to Him as the God of battles. David understood the greatness of God when he went up against Goliath with a sling and five smooth stones. David said to the giant, "You come to me with a sword, with a spear, and with a javelin. But I come to you in the name of the Lord of hosts, the God of the armies of Israel, whom you have defied." You are a soldier in the army of the Lord and with God on your side there is no way you can be defeated. To walk in victory you've got to follow the Captain of the army wherever He may go for He will always lead you in triumph in Christ (2 Cor. 2:14).

Don't get entangled with the affairs of this life so that you can please the one who enlisted you as a soldier (2 Tim. 2:4). Remember, God is not here to please you, you are here to please Him. In order to live a good life you've got to come up higher and make God your every-thing. Acts 17:28 says, "For in Him we live and move and have our being." He is a good God and good is all He ever does. He is Jehovah Nissi which means The Lord Our Banner. In Ex. 17:15 Moses recog-nized that the Lord was Israel's banner under which they defeated the Amalekites. He then built an altar and named it Jehovah Nissi. The word "Nissi" is derived from the Hebrew word "nes" which is trans-lated as a pole with an insignia attached to it. In battle opposing na-tions would fly their own flag on a pole at each of their respective front lines. This was to give their soldiers a feeling of hope and a focal point. This is what God is to you. He is a banner of encouragement to give you hope in times of trouble.

He goes before you and leads you to victory in all the circumstances of life. David understood this when he wrote, "You prepare a table be-fore me in the presence of my enemies" (Ps. 23:5). David knew that when attacked by the enemy, the Lord would hold up a banner be-fore him. The most important thing banners do is mark victory. It is well understood that the conquering army in any battle has the right to remove the defeated country's flag and replace it with their own. The victor's flag was usually put in the highest spot possible for all to see. The country with the conquering flag has won the battle and now they are in control. God wants you to have a revelation that He is your banner. He is the one that wins your battles. He is everything you need and in times of battle He is your victory. He's the one who causes you to be the head and not the tail, above and not beneath. Dan. 11:32 says, "The people who know their God shall be strong, and carry out great exploits."

The Message Bible says, "Those who stay courageously loyal to their God will take a strong stand." Never again allow the enemy to convince you that your problems are bigger than God. He is your banner and has the Name that is above all names. His name is bigger than cancer, diabetes, divorce, and poverty. He is Jehovah Nissi, your victory and everything else you need. Look around you. The ravages of sin are everywhere. It's even gotten to the point that homosexuals are now becoming pastors in the local church. This should not be for it was God who said in Lev. 20:7,8, "Sanctify yourselves therefore, and be holy, for I am the Lord your God. And you shall keep My statutes, and perform them: I am the Lord who sanctifies you." Your God is Jehovah M'Kaddesh, the one who sets you apart for His purposes. It can be argued that no other name more accurately expresses the nature and character of God and the requirements He places on His people than this name.

The most fundamental, solemn, and impressive of all the attributes of God is His holiness. It is this holiness that gives Him splendor and majesty and more than anything else constitutes His fullness and perfection. His holiness is so pure and intense that Ps. 29:2 says you are to "worship the Lord in the beauty of holiness." Because you are His child, it is the desire of God to impart the glory and beauty of His holiness to you. He wants you to be just as holy as He is. Lev. 20:26 says, "And you shall be holy to Me, for I the Lord am holy, and have separated you from the people, that you should be Mine." The word "sanctified" means 'set apart' and refers to the active participation in the divine nature of God. What's so exciting about all this is that this holy God won't leave you struggling in your own strength trying to achieve a state of holiness that's impossible to attain. No, He is Jehovah M'Kaddesh, the God who makes people holy.

What you cannot do on your own, He is willing to do in you if you will let Him do it (Phil. 2:13). The impossibility of becoming holy on your own is the very thing that should drive you into the arms of the only one who is holy (Rev. 15:4). When you get born again, God transforms you and uses His own holiness to make you holy like Him. He shares His own character and nature with you through your union with Jesus. He'll wrap you in the cloak of His holiness until you are totally transformed into something you could not be except for His great grace toward you. God is everything you need and you've got to submit to Him and let Him be all that He is. God never asked you to live the Christian life apart from Him. He wants to be your strength, your provider, and your healer. He wants to do for you what you could never do for yourself. Heb. 12:14 says that without holiness no person will see God.

This is not hard to comprehend when you consider what Paul said in 2 Cor. 5:21, "For He made Him who knew no sin to be sin for us, that we might become the righteousness of God in Him." You cannot be righteous in and of yourself for righteousness comes from God and God alone. He is Jehovah Tsidkenu, The Lord Our Righteousness (Jer. 23:5,6). The word "Tsidkenu" is a form of the word "tsedek" and means 'to be stiff; to be straight; righteous.' An understanding of this name will create in you a heart bursting with gratitude. Jesus lived a sinless life and the Father accepts His righteousness as if it were your own. All you have to do is accept it. It is not forced on anyone for God desires that your relationship with Him be sought after with a heart of love. Ps. 119:42 says, "Your righteousness is an everlasting righteousness."

When God revealed Himself as Jehovah Tsidkenu the people were anything but sinless. In fact, they were in the process of being hauled off into exile and captivity for their constant sin and unfaithfulness to the Lord. In the midst of all this devastation, God still comforted the people by revealing Himself to them in a new way that would carry them through the tough times ahead. The promise given to the people of Israel was that He was going to send a Messiah, one who would sit on the throne of David again and provide a permanent solution to sin. This prophecy was fulfilled in the person of Jesus Christ. Bow down in reverence to Him. Call upon the Lord your righteousness today. His arms are wide open to you. James 1:17 says, "Every good gift and every perfect gift is from above." Jesus and His righteousness is a gift to you from the Father above. Embrace Him with all your heart and soul. He is your shepherd. In Him you shall not want for He is everything you need.

| 15 |

"THE LORD IS MY SHEPHERD"

The best way for people to come to know God intimately is to see His character displayed in the lives of those who know Him in a personal way. Who better to show the world what the Father is like than the Lord Jesus Himself? In His words, His compassion, and His sacrificial love, we see the heart of God made visible. To know Jesus is to know the Father, revealed not in theory, but in living truth and grace. John 14:8,9 says, "Philip said to Him, 'Lord, show us the Father, and it is sufficient for us.' Jesus said to him, 'Have I been with you so long, and yet you have not known Me, Philip? He who has seen Me has seen the Father; so how can you say, "Show us the Father"?'" What is so amazing about Jesus is that not only does He want to show you what the Father is like, He also wants to identify with you and personally know what it's like to be a human being in a world that has turned its back on God.

Heb. 2:17,18 (NLT) says, "Therefore, it was necessary for Him to be made in every respect like us, His brothers and sisters, so that He could be our merciful and faithful High priest before God. Then He could offer a sacrifice that would take away the sins of the people. Since He himself has gone through suffering and testing, He is able to help us when we are being tested." It is the nature of all people to want to feel safe from all harm and to be well cared for in this sinful and fallen world. Life is just too difficult to make it on your own but you can take comfort knowing that Jesus is forever by your side. David said it best in Ps. 23:1, "The Lord is my shepherd; I shall not want." Throughout the Bible the children of God are often depicted as a flock of sheep. Ps. 100:3 says, "We are His people and the sheep of His pasture." Every flock needs a shepherd to guide them and protect them and to make them feel safe.

Jesus said in John 10:14, "I am the good shepherd; and I know My sheep and am known by My sheep." Not only is Jesus a shepherd, but here also He calls himself a good shepherd because He always provides what His sheep need. David said, "I shall not want." The word "want" means 'lack' and Ps. 84:11 says, "No good thing will He withhold from those who walk uprightly." You will lack no good thing because Jesus is the Good Shepherd and you are walking the straight and narrow path. A good shepherd does more than stand around under a hot sun all day keeping an eye on his sheep. No, he is much more than that. He is a manager, caretaker, protector, and provider. You are not your own for Jesus paid for you with the blood He shed on the cross. 1 Cor. 6:20 says, "For you were bought at a price; therefore, glorify God in your body and in your spirit, which are God's." Because you belong to Him, Jesus wants to manage your life and care for you each and every day.

Ps. 61:3,4 says, "For You have been a shelter for me. and a strong tower from the enemy. I will abide in Your tabernacle forever; I will trust in the shelter of Your wings." Jesus wants to be involved in everything that pertains to your life. You can talk to Him about anything, big or small. He said in John 6:37, "All that the Father gives Me will come to Me, and the one who comes to me I will by no means cast out." The Message Bible says, "Every person the Father gives Me eventually comes running to Me. And once that person is with me, I hold on and don't let go." Most animals in the wild take care of themselves but sheep instinctively do not do that. Sheep need endless attention and special care. They are prone to diseases and parasites representing sin and every other dreadful thing on the earth today. They're fearful, timid, stupid, and very stubborn. A small rabbit can cause an entire flock of sheep to run away in fear.

Even though the sheep have many faults, the shepherd loves them anyway and forever stands by their side. He delights in taking care of them and in no way does he consider it a burden to do so. It's something he does gladly and willingly. Jesus knew everything you would say and do in your life before you were even born so whatever you bring before Him is no surprise. Ps. 139:3 (MSG) says, "You know everything I'm going to say before I start the first sentence." Every thought you haven't even had yet He already knows what they are. Vs. 16 says, "Your eyes saw my substance, being yet unformed. And in Your book they all were written, the days fashioned for me, when as yet there were none of them." The love Jesus has for you is unconditional and everlasting. He wants to care for you but there is something you must do first before this can happen. 1 Peter 5:7 (NLT) says, "Give all your worries and cares to God, for He cares about you."

A simple guideline to follow is that you do what's possible and then cast your care on Him and He'll do the impossible. Too many times people want to do God's part and expect Him to do their part. It doesn't work that way. God will hold you responsible for doing your part and, more times than not, you must do your part first. Faith without works is dead (James 2:17) which means God wants to see you act on what you believe before He'll step in and bring into manifestation that which is impossible for you to achieve on your own. There comes a time when you have to back off and let God be God. This is when you cast all your care on Him. The good news is that God can do in one moment what you can't do in an entire lifetime. All you have to do is trust Him and believe that He will do it. Jesus is the Good Shepherd and He has His eye on you at all times.

Gen. 28:15 says, "Behold, I am with you and will keep you wherever you go, and will bring you back to this land; for I will not leave you until I have done what I have spoken to you." If you're struggling in your effort to fulfill your destiny, then cast all your care on Him and confess out loud this verse every day. The Lord is with you all the time whether you feel His presence or you don't. Moses told Joshua, "And this Lord, He is the one who goes before you. He will be with you; He will not leave you nor forsake you; do not fear nor be dismayed" (Deut. 31:8). Say that which David knew to be true, "The Lord is my shepherd. I shall not want." Ps. 121:2,3 says, "My help comes from the Lord, who made heaven and earth. He will not allow your foot to be moved; He who keeps you will not slumber." Vs. 7,8 says, "The Lord shall preserve you from all evil; He shall preserve your soul. The Lord shall preserve your going out and your coming in from this time forth, and ever forevermore."

A shepherd puts a special mark on each one of his sheep so that those who pass by know they belong to him. Eph. 1:13 says you are marked, branded, and sealed by the Holy Spirit. The NLT says, "And when you believed in Christ, He identified you as His own by giving you the Holy Spirit, whom He promised long ago." You have been set apart for the Master's use and the Good Shepherd has put His mark on you. You belong to Him and this is why His will must now become your will. Stop running around trying to do what you want to do all the time. Doing this takes you out from under the care of Jesus and will leave you vulnerable to the attacks of the enemy. There are hungry wolves and slithering serpents in the world seeking to sink their sharp teeth into you. The devil roams about like a roaring lion seeking whom he can devour (1 Peter 5:8). He can't devour everybody, only those who leave the sheepfold of Jesus.

Those who stay close to Jesus are well protected for the enemy will see His mark on them and will know he has no chance to do them harm. Ps. 23:2 says, "He makes me lie down in green pastures; He leads me beside the still waters." One of the first things the Good Shepherd provides for you is peace and contentment. These two things are the mark of a true believer. If you feed on the Word of God you will not worry about anything and will have no fear. The Good Shepherd will always lead you to the rest of God and this is a very wonderful place to be. The rest of God is not a rest from activity, it's a rest in the midst of activity. Remember, there is always something you should be doing in your walk with the Lord. You do the possible and, when you've done all that you can do, God will give you rest as you wait on Him to do the impossible. Rest comes when you know what to do and what not to do. It's when you have the confidence on the inside of you everything is going to turn out for your good.

You love God and you know He loves you. God has the answer for whatever problem you have and casting your care on Him allows you to lie down in those green pastures that are beside the still waters. Resting in the Lord enables you to enjoy your life each and every day as you actively pursue the fulfillment of your destiny. Jesus is asking you to do the exact same thing He did. He came to earth with a specific call on His life and when He did all He could do the Father said to Him, "Sit at My right hand, till I make Your enemies Your footstool" (Heb. 1:3). Jesus did His part and now He's waiting for the Father to do His part. You will be amazed at the wonderful life you can have if you will learn to do everything while you're resting in God. You're trusting Him to manage your life and no longer are you trying to figure things out on your own. You're doing what you can do and letting God do what you cannot do.

Trust is the soil in which your faith will grow and with the help of the Good Shepherd you can accomplish everything you need to do. Resting in God doesn't mean you don't do anything. What it does mean is that you don't carry the burden of care on your shoulders trying to figure out how what you need to do is going to get done. No, you cast this care on the Lord, and this allows you to enter His rest. Some people miss the plan of God for their lives because they get so driven by the pursuit of their dreams that they don't enjoy their everyday life.

The problem is they've stepped beyond doing only what they can do. They've taken on the burden of trying to get what they think they need instead of trusting God and submitting to His perfect will and timing. This is why David said, "He makes me lie down in green pastures." If you'll enter His rest on your own, God won't have to make you do it.

The good news is that as you're resting beside the still waters, the Shepherd of your soul will lead you to the fulfillment of your destiny and you'll enjoy your life a whole lot more. Your inner man will be on a continual carefree holiday while on the outside you're having fun doing that which you can do. This is the rest of God. If you have unrest in your soul, then you're not truly trusting God. Heb. 4:3 says, "For we who have believed do enter that rest." Don't make the silly mistake of thinking God needs your help in doing His part. Enter His rest and let God be God. Ps. 23:3 says, "He restores my soul; He leads me in the paths of righteousness for His name's sake." Your soul is that part of you that determines what you think, what you want, and how you feel. It is sad but true that most people are led by what they want and feel more than any single thing. Feelings can be either good or bad but they are fickle and keep changing like the blowing of the wind. This is why you can't trust them or be led by them.

So you won't be led astray, God has given you a free will with which you can choose to do whatever it is you want. It is, however, His desire for you to use your will to choose to do His will. Having a free will is a wonderful gift to have but with it comes a great responsibility. There is great power in the choices you make. The outcome of your life is determined by whether you choose life or death, blessing or cursing. Will you do things God's way or your way? If you'll allow Him to direct your steps, the Good Shepherd will correct your mistakes and lead you in paths of righteousness all because He loves you and wants what's best for your life. The last thing you want to do is ask yourself how you feel about doing what you're supposed to do.

Don't ask yourself how you feel, tell yourself how you feel. Use your free will to follow the direction of the Lord knowing that your feelings can change in a moment's notice anyway.

The bottom line is it doesn't matter how you feel as long as you're doing what God told you to do. As you trust Jesus to restore your soul, before long your feelings will catch up to your obedience and you'll be happy doing what you're doing. There is power being committed to the will of God for your life and it is this power that enables you to keep going forward even when you don't feel like doing so. Become like Jesus who said to the Father in John 17:4, "I have glorified You on the earth. I have finished the work which You have given Me to do." If nothing else, be committed to do what God is calling you to do. Don't give up in a couple of weeks because you don't feel like doing it anymore. Lay your feelings aside so you can run your race and finish your course. Jesus is the Good Shepherd and He really does love you. One way this love is shown is that He will lead you in paths of righteousness by correcting you when you've stepped off the beaten path.

Most people in prison today will tell you that when they were young they were either corrected very violently of not corrected at all. It is interesting to note that those who were not corrected felt like they were not loved and that nobody cared about them. This is not the case with the Lord your God. Heb. 12:5-8 (MSG) says, "My dear children, don't shrug off God's discipline, but don't be crushed by it either. It's the child He loves that He disciplines; the child He embraces, He also corrects. God is educating you; that's why you must never drop out. He's treating you as dear children. This trouble you're in isn't punishment; it's training, the normal experience of children. Only irresponsible parents leave their children to fend for themselves. Would you prefer an irresponsible God?" The worst thing that could ever happen to you is for God to leave you alone in the mess you're in making it impossible for you or your situation to change.

Think about it. God is running the entire universe yet He takes the time to lead you in paths of righteousness. That alone shows you how much you mean to Him. You need to thank Him for this loving concern for you and then submit to His correction. Rev. 3:19 (NLT) says, "I correct and discipline everyone I love. So be diligent and turn from your indifference." The Message Bible says, "The people I love, I call to account - prod and correct and guide so that they'll live at their best. Up on your feet, then! About face! Run after God!" If your destiny involves you doing great things in the kingdom of God, then great change will have to come to your life. You can't be a good witness for Jesus if your life is a sinful mess. This is why you have to come up higher and have a willingness to change. You can't straddle the fence by having one foot in the kingdom and the other foot in the world.

The Bible says be hot or cold (Rev. 3:15,16). When the Lord gives you His correction you need to burn with zeal and get excited about it knowing that great things are coming your way. When you got born again you were given an open invitation to get intimate with God. Because of what Jesus did for you on the cross you have "become the righteousness of God in Him" (2 Cor. 5:21). Being led in paths of righteousness means you're daily in the process of becoming what you already are. Prov. 4:18 says, "But the path of the just is like the shining sun that shines ever brighter unto the perfect day." The Message Bible says, "The ways of right-living people glow with light; the longer they live, the brighter they shine." Jesus came to give you life and life more abundantly (John 10:10) which means you shouldn't be satisfied with the level of life you are now living. The life of God is dynamic and people are experiencing various degrees and measures of that life.

They have life but Jesus wants them to come up higher and have life more abundantly. The Message Bible says, "I came so they can have real and eternal life, more and better life than they ever dreamed of." God wants you blessed every single day of your life, and those blessings are found on the paths of righteousness. Ps. 24:5 says, "He shall receive blessing from the Lord, and righteousness from the God of his salvation." To experience this higher level of blessing you've got to understand how to live the Christian life more abundantly. Gal. 3:11 says, "The just shall live by faith." A deeper meaning of what Paul is saying here is found in the original Greek text, "The righteous by faith shall live." When you use your faith to believe that you have right standing with God, you will begin to live a more abundant life. Don't just use your faith to try to get a new house or a new car. No, use your faith to believe that you are accepted in the eyes of the Heavenly Father.

Ps. 119:40 (ESV) says, "Behold, I long for Your precepts; in Your righteousness give me life!" You will experience the abundant life of God when you believe that you are righteous in His eyes. You need to treasure the reality of what Jesus did for you on the cross. Go before the throne of grace and enjoy the tremendous pleasure of approaching your Daddy and speaking to Him face to face. It's what He longs for and so should you. To be established in righteousness you've got to get over the belief that it's based on the good works you do. Too many people are performance conscious and not faith conscious. They feel good driving home from church on Sunday because they believe they just did a good deed. Yes, it is a good thing to not forsake the assembling of yourselves together but this is not what makes you righteous. You are made righteous by faith and faith alone. Good works don't make you righteous just like missing the mark once in a while don't make you unrighteous.

It's when you believe that you will experience the life of God. Jesus is righteous and by faith you are just as righteous as He is. Because of that you can now expect good things to happen to you all the days of your life. You'll face life with confidence knowing that no good thing will He withhold from them that walk uprightly. If you're having a bad day, the life of God will swallow it up with His goodness. You are one with God, He is one with you, and nothing shall by any means hurt you (Luke 10:19). Ps. 23:4 says, "Yea, though I walk through the valley of the shadow of death, I will fear no evil; For You are with me; Your rod and Your staff, they comfort me." Jesus is the Good Shepherd. He's the Lion of Judah and He will fight your battles for you. The battle truly does belong to the Lord so determine ahead of time to seek Him out in time of trouble. If you'll do that you will fear no evil.

Because the Good Shepherd protects His sheep, you can remain stable in the midst of your trial and not be moved by what you see and feel. David said in Ps. 27:4-6, "One thing I have desired of the Lord, that will I seek: That I may dwell in the house of the Lord all the days of my life, to behold the beauty of the Lord, and to inquire in His temple. For in the time of trouble He shall hide me in His pavilion; In the secret place of His tabernacle He shall hide me; He shall set me high upon a rock. And now my head shall be lifted up above my enemies all around me; Therefore I will offer sacrifices of joy in His tabernacle; I will sing, yes, I will sing praises to the Lord." David was walking through the valley of the shadow of death but he feared no evil because he knew the shadow of a dog never bit anybody. The devil is a deceiver and he will always try to get you to think your trial is worse than it actually is. This is why there is no need to be afraid of trouble when it comes.

In 2 Chron. 20 a great multitude came against the children of God and Jehoshaphat sought the Lord and said to Him, "O Lord God of our fathers, are You not God in heaven, and do You not rule over all the kingdoms of the nations, and in Your hand is there not power and might, so that no one is able to withstand You?" (vs. 6). Seek the Lord knowing that no weapon formed against you shall prosper. Col. 3:2 says, "Set your mind on things above, not on things on the earth." The Message Bible says, "Don't shuffle along, eyes to the ground, absorbed with the things right in front of you. Look up, and be alert to what is going on around Christ - that's where the action is. See things from

His perspective." It should be natural for you to experience the supernatural power and provision of the Good Shepherd. After all, you are in His flock and He's with you every day of your life. You resist the devil by putting one foot in front of the other as you allow the Lord to lead you down the path of life.

You follow Him wherever He may lead and this is how you experience victory in your life. Jesus said in John 10:2-5, "But he who enters by the door is the shepherd of the sheep. To him the doorkeeper opens, and the sheep hear his voice; and he calls his own sheep by name and leads them out. And when he brings out his own sheep, he goes before them; and the sheep follow him, for they know his voice. Yet they will by no means follow a stranger, but will flee from him, for they do not know the voice of strangers." If you will pray and set your heart to seek the Lord, He will lead you and guide you and direct your steps. No longer do you have to live in the dark not knowing what to do. The Good Shepherd will call you by name and, when He's got your full attention, He'll give you the direction you need. Don't forget, sheep are stupid animals compared to other creatures and sometimes people do stupid things. Still, the shepherd loves his sheep and will use his rod and staff to comfort them.

David paints a picture of a strong, protective shepherd whom you can trust to not only care for you but to lay down his life to protect you at all costs. Jesus said in John 10:11, "I am the good shepherd. The good shepherd gives His life for the sheep." He then said in vs. 15, "As the Father knows Me, even so I know the Father; and I lay down My life for the sheep." Never did the Lord promise to keep you out of the valley but He did promise to go with you through the valley. David had no fear because he knew the Lord had His rod and His staff with Him. These were tools of the shepherd's trade and he would use them to protect his flock and to guide them to green pastures. The sight of the rod and staff comfort the sheep because they know the shepherd is there. They impart confidence showing that he will not leave them or forsake them and will defend them at all times.

The shepherd carried the rod tucked in his belt. It was a thick piece of wood about three feet long with a lump of wood the size of an orange at the end of it. With this weapon the shepherd fought the battles of the flock, using it to drive off wild beasts and to defend the flock against robbers who would try to steal the sheep. David was a shepherd in his youth and he described his use of the rod to King Saul. "Your servant used to keep sheep for his father. And when there came a lion, or a bear, and took a lamb from the flock I went after him and struck him and delivered it out of his mouth. And if he arose against me, I caught him by his beard and struck him and killed him" (1 Sam. 17:34,35). The rod is a symbol of the shepherd's strength, his power, and his authority in any given situation. The spiritual parallel to the rod is God's Word. It serves as an extension of the shepherd's mind, will, and his intentions for the sheep.

The clarity of God's Word will keep your life from confusion and chaos and will bring peace and quiet serenity. Ps. 110:2 says, "The Lord shall send the rod of Your strength out of Zion. Rule in the midst of your enemies." In the same way that the sheep learn to rely on the shepherd's rod to protect them, you can learn to rely on the Word to bring you protection, comfort, and security. The gospel is the rod of His strength and the Lord will use His Word to comfort you when all is going well and in the midst of your greatest troubles. As you put your trust in the Good Shepherd you can have the confidence that He will lead you on the paths of righteousness so that your life will bring glory to God. Jesus knows how to comfort you. You can find comfort in the power and authority of the Word and through the gentleness and guidance of the Holy Spirit. The Holy Spirit is the great Comforter and where He is, support and comfort is not lacking.

Peace will come to you knowing that the rod and staff of the Good Shepherd will always take care of any problem that comes your way.

He'll defend you with His rod and He'll direct your steps with His staff. Micah referred to the staff when he wrote, "Shepherd Your people with Your staff, the flock of Your inheritance, who dwell alone in a forest in the midst of a garden land" (Micah 7:14). A shepherd's staff has a gradual curved end that fits around the neck of the sheep perfectly. The shape of the staff allows the shepherd to take hold of little lambs as well as full grown sheep. With the staff the shepherd will draw the sheep close to himself so they can have a close relationship together. He pulls the timid sheep in who would typically keep their distance from him and the other sheep. The shepherd also uses his staff to gently guide the sheep, reaching out to rest it tenderly upon their back. God's guidance is not harsh or forceful, but loving, reassuring, and meant to keep us on the right path.

The sheep receives comfort from this gentle touch and with a small amount of pressure the shepherd guides the sheep in the direction it should go. The Lord is directing your steps and as you comply with His gentle promptings a sense of safety and well-being will be all around you. Take comfort knowing the Lord is there to give you direction even in the smallest details of daily living. Ps. 23:5 says, "You prepare a table before me in the presence of my enemies; You anoint my head with oil; My cup runs over." In shepherd's terms, a table was a high plateau on top of a mountain. It's hard to reach but the shepherd knows good, healthy grass grows up there. Sometimes the journey of life is hard but the greatest blessings in life are in those places that are hard to reach. The shepherd goes before the sheep and prepares the ground for the arrival of the flock.

Snakes are on this mountain so the shepherd pours a special oil around the boundary of the feeding area. The snakes will not cross over this oil and when the shepherd leads the sheep into this marked area they're able to eat to their heart's content. A table was prepared for them in the presence of their enemies and their cup is running over. You can rest beside the still waters, knowing the Lord invites your heart into a place of peace and renewal. He stands as your faithful protector, watching over you and guarding you from all harm. In every season, His presence is a shield that surrounds your life. He knows your needs before you speak them and provides with perfect wisdom and care. As you trust Him, your soul is refreshed, strengthened, and made whole in His unfailing love. Have confidence in what David said in Ps. 23:6, "Surely goodness and mercy shall follow me all the days of my life; And I will dwell in the house of the Lord forever."

"YOUR CONSTANT COMPANION"

There are many false religions in the world today which prove that having a relationship with a higher entity is something man cannot live without. Somewhere, somehow, people need a source of power higher than themselves to turn to in time of need. For some people it's a bottle of alcohol, to others it's a wooden statue carved from some tree. For many, it's a prayer rug on which they can bow down and pray five times a day while facing in a certain direction. None of these things satisfy the wants and needs that people so desperately crave so, in spiritual blindness, they keep looking in all the wrong places and doing all the wrong things. What these hurting people need is not some false religion but a living relationship with the one true God. They don't realize it yet but Christianity has the one thing no other religion has. It has the presence of the Holy Spirit. In fact, there is no Christianity without the Holy Spirit.

Without His presence the Christian church will turn into a dry, mundane religion where the gathering of people on Sunday will morph into a social club with thoughts of God pushed into the background. The most important person on the earth today is the Holy Spirit. He is the one sent by Jesus to do the will of the Father and to finish the work He started two thousand years ago. The Old Testament basically describes the work of the Father, the four gospels describe the work of the Son, and the book of Acts up to this present time is known as the workings of the Holy Spirit. At the last supper Jesus spoke to His disciples after Judas left to betray Him and He began by saying, "Let not your heart be troubled; you believe in God, believe also in me" (John 14:1). His crucifixion was only hours away and the Lord wanted to impart to them hope that would hold them over in the days to follow.

He said in vs. 16,17, "And I will pray the Father, and He will give you another Helper, that He may abide with you forever, even the Spirit of truth, whom the world cannot receive, because it neither sees Him nor knows Him; but you know Him, for He dwells with you and will be in you." The first thing you need to learn is that the Holy Spirit is here to help you with whatever you need help with. He is an ever-present help in time of need. The Christian church was birthed in the book of Acts and as you read through its pages you will see that the Holy Spirit was a vital part of their individual lives. The early church depended on and interacted with the Holy Spirit for He was preeminent in everything they did. He was literally with them and partnered with them each and every day. Sad to say, what was very common to them seems to be uncommon in the church today. The Holy Spirit is the most active member of the Godhead yet is the most ignored and the most understood.

This is why it is a crucial thing for you to know Him and understand Him as a person without making the common mistake of only focusing on the manifestation of His power. You must see Him as being more than a ghostlike vapor floating through the cosmos with unlimited influence and spiritual energy. No, He is a real live person and if you don't see Him as such you will never have a personal relationship with Him. He is a person and not some cosmic force field because He has a soul and a personality. He has thoughts, desires, and feelings. Most people say they want the power of the Holy Spirit but shy away from having intimacy with the most misunderstood person in the Bible. He is the Spirit of the Living God, the third person of the Godhead, and you wouldn't know who Jesus is were it not for Him. It is the Holy Spirit who convicts the world of sin (John 16:8) and draws people to have a relationship with Jesus (1 Cor. 12:3).

The truth is, He's the most ignored person in the church yet He still loves you and has a yearning for you that cannot be measured. The Holy Spirit is a wonderful, kind, sensitive person and He wants to be your best friend. He wants you to have a daily experience with Him because you cannot live the Christian life successfully without Him. He is God and is just as much a part of the Trinity as the Father and the Son. Still, there are many misconceptions about who He is and what He does and this causes many people to shy away from having an intimate relationship with Him. This is all the workings of the enemy because he knows the Holy Spirit is the only one who can reveal to people who they truly are in Christ. The function of the Godhead can be compared to the building of a house. The Father is the architect who designs the house, Jesus is the foreman who oversees the construction, and the Holy Spirit is the team of workers who actually build the house.

He is the one who manifests what the Father wants done. Jesus said in Matt. 12:28, "If I cast out demons by the Spirit of God, surely the kingdom of God has come upon you." Luke sheds more light on the working of the Holy Spirit when he recorded the words of Jesus in Luke 11:20, "If I cast out demons with the finger of God, surely the kingdom of God has come upon you." The Holy Spirit is the finger of God, the hand that does what the Father wants done. Jer. 32:21 says, "You have brought Your people Israel out of the land of Egypt with signs and wonders, with a strong hand and an outstretched arm." Ps. 8:3 says, "When I consider Your heavens, the work of Your fingers. The moon and the stars, which you have ordained." In the beginning, the Father and the Son spoke creation into being through the power of the Holy Spirit, bringing order out of nothing and light out of darkness. The universe exists because the triune God willed it, formed it, and filled it with life by His Spirit.

Jesus is the Word of God and in the beginning He said "Let there be light" because this is what the Father wanted done. The Son spoke the command, and the Holy Spirit brought it into manifestation. He was "hovering over the face of the waters" (Gen. 1:2) waiting for Jesus to tell Him what the Father wanted Him to do. The Holy Spirit is the finger of God and He is powerful. So powerful is He that Isaiah writes, "Who else has held the oceans in His hand? Who has measured off the heavens with His fingers? Who else knows the weight of the earth or has weighed the mountains and hills on a scale? Who is able to advise the Spirit of the Lord? Who knows enough to give Him advice or touch Him? Has the Lord ever needed anyone's advice? Does He need instruction about what is good? Did someone teach Him what is right or show Him the path of justice? No, for all the nations of the world are but a drop in the bucket. They are nothing more than dust on the scales. He picks up the whole earth as though it were a grain of sand" (Is. 40:12-15 NLT).

What is the Holy Spirit like? Consider Gen. 1:27, "So God created man in His own image; in the image of God He created him; male and female He created them." Both man and woman were created in the image of God. This means that God took some of His attributes and put them in man. He then took some of His other attributes and put them in woman. Men and women are completely different from one another yet each display the character traits of a loving God. It is the responsibility of Jesus to show the world what the Father is like and man was created to show what Jesus is like. Eph. 5:25 says, "Husbands, love your wives just as Christ also loved the church and gave Himself for it." What about the woman? Could it be that God created woman to show the world what the Holy Spirit is like? A child scraps his knee and goes to his mother for comfort. The Holy Spirit is the great Comforter. The woman is a helper to her husband and Jesus said the Holy Spirit would be a Helper to the church.

The Holy Spirit is a real person and you can know His personality and how He does things. He is not a white dove but is God, the third person of the Trinity. He lives in the heart of every born again believer and is forever endeavoring to get them to think how God thinks, desire what God desires, and feel what God feels. He has a mind of His own (Rom. 8:27), a will (1 Cor. 2:11), and emotions. He feels love (Rom. 15:30) and grief (Eph. 4:30). He speaks (Rev. 2:7), teaches (John 14:26), leads (Rom. 8:14), comforts (Acts (9:31), appoints (Acts 20:28), and empowers (Acts 1:8). A mere influence cannot do all these things. The Holy Spirit is God and He knows all truth and has all knowledge. He can never think of something He's never thought of before. If He could do that then He might learn something new but that's not possible because He already knows everything there is to know.

The good news is that you have someone living inside of you who knows everything about everything and He has committed Himself to be your teacher and guide. The apostle Paul wrote two letters to the Corinthian church telling them how to live effective, Christian lives. The last words he says to them is recorded in 2 Cor. 13:14, "The grace of the Lord Jesus Christ, and the love of God, and the communion of the Holy Spirit be with you all. Amen." Paul is highlighting here the roles of each person in the Godhead in your life. The Greek word for "communion" is 'koinonia' and this word means 'fellowship, companionship, communication, intimacy, sharing together, social intercourse, partnership, joint participation, close mutual association." The Holy Spirit is on the earth today and He wants to be your constant companion where the two of you share your most intimate thoughts with one another. You need to talk to Him the same way you talk to the Father and to Jesus.

The greatest sin against Him is when He is ignored. He is a person with intellect. He has His own mind, and He makes His own decisions. He has emotions and feelings and is grieved when you ignore Him. You need to fellowship with Him and share things together on a friendly basis with mutual recognition and common interests. You need a personal relationship with the Holy Spirit and He needs to be more real to you than anything you see or feel with your physical senses. In some places the Holt Spirit is unknown and unwanted and people get offended when you talk about Him. Some people live their entire Christian life and never give any serious thought to the Holy Spirit yet the Bible talks about Him from cover to cover. People need to understand who He is because they are in danger of losing everything. They're drawn to miracles and the supernatural yet Zech. 4:6 says, "'Not by might nor by power, but by My Spirit,' says the Lord."

People who want to know the Holy Spirit need to realize that they already know Him, they just don't recognize Him. He is the Spirit of Jesus. In John 14:16 Jesus said He would pray to the Father "and He shall give you another Comforter, that He may abide with you forever." In Greek this means "one just like Me" thus the Holy Spirit can be described as "Jesus unlimited." When Jesus walked the earth He could only be where His physical body would take Him but the Holy Spirit can be everywhere at once. Jesus is now in heaven seated at the right hand of the Father (Mark 16:19) but the Holy Spirit is on the earth today for He was sent to be your constant companion. Begin to put the Holy Spirit first in your life and talk to Him every day. It should be natural for you to not do anything until you've first taken the time to talk to the Holy Spirit. Talk to Him about everything that concerns you for He is your helper, comforter, and guide.

He has the answer to every problem you're facing and through Him you can know what the will of God is for your life. He is ready, willing, and able to help you accomplish and achieve your goals and to become the person God wants you to be. It is He who helps you do what God has called you to do. He'll tell you what to say and do in certain situations and how to be at the right place at the right time. The Holy

Spirit is alive and inside of you all the time. He is the same Spirit that was on Jesus when He walked the earth, the same Spirit that anointed Jesus to teach and preach, to perform miracles, and to heal people and deliver them from the bondage of the enemy. Fellowship means to have a friendly relationship with someone. Friends have compassion for one another and share their deepest thoughts and feelings. There is nothing they're not willing to share because the person they're talking to is their best friend. This is the type of relationship the Holy Spirit wants to have with you.

He wants to talk to you but first you must deliberately engage Him in a conversation. Talk to Him like you would talk to a best friend because that is what He is. Talk to Him and you will be amazed at how He will respond. He will give you eyes to see and ears to hear and a heart that is receptive. He'll give you answers to questions, solutions to problems, and light where there was once darkness. He'll give you peace where there was once unrest and He will show you how to respond personally to the truths you read in the Bible. He will show you things to come and will direct your steps as you seek to fulfill your destiny. He'll show you what to do and tell you what to say in every circumstance you find yourself in. This is what a best friend does. Intimacy with the Holy Spirit can't be developed unless you first have fellowship with Him. Intimacy goes beyond fellowship for it deals with the thoughts, secrets, and desires of the heart. Intimacy is the avenue that leads to a deep friendship.

The Message Bible says in 2 Cor. 13:14, "The amazing grace of the Master, the extravagant love of God, the intimate friendship of the Holy Spirit, be with all of you." Your life will change when you realize that the Holy Spirit wants to be an intimate friend with you. James 4:5 says, "Or do you think that the scripture says in vain, 'The Spirit who dwells in us yearns jealously'?" The word "yearn" means 'to long for intensely and consistently.' The Holy Spirit yearns for you jealously. He wants you to put nothing else before Him for He will not share with you the most intimate secrets of His heart if you're pursuing a friendship with the world. James 2:4 says, "Adulterers and adulteresses! Do you not know that friendship with the world is enmity with God? Whoever therefore wants to be a friend of the world makes himself an enemy of God." Intimacy deals with the desires, intentions, and thoughts of the heart. To have intimacy with someone you must first know who they are and this happens through fellowship.

Depending on how you interact with someone will determine how close you become. There are couples who have been married for thirty years but they act like strangers because they don't interact with one another nor do they go to those high levels of intimacy. In like manner, there are Christians who have been saved for years yet really don't know Jesus all that well because it's the Holy Spirit who reveals Him to people. Paul never physically walked with Jesus but he came to know Him intimately through fellowship with the Holy Spirit. Peter later testified that Paul knew Jesus so well that some of his letters were hard for him to understand (2 Peter 3:16). The Holy Spirit can bring you to realms of understanding that Jesus couldn't even do personally because He communicates with your inner man. The problem is that many people want to know God in their minds and not their hearts.

Your body is the temple of the Holy Spirit (1 Cor. 6:19). Jesus said He is "the Spirit of truth, whom the world cannot receive, because it neither sees Him nor knows Him; but you know Him, for He dwells with you and will be in you" (John 14:17). Jesus said you know Him so the question must be asked, "How well do you know the Holy Spirit?" Not how well do you know about Him, but how well do you know Him personally? People learn the doctrine of the Holy Spirit in their minds yet don't fully receive Him in a personal way in their heart. He is received when you allow Him to take His place of ministry in your life, the ministry Jesus said He would have when He comes. He is the Comforter but He is not here to manipulate your feelings. He is the

Spirit of truth and the truth of God's Word will overwhelm all your feelings. The devil will use your wayward feelings to bring you guilt and shame and cause you to walk in doubt and fear.

No matter how you feel, you can know that the Spirit of truth is at work inside of you. Jesus said, "And you shall know the truth, and the truth shall make you free" (John 8:32). You know the Holy Spirit by what He's doing in your life, by the fruits of His ministry. You know He is at work in your life because it is the Holy Spirit who plants in your heart the hunger and thirst to get to know Jesus in a more intimate way. Jesus came to point people to the Father and the Holy Spirit was sent to point people to Jesus. On the Day of Pentecost, Peter preached to the people about Jesus and three thousand people gave their lives to the Lord (Acts 2:41). The Holy Spirit will take you from glory to glory and will be to you what Jesus was to those who knew Him when He walked the earth. Everything Jesus was to His disciples, the Holy Spirit will be to you. Jesus taught them, comforted them, helped them, and gave them resources. He was their everything, their all in all.

He was their friend and this is what the Holy Spirit desires to be to you. He comes to search your heart and, when He finds the good that is there, He brings it out into the open and presents it to the Heavenly Father. It is He who will take you to the higher realms of glory and when you recognize what He's doing in your life you will begin to know him better and better. The Holy Spirit is tender and true and will do for you that which you can gratefully receive. Rest in peace knowing that no distance and no circumstance can separate you from the heavenly Comforter. Wherever you go and whatever you do, the Holy Spirit will be your constant companion. He was sent to take the place of Jesus on the earth and He will forever be with you and never will He forsake you. He works in and through every person who has made Jesus the Lord of their life. The ministry of the Holy Spirit is a ministry of comfort. He will comfort you by bringing you to the knowledge of who you are in Christ.

Rom. 8:15,16 (NLT) says, "So you have not received a spirit that makes you fearful slaves. Instead, you received God's Spirit when He adopted you as His own children. Now we call Him, 'Abba, Father,' For His Spirit joins with our spirit to affirm that we are God's children." If that doesn't give you comfort then nothing will. Jesus said to the Father, "I in them, and You in Me; that they may be made perfect in one, and that the world may know that You have sent Me, and have loved them as You have loved Me" (John 17:23). Acts 9:31 says, "Then the churches throughout all Judea, Galilee, and Samaria had peace and were edified. And walking in the fear of the Lord and in the comfort of the Holy Spirit, they were multiplied." The Holy Spirit enriches the church with His comfort. Every word in the Bible that brings peace to your soul was inspired by the Holy Spirit. Jesus said in John 6:63, "The words that I have spoken to you are spirit and are life."

When you read God's Word, the Holy Spirit will minister comfort to you. When you go to church and hear anointed messages inspired by the Holy Spirit, your life will be changed. You will be encouraged to come up higher, to never give up, and to keep pressing forward in your walk with God. The Holy Spirit will comfort you with thoughts that He originates. As you meditate on what He is saying, you will learn to hear His voice and discover the will of God. You can act without misgivings because of what the Holy Spirit has said and this will bring you comfort and peace. He alone can turn the darkness of night into the brilliance of a new day that shines brightly with the light of truth that comes from God's Word. The Greek word for "Comforter" is 'parakletos' and means "one called to the side of another." During His earthly ministry, Jesus walked daily with His disciples, sharing life with them - teaching, guiding, correcting, and modeling the heart of the Father through constant presence.

As He was preparing to leave them, He promised that "another Comforter" would come and dwell in them, taking the place of His physical presence. In the Old Testament the Spirit of God would come on people and then leave. God's Spirit departed from King Saul (1 Sam. 16:14) and when David confessed his sin he asked that the Spirit be not taken from him (Ps. 51:11). But when the Spirit was given at Pentecost, He came to God's people to be with them forever. The Holy Spirit can be grieved but He will never leave. To have the Holy Spirit as your Comforter is to have God Himself indwelling your mortal body. He will teach you the Word and will guide you into all truth. He will remind you of what Jesus taught so that you can depend on His Word in the difficult times of life. He'll give you peace (John 14:27), love (John 15:9,10), and joy (John 15:11). He will comfort your heart and mind in a troubled world (2 Cor. 1:4).

The Holy Spirit was sent to enable you to be fulfilled in your inner man and in your Christian life. Life is to be celebrated and not tolerated, therefore, it is the will of God that the character traits of the Holy Spirit be evident in your life every single day. Gal. 5:22,23 says, "But the fruit of the Spirit is love, joy, peace, longsuffering, kindness, goodness, faithfulness, gentleness, self-control. Against such there is no law." You cannot produce these things on your own but since the Holy Spirit is your constant companion you can trust Him to manifest Himself in your life to the point where the fruit He produces is evident in your life. When you allow the Holy Spirit to work in your life you'll become more like Jesus and become the person God wants you to be. Christians everywhere want to know the will of God for their lives not realizing that the One who lives inside of them knows the will of God. If you will spend time with the Holy Spirit and have a close, mutual association with Him, you will hear Him speak and He will tell you what God's specific will is for your life.

Before Jesus ascended into heaven He gave His disciples instructions on what they should do for the rest of their lives. Mark 16:15 says, "Go into all the world and preach the gospel to every creature." The world they lived in was ruled by the Romans and it was an evil, wicked, and brutal world. Jesus knew they would not be able to fulfill their destiny with their own ability and in their own strength so He told them "not to depart from Jerusalem, but to wait for the Promise of the Father" (Acts 1:4). "For John truly baptized with water, but you shall be baptized with the Holy Spirit not many days from now" (vs. 5). "But you shall receive power when the Holy Spirit has come upon you; and you shall be witnesses to Me in Jerusalem, and in all Judea and Samaria, and to the ends of the earth" (vs. 8). You are never alone in the journey of life for the Holy Spirit is in you, with you, and upon you. He goes with you wherever you may go. He is your constant companion and He'll enable you to do the things that God would have you do.

| 17 |

"YOU SHALL RECEIVE POWER"

God knows what you need more than you do and this is why you need to seek His direction in everything that pertains to your life. He knows what's important and what's not important and, if you will read and study your Bible consistently, He will show you what those things are. He knows that living in this sinful world is too tough to make it on your own and this is why Jesus said in John 14:16, "And I will pray the Father, and He will give you another Helper, that He may abide with you forever." Without a doubt, there is nothing more important to you and your walk with God than the indwelling presence of the Holy Spirit. The last thing Jesus said to His disciples before He ascended into heaven is found in Acts 1:8, "But you shall receive power when the Holy Spirit has come upon you; and you shall be witnesses to Me in Jerusalem, and in all Judea and Samaria, and to the end of the earth."

You need the help of the Holy Spirit to fulfill your destiny, and this is why the enemy consistently tempts the children of God with the deceptive sin of self-effort. Rom. 8:1 says, "There is therefore now no condemnation to those who are in Christ Jesus, who do not walk according to the flesh, but according to the Spirit." Those who walk according to the flesh are walking in self-effort. There is a war raging on the inside of you. God wants you to receive help from the Holy Spirit and the devil wants you to try to serve God with your own power and ability. The greatest temptation you will ever face is not to sin but to walk in self-effort. Your heart may be full of good intentions but if you try to serve God with self-effort you are walking in the flesh. When this happens it will only be a matter of time before the works of the flesh get manifested in your life. Abraham had two sons, one born according to the flesh and the other according to the Spirit (Gal. 4:29).

God promised Abraham a son but before it happened he walked in the flesh and had a son with his wife's handmaiden named Ishmael (Gen. 16). God and His miraculous power was not involved with the birth of this child. It was all a work of self-effort and to this day the descendants of Ishmael continue to persecute the descendants of Isaac, the son born according to the Spirit. You are to have no confidence in those achievements that come through self-effort. The world will tell you that to be successful in life you need a lot of self-confidence and this is precisely what the devil wants you to believe. He knows that in order for you to be a leader in the kingdom of God you can have no self-confidence whatsoever. He also knows that the Christian life is impossible to live if all you have is self-effort. The only thing you can do is rest in Jesus and allow the power of the Holy Spirit to work in your life.

Don't be like Moses who at the age of forty tried to fulfill his destiny with self-effort when he killed an Egyptian who he saw beating a Hebrew slave (Ex. 2:11,12). Paul says in Phil. 3:3 to "rejoice in Christ Jesus and have no confidence in the flesh." Humble yourself and admit you really do need help in this sin-stained world. Jesus said you needed a Helper for a reason and His coming is recorded in Acts 2:1-4, "Now when the Day of Pentecost had fully come, they were all with one accord in one place. And suddenly there came a sound from heaven, as of a rushing mighty wind, and it filled the whole house where they were sitting. Then there appeared to them divided tongues, as of fire, and one sat upon each of them. And they were all filled with the Holy

Spirit and began to speak with other tongues, as the Spirit gave them utterance." Special abilities were given to those in that upper room with which they used to turn their world upside down (Acts 17:6).

They were ordinary people whom God enabled to do extraordinary things. They made a radical difference in the world in which they lived for they chose to not leave their world the same way they found it. With fearless preaching and a willingness to obey, they began a movement that continues to this very day. They were radical then and you can be just as radical today. You can be that way with the help of the Helper. The book of Acts shows what normal Christianity should look like. While the four gospels tell the story of Jesus, the book of Acts tells the story of the disciples carrying on His work through the power of the Holy Spirit. Jesus did many great works when He walked the earth and He said in John 14:12, "Most assuredly, I say to you, he who believes in me, the works that I do he will do also; and greater works than these because I go to My Father." Jesus preached the gospel, healed the sick, cleansed the unclean, raised the dead, and drove out demons.

This is what normal Christianity looks like and Jesus said that you would do greater works than these. The same power that raised Jesus from the dead and dwelt in the early disciples now dwells in you. Allow the Holy Spirit to put a fire down on the inside of you and then go out and turn your world upside down. It was the power of the Holy Spirit that enabled the disciples to do the work of Jesus and you need to desire this same power to move and work in your life also. God is a consuming fire and you get on fire for Him by immersing yourself in the flame. The last thing you want to do is try to turn your world upside down with self-effort. Acts 19:11-20 tells how the seven sons of Sceva tried to cast a demon out of a man with their own strength and ability and vs. 16 tells what happened next, "Then the man in whom the evil spirit was leaped on them, overpowered them, and prevailed against them, so that they fled out of that house naked and wounded."

As religious as these men were, they had no relationship with God, they were not believers in Christ, and they did not possess the power or the presence of the Holy Spirit. There was nothing in them or in their words that would cause a demon to pay them the slightest heed. This story can't be taken lightly because the sons of Sceva are like many in the church today. They have a form of godliness but deny its power (2 Tim. 3;5) and influence in their life. These people are filled with religion, they promote religious activity, but they reject the power of the Holy Spirit. They talk the talk not realizing what Paul said in 1 Cor. 4:20 (NLT), "For the kingdom of God is not just a lot of talk; it is living by God's power." Phil. 2:13 (NLT) says, "For God is working in you, giving you the desire and the power to do what pleases Him." This is what happens when you are filled with the Holy Spirit.

The Message Bible says, "Be energetic in your life of salvation, reverent and sensitive before God. That energy is God's energy, an energy deep within you, God Himself willing and working at what will give Him the most pleasure." The Christian life is a life of power and everything you do for God must be done with the power of the Holy Spirit. This is the same supernatural power that parted the Red Sea and brought down the walls of Jericho. It was the power of God that transformed Moses from being a person who could kill in anger to being the meekest man on the earth. The power of God came mightily on Samson and he tore a lion apart with his bare hands and single-handedly killed a thousand men in a single day. More than that, it was the supernatural power of the Holy Spirit that raised Jesus from the dead and is now working inside of you. The Message Bible says, "He'll do the same thing in you that He did in Jesus, bringing you alive to Himself" (Rom. 8:11).

It is impossible to live a victorious Christian life without the power of God operating in your life. It's this power that allows you to come up higher and experience the reality of God and live in the supernatural. It will transform you from the inside out and allows you to overcome death, sickness, poverty, fear, doubt, rejection and persecution. It gives you boldness to tell others about Jesus and it's what enables you to fulfill your destiny. Jesus operated in this same power and although He was the Son of God He didn't begin His ministry until after He was baptized and filled with power from on high. Because of this power, He preached the Word fearlessly with signs and wonders following. In other words, He turned His world upside down. What happened is that the Holy Spirit had taken over. Acts 10:38 (NLT) says, "And you know that God anointed Jesus of Nazareth with the Holy Spirit and with power. Then Jesus went around doing good and healing all who were oppressed by the devil, for God was with Him."

Adam was clothed with the glory of God and Jesus came to restore God's glory back to man. When you are filled with the Holy Spirit you will rule and reign as God had originally intended. The Holy Spirit was sent to transform you into a person of boldness, power, and authority. You'll be able to look the devil in the face and fear no evil because you are strong in the Lord and in the power of His might (Eph. 6:10). Rivers of living water are flowing out of you and nothing can stop you from doing what you've been called to do. Jesus said in Luke 4:18,19, "The Spirit of the Lord is upon Me, because He has anointed Me to preach the gospel to the poor. He has sent Me to heal the brokenhearted, to preach deliverance to the captives and recovery of sight to the blind, to set at liberty those who are oppressed, to preach the acceptable year of the Lord." These were all rivers that were flowing out of Him into the lives of hurting people and these same rivers can flow out of you.

The devil is a bully and you can't let him push you around. This power was given to you so you can put him in his rightful place which is under your feet. Rivers of living water are flowing out of you. Ezek. 47 tells of a river that flows from the Temple of God and vs. 9 says "everything will live wherever the river goes." The Message Bible says, "Wherever the river flows, life will flourish. Where the river flows, life abounds." You have been anointed to help suffering humanity and you've got to step up and let the rivers flow. Allow the Lord to use you to give light to those in darkness. There is a great work to be done and many don't realize what God is willing to do for them. It is therefore your responsibility to show them by letting the rivers flow out of you. The biggest lie a person could ever believe is that God closed the reservoir of His power after He poured His Spirit upon the early disciples. No, the Holy Spirit is alive and well on the earth today for there is still a great work to be done.

Be filled with the Holy Spirit and allow God to use you in a powerful way. The evil that has been accumulating for centuries has to be confronted and resisted and God wants to use you to do it. From the Day of Pentecost to this present time the Holy Spirit has been available to all those who would receive Him. Jesus openly declared that the divine influence of His Spirit would be with His followers until the end of time. The problem in the church today is that most people don't desire the Holy Spirit and therefore don't seek His presence in their lives. They're content to go to church occasionally and maybe, just maybe, they may read a Bible verse on some prayer card they have sitting on the shelf. As long as the church is satisfied with small things they will forever be disqualified from receiving the great things of God. This is why there has to be a hunger and a thirst for the Holy Spirit. He is a gentleman to the highest degree and won't force Himself on anybody.

Rivers of living water will only flow out of you when you respond and yield to His promptings. If you will read your Bible and search the scriptures with a teachable spirit then your efforts will be richly rewarded. Ps. 119:18 (GWT) says, "Uncover my eyes that I may see the miraculous things in your teachings." Jesus wants to impress upon your heart that when you are filled with the Holy Spirit you will be given the same power and glory that He had. The Greek word for "power" is 'dunamis' and is where the word "dynamite" comes from. Consider happening to you what happened to Jesus in Luke 6:19, "And the whole multitude sought to touch Him, for power went out from Him and healed them all." It was this same power that healed the woman with the issue of blood who pressed through the crowd and touched the hem of His garment (Mark 5:25-34).

People marveled at this power and before Jesus ascended into heaven He commanded His disciples to not leave Jerusalem until they received this same power (Acts. 1:4). This same command is given to the church today. God is commanding you to be filled with the Holy Spirit from whom this power comes. It is this dynamite power that will allow you to lay hands on the sick and they will recover, to go to the uttermost parts of the earth and be witnesses for Him. On this power He will build His church and the gates of hell will not prevail against it. Just because you're born again does not mean you don't need the power of the Holy Spirit. The devil don't fear people who are saved, he fears those who have the power of God operating in their lives. The devil fears this power but the problem is there are born again believers who fear this power as well. They don't understand it and are thus intimidated by it and don't thirst for it as they should.

They don't understand that they don't have to struggle day in and day out always being overcome by the devil. Jesus said in John 16:33, "In the world you will have tribulation; but be of good cheer, I have overcome the world." In Greek this verse says the Lord "deprived the world of its power to harm you." Jesus overcame the world because He was anointed with power and this same power is available to you. Don't run from this power because you don't understand it with your mind. Trust God and thirst for it and run after it. Ask Him today to fill you with the Holy Spirit, releasing the same supernatural power that enabled Jesus to overcome the world through faith, obedience, and love. That power is not distant or reserved for a few—it is available now to every heart that hungers and thirsts for God. And if you are not thirsty yet, stir your hunger, open your heart, and seek Him today until your soul is filled.

A lost sinner cannot get born again and filled with the Holy Spirit at the same time. Jesus said in John 14:16,17 (NLT), "And I will ask the Father, and He will give you another Advocate, who will never leave you. He is the Holy Spirit, who leads into all truth. The world cannot receive Him, because it isn't looking for Him and doesn't recognize Him." The Message Bible says, "The godless world can't take Him in because it doesn't have eyes to see Him, doesn't know what to look for." A lost sinner can only receive Jesus as Savior but it's the born again believer who can be filled with the Holy Spirit. When you receive Jesus, you're born of the Spirit of God and are now ready to receive the fullness of all that's available to you. Seminaries and false teachers will tell you that this power with signs and wonders have been done away with. The problem with that is these people have no scripture to back up what they're saying. Jesus said if you believe in Him, out of your heart will flow rivers of living water.

People still believe today so the power of the Holy Spirit is available today also. The misinformed don't have an answer for that, only excuses and false doctrine. Notice that Jesus cried out with a loud voice, "If anyone thirsts, let Him come to Me and drink" (John 7:37). He didn't say this passively. No, He cried out so the people would listen and pay attention to what He had to say. He is crying out to you also. He is telling you to not be satisfied to simply having your name on some church roster somewhere. He is telling you to thirst for more of the things of God, to thirst for the Holy Spirit. The Lord does not refuse to give His Spirit to those who ask Him. Jesus is speaking to you and you need to take heed to what He is saying. With every excuse you make, with every hesitation and delay, you put yourself in a position where it will be more difficult to accept this free gift from heaven. Don't be like Felix who said to Paul, "Go away for now; when I have a convenient time I will call for you" (Acts 24:25).

Those who shy away from the Holy Spirit bring upon themselves the consequences of living life with self-effort, doing what they want, when they want. How dark and sullen is this independence for the sentence of death is on their lives. It is a serious thing to refuse this invitation to be filled with the Holy Spirit. He seeks to come and abide in your heart and is grieved when He is not welcomed as an honored guest. Jesus said in John 12:35, "Walk while you have light, lest darkness overtake you." You've got to live by every word that proceeds out of the mouth of God and Jesus specifically commanded you to be filled with the Holy Spirit. When you invite Him into your heart you will be made complete in Christ and the good work He began in you will be finished. Heavenly thoughts and Christlike actions will take the place of rebellious acts brought about through the perverseness of self-effort.

Those who turn their back on the Holy Spirit do not know what lengths the devil will go to lead them down the dark path. They'll do things today that they knew was wrong yesterday. They'll make decisions they shouldn't be making and do things they shouldn't be doing. They'll then wonder why their life is caving in around them. The problem is they didn't answer the door when the Holy Spirit came knocking. To be filled with the Holy Spirit is the most urgent of all your needs. The Heavenly Father is more than willing to give you His Holy Spirit but an earnest effort must be made on your part in order to receive this blessing from above. You must hunger and thirst for His presence in your life while basing your faith on the fact that God has promised to grant you your request. Take comfort in knowing that when you are filled with the Holy Spirit it will be impossible for God to give you more. To this gift nothing can be added for through Him all your needs are supplied.

Paul said in 2 Cor. 1:21,22 (NLT), "It is God who enables us, along with you, to stand firm for Christ. He has commissioned us, and He has identified us as His own by placing the Holy Spirit in our hearts as the first installment that guarantees everything He has promised." He is not glorified when people ask for small things which show nothing is really expected. No, He wants you to come up higher with earnestness and zeal asking for everything He has to offer. Jesus said in Matt. 7:11, "If you then, being evil, know how to give good gifts to your children, how much more will your Father who is in heaven give good things to those who ask Him!" In the eyes of God, all good things are given to you when you are filled with the Holy Spirit. The more you consider what your needs are, the more you should desire the gift of the Holy Spirit. It is in proportion to you needing Him that you will seek to receive Him.

Those who don't seek Him think they can gain victory with their own strength and wisdom not realizing that their self-effort is being controlled by the devil himself. There is a vacuum inside of them that can only be filled by the Holy Spirit. These people must have the Spirit of the living God in their heart for they can never go forward and do great things in the kingdom until they do. They must die to themselves and empty their hearts of all selfishness. With a humble heart they must ask the Lord to fill them with His glorious Holy Spirit. Jesus said, "Ask, and it will be given you; seek, and you will find; knock, and it will be opened to you" (Matt. 7:7). You must receive the Holy Spirit the same way you received Jesus into your heart. Both come by invitation and a surrendering of the will. People say they love God yet continue to manage their own lives. They only approach God when they want Him to do something for them. This is not right for you cannot use the Holy Spirit, the Holy Spirit is to use you.

Phil. 2:13 (NLT) says, "For God is working in you, giving you the desire and the power to do what pleases Him." Only to those who surrender their will to the will of God will the Holy Spirit be given. He must be asked for and claimed by faith. When He comes, all the blessings of life come with Him. He'll be a breath of life in your soul for the impartation of the Holy Spirit is the impartation of the very life of Jesus. He'll influence every decision you make and every action you take. You will walk in love as you conform your will to the will of the Father. The Holy Spirit will be your permanent connection to the throne of grace. Through Him you will fulfill your destiny and do great exploits in the kingdom of God. There is no limit to what you can do for the kingdom of God when you lay your life aside and make room for the working of the Holy Spirit. Your heart will be so full of compassion and power that you'll be willing to go to the ends of the earth to tell people how good God truly is.

Sinners will give their lives to Jesus and backsliders will go back to their former ways. You'll labor with holy zeal and much fervor accompanied by the Holy Spirit in greater measure. Where He goes, you go and where you go, He goes. When you are filled with the Holy Spirit you will bear witness to the truth of the gospel with mighty power and signs following. The end is near and special grace and divine favor will be upon you as you prepare others for the coming of the Lord Jesus Christ. Jesus said, "Watch, therefore, for you do not know what hour your Lord is coming. Therefore you also be ready, for the Son of Man is coming at an hour when you do not expect Him" (Matt. 24:42,44). So much time has been wasted by people giving too much attention to trivial things. No more. It's time for your destiny to be fulfilled. It's time to be filled with the Holy Spirit. Yield yourself to the control of the Holy Spirit and be open to all the wonderful things He would have you do.

You can't put Him in a box because He works in mysterious and unexpected ways. The Jews refused to receive Jesus because He did not come in accordance with their expectations. Do not allow the limitations of a finite mind to determine the boundaries in which the Holy Spirit will work in your life. Be open to anything and everything He would have you say and do. The Holy Spirit has a mind of His own and never works according to the plans and expectations of man. He is here to do the work of the Heavenly Father and no human can restrict and limit what He can and will do. Acts 2:2 says, "And suddenly there came a sound from heaven, as of a rushing mighty wind, and it filled the whole house where they were sitting." Just as a mighty wind moves across the earth, bending and breaking giant trees that are in its path, so does the Holy Spirit change and influence the hearts of those who are submitted to Him. He is not here to modify your old life, He is here to give you a new life altogether.

The busiest person on the planet today is the Holy Spirit and Paul says in 1 Cor. 3:9 that "we are God's fellow workers." This means that nothing will be impossible for you and the Holy Spirit. The boundaries of self-effort will be swept away as the Holy Spirit takes over and works through you with great and convincing power. Rivers of living water are flowing out of you and suddenly the world around you is becoming a better place. There is a fountain of blessings inside of you whose name is the Holy Spirit and He wants you to be a vessel through which the rich treasures of heaven can flow into the lives of other people in unexpected ways. The Holy Spirit is in you and He is flowing out of you in a mighty way. God has a work for you to do and it is only through the working of the Holy Spirit that your destiny will be fulfilled. Jesus commanded the disciples to not leave Jerusalem until they received power from on high. This same power is available to you. Don't leave home without it.

| 18 |

"A HEAVENLY LANGUAGE"

Where would you be today were it not for the Holy Spirit? Very rarely, if ever, does He get the recognition for all that He does but still, it is He who is responsible for taking you to where you are today in your Christian walk. When you asked Jesus into your heart and got born again you were changed on the inside. As wonderful as that is, that alone is not all there is to the Christian experience. God says you must also change on the outside and for that to happen you must be filled with the Holy Spirit. When that happens then, and only then, will you begin to change on the outside. Being changed on the inside alone will do you little good in this life if all you do is apply self-effort to become more and more like Jesus. No, your life must also change on the outside and this you cannot make happen with your own strength and ability. To become the person God wants you to be, you will need power from on high which you receive when you are filled with the Holy Spirit.

Jesus said in Acts 1:8, "But you shall receive power when the Holy Spirit has come upon you." The power to live the Christian life comes from the Holy Spirit. Living a good life in this dark, sinful world is not only difficult to do but, in fact, is outright impossible. You were never designed to live for God on your own and this is why Jesus told the disciples to not go anywhere or do anything until they received this power from the Holy Spirit (Acts 1:4). When you are filled with the Holy Spirit, you will receive this power that will allow you to live for God that goes way beyond anything you could ever do on your own. Receiving this power is described in scripture as being baptized in or with the Holy Spirit. There are three baptisms in the Bible and each one of them is a separate event. The word "baptize" in Greek means 'to immerse' and, when you gave your life to Jesus, 1 Cor. 12:13 says the Holy Spirit baptized you into the body of Christ.

Once you are born again, Jesus says in Matt. 28:19 that you need to be baptized in water as an outward sign of what happened in your heart. And third, when asked, Jesus will baptize you with the Holy Spirit. John the Baptist said in Matt. 3:11, "I indeed baptize you with water unto repentance, but He who is coming after me is mightier than I, whose sandals I am not worthy to carry. He will baptize you with the Holy Spirit and fire." There are two spiritual experiences every person should go through. They should receive the baptism "of" the Holy Spirit which is the born-again experience and then they need to be baptized "in" the Holy Spirit. Acts 8:5,6 says, "Then Philip went down to the city of Samaria and preached Christ to them. And the multitudes with one accord heeded the things spoken by Philip, hearing and seeing miracles which he did."

These people got born again through the preaching of Philip (vs. 12) but look what happened next, "Now when the apostles who were at Jerusalem heard that Samaria had received the word of God, they sent Peter and John to them, who, when they had come down, prayed for them that they might receive the Holy Spirit. For as yet He had fallen upon none of them. They had only been baptized in the name of the Lord Jesus. Then they laid hands on them, and they received the Holy Spirit" (vs. 14-17). Getting born again and being filled with the Holy Spirit is not the same thing even though many theologians will tell you that they are both one and the same. They're not. You getting born again is a work of the Holy Spirit and getting filled with the Holy Spirit is a work of Jesus. He wants to immerse you and surround you and get you completely filled with the Holy Spirit until He abundantly flows out of you.

Jesus said in John 7:38, "He who believes in Me, as the Scripture has said, out of his heart will flow rivers of living water." Vs. 39 then says, "But this He spoke concerning the Spirit, whom those believing in Him would receive." When you got born again you got a well of water for your own satisfaction (John 4:14) but when you're filled with the Holy Spirit you get rivers of living water that will flow out of you to help meet the needs of a dark and hurting world. God wants you to have the power to witness, power to act, power to live, and power to show forth the divine manifestation of God. The power of the Holy Spirit will take you out of your own plans and put you into the plan of God. Many people who consider themselves to be religious get offended when they're asked if they received the Holy Spirit when they first believed not realizing that this is the exact question Paul asked some disciples in Acts 19:2.

Getting the Spirit inside of you at your conversion is not the same as being filled with the Holy Spirit. There is a difference between drinking a glass of water and jumping into a pool of water. In one instance the water is in you and in the other you are in the water. This is how it is with the Holy Spirit. He may be in you but that does not mean you have been immersed in Him. This is why Paul told born again believers in Eph. 5:18 (NLT), "Don't be drunk with wine because that will ruin your life. Instead, be filled with the Holy Spirit." These people were saved yet Paul said they needed to be filled with the Holy Spirit. Being baptized in the Holy Spirit means you give Him permission to exercise authority and power over your circumstances and to use you in ministry and to control the choices you make in life. Anybody can be filled with the Holy Spirit but you've got to want it to happen.

God doesn't force Himself on anybody and this is why Jesus said in John 7:37, "If anyone thirsts, let him come to Me and drink." Are you satisfied with where you're now at or are you thirsty for more of God?

Are you thirsty for the Holy Spirit? If so, then rivers of living water will flow out of you. This includes rivers of speaking in tongues, rivers of miracles, rivers of healing, rivers of divine revelation, and rivers and rivers of supernatural power. Reject those teachings that say the baptism of the Holy Spirit was only for those in the upper room on the Day of Pentecost. In Acts 1:4 the Holy Spirit is called "the Promise of the Father" and Peter later said in Acts 2:38,39, "Repent, and let every one of you be baptized in the name of Jesus Christ for the remission of sins; and you shall receive the gift of the Holy Spirit. For the promise is to you and to your children, and to all who are afar off, as many as the Lord our God will call." Clearly, the Holy Spirit is available to all those who thirst for Him.

Jesus said in Luke 14:28 that a wise man counts the cost before he begins to build a tower. The baptism in the Holy Spirit is a free gift but you first must be willing to submit fully to God to receive it. It is a gift that cannot be earned for you will never be good enough to receive it. No, it is a free gift from God to those who sincerely desire this beautiful experience. The same power that enabled Jesus to open blind eyes, raise the dead, calm the storm, and to live a life pleasing to the Father during His ministry on earth is available to you today. Jesus said, "Ask, and it shall be given to you" (Luke 11:9). Pray this prayer right now, "Heavenly Father, I thank you that Jesus saved me and I pray for the Holy Spirit to come upon me. Lord Jesus, baptize me now in the Holy Spirit. I receive the baptism in the Holy Spirit right now by faith. May the anointing, the glory, and the power of God come upon me and into my life right now. May I be empowered for service from this day forward. Thank You, Jesus, for baptizing me in Your Holy Spirit. Amen."

Begin praising God out loud and tell Him how much you love Him. Thank Him, worship Him, and yield your voice to Him. Let Him give you new words of praise that you never heard before and speak out loud whatever words come to you. In the book of Acts every time somebody got filled with the Holy Spirit they began to speak in tongues. When this happens rivers of living water will flow out of you. Water is for cleansing and Prov. 18:4 says, "The words of a man's mouth are deep waters; The well-spring of wisdom is a flowing brook." Prov. 15:4 says, "A wholesome tongue is a tree of life." The Hebrew word for "wholesome" means 'healing' and this verse is saying that the healing of your tongue is a tree of life. James 3:8 says the tongue "is an unruly evil, full of deadly poison" and this is why on the Day of Pentecost the first thing God did was heal the tongues of those who were filled with the Holy Spirit.

Acts 2:4 says, "And they were all filled with the Holy Spirit and began to speak with other tongues, as the Spirit gave them utterance." When the disciples got filled with the Holy Spirit they yielded their tongues to Him for He requires our cooperation in everything He does. And it was this yielding that allowed a new language to come out of them. In Greek the word "tongues" means 'language' therefore, according to the Bible, speaking in tongues is not gibberish but in fact is a language that you can speak. Because it is a language there are many myths associated with it that simply are not true. Speaking in tongues is a heavenly language yet many say it means to speak in the language of another country or culture. This is not true even though people quote Acts 2:6 to back up what they say. "And when this sound occurred, the multitudes came together, and were confused, because everyone heard them speak in his own language."

This verse does not say the disciples spoke fluently in the different languages of the people who were there. No, they spoke one heavenly language and the scripture says the people "heard" and understood what was being said in their own separate language. The miracle was in the hearing and not the speaking. Understand also that your will is involved in everything you do. 1 Cor. 14:32 says, "And the spirits of the prophets are subject to the prophets." The Holy Spirit doesn't make you do anything you don't want to do. You are not a mindless robot or a puppet on a string. Speaking in tongues is an act of your will and you control if and when you allow this to happen. The words of this heavenly language are not just going to jump out of you on their own. No, you and the Holy Spirit are a team and He will give you the unction to speak but it is up to you to cooperate with Him when this prompting occurs.

Remember, speaking in tongues is a language of the Spirit. It's His language and He gives you the words to say. 1 Cor. 14:2 says, "For he who speaks in a tongue does not speak to men but to God, for no one understands him; however, in the spirit he speaks mysteries." Here it says that no one understands a person who is speaking in tongues yet the people understood on the Day of Pentecost. This is further proof that the miracle was in the hearing and not the speaking. 1 Cor. 14:14 says, "For if I pray in a tongue, my spirit prays, but my understanding is unfruitful." Notice that Paul said "if I pray." He had a choice to pray in tongues or not to pray. His will was involved and so is yours. He also said his understanding was unfruitful. He didn't understand with his mind what was being said but he did it anyway in obedience to God. Vs. 15 says, "What is the conclusion then? I will pray with the spirit, and I will also pray with the understanding. I will sing with the spirit, and I will also sing with the understanding."

This is so very clear that there should be no room for any confusion whatsoever. Paul is saying that when you pray in tongues that your spirit is praying. You can pray with your mind where you understand everything that is being said. Just understand that your mind is very limited in what it can do but your spirit man is not. Your spirit has much more understanding about what's going on in your life than your mind does. This is why those who pray with their mind only have a limited capacity to what they can pray for and this in turn limits what they can receive from God. A lot of believers don't realize this but praying in the Spirit is part of the armor of God. Eph. 6:17,18 says, "And take the helmet of salvation, and the sword of the Spirit, which is the word of God; praying always with all prayer and supplication in the Spirit." The NLT says, "pray in the Spirit at all times and on every occasion." Jude 20 then goes on to say, "But you, beloved, building yourselves up on your most holy faith, praying in the Holy Spirit."

Christians are losing battles because they're not building themselves up spiritually. When they don't pray in the Spirit they're not putting on all of their armor and this leaves an opening for the enemy to come in and hinder their efforts to fulfill their destiny. The enemy knows that when you pray in the Spirit that nothing will be withheld from you. Why is that? Because you're praying the perfect prayer. Your soul isn't praying a selfish prayer but your spirit is praying a Spiritual prayer and there is nothing selfish about the Holy Spirit. This is why you need to submit your tongue to the Holy Spirit every single day and allow Him to pray through you. The language of the Holy Spirit is a heavenly language that is pure and undefiled. There was a time when "the whole earth had one language and one speech" (Gen. 11:1). Adam and Eve had a language that was pure because they talked with God face to face. Sin then entered in and got so bad that God destroyed the entire planet with a flood.

Not long after the time of Noah the people of Babel wanted to build a tower whose top is in the heavens. This was not pleasing to God and He said in Gen. 11:7, "Come, let Us go down and there confuse their language, that they may not understand one another's speech." This is where all the different languages that are in the world today came from. This was not God's perfect will and He said in Zeph. 3:9 what would one day happen, "For then I will restore to the peoples a pure language, that they all may call on the name of the Lord, to serve Him with one accord." This was fulfilled on the Day of Pentecost where Acts 2:1 says, "They were all with one accord in one place." On that day God gave back to the people a pure language that will cause nothing to be withheld from those who pray in the Spirit. Every believer can and should pray in a prayer language to God. Prayer is important to God for when you pray it brings Him into your life and circumstances.

In fact, it is so important that 1 Thess. 5:17 says to "pray without ceasing." You cannot do this with the limitations of a finite mind and this is why believers are told to pray in the Holy Spirit. When you pray in tongues, you are speaking a pure language that you don't understand with your intellect for it is a heavenly language that comes from the Lord above (Acts 2:33). He creates this language and puts it down in your spirit where it becomes your responsibility to speak it out your mouth. Speaking in tongues is a manifestation of the Holy Spirit and 1 Cor. 13:1 calls it the tongues of angels. It is supernatural and only true believers can speak this heavenly language. Paul said in 1 Cor. 14:5, "I wish you all spoke with tongues." This is God speaking to you personally so don't allow others to tell you otherwise. How can you pray without ceasing if you don't first obey God? You need to become like Paul who said in 1 Cor. 14:18, "I thank my God I speak with tongues more than you all."

God wants you to pray to Him in tongues for it causes you to have an intimate and personal time of fellowship with Him. How better to speak to the Heavenly Father than in a heavenly language? This alone should give you the motivation to be filled with the Holy Spirit with the evidence of speaking in tongues. It is a difficult thing to find the right words in a known language to describe to God how you feel about Him. Human words just don't have the capacity to tell God how it is you actually feel. But speaking in a heavenly language will solve that problem for you. God hears and understands what you're saying even if you don't and He is well pleased with what you're telling Him. You can know the subject of what you're saying even though in your mind you don't know precisely what's being said. But that's okay. You're praying in faith and doing precisely what God is telling you to do. For that He is well pleased because as you pray in a heavenly language you are drawing near to Him and now He is drawing near to you (James 4:8).

Speaking in tongues is the key to a spirit-led life. Rom. 8:26 says, "Likewise, the Spirit also helps in our weaknesses. For we do not know what we should pray for as we ought, but the Spirit Himself makes intercession for us with groanings which cannot be uttered." This is why God wants everybody to pray in tongues. Simply put, people don't know what to pray for because of the limitations of the soulish mind. But God knows and this is why He has given you a heavenly language with which you can pray the perfect prayer. The reason many people don't pray in tongues is because they've never been taught the mechanics of how to do it so they turn away frustrated and confused. The first thing you need to understand is that some mythical power is not going to come over you and take control of your vocal cords. No, God has given you a free will and you can speak in tongues if and when you want to. You are the one who is in control of your vocal cords, not God and certainly not the devil.

You choose to speak in tongues the same way you choose to speak in your native language. You have been filled with the Holy Spirit and as an act of your free will you have to move your lips and begin speaking words and sounds out of your mouth. Know ahead of time that you're not going to understand with your mind the words that you're saying but do it anyway. You are speaking a new language, a heavenly language, so of course you're not going to understand it. Don't allow yourself to think this is senseless babbling and gibberish coming out of your mouth. It's not. It's a pure language that God gives you to speak out of the depths of your inner man. If you can get over the initial shock of hearing strange words coming out of your mouth then you are on your way to becoming a powerful Spirit-filled, tongue-talking believer and God is going to use you to do many great and wonderful things in the kingdom.

Know also that many people will try to tell you that what you're doing is foolish and some may no longer wish to associate with you. That's okay. These people have never spoken in tongues and don't know what they're talking about. Speaking in tongues is Biblical and there is scripture and verse commanding you to do it. Will you still go to heaven if you choose not to speak in tongues? Of course you will but why own a car if you don't have a battery that gives it power to operate? That's what being filled with the Holy Spirit and speaking in tongues does for you. Remember, Jesus said you shall receive power when the Holy Spirit comes upon you. There is no power in self-effort. You can put your car in neutral and push it for a while but how far is that going to get you? No, come up higher and speak in a heavenly language that is pure and undefiled and full of power. God is telling you to speak in tongues so use your faith to believe that the words you hear yourself saying are in truth coming from Him.

Also, don't be surprised if at first only one or two words come out of you. A young child learns to speak a word or two at a time and so it is with your heavenly language. Keep at it and keep practicing doing it. God will see your effort and before long entire sentences will be coming out of your mouth. You'll pray for a minute, then ten minutes, then an hour. Before long speaking in tongues will be just as natural as speaking in your native language. God is telling you to speak in tongues and, as you obey Him, in time you will be able to do so without any forethought or meditation. It will just automatically be natural for you to do so. When you speak in your native language you don't meditate for twenty minutes figuring out what to say. No, you know in your mind what you want to say and the words just naturally come out of you. It's automatic for this is what talking is all about. It's the same way with speaking in a heavenly language. It's just like speaking in a known language except now you're speaking in a language from above.

There is no difference if you can get over those mental barriers that will try to confuse you and get you to not obey God in this area. Don't think about what you're doing, just do it. Move your lips and speak knowing that you're doing what God is telling you to do. Words form syllable by syllable and, when a syllable comes to you, speak it out. Syllables turn into words and words turn into sentences. It gets easier with practice but you've got to take the first step. When you first begin to speak in tongues it may seem strange to you but stay in faith and keep doing it anyway. What's happening is that Jesus, through the Holy Spirit, is giving you a heavenly language to speak and He's bypassing your mind and putting these words directly into your spirit. In the upper room the disciples "began to speak with other tongues, as the Spirit gave them utterance" (acts 2:4).

Your mind wants to be in control and this is where the confusion comes in. So relax, take a deep breath, think about Jesus, and then open your mouth and speak out whatever comes to you. It's as simple as that. It's not hard, it's not difficult, and it's not confusing. God's truth was never meant to overwhelm you. It becomes clear when you stop overthinking and start trusting what He has already made plain. All you have to do is learn how to turn your mind off and let the words flow out of your inner man. A baby struggles at first to talk but before long you can't keep them quiet. This is how it should be with your heavenly language. Don't allow your mind and the devil to keep you quiet. Resist the devil and he will flee from you (James 4:7). Then open your mouth and let the words flow out. You can do it so don't let any person or any devil tell you otherwise.

| 19 |

"DESIRE THE BEST GIFTS"

You have been called by God to faithfully serve Him and He sent the Holy Spirit to give you special abilities with which you can accomplish the task He has called you to do. These abilities are called the "gifts of the Spirit" and are listed in 1 Cor. 12:8-10. These gifts include wisdom, knowledge, faith, healing, miracles, prophecy, discerning of spirits, speaking in tongues, and interpretation of tongues. The gifts of the Spirit are simply God enabling you to come up higher - lifting you beyond natural limits so you can walk in His power and purpose. Through these gifts, He equips you to fulfill your God-given destiny and make an eternal impact. 2 Peter 1:3 says, "His divine power has given us everything we need for life and godliness through our knowledge of Him who called us by His own glory and goodness." One of the biggest reasons the church hasn't made a greater impact on the world today is because of its failure to operate in the gifts of the Holy Spirit.

Heb. 2:3,4 says, "How shall we escape if we neglect so great a salvation, which at the first began to be spoken by the Lord, and was confirmed to us by those who heard Him, God also bearing witness both with signs and wonders, with various miracles, and gifts of the Holy Spirit, according to His own will?" One of the first things you need to understand is that the working of the gifts of the Spirit does not come forth from the mind of man but is a supernatural move of the Holy

Spirit in a person's life. The gifts of the Holy Spirit are called that because they're His gifts. 1 Cor. 12:7 says, "But the manifestation of the Spirit is given to each one for the profit of all." You were born to be great but greatness is not for oneself. Greatness comes when you are used by God to operate in the gifts of the Holy Spirit to be a blessing to someone else. These various gifts are handed out to people all over the world and they originate in the Holy Spirit.

You can operate in these gifts but don't go around saying they're your gifts because they're not. You have none of these gifts but the Holy Spirit has all of them and He alone decides which gifts each person should have. Vs. 11 says, "But one and the same Spirit works all these things, distributing to each one individually as He wills." The Message Bible says, "All these gifts have a common origin, but are handed out one by one by the one Spirit of God. He decides who gets what, and when." You have been called to turn your world upside down and if your life is not supernatural then it will only be superficial. Jesus said in Mark 16:17,18 that all believers would flow in the miraculous, "And these signs will follow those who believe: In My Name they will cast out demons; they will speak with new tongues; they will take up serpents; and if they drink anything deadly, it will by no means hurt them; they will lay hands on the sick, and they will recover."

One of the most important steps to flowing in the gifts of the Holy Spirit is to earnestly desire them. Paul said in 1 Cor. 12:31, "But earnestly desire the best gifts." He repeated this thought in 1 Cor. 14:1 when he said to "desire spiritual gifts." The gifts of the Holy Spirit are always flowing but to get them to operate in your life you have to seek them with all your heart and soul. Understand that this is not a suggestion but a command from on high. God does not give you the option of either seeking them or nor seeking them. Once you realize this and desire to flow in the supernatural, you will put yourself in a position where God can use you and He'll release more of His power and ability into your life. God never intended for you to operate in the natural realm. No, He is a supernatural God and He wants you to operate in the supernatural realm.

Speaking in tongues is supernatural and so is operating in the gifts of the Holy Spirit. If you will live spiritually, and not naturally, you will function and operate in that which is beyond yourself. This makes for an exciting life for you will always be watching to see what the Holy Spirit is going to do next. The problem in most churches today is that the people already know what's going to happen next. The outline of the church service is printed out in their bulletin and it is faithfully followed with no room or time given for the moving of the Holy Spirit. These are the services where people constantly glance at their watches, counting down the minutes until they can finally leave. Instead of hearts being stirred, time is being endured and everyone feels it. These churches are operating in the natural and not the supernatural and people leave these services in the same condition as when they went in.

The greatest untapped power in the world today is in the local church. The devil mocks those churches whose doors are only open for an hour a week where the preachers talk for a few minutes and the people sing songs that are four hundred years old. The people have fake smiles on their face and then walk out of these services thankful that their spiritual obligation for that week is over with. They then go home and live like the devil until the following Sunday when they go back to church and play this silly religious game all over again. Is it any wonder that the devil is laughing at these people? He told the sons of Sceva, "Jesus I know, and Paul I know, but who are you?" (Acts 19:15). These people don't know anything about what true Christianity is all about and it's especially sad concerning the hour in which the world is now living. Jesus is coming soon and the true believers get persecuted by the church and are asked to leave when they show an interest in tapping into the power of God.

They know that it's the power of God that will bring the world to its knees so they need to leave that church and go where the Holy Spirit is made to feel welcome. Those who speak in tongues and operate in the gifts of the Spirit are often labeled as being charismatic and that is not a bad thing. The word "gift" comes from the Greek word "charisma" and is defined as 'the instantaneous enablement of the Holy Spirit in the life of any believer to exercise a gift for the edification of others.' The word "charis" means 'grace' and "ma" means 'gift.' Put the two together and the word "charisma" means 'grace gift.' Therefore, if you are charismatic then that means God is using you in a powerful way to minister grace to other people. In fact, according to the Bible, all Christians are charismatic for all believers have gifts God gave them through grace (1 Cor. 12:7). You must be open and willing to be used by God because the next great revival to come to planet Earth will be the revival of the gifts of the Holy Spirit.

What happened in the book of Acts will happen again when believers are willing to come up higher and become charismatic for the purpose of being used by Almighty God on the earth. You can change the world if you want to. All it takes is a heartfelt desire to be used by God and a willingness to flow and operate in the gifts of the Holy Spirit. You must take the time and make an all-out effort to understand what these gifts are because the Holy Spirit never operates in ignorance. These nine gifts are divine and supernatural and if the church operated consistently in these gifts it wouldn't be in the condition it's in today. The church is the most underappreciated institution in the world, not because it lacks power, but because many local churches no longer thrive in the active operation of heaven's gifts. When spiritual gifts are neglected or dormant, the church's God-given influence fades, leaving untapped potential where life, transformation, and impact should abound.

The problem is they don't understand them nor do they desire them as they should. If these gifts were in operation the people would know the future, they would supernaturally know what's happening in the present, faith would abound, hearts would be cleansed, and miracles and divine healings would occur. Each and every service would be packed full with a long line of people standing outside waiting to get in. When this happens, the world will change its attitude toward God and the church. Heb. 6:5 says there are those who "have tasted the good word of God and the powers of the age to come." This verse is saying you don't have to wait until you get to heaven to have some miraculous things happen in your life. You can have the gifts of the Spirit manifested in your life right now but first you must hunger for them and earnestly desire the best gifts. The problem in the church today is that people shy away from things they don't understand.

The Holy Spirit is the most misunderstood person in the Bible as are the manifestations of His power. Still, that is no excuse to stay ignorant in these matters. Paul said in 1 Cor. 12:1, "Now concerning spiritual gifts, brethren, I do not want you to be ignorant." The Message Bible says, "What I want to talk about now is the various ways God's Spirit gets worked into our lives. This is complex and often misunderstood, but I want you to be informed and knowledgeable." Use your faith to believe that knowledge will come as you set out to desire the best gifts. Luke 25:48 says, "And He opened their understanding, that they might comprehend the scriptures." You were born to change the world you live in so become the person God created you to be. Don't let the environment change you to the point you blend in with everybody else. No, you go out in the power of the Holy Spirit and change the environment. You are the light of the world and anything that needs brightened up needs you.

Not only are you to learn about the gifts of the Holy Spirit, you also need to desire the best gifts to be operational in your life. It only stands to reason that you can't desire what you don't know about and this is why Paul said he didn't want you to be ignorant concerning spiritual gifts. The word "spiritual" comes from the Greek word "pneumatikos" and means 'empowered by breath or wind.' On the Day of Pentecost there suddenly came a sound from heaven, as of a rushing mighty wind (Acts 2:2). Paul is saying that he wants you to learn about and operate in those gifts that are empowered by the breath of God. These are the gifts that you can only move in if you allow the Holy Spirit to breath in you. The gifts of the Spirit are for divine communication. They are used to destroy the work of the enemy, to tear down those things that are ungodly. The operation of these gifts will make you a powerhouse for God, an invincible force stronger than any power known on the face of the earth.

God is all powerful and Jesus came to the earth to make you more than a conqueror. It is a shame that so many believers are suffering defeat in their lives. This is not good for if the devil can make you feel defeated then how can you flow in the gifts of the Holy Spirit and tell others that they don't have to be defeated? Jesus operated in all nine gifts of the Holy Spirit and He sent the Comforter so that you might also operate in the same gifts He had. His life was guided and empowered by the Holy Spirit and yours should be as well. The world is waiting for you to step out and be used by God in the operation of these gifts. In other words, the world is waiting for you to fulfill your destiny. Don't put it off a moment longer. Rise up and be all you were meant to be. The world is hungry for the moving of the Holy Spirit and most people in the church today are waiting for someone else to function in these spiritual gifts. They don't realize that the manifestation of the Spirit is given to every person for the profit of all (1 Cor. 12:7).

This verse is talking about you. You need to look inside yourself and ask why you're not operating in the gifts of the Holy Spirit. God is giving you the opportunity to do so and it can happen if you'll have the same attitude as Isaiah who said, "Here am I! Send me" (Is. 6:8). You must have a willingness and an earnest desire for God to use you in this area. If the gifts of the Holy Spirit are not being taught in your church then ask God to lead you to a church that does. Many churches ignore the Holy Spirit completely and those who teach and go there are poor in spirit and will never operate in the fullness of all that God has for them. Now is not the time to play these religious games. God wants your desire to be sincere because if you are to operate in the gifts of the Spirit then everything that pertains to your life must be lined up and in harmony with the supernatural. Don't spend your life seeking fortune and fame and to be friends with the world. No, seek for the power of God to be in operation in your life.

The world and those who claim to be religious will turn their backs on you in an instant but Jesus is a friend who sticks closer than a brother. Paul said in Gal. 1:10 (NIV), "Am I now trying to win the approval of human beings, or of God? Or am I trying to please people? If I were still trying to please people, I would not be a servant of Christ." God has promised to reward your faithfulness and earnest desire by giving you opportunities to flow in the gifts of the Holy Spirit. Don't be satisfied with where you're now at or with what God did through you in the past. No, be hungry for more and more of the Holy Spirit in your life. Desire Him and seek Him out and you'll receive as much power as you have faith for. The wells of His goodness are bottomless and there is no limit to what you can do in and for the kingdom of God when you come up higher and operate in the gifts of the Holy Spirit. Rest assured, God wants you to be a part of this great end-time revival.

Paul said in 1 Cor. 12:31, "But earnestly desire the best gifts. And yet I show you a more excellent way." He then went and wrote an entire chapter about walking in unity and love. You've got to come to a place where you sincerely love and care for people for it's in this type of atmosphere where the great gifts of the Holy Spirit can be demonstrated. The gifts will not flow when there is strife, envy, and criticism among the people. On the Day of Pentecost the disciples "were all with one accord in one place" and this shows that the church was birthed in a spirit of unity. People who quarrel with their family or their fellow church members can be the reason the Holy Spirit doesn't move in that particular church. Some people are negative about almost everything and this spirit of disunity can affect those around them. There is perfect unity in heaven and there needs to be unity in the church on earth.

1 Cor. 12:12 says, "For as the body is one and has many members, but all the members of that one body, being many, are one body, so also is Christ." There is power in unity and the church must not allow strife to come through its doors. A small church with few members can do a mighty work for God if their unity is strong. Jonathan told the young man who bore his armor, "For nothing restrains the Lord from saving by many or by few" (1 Sam. 14:6). The Message Bible says, "There is no rule that says God can only deliver by a big army. No one can stop God from saving when He sets His mind to it." There is no greater plea for unity in the church than in the words Paul wrote in 1 Cor. 12:13 (NLT), "Some of us are Jews, some are Gentiles, some are slaves, and some are free. But we have all been baptized into one body by one Spirit, and we all share the same Spirit." When there is unity, the power of the Holy Spirit will flow and this is why all strife and division must be confronted.

Do not stay in an environment that abounds with disunity, whether it be your place of employment or the local church. Paul also said in Rom. 12:18, "If it is possible, as much as depends on you, live peaceably with all men." Heb. 12:14 (NLT) says, "Work at living in peace with everyone, and work at living a holy life, for those who are not holy will not see the Lord." It is in this spirit of unity that you are to earnestly desire the best gifts. The word "earnest" means 'to be passionate; to contend; to excel; to strongly exert yourself in the pursuit of something you want.' You must desire these gifts and the better you understand them the more you'll unlock their power and the manifestation will abound. God wants you to move in the supernatural and you must not remain ignorant of the gifts of the Holy Spirit and their proper use and purpose. The Holy Spirit is present in every believer to help them fulfill their destiny and do what they are called to do.

Paul said in 1 Cor. 1:7 (NLT), "Now you have every spiritual gift you need as you eagerly wait for the return of the Lord Jesus Christ." The Holy Spirit is moving on the earth today and God is expecting you to cultivate and develop your capacity to flow with Him. Paul told Timothy, "Therefore I remind you to stir up the gift of God which is in you through the laying on of my hands" (2 Tim. 1:6). The words "stir up" means 'to kindle glowing embers back into a roaring fire; to ignite a flame by providing fresh fuel and air.' It takes effort and commitment to gain knowledge and experience in the moving of the Holy Spirit. You can't just sit back and expect all this to happen on its own. It won't. The Holy Spirit only goes and moves where He is made to feel welcome. 1 Cor. 14:12 says you must be "zealous for spiritual gifts." It's the level of your desire that determines how much effort you'll put forth.

If you have a deep passion for the things of God then you will read your Bible and stir your faith up as you believe to receive and operate in the gifts of the Holy Spirit. This deep desire you have brings God on the scene and it's in His presence that the power will flow. As you get still before the Lord know that your spirit is joined to the Holy Spirit (1 Cor. 6:12) and that He will speak to you spirit to spirit. "Deep calls unto deep" (Ps. 42:7). Get alone with God and be still and quiet. Open your heart up and down in your spirit you will perceive that He is talking to you. Do this often and spiritual sensitivity will be developed in your life and you'll know what you're supposed to do and say. Paul told Timothy to "fan into flames the spiritual gift God gave you" (NLT). Paul is saying that the gifts of the Spirit can be activated. This means you can take practical steps that will stir up your faith and energize your spirit to be responsive to the Holy Spirit.

An important foundation for operating in the gifts of the Spirit is to cultivate a strong spirit through prayer, worship, reading the Bible, and pursuing intimacy with God. You need to pray in tongues often for this will energize your inner man. As you pray in tongues the Holy Spirit is moving through you so you need to keep praying until you feel a stirring inside of you. Expect to hear the voice of God for expectation is what draws the Holy Spirit into your life. Don't allow your mind to wander or be distracted but instead focus your full attention on hearing that still, small voice on the inside of you. God will speak to you and at some point you will have to take what appears to be a risk and act upon what you feel the Holy Spirit is showing you. It is God's desire for you to be a channel through which the power of heaven can come to earth and flow into the lives of other people. Have confidence knowing that you can start from wherever you're at right now in your spiritual journey.

Day by day you can grow in intimacy with God and in your faith as you earnestly desire to operate in the gifts of the Holy Spirit. As you make the effort and put into practice those things you've learned, you will quickly find that God is far more willing to work with you than you realize. It is His plan for your life that the kingdom of God get manifested on the earth through you. You are a supernatural person and inside of you is the power of the Holy Spirit. However, that power will not work until you put it to work. Spend time alone with God and allow your prayers to activate the power that is at work inside of you. Eph. 3:16,20 (NCV) says, "I ask the Father in His great glory to give you the power to be strong inwardly through His Spirit. With God's power working in us, God can do much, much more than anything we can ask or imagine." It has been said that the journey of a thousand miles begins with a single step. That vital step is preceded by a decision to move forward.

You can activate these gifts when you acknowledge before God that you are willing to move ahead in this area, and then have the courage to move forward in your journey. Show God that you're serious about this by studying your Bible every day and listening to what He is telling you down in your spirit. Take notes and write down everything God is telling you. The gifts of the Spirit are for the profit of all so develop a lifestyle of encouragement and walk in love with those around you. Exhort people and share scriptures with them that God puts on your heart. As you do this, ask God if there is something He wants to show you or speak to you about that person and the situation they may be in. If so, then down in your spirit you will know what to do or say. If not, keep doing what you're doing and, as you continue to desire the best gifts, the day will come when you'll operate in the supernatural as the Spirit wills.

Learning how to operate in the gifts of the Spirit is not hard or complicated. Everything God does is incredibly simple and all He requires is an open heart to receive and an earnest desire to be used by Him in a powerful way. You don't have to be highly educated to flow in the supernatural. In fact, Paul says in 1 Cor. 1:27, "But God has chosen the foolish things of the world to put to shame the wise, and God has chosen the weak things of the world to put to shame the things that are mighty." God can and will use anybody who has an earnest desire for Him to do so. Go to the Father and tell Him you want to be used by Him believing that your request will be granted. God is looking for and waiting for you to come to Him. 2 Chron. 16:9 says, "For the eyes of the Lord run to and fro throughout the whole earth, to show Himself strong on behalf of those whose heart is loyal to Him." The Message Bible says, "God is always on the alert, constantly on the lookout for people who are totally committed to Him."

God wants to use you and He will when your desire causes you to seek Him with all your heart and soul. You need to live each day with the realization that you have access to the realm of the supernatural. Your body is the temple of the Holy Spirit and your life is to be a gateway through which His power flows into all the world. People in the world today are blinded to the truth of the gospel message and God is calling you to manifest the kingdom of God to everyone around you. Paul prayed in Eph. 3:19 that you would "be filled with all the fullness of God." A cup is not completely full until it is overflowing. Likewise, you are not completely full until the Holy Spirit overflows in your life with great demonstrations of heavenly power and glory. The angel Gabriel told Mary in Luke 1:35. "The Holy Spirit will come upon you, and the power of the Highest will overshadow you." Mary responded by saying, "Let it be to me according to your word" (vs. 38).

You must say the same thing to God for He is ready and willing to use you in a powerful way. It's the Holy Spirit working through you that will bring the manifestation of heaven to the earth. David hit the giant with a smooth stone, you hit the enemy with the gifts of the Spirit. David used what he had and God brought forth the victory. The same thing will happen to you when you learn how to fight and confront the enemy. God can take that which is least and make it big and powerful and victorious. He is a great and mighty God and without the gifts of the Holy Spirit, these gifts of God's power, the church will not be able to win the world from the bondage of the enemy. Without these instruments of God's power it would be the same as trying to defeat a modern army bare-handed and without weapons. To fulfill your destiny you must come up higher and live a supernatural life.

The world is mocking the church today because people have a form of godliness but have no power to back up what they say they believe. These mockers are the very people God is sending you to. Jesus said in Matt. 12;29 (NLT), "For who is powerful enough to enter the house of a strong man like Satan and plunder his goods? Only someone even stronger - someone who could tie him up and then plunder his house." You change the world by sharing with others the gifts God has so graciously given you. 1 Peter 4:10 (NLT) says, "God has given each of you a gift from His great variety of spiritual gifts. Use them well to serve one another." There will one day be millions of believers standing before the judgment seat of Christ who received a special gift from God but they buried it and did not share it with others. Do not allow yourself to be one of these people because each person will one day be held accountable for what they did with the gift God gave them.

It is time to come up higher - leaving behind comfort, complacency, and fear - to walk boldly in faith and obedience. The Lord Jesus Christ is calling you not to be a passive believer, but a dynamic disciple who lives with purpose, power, and unwavering devotion. As you rise to His call, your life becomes a testimony of His truth, love, and transforming grace to the world. It is time to put away those golf clubs and time to stop working so many hours just so you can earn more money to support the lusts of the flesh. It is time to fear the Lord and do what He told you to do. The end is near and God wants you to be a part of the Spirit-filled army of believers from every denominational background who are marching toward the glorious return of Jesus. The gifts of the Holy Spirit are operating in their lives and the world they live in is being turned upside down.

| 20 |

"THE GIFTS OF THE SPIRIT"

The gifts of the Spirit are real, active, and alive, given by God to empower His people today. When you believe, desire, and walk in obedience, these gifts move from doctrine on a page to divine power working through your life. The world around you becomes brighter and the sounds of life have more clarity and meaning. What once felt distant or muted now resonates with purpose, reminding you that you are fully present and alive. The foods you eat taste better and the everyday chores of life bring a joy you never thought possible. You will never possess what you refuse to desire, so allow your heart to be awakened by what God has promised. Stir yourself up and let a holy hunger rise within you - a hunger that refuses to settle for less than God's best. As you hunger and thirst for the gifts of the Spirit, trust that God is faithful to fill every longing He has placed inside you.

There are nine gifts of the Holy Spirit listed in 1 Cor. 12:8-10. There are three categories of gifts and three gifts per category. The number three is the number of divine perfection in the Word of God. Nine is three times three, perfection times perfection. There are revelation gifts that allow you to supernaturally see and know things that you could not know unless the Spirit revealed them to you. There are gifts of power that allow you to do miraculous things that no human could ever do on their own. And then there are speaking gifts where you say things by inspiration from God that didn't come from your own intellect. All nine gifts of the Spirit are perfect, they are all supernatural, and they are all operating in the world today. As it was in the acts of the apostles, so should the gifts of the Spirit be in manifestation in the here and now. Take time to study the book of Acts and you will find over fifty demonstrations of the gifts of the Spirit.

Put yourself in their shoes and believe that you will be used by God and do even greater things than they did. Once again, there are revelation gifts, power gifts, and inspiration gifts. God wants you to be inspired because you can't have any power without inspiration. At the same time, you can't have any inspiration without some form of revelation. There is unity in the gifts of the Spirit for they all work together. Through these nine gifts the Holy Spirit is continually revealing something, doing something, or saying something. It is your responsibility to desire these gifts and to operate in them and then trust the Holy Spirit to distribute "to each one individually as He wills" (1 Cor. 12:11). He will not use everybody in the same way and people get into trouble when they decide for themselves what it is they want to do. This is why you have to say to the Lord, "Not my will, but Your will be done."

The Bible says you are to earnestly desire to operate in these gifts which means you have a responsibility to ask for them. Yes, the Holy Spirit decides what gifts He gives and to whom He gives them but that is not supposed to stop you from asking Him for these gifts. God has given you the opportunity to do so and asking for them is your right as a born again believer. These gifts are special endowments of supernatural power and energy and the Holy Spirit won't even consider using you in these gifts unless the desire is first there. It is God's plan and will to use you in a mighty way and you already have the power inside of you to move in signs, wonders, and the gifts of the Holy Spirit. One way that you show God you earnestly desire to be used by Him is to study the Bible so that you can understand the correct operation of the nine gifts of the Spirit. You must not be spiritually lazy but grow in faith and continually express your desire to God that you want to be used by Him here in His kingdom on the earth.

God does not want you to just sit back and watch others do all the work of the ministry. No, you are in the army of the Lord and the Spirit anoints you to participate and join in on the fight. You've been called to wage war against the enemy and not just sit down and watch others do it. Your part is to be open to God and to be sensitive to the leading of the Holy Spirit. If you're not obedient to the voice of God then you will probably not see a great measure of the gifts operating through you. Submit to God believing that when He gives you something to do, the Holy Spirit will come and equip you for the task at hand. The key is not to focus on the gifts, but to focus on the One giving the gifts. There is nothing more important than your relationship with God. You get closer to Him by spending quality time alone with Him and by doing what He tells you to do. Your approach to spiritual gifts must be God-centered and, the closer you get to Him, the more you will find Him using you in the gifts of the Spirit.

This happens as you earnestly desire for Him to use you more effectively for His purposes and His glory. Paul said in 1 Cor. 12:31 to "earnestly desire the best gifts." The most important gift is the gift you need at the time you need it. All the gifts of the Spirit are for the benefit of the church and not the individual operating in the gifts. They are always associated with human need and are not restricted to the Sunday morning church service. You can flow in the gifts of the Spirit at home, at work, or at the shopping mall. Wherever there is a need, the Holy Spirit wants to use you to help meet that need. All nine gifts operate through faith in the lives of Spirit-filled believers who are readily obedient to the leading of the Holy Spirit. Gal. 5:6 says faith works through love and, as you fulfill the command to love your neighbor as you love yourself (Mark 12:31), down in your heart will come the desire to tell others about Jesus so they can grow and be strong and experience His presence with you.

Pursuing love and desiring spiritual gifts always go together. Love is the aim of all these gifts and, if you don't earnestly desire and pursue them, then you are neglecting some aspect of your love walk and Christ is not glorified. All the gifts of the Spirit are necessary, they are all good, and all of them will change your life and the lives of those in the church. God is all powerful and it is a humbling thought that He wants to use you as a channel to bless this hurting and dying world. One of the ways in which He will use you is through the inspirational gift of prophecy. The Holy Spirit is the voice of God and the words He tells you to speak are powerful and highly anointed. Words inspired by the Holy Spirit can change nations, churches, and the lives of individual people. By faith you know that you know the words you're speaking are coming from the Holy Spirit and not your own intellect.

2 Peter 1:21 says "for prophecy never came by the will of man, but holy men of God spoke as they were moved by the Holy Spirit." The gift of prophecy is a spontaneous message given by the Holy Spirit to a believer to speak forth the mind and counsel of God to a specific person or group of people at a specific time. Words of prophecy should be spoken with enthusiasm and excitement for they are given to build up and not tear down. The Hebrew word for "prophecy" means 'to flow forth, to bubble forth like a fountain, to let drop, to life up, to tumble forth, and to spring forth.' In Greek the word means 'to speak for another' so the word "prophecy" means to speak for God or to be His spokesman. The gift of prophecy should not be confused with the office of a prophet where God uses someone to foretell the future. Paul said in 1 Cor. 14:3, "But he who prophesies speaks edification and exhortation and comfort to men."

Prophecy is inspired utterance and goes beyond speaking by your own reasoning and intellect. God will use you to tell things to people that will promote their spiritual growth and to comfort them and give them hope in time of grief or pain. When the gift of prophecy flows there is a change in the atmosphere for the better. Prophecy is never used to scold or rebuke people and if there is any discomfort then the words spoken were not the gift of prophecy. Putting people down does not promote spiritual growth but when a person is built up and made to feel better they'll be motivated to press forward into the good things of God. The gift of prophecy brings comfort to the heart and it heals the wounds of the past. This gift is so important that Paul says in 1 Cor. 14:1, "Pursue love and desire spiritual gifts, but especially that you may prophesy." God wants every believer to be a light to a dark and hurting world and that includes you.

All people can prophesy but you must have a passion to do so. Be sensitive to the Holy Spirit and down inside of you words of encouragement will bubble up and will be expressed through the words you speak. As you respond to this unction, more words will flow out of you like a sweet flowing river and people will be blessed as a result of what you say to them. When words of prophesy are spoken the presence of God is present and lives get changed for the better. People feel His love and their lives are touched in a meaningful way. They believe God is speaking directly to them which, in fact, He is doing through the words He is telling you to say to them. You are God's spokesman, entrusted with words that carry heaven's authority and life-changing power. When you speak in alignment with His truth, your voice becomes a vessel through which God Himself reaches hearts, transforms lives, and releases His will into the world.

The other two inspirational gifts are speaking in tongues for public ministry and the interpretation of what was spoken. The gift of tongues is not the prayer language of the Spirit-filled believer but is an anointed message given by the Holy Spirit in a language the speaker has not learned. The gift of tongues is a supernatural sign, it's a vocal miracle of the Holy Spirit that should be accompanied by an interpretation. Your prayer language is used when you talk to God but the gift of tongues is when God talks to people. 1 Cor. 14:5 (NLT) says, "I wish you could all speak in tongues, but even more I wish you could all prophesy. For prophesy is greater than speaking in tongues, unless someone interprets what you are saying so that the whole church will be strengthened." What Paul is saying here is that to speak with tongues and to interpret the tongues is equivalent to prophecy.

The reason prophecy is the most important of these three gifts is because it doesn't require another gift to complete it. Prophesy is a supernatural utterance in a known tongue whereas interpretation of tongues is a supernatural revelation of what was said in an unknown tongue. The gift of tongues is energized by the Holy Spirit and it is the responsibility of the believer to speak out when the Holy Spirit comes upon them. Understand that the Holy Spirit is a true gentleman and He does everything decently and in order (1 Cor. 14:40). Never will He have a person stand up in a church service and interrupt the pastor while he's teaching an anointed message. The gift of tongues operates only as the Spirit wills and nobody should try to operate this gift in the public assembly without the unction of the Holy Spirit. The Holy Spirit will never interrupt Himself and this is why it is so imperative that time be given in the church service for Him to move.

After a time of praise and worship would be a good moment for the entire congregation to be still and quiet as they invite the Holy Spirit to move in their midst. It is during this time of giving Him reverence that He will move in a person and have them speak a specific message to that group of people in an unknown tongue. When this happens continue to remain still and quiet for the Holy Spirit will move on the speaker or someone else to give the interpretation of what was spoken. The church is edified when someone speaks with other tongues in a public service and there is an interpretation. So order can be maintained Paul said in 1 Cor. 14:27,28, "If anyone speaks in a tongue, let there be two or at the most three, each in turn, and let one interpret. But if there is no interpreter, let him keep silent in church, and let him speak to himself and to God."

Chaos would abound if thirty people all stood up and began to speak in tongues and Paul is simply saying that not more than two or three people should speak in a service. He is also saying that there should be no prolonged praying in tongues in public services if there is no interpretation because the people won't know what's being said and won't be edified. People who operate in these gifts need to know how to use what they've been given to the greatest advantage so that the people are blessed and edified. The key is to remain sensitive to the Holy Spirit, allowing His guidance to shape every word, action, and decision. When we yield to Him, all things are done decently and in order, bringing clarity, peace, and lasting fruit to everything we put our hands to. God is not the author of confusion and when order is maintained the people get blessed in a greater measure.

The revelation gifts of the Spirit are a word of wisdom, a word of knowledge, and the discerning of spirits. God has all wisdom and all knowledge and He doesn't reveal to anybody everything He knows. Ps. 147:5 says, "Great is our Lord, and mighty in power, His understanding is infinite." There is no such thing as a gift of wisdom and a gift of knowledge. Some people think Solomon's wisdom was a manifestation of the word of wisdom but it wasn't. Yes, God did give Solomon wisdom but that was in line with James 1:5, "If any of you lacks wisdom, let him ask of God, who gives to all liberally and without reproach, and it will be given to him." There is wisdom that is gained through the knowledge of God's Word but that is not the supernatural manifestation of the gift of the word of wisdom. What God does do through these gifts is impart a small portion of what He knows to His people thus giving them a "word" of His wisdom and a "word" of His knowledge.

These gifts are given to a person as the Spirit wills inferring that not everyone is going to have these manifestations whereas everybody can gain wisdom and knowledge from the study of the Word of God. Operating in these revelation gifts has nothing to do with academic excellence or how many college degrees you may have obtained. It's true, God does not bless ignorance but the knowledge He does bless and move in is that what you've learned pertaining to the Word of God. This knowledge, along with an earnest desire, is what moves the hand of God. All these gifts are supernatural and they produce results that can be perceived with your senses and are always on a level higher than what you can achieve with your own natural ability and intellect. Of the three revelation gifts the word of wisdom is listed first for it is the greatest gift of all, bringing forth revelation about the divine plan and purpose of God. If the church today operated in this gift it could change the world.

Paul said in 1 Cor. 2:6,7, "However, we speak wisdom among those who are mature, yet not the wisdom of this age, nor of the rulers of this age, who are coming to nothing. But we speak the wisdom of God in a mystery, the hidden wisdom which God ordained before the ages for our glory." The Message Bible says, "God's wisdom is something mysterious that goes deep into the interior of His purpose." A word of wisdom is a fragment of God's wisdom with which He'll tell you what the future will look like, often going into great detail so there will be no doubt that the revelation came from Him. The word of knowledge deals with the past or present whereas the word of wisdom always speaks of the future. In the Old Testament Noah received a word of wisdom being told of God's future judgment on the world through a flood. God spoke to Joseph through dreams concerning his own future and gave Pharaoh a dream foretelling a coming drought in Egypt.

God spoke to Jonah and gave him a word of wisdom saying that Nineveh was going to be destroyed if the people didn't repent and turn to God. In Acts 9 the Lord told Ananias to go pray for Paul who was blinded on the road to Damascus. The Lord said to him, "Go, for he is a chosen vessel of Mine to bear My name before Gentiles, kings, and the children of Israel" (vs. 9). This was a divine revelation of what Paul was eventually going to do for the Lord. It was a word of wisdom because it looked toward the future and revealed the plans and purposes of God. Again it needs to be emphasized that the word of wisdom is not the same thing as having wisdom that shows you what to do or how to deal with a specific situation. This type of wisdom that shows you what steps you should take in the affairs of life is not a spiritual gift. Yes, it is wisdom that comes from above but it is not the supernatural manifestation of the gift of the word of wisdom.

The word of wisdom always looks to the future. For example, Jesus said "In three days I will arise" and He later told the disciples "You shall receive power when the Holy Spirit has come upon you." This was the word of wisdom operating in the life of Jesus. What some people call prophecy is really a word of wisdom in manifestation. God may use the office of a prophet to predict future events but his prophetic words are just the vehicle through which the word of wisdom comes. Also, be sure to stay humble if and when the Holy Spirit uses you in this gift and don't get puffed up thinking that you are now some holier-than-thou prophet. When pride rises and we become high-minded, we close ourselves off from the flow of the Spirit, because God entrusts His power to the humble. Stay low before Him, and the supernatural gifts will continue to operate through a surrendered and obedient heart.

The second revelation gift is the word of knowledge and it is a supernatural revelation concerning people, places, or things and deals with the past or present. It's when the Holy Spirit allows you to know something specific without having learned it by natural means. Jesus operated in the word of knowledge when He told the woman at the well of Samaria that she had been married five times and the man she was now with was not her husband (John 4:17,18). The Holy Spirit revealed this to Him for Jesus had no way of knowing this on His own.

Remember, Jesus lived as a man but operated and ministered in the power of the Holy Spirit. Peter was also used in this gift when he supernaturally knew that Ananias and Sapphira were lying to the congregation about giving the church the full price they had received for the land they had recently sold (Acts 5:1-11). On the Isle of Patmos, John was in the Spirit on the Lord's day and Jesus revealed to him in a vision the condition of the seven churches in Asia Minor (Rev. 1-3).

John couldn't possibly have known what was going on in these churches but Jesus revealed to him their spiritual condition. This was a word of knowledge. The word of knowledge uncovers the true situation as seen from God's perspective and enables you to minister more effectively to the needs of people. It is vitally important that you remain still and stay in God's presence when this revealed fact is given to you. You don't want to run off and get ahead of God by telling people what you think they need to hear. No, wait on God and allow Him to open the door of communication between you and that other person. Be led by the Spirit because no matter how important the words are that you want to say, they won't be received unless you know how and when to say them. Words spoken at the wrong time with the wrong tone of voice can do more harm than good. Wait on God and then with a spirit of meekness minister to the needs of the person in front of you.

The gift of discerning of spirits reveals the kind of spirit that is in operation behind a particular event. To discern something means "to perceive by seeing or hearing" and this gift gives you supernatural insight into the spirit world. In Acts 16:16-18 a girl with a spirit of divination followed Paul around for many days thus making him greatly annoyed. He discerned the presence of an evil spirit in her and he turned and commanded the demon to come out of her. This was the gift of discerning of spirits and not the gift of discernment. There is no gift in the Bible called the gift of discernment and people who falsely believe they have this gift are actually being influenced by a spirit of criticism. They are critical of other people and believe their opinion is God's opinion when it's not. They cover up their behavior by saying they have the gift of discernment and this is a lie from the devil himself. There is no such gift and these people need to remember that love "covers a multitude of sins" (1 Peter 4:8).

The divine purpose of this special gift is to discern the spirit that motivates a person, whether it be a good spirit from God or an evil spirit from the devil. There are wolves in sheep's clothing and the veil that covers the unseen world is lifted and the schemes and deceptions of the enemy are exposed. Just remember that this gift is not the ability to discern the faults of others. Matt. 7:1 says, "Judge not, that you be not judged." This gift is called the discerning of spirits because its revelation is limited to a single group of objects. It deals with spirits that exist in the spirit realm whether they are divine, satanic, or human. When this gift is in operation, the Holy Spirit may tell you that a demonic spirit is coming against your family and business and this in turn will give you direction and clarity on what to pray for. Never forget that the devil works overtime when the body of Christ does nothing. Wake up and realize the potential you have to tear down the kingdom of darkness through the operation of this gift.

There are three spiritual gifts that do something and these power gifts are the gift of faith, the gifts of healings, and the working of miracles. The gift of faith is not the same faith that comes by hearing and hearing by the word of God (Rom. 10:17). Normal faith comes from hearing a promise of God whereas the gift of faith comes from a sudden impartation by the Holy Spirit. Yes, the faith you got saved with is 'the gift of God" (Eph. 2:8) but it is not one of the nine gifts of the Spirit. The gift of faith is a special faith that enables a person to receive a miracle beyond the capacity of ordinary faith to receive. It is given as the Spirit wills so that a person can receive a miracle whereas the gift of the working of miracles is given to a believer that he might receive faith to work miracles. One gift receives, the other ministers to another person.

The gift of faith doesn't work a miracle but passively receives a miracle. Those who operate in the gift of faith can believe God in such a way that God will honor their word as His own and, as a result of that, miracles happen. The gift of faith is in operation when God, through the power of the Holy Spirit, performs supernatural exploits for a person when there is no human strength or intellect involved. God does the work and you receive the miracle. Throughout the Bible the gift of faith was given to people who were in danger and through this gift they possessed a quiet assurance that was supernatural. The three Hebrew children had this gift when they were thrown into the fiery furnace as did Jesus when He slept in the back of the boat in the midst of a raging storm. Scripture tells how Daniel was placed in a den of lions and immediately he mastered the situation. A force radiated out of him that caused the lions to lay down and do him no harm. This force was the gift of faith that God supernaturally gave to him.

Daniel didn't do anything except receive it and soon he laid down and went to sleep in the midst of his hairy friends. In the face of danger Daniel slept in perfect peace and calm assurance and Dan. 6:23 then says, "Daniel was taken up out of the den, and no manner of hurt was found upon him, because he believed in his God." The gift of faith expects great things from God. It looks not at a promise in the Word but to the One who makes the promise. It is an elevated level of faith that releases God's power beyond normal expectations. It is given by God for supernatural results in a specific situation. With the gift of faith David boldly and confidently told the giant, "This day the Lord will deliver you into my hand" (1 Sam. 17:46). It was this same gift of faith that gave Elijah his victory over the prophets of Baal (1 Kings 18). God will supernaturally do things for you that you couldn't do on your own and then He'll perform miracles through you to bless other people.

The gifts of healings and the working of miracles are both supernatural events with supernatural outcomes. Acts 5:12 says, "And through the hands of the apostles many signs and wonders were done among the people." A miracle can be defined as a supernatural intervention by God that interrupts, disregards, and displaces the natural laws of nature. These power gifts interrupt the way things naturally occur. When these power gifts are in operation there will be an explosion of divinity that reaches beyond the human and natural laws of nature. It reaches into the supernatural world of God where His power, operating through you, intervenes in the ordinary course of daily living. The gifts of healings have nothing to do with medical science or human learning. Doctors and medical science can help bring about natural means of healing but the power gifts of healings are supernatural. Divine healing comes by laying on of hands, anointing with oil, or sometimes just by speaking the Word over the situation.

The gifts of healings were prominent in the life of Jesus and the rest of the New Testament saints and its purpose was to deliver the sick and destroy the works of the devil in the human body. Notice that both the words "gifts" and "healings" are plural. Science will tell you that there are thirty-nine types of diseases in the world, and God provides a gift of healing for each one. Also, according to Old Testament law, it is believed that Jesus received thirty-nine stripes on His back, one stripe for each disease (see Deut. 25:1-3; 2 Cor. 11:24). The word "miracle" comes from the Greek word 'dunamis' and is defined as God's miraculous, wonder-working power. The working of miracles is allowing the mighty power of God to work and flow through you. Earnestly desire to be an instrument on the earth of this great power. Ask Him to use you to do things that other people say can't be done.

Jesus said in John 14:12, "Most assuredly, I say to you, he who believes in Me, the works that I do he will do also; and greater works than these he will do, because I go to the Father." Jesus promised that after He returned to the Father, He would send the Holy Spirit to indwell those who believe. The greater works that can be done today is the direct result of the Spirit working in and through those who earnestly desire for Him to do so. The gifts of healings and the working of miracles should be a common occurrence in the world today. God is real and His power is real. Just as real as all that is God's desire to use you to flow and operate in all nine gifts of the Spirit. Submit yourself fully to Him, earnestly desiring that He would use your life for His glory and purposes. Then step back in faith and watch what He will do for surely what unfolds will be nothing short of miraculous.

| 21 |

"A MATTER OF HONOR"

What time is it? It is time to honor God like never before. The world as we know it is rapidly coming to an end and the return of Jesus is upon us. God wants to do many great things on the earth before this glorious event but the church isn't cooperating. Scripture reveals that before God would manifest Himself in times past He would first tell the people to get ready and to prepare their hearts for what He was about to do. As a whole, the church is not doing this today for the people do not have the same reverence for God that believers had in recent generations. A lack of reverence reveals a lack of faith and Heb. 11:6 says that "without faith it is impossible to please God." God always responds to faith and He will also respond when you give Him the reverence and honor that He so richly deserves. When you draw near to God, He will draw near to you (James 4:8). Why settle for less than what God has for you?

Don't be like those people who don't mind being a Christian as long as it don't interfere with their lives. No, it's time to honor God like never before. There is more to the Christian life than going to church for a few minutes on Sunday morning. The manifested presence of God should be in your life seven days a week. You should feel His presence and communicate with Him in your house, in your car, at the grocery store, and at the workplace. Honoring Him should be the first thing you do when you wake up and the last thing you do when you go to bed. God needs to become real to you and Jesus needs to become more than just a picture you hang on the wall. People need to walk by you and sense that there is something different about you. There is a peace and a calm about you that nobody else has. For some reason you're happy all the time and the cares of this world never get you down. You're just different than everybody else around you.

People want what you have but don't want to do what you do in order to get it. These are the people who wish the church service would hurry up and get over so they can go home and watch the ballgame on TV or gossip on the telephone all afternoon. What does God think about all this? He said in 1 Sam. 2:30, "For those who honor Me I will honor, and those who despise Me shall be lightly esteemed." The BBE says, "I will give honor to those by whom I am honored, and those who have no respect for Me will be of small value in My eyes." The universal law of sowing and reaping is found in this verse. If you honor God, He will honor you and the greatest way He does that is with His glorious presence. He talked to Moses about going into the Promised Land and said to him, "My presence will go with you, and I will give you rest" (Ex. 33:14). Moses then said, "If Your presence does not go with us, do not bring us up from here" (vs. 15).

This is how it should be in your life. You shouldn't even want to get out of bed in the morning unless the presence of God is manifested in your life. Life just has no meaning without God in it and, thankfully, there are things you can do that will initiate a greater manifestation of His presence in your life. No, you don't have to wait for God to move for it is He who is waiting for you to move. They don't realize it but the presence of God is what the drug addicts and the alcoholics and the lovers of money are all searching for. You are a spiritual being, God is the "Father of spirits" (Heb. 12:9), and His presence is what your heart is craving for. You can have all the riches in the world and still feel empty and at unrest if the presence of God is not manifested in your life. David, great as he was, earnestly prayed, "Do not cast me away from Your presence, and do not take Your Holy Spirit from me" (Ps. 51:11).

Jesus prayed to the Father and Heb. 5:7 (NLT) says, "And God heard His prayers because of His deep reverence for God." The NIV says, "He was heard because of His reverent submission." You reverence God by yielding to Him and by being in subjection to Him and this is what brings about a greater manifestation of His presence in your life. Those who are not close to God have some form of rebellion in their life and God will not draw near to somebody who is in defiance to His will and authority. Jesus submitted to the Father and for this reason He could say in John 10:30, "I and the Father are one." The more you respect somebody, the more access you give them to your life. Those who are proud and rebellious are limited in what God can do in their life for they have closed the door on the presence of God. Like Joshua at Jericho, you need to knock down those walls of rebellion and begin to reverence God with all your heart and soul.

If you'll do that, you are giving Him an open invitation to move in your midst and to make His presence known to you. Become like Obadiah who "feared the Lord greatly" (1 Kings 18:3). People who know God and have had some experience with Him will reverence Him in a greater measure than those who only have a passing knowledge of who He is. Jesus was close to the Father because He submitted His will to the will of the Father. In order to reverence God you must do the same thing. Heb. 12:28,29 says, "Therefore, since we are receiving a kingdom which cannot be shaken, let us have grace, by which we may serve God acceptably with reverence and godly fear. For our God is a consuming fire." The Message Bible says God is "actively cleaning house, torching all that needs to burn, and He won't quit until it's all cleansed."

You can't be casual when it comes to honoring God. In today's world people go to church dressed like they're going to the beach. Even ministers look sloppy when they preach in sandals and wear pants with holes ripped in them. People say God still loves them no matter what clothes they wear. That's true, but this is not about clothes and love. This is about the condition of your heart and your attitude toward your Lord and Savior. How you present yourself is a reflection of what's inside of you and know with certainty that there is nothing casual about honoring God. Church is not the place to wear tank tops while you're chewing gum and clipping your fingernails and sending a text to your best friend. People are always disrespecting God and then turn around and make excuses for why they're doing so. People have crossed the line and have become too casual and too loose in their appearance and attitude toward the things of God and it is costing them dearly.

Remember, God honors those who honor Him. God is awesome and worthy to be praised and honored. Tell Him every day how much He means to you and then go out and serve Him with reverence and godly fear. God is asking, "Where's My respect?" He said in Mal. 1:6, "A son honors his father, and a servant his master. If then I am the Father, where is My honor? And if I am a Master, where is My reverence? Says the Lord of hosts to you priests who despise My name." It should touch your heart to hear the Lord ask this question. Live your life in such a way that God will never ask this question to you. Stop being casual in your approach to God and give Him honor morning, noon, and night. Honor Him with your substance, honor Him with your time, honor Him with your words and actions. Honoring God is what causes you to come up higher where you'll have greater influence in the world in which you live.

If you will honor God then He will honor you with His manifested presence and along with that comes the power and ability to fulfill your destiny. It's all a matter of honor for honor is what makes God who He is. When you honor God, you touch Him on the inside for He is honor. Honor and glory go together, and Paul said in 1 Cor. 10:31 (NLT), "Whatever you do, do it all for the glory of God." Rom.

13:7 says, "Render therefore to all their due: taxes to whom taxes are due, customs to whom customs, fear to whom fear, honor to whom honor." The GWT says, "Pay everyone what you owe them. If you owe taxes, pay them. If you owe tolls, pay them. If you owe someone respect, respect that person. If you owe someone honor, honor that person." You owe God a debt of honor and it needs to be paid in full. It is a wicked thing to not pay what you owe. Ps. 37:21 says, "The wicked borrows and does not repay."

You need to pay what you owe. You owe God respect and honor so give it to Him and don't be casual about it. If God is important to you then make a big deal out of the reverence you give Him. Do not be like those who today are suffering the effects of the previous generation of people who were rebellious and wanted to have free love and go off and do their own thing. These people are described in 2 Tim. 3:1,2 (GWT), "In the last days there will be violent periods of time. People will be selfish and love money. They will brag, be arrogant, and use abusive language. They will curse their parents, show no gratitude, have no respect for what is holy." A lack of respect is a common trait in today's evil and wicked generation. People tend to think of themselves as gods in their own right, so they think they don't have to respect anybody. Paul says, "From such people turn away!" (2 Tim. 3:5). God says to give honor to whom honor is due and nobody deserves more honor than the Lord Himself.

It's a matter of honor so come up higher and give God His just due. There is a price to pay for not honoring God for, if you don't honor Him, He won't honor you. If you want more of the presence of God manifested in your life, then honor Him more and more each and every day. This is not about following rules and regulations, it's about how valuable and how precious God is to you. When God is important to you, it shows in the way you talk and how you conduct yourself in front of other people. Phil. 2:13 (MSG) says, "Be energetic in your life of salvation, reverent and sensitive before God. That energy is God's energy, an energy deep within you, God Himself willing and working at what will give Him the most pleasure." The key to living a good life is to learn what's important and what's not important. Some things are precious and valuable while other things are completely worthless. Some things you need to pursue with all your heart and soul and other things you need to run away from with all your might.

When you honor God, He will give you the wisdom to know what to do and what not to do. You become a person of substance with great influence in the world when you choose to value and honor the right things. What or who you highly esteem reveals who you are on the inside and it all comes down to how much you honor the Lord your God. 1 Sam. 13:14 says, "The Lord has sought for Himself a man after His own heart." Does this describe you? If so, you need to learn as much as you can on how to give God reverence and glory. Regarding the book of the law Deut. 17:19 says, "And it shall be with him, and he shall read it all the days of his life, that he may learn to fear the Lord his God and be careful to observe all the words of this law and these statutes." You need to learn how to fear the Lord and how to give Him honor. Jesus said in Mark 4:24, "Take heed what you hear. With the same measure you use, it will be measured to you; and to you who hear, more will be given."

The NLT says, "The closer you listen, the more understanding you will be given." How you hear is measured by how much value and reverence you give to what you're listening to. This is what determines how much revelation you'll receive along with the manifested presence of God. Stop being in such a hurry when you go to church on Sunday hoping the service will soon get over with so you can go home and have a cookout on the backyard grill. God deserves more honor than that. If this is how people feel then why go to church in the first place? They're certainly not fooling God. 1 Sam. 16:7 says, "For man looks at the outward appearance, but the Lord looks at the heart."

People with dignity read their Bible and go to church for the purpose of learning how to fear the Lord and how to give Him reverence and honor. And when they learn it, they then do it with all their heart and soul.

Ps. 33:8 says, "Let all the earth fear the Lord; Let all the inhabitants of the world stand in awe of Him." People are to praise the Lord but standing in awe of Him goes deeper than that. It's giving Him glory and recognition for who He is and for all He has done that allows you to stand in awe of Him. Ps. 89:7 says, "God is greatly to be feared in the assembly of the saints, and to be held in reverence by all those who are around Him." God will honor you with His presence and you are to honor Him with your presence. Commit yourself to seek the Lord every minute of every day. If you'll do that, Jer. 29:13 says, "And you will seek Me and find Me, when you search for Me with all your heart." When you give your all to God, He will give His all to you. When you honor God, He will honor you. What do you think your life would be like if you were publicly honored by God?

God is expecting you to be completely committed to Him and, when that happens, His will for your life will be done just as it is in heaven. He will honor you and you'll live a good life basking in the fullness of God and the manifestation of His presence. You honor God when you surrender your will to Him and your purpose for living lines up with His eternal purpose for your life. The highest form of honor is to lay your life into His loving hands and to fully trust Him at all times. Boaz said to Ruth, "The Lord repay your work, and a full reward be given you by the Lord God of Israel, under whose wings you have come for refuge" (Ruth 2:12). Boaz was saying that when you honor God, He will honor you. God is a jealous God and His jealousy has to do with His honor. When He closed up the Red Sea, He said in Ex. 14:18, "Then the Egyptians shall know that I am the Lord, when I have gained honor for Myself over Pharaoh, his chariots, and his horsemen."

Your body is the temple of the Holy Spirit, and the house of God should be a place where God is truly honored. David wrote in Ps. 26:8, "Lord, I have loved the habitation of Your house, and the place where Your honor dwells." When Christians walk in fear and worry about the economy, they are in fact dishonoring the Lord before the eyes of this wicked world. It's a dishonor to His name when people murmur and make Him out to be powerless against what's going on around them. Another way to honor God is with the words you speak. Saying the right things can honor God just like saying the wrong things dishonor Him. The Jews accused Jesus of being a Samaritan and having a demon to which He responded, "I do not have a demon, but I honor My Father, and you dishonor Me" (John 8:49). Words are important and they are powerful. Prov. 18:21 says, "Death and life are in the power of the tongue" so watch what you say and think before you speak.

Whether or not you are honoring God is revealed by the words that come out of your mouth. Jesus said in Matt. 12:33,34 (NLT), "A tree is identified by its fruit. If a tree is good, its fruit will be good. If a tree is bad, its fruit will be bad. You brood of snakes! For whatever is in your heart determines what you say." The next time you speak remember that what's at stake here is the honor of God. Make sure your words line up with the honor of God that's in your heart. Vs. 35 (NLT) says, "A good person produces good things from the treasury of a good heart, and an evil person produces evil things from the treasury of an evil heart." You, and you alone, are responsible for the words that come out of your mouth. When you say something bad about somebody, you are dishonoring God. When you murmur and complain, God also is not honored.

This is why Paul said in Eph. 4:29, "Let no corrupt communication proceed out of your mouth, but what is good for necessary edification, that it may impart grace to the hearers." The Message Bible says, "Say only what helps, each word a gift." Paul is saying to use your words as a means of ministering grace to other people whereby you'll be able to help meet a need and build up the faith of those you're speaking to. Use your words to communicate happiness, to cheer up the faint-hearted, and to inspire those who are discouraged. Eliphaz paid Job a great compliment when he said, "When someone stumbled, weak and tired, your words encouraged him to stand" (Job 4:4 TEV). Solomon spoke of words such as these in Prov. 25:11, "A word fitly spoken is like apples of gold in settings of silver." The same God who gave birds the power of song gave you the power of speech so use your words to bring honor to His name.

Jesus said in Matt. 12:34, "For out of the abundance of the heart the mouth speaks." What is in the well of your heart will always come up in the bucket of your mouth. Your words will minister either grace or disgrace to people so watch what you say knowing that every careless word you have spoken will someday come back to haunt you. Jesus continued, "But I say to you that for every idle word men may speak, they will give account of it in the day of judgment. For by your words you will be justified, and by your words you will be condemned" (vs. 36,37). Wisdom is knowing when to speak your mind and when to mind your speech. People will fight for the right to say what they want not realizing that Prov. 10:19 says, "In the multitude of words sin is not lacking, but he who restrains his lips is wise." The minds of most people are like wagons: the lighter the load, the noisier they sound.

Watch what you say and honor God with the words you speak. Col. 4:6 says, "Let your speech always be with grace, seasoned with salt, that you may know how you ought to answer each one." Not only can you honor God with your speaking, you can also honor Him with your hearing. Jesus said in Luke 10:16, "He who hears you hears Me, he who rejects you rejects Me, and he who rejects Me rejects Him who sent Me." You need to be able to recognize those people God sends into your life who have come to give you a word from the Lord above. If you will listen to what they have to say and give them honor, by doing so you will also be giving honor to God. James 1:19 says, "Therefore, my beloved brethren, let every man be swift to hear, slow to speak, slow to wrath." The Message Bible says, "Post this at all intersections, dear friends: Lead with your ears, follow up with your tongue, and let anger straggle along in the rear."

People who do not honor God obey this scripture in reverse. They're slow to hear and quick to speak and get angry. These are the people who always want to give you a piece of their mind with no interest in hearing what you or God have to say to them. They dishonor you and in turn they are dishonoring God. Ps. 4:4 says, "Meditate within your heart on your bed, and be still." One way to show respect is to be still and listen. Stop trying to get the first and last word in all the time. The Message Bible says, "Keep your mouth shut, and let your heart do the talking." Stop talking when you should be listening. To grow in honor, you've got to grow in your ability to be quiet. When you interrupt somebody, you are in truth despising what they're saying to you. You're giving that person no honor and in turn you are dishonoring God because He was the one who sent that person to you in the first place.

You need to be quiet and pay attention to what's being said to you. By listening to them, you are listening to God. By giving them honor, you are giving honor to God. Keep before you the words of Ps. 46:10, "Be still, and know that I am God." You can't be still if you're talking all the time. Be careful because if honor is not given then God may cease in His effort to talk to you. Jesus said, "Do not give what is holy to the dogs; nor cast your pearls before swine" (Matt. 7:6). Be aware that God will not give precious things to people who don't appreciate them. In the eyes of God, everything you say and do is a matter of honor. Live your life in such a way that your body, which is a temple, will become a vessel of honor unto the Lord. 2 Tim. 2:20,21 says, "But in a great house there are not only vessels of gold and silver, but also of wood and clay, some for honor and some for dishonor. Therefore, if anyone cleanses himself from the latter, he will be a vessel for honor, sanctified and useful for the Master, prepared for every good work."

The Message Bible says, "Become the kind of container God can use to present any and every kind of gift to His guests for their blessing." It is your responsibility to cleanse yourself of all things that would dishonor God so that you can become a vessel of honor unto His holy name. This is something that only you can do. You must separate yourself from those things that defile and drive a wedge between you and God. 2 Cor. 6:14 says, "Do not be unequally yoked together with unbelievers. For what fellowship has righteousness with lawlessness? And what communion has light with darkness"? The answer is none whatsoever. It is a shame how many believers seek and crave the approval of others, even from those who despise the name of the Lord they serve. This is not right for you dishonor God when you become friends with the world.

James 4:4 says, "Adulterers and adulteresses! Do you not know that friendship with the world is enmity with God? Whoever therefore wants to be a friend of the world makes himself an enemy of God." Paul was honoring God when he wrote in Gal. 1:10 (NLT), "Obviously, I'm not trying to win the approval of people, but of God. If pleasing people were my goal, I would not be Christ's servant." To be a vessel of honor you must separate yourself from the world and make pleasing God your highest aim in life. There is much work to be done before the Lord's glorious return and vessels of honor are committed, reliable, and consistent in all that they do. Ps. 110:3 says, "Your people shall be volunteers in the day of Your power." In Hebrew this verse says, "Your people are free will offerings." Vessels of honor willingly and quickly present themselves to the Lord for His service with a cheerful readiness that comes from within.

Eph. 2:10 (MSG) says, "He creates each of us by Christ Jesus to join Him in the work He does, the good work He has gotten ready for us to do, work we had better be doing." God is honored when you're willing to sacrifice your comfort and convenience for the benefit of someone else. All it takes is a willing heart that is full of grace and a soul that is motivated by love. Make time in your busy schedule and use whatever abilities and resources you have for the glory of God and the support of others. Bloom where you're planted for the greatest opportunities to serve are oftentimes right in front of you. Don't wait for someone to ask you to serve but be proactive and look for things that need to be done. Arthur Ashe once said, "Start where you are. Use what you have. Do what you can." Also, don't be afraid to start with small things. If the toilet at church needs cleaning, then clean it so that it sparkles like a diamond.

Believe that God will bless all the work of your hands and one day He will say to you, "Well done, good and faithful servant; you have been faithful over a few things, I will make you ruler over many things" (Matt. 25:23). The truth be told, the church of Jesus Christ has largely lost its influence and effectiveness in the world today. The problem is that, as a whole, the church does not honor God as it once did and because of that the world is sinking into the abyss of unchartered waters. Sin abounds morally, socially, and politically and the church refuses to stand up and take a stand against the atrocities that abound. A majority of believers fear man more than they fear God and because of this cowardice God is greatly dishonored. The church today needs to rise up from the muck and mire of complacency and begin to honor God once again for there is no other option.

When people fail to honor God, confusion settles into their hearts, distorting their sense of purpose and direction. What begins inwardly soon manifests outwardly, leaving lives marked by defeat rather than clarity, strength, and victory found in Him. These are the people who fold their hands and step back from doing what they've been called to do not realizing that they've fallen into the trap of the evil one. Sin abounds when the people of God do nothing but it's those who honor God who are being called to push back the power of darkness. Once and for all, the children of God must reject passivity and refuse to live beneath the calling placed on their lives. This is the hour to rise higher, shake off complacency, and walk boldly in faith, obedience, and purpose. God is worthy of more than half-hearted devotion—He deserves our full surrender, courage, and commitment. When we honor Him like never before, our lives become a clear declaration of His glory to the world.

| 22 |

"YOUR FRIEND GOD"

The Heavenly Father is everything you need, Jesus is the Good Shepherd, and the Holy Spirit is your constant companion. All these titles reveal the various relationships God wants to have with you. He wants to be your Father, your Savior, your Lord and Master, and your Guide in the everyday affairs of life. Because of who He is and for all He has done, it is your responsibility to honor Him with all your heart and soul and to give Him reverence and glory. When you do all that, the day will come when you will receive from God an open invitation to partake in the greatest relationship of all. He will invite you to become His friend. Let it come as no surprise to you that God wants to have the same close, personal relationship with you that He had with Adam and Eve before sin entered into the world. Together they delighted in God and He delighted in them. Make no mistake about it, God wants to be your friend. Life was glorious then and it can still be glorious today.

Sad to say, there are not too many people who have this type of relationship with God but it's available to everybody. To become friends with God you must first understand what friendship is. Prov. 18:24 says, "A man who has friends must himself be friendly, but there is a friend who sticks closer than a brother." The Living Bible says, "There are friends who pretend to be friends." There are two types of friends. There are "pretenders" and there are those "who stick closer than a brother." Most of the people you call friends are not friends at all. They'll talk to you, laugh with you, work with you, and play with you. They appear to be friends with everybody, but the Amplified Bible says, "A person who is a friend to everybody in the world is a bad friend." They are there during the good times but are nowhere to be found when things get rough.

There is, however, a kind of friend who will stick by you through any problem, circumstance, and trial. They're there for you during times of sickness, financial woes, marital problems, and any other type of need. David and Jonathan had a friendship like this. They laid their lives down for one another and their relationship went far beyond the bonds of blood kinship. This is the type of relationship God wants to have with you. There are certain kinds of friendships that you can enter into and be involved in that when you get into a bad situation, you'd rather get hold of your friend than your own brother or sister. This is the kind of friend that God would like to be with you, the kind of friend that won't run away during times of trouble. God wants to enter into this type of relationship with you, and He wants you to enter into this type of relationship with Him. You need to have this "stick closer than a brother" attitude with your spouse, other believers, and especially with God.

This type of relationship with God goes beyond the normal father/child relationship. It goes way beyond that. Yes, it encompasses that relationship, but it encircles more than that. You must, however, let God be your friend. If you don't want this type of relationship with God, then know that He won't force Himself on you. When Jesus set free the mad man of Gadara the people asked Jesus to leave and go away from them (Mark 5:17). They didn't want to be friends with Him, so what did Jesus do? He left. He didn't argue with them, and He didn't force Himself on them. Why did the people of Gadara tell Jesus to leave their presence? People come against what they don't understand. Even today people reject Jesus and don't accept Him with opened arms because they don't understand Him. They think He's standing over them with a baseball bat ready to clobber them on the head if they trip up and fail. They don't understand that God is a loving God, that He is kind and merciful.

The problem in marriages and most other relationships is some form of misunderstanding. What people don't understand they will come against. Too many people don't understand God and what He is like, who He is, and how He does things. Because of their lack of knowledge and understanding, they're against having a close relationship with Him. It takes time and effort to understand God and what He wants to do in your life. Also, most people don't want to make the commitment to do this. The good news is that when you understand that God wants to become your friend then you won't have any problem becoming His. Exodus 33:11 says, "So the Lord spoke to Moses face to face, as a man speaks to a friend." A friend is a person you can talk to about anything, and the Lord talked to Moses as a friend, face to face. Why did God do this with Moses? Because of the desire in the heart of Moses to know Him.

Vs. 13 says, "Now therefore, I pray, if I have found grace in Your sight, show me Your way, that I may know You and that I may find grace in Your sight." Moses wanted to be friends with God. He wanted to know God in a personal way. He longed for a personal connection with God, desiring to walk with Him, hear His voice, and understand His heart. When he said, "Show me Your way" he was saying he wanted to know God better and have an intimate knowledge of who He is. He wanted to know God personally! How did God respond to his request? "Then the Lord said to Moses, 'I will also do this thing that you have spoken; for you have found grace in My sight, and I know you by name.'" The more you know God and understand Him, the more His grace will be poured into your life. The question to be asked is this: Does God know you by name? Do you know Him by name?

Jesus said in John 15:15, "No longer do I call you servants, for a servant does not know what his master is doing; but I have called you friends, for all things that I heard from My Father I have made known to you." Think about it. You are "called" to be a friend of God and as God's friend you can know everything Jesus knows. Friendship with God is the reason you were created. Abraham is the only man in the Bible called "the friend of God" (2 Chron. 20:7). In Hebrew the word "friend" means 'to have affection for' and three times God called Abraham His personal friend. God treasured their friendship so much that He took time out to discuss His plans with His friend Abraham (see Gen. 18:16-33). Abraham had input on what God did as Moses also did in later years. And because Abraham was His friend, God did everything Abraham asked of Him. This is why Abraham was so abundantly blessed and was able to live the good life.

God treasured their friendship and He wants to have the same type of relationship with you. If you are God's friend, you will abide and continually stay in His love (John 15:9,10). That's a good place to be for this is where you become the object of God's affection. This is where Jesus was, as was Abraham. The Bible records that God unloaded His affection and blessings on Abraham and you can enter into the same type of relationship. Gen. 1:26 says, "Then God said, 'Let Us make man in Our image, according to our likeness.'" Why did God do this? Why didn't He make a monkey in His image instead? Because He wanted somebody to be friends with. God wasn't lonely but having a true friend was the desire of His heart. He wanted somebody in His image that He could fellowship with and be friends with. In the garden of Eden, He came down in the cool of the evening and had fellowship with His friend Adam. They walked together and they talked together.

Adam was made in the image of God, and this means he knew how God did things. When you are God's friend, He knows how you function and you know how He functions. This gives you something to talk about. When you're friends with somebody their interests become your interests. When you are God's friend He'll show you things to come. He'll talk to you about His plans. This is why He created you, to be His friend. It is important to understand that just because God loves you doesn't mean He enjoys hanging around with you. You "pal around" with friends. Yes, God loves you, but He wants to get friendly with you. You tell friends your secrets and plans. You visit your friends just to hang around with them. God is your Heavenly Father, but He wants to take it beyond the Father/child relationship. He wants to take it a step further and this takes time and effort. You don't become friends overnight. To become friends with God takes instruction, discipline, training, time, and a whole lot of love.

There are no short-cuts. There are things that only time and experience can mature you in. Some things you can't learn in a book. Today there are many who love to hang around with people for the crumbs that fall from their table. Friendship with God will give you more than crumbs. It will bring true riches and blessings into your life. It will allow you to live the good life. David asked in Ps. 15:1, "Lord, who may abide in Your tabernacle? Who may dwell in Your holy hill?" The Message Bible says, "God, who gets invited to dinner at Your place? How do we get on Your guest list?" King David had a deep desire to be included on God's guest list because he placed high value on his friendship with God. His spirit was sensitive to the blessing and approval of God. All his life David vigorously pursued God's friendship. He said in Ps. 27:4, "One thing I have desired of the Lord, that I may dwell in the house of the Lord all the days of my life, to behold the beauty of the Lord, and to inquire in His temple."

David was a man after God's own heart, and this is what qualified him to be a friend of God. David knew that God chooses His friends carefully and blesses them liberally. Friendship with God gives your life stability. It's like a shelter in the time of storm. With God as your friend your feet will be planted on the Rock of your salvation, and He will give you a good name. Eccl. 7:1 says, "A good name is better than precious ointment" and Prov. 22:1 says, "A good name is to be chosen rather than great riches." God's friendship gives your life direction in the midst of confusion and uncertainty. Ps. 31:3 says, "For You are my rock and my fortress; Therefore, for Your name's sake, lead me and guide me." Also, God says in Ps. 32:8, "I will instruct you and teach you in the way you should go; I will guide you with My eye." Seek God's guidance for all the decisions you have to make about your destiny.

A person is known by the friends they keep and friendship with God is like being a blind man who gets his sight. God's friendship will give you a reason to live, a reason to get up in the morning. Some people die at age 20 and stop breathing at age 80. For 60 years they work at a job they hate for a boss they envy. Why do they do this? So they can go home and get drunk, fight with their spouse, and fall asleep in front of the television set. But if you are God's friend, He will have a different plan and purpose for your life. Jesus said in John 15:16, "You did not choose Me, but I chose you and appointed you that you should go and bear fruit, and that your fruit should remain, that whatever you ask the Father in My name He may give you." Eph. 2:10 says, "For we are His workmanship, created in Christ Jesus for good works which God prepared beforehand that we should walk in them." The reason to live a good life is so you can perform good works unto your Lord and Savior.

Friendship with God will transform your life so that you will be a blessing to those you come in contact with. This is all part of living the good life. God's friendship will also help you finish life well. Ps. 112:5,6 says, "A good man deals graciously and lends; He will guide his affairs with discretion. Surely he will never be shaken; The righteous will be in everlasting remembrance." If you want stability, a good name, life-long direction, a reason to live and the rich reward of finishing life well, then determine to be a friend of God and make proper lifestyle choices. In every relationship there is an unwritten code of conduct that you must submit to and follow. Realize that it's your right choices that qualify you to be called the friend of God. Ps. 25:14 (TLB) says, "Friendship with God is reserved for those who reverence Him. With them alone He shares the secrets of His promises."

Friendship with God is promoted by clean moral living. David said the person who may dwell in the presence of God in His holy hill is "he who walks uprightly, and works righteousness, and speaks truth in his heart" (Ps. 15:2). To be blameless does not mean to be sinless. It means to have a manner of life that is upright. Ps. 84:11 says, "For the Lord God is a sun and shield; The Lord will give grace and glory; No good thing will He withhold from those who walk uprightly." Personal integrity is so important and God insists on having a friendship with you that is based on the foundation of truth (Eph. 4:25). David continues in Ps. 15:3, "He who does not backbite with his tongue, nor does evil to his neighbor, nor does he take up a reproach against his friend." Friendship with God is promoted not by gossip or backbiting but by speaking positive words of blessing to others.

James 4:11 says, "Do not speak evil of one another, brethren. He who speaks evil of a brother and judges his brother, speaks evil of the law and judges the law. But if you judge the law, you are not a doer of the law but a judge." People all over the world share a deep need to be loved, seen, and valued, and God has not left that need unanswered. He has entrusted His friends with the sacred task of reflecting His love through compassion, kindness, and selfless action to a hurting world. People everywhere crave acceptance, affection, appreciation, approval, and attention. Loving your neighbor as you love yourself all begins by keeping watch over the words you speak. Paul says in Phil. 4:8, "Finally, brethren, whatever things are true, whatever things are noble, whatever things are just, whatever things are pure, whatever things are lovely, whatever things are of good report, if there is any virtue and if there is anything praiseworthy - meditate on these things."

Also, friendship with God is strengthened when we choose good role models who live out their faith with integrity and obedience. By following those who walk closely with Him, we are inspired to grow deeper in trust, character, and devotion to God each day. Ps. 15:4 (NLT) says, "Those who despise flagrant sinners, and honor the faithful followers of the Lord, and keep their promises even when it hurts." Who are your role models? Immoral actors in Hollywood or drug-taking rock musicians? Do you idolize professional athletes who cheat on their wives and often get arrested for drunk driving? It is wrong if you do. The friends of God choose to honor those who walk in righteousness, wisdom, and humility, rather than giving influence to scoundrels and fools. They recognize that who they esteem and associate with shapes their character and direction. By valuing godly people, they align their hearts with God's ways and invite His wisdom and blessing into their lives.

Psalm 15:4 says, "He who swears to his own hurt and does not change." Friendship with God is promoted by keeping your word and the vows you make. Another important truth is that God's friends don't hit people when they're down. Ps. 15:5 says, "He who does not put out his money at usury, nor does he take a bribe against the innocent." God's friends don't take advantage of poor people and those who are struggling. Lev. 25:35-37 says, "And if one of your brethren becomes poor, and falls into poverty among you, then you should help him, like a stranger or sojourner, that he may live with you. Take no usury or interest from him; but fear your God; that your brother may live with you. You shall not lend him money for usury, nor lend him food at a profit." Friendship with God is promoted by treating people justly. Yes, God loves friends who live by the Golden Rule, those who are a doer of the Word of God and not hearers only.

2 Peter 1:10 says, "Therefore, brethren, be even more diligent to make your calling and selection sure, for if you do these things, you will never stumble." The Message Bible says, "So, friends, confirm God's invitation to you, His choice of you. Don't put it off; do it now. Do this, and you'll have your life on a firm footing, the streets paved and the way wide open into the eternal kingdom of our Master and Savior, Jesus Christ." God said about David, "I have found David the son of Jesse, a man after My own heart, who will do all My will" (Acts 13:22). Your actions are the determining factor as to whether or not you become a friend with God and live a good life. It all begins with you. You can wake up each morning knowing that God wants to be a friend to you that sticks closer than a brother. He sent Jesus to die for you so that you could be His friend.

Still, you can have a relationship with somebody from a distance and not be their friend. The reason this is true is that it takes time, effort, desire, and sacrifice to cultivate such a friendship. Most people don't take the time to seek God in a proper way. They're always in a hurry doing this and doing that not realizing that if they're too busy for God, they're too busy. People need to sacrifice whatever it is they're doing and seek God like never before. They need to know Him and who He is. Moses and David both had a desire to know God in a close and personal way. Abraham was willing to offer up his son Isaac because he wasn't going to let anything interfere with his friendship with God. To "seek God" means to have a face-to-face relationship with Him. This means God has your undivided attention and you have His. Heb. 11:6 says that God "is a rewarder of those who diligently seek Him." What does He reward you with? A good life.

Too many people know about God but don't know God in a personal way. Why? Because they don't seek, crave, and pursue Him with all their heart and soul. God must be sought after to be found. Meeting somebody doesn't mean you know them. It takes a face-to-face relationship to get intimate with somebody and fellowship is the key to really getting to know someone. When you know somebody in a close, personal way you will stick to them like glue. You become one with them and before long your lives will mingle with one another. When you know God you'll start conceiving things down in your spirit. You'll get pregnant with a vision that God wants you to live a good life. A miracle is inside of you and it will be confirmed with signs following. Jesus prayed in John 17:3, "And this is eternal life, that they may know You, the only true God, and Jesus Christ whom You sent." Eternal life is a good life and comes when your life is intertwined with the life of your friend God.

It is interesting to note that when you mingle with God the devil can't tell you apart. You'll look like God, talk like God, act like God, think, love, forgive, walk, and have dominion like God. This is all part of God's plan to give you a good life and fellowship is the key that will cause this to become a reality in your life. There are four decisions you can make that will help you cultivate a strong, binding friendship with God. The first decision you can make is to become a worshiper of God. Paul told the church at Rome to "greet one another with a holy kiss" (Rom. 16:16). To become friends with God, you must do the same thing to Him. How does one "kiss" God? Through praise and worship. Jesus said in John 4:23, "But the hour is coming, and now is, when the true worshipers will worship the Father in spirit and truth; for the Father is seeking such to worship Him."

2 Chron. 16:9 says, "For the eyes of the Lord run to and fro throughout the whole earth, to show Himself strong on behalf of those whose heart is loyal to Him." God is searching for those who will be loyal to Him and become His friend. Tell the Lord to search no more. Tell Him you're ready, able, and willing to become His friend. What do you think will happen when you become God's friend? He'll "buddy" up to you. He'll "pal around" with you night and day. God inhabits the praises of His people (Ps. 22:3). The word "inhabit" means 'to settle, sit down, dwell." When you praise God and become His friend, He'll

sit down and dwell with you. Let's face it, everybody likes praise. People like praise, cats and dogs like praise, and God likes praise. When a person compliments you something rises up on the inside of you causing you to respond back in a positive way. You just naturally want to bless them back and this is how God is.

Praise God continually because He wants to do something good to you. During times of trouble back off from the situation and praise God. You don't have to memorize and quote every verse in the Bible concerning the trial you're going through. No, just praise God for who He is. When you do that God will show up and sit down and dwell with you. He is forever looking to give something to somebody so, if you decide to be a worshiper, you'll be right in the center of what He wants to do. It will put you in the secret place of the Most High, a place that brings promotion and gives to those who dwell there a good life. The second decision you must make to become a friend of God is to always live by faith. You can't please Him without it (Heb. 11:6) so when you choose to live by faith you've made the decision to please God and to become His friend.

Rev. 4:11 (KJB) says, "Thou art worthy, O Lord, to receive glory and honor and power: for Thou hast created all things, and for Thy pleasure they are and were created." Why do you think you were born in the first place? You were created to give God pleasure and your friendship with Him is what He values most. Never forget, you were created to be God's friend and nothing pleases Him more than when His friends live by faith. Faith is a lifestyle so live totally and completely by faith all the time. The just shall live by faith for it is a constant expression that you believe God and what He says. When you believe God with all your heart then surely your friendship with Him will surely blossom. Walking by faith is not hard. God lives by faith and He won't ask you to do something He doesn't do Himself. When you begin to call those things that be not as though they were, when you do the same thing He does, you are on your way to becoming a friend of God.

Rom. 4:18 (MSG) says, "When everything was hopeless, Abraham believed anyway, deciding to live not on the basis of what he saw he couldn't do but on what God said He would do." Abraham was a man of faith. In fact, he is called "the father of our faith." Is it any wonder that God called him His friend? The third thing you can do to cultivate a friendship with God is to make the decision to obey Him at all costs. Jesus set the example in the Garden of Gethsamane when He said to the Father, "Nevertheless, not My will but Your will be done" (Luke 22:42). God called Abraham His friend because he walked by faith and was willing to obey God even to the point of offering up his own son as a sacrifice. Walking by faith requires actions of obedience. When God told Abraham to sacrifice his son, he got up early the next morning. That's faith. When he reached the place where the sacrifice was to take place he told his servants, "Wait here and we'll return." That's faith.

Isaac asked, "Where is the sacrifice?" and Abraham said the Lord would provide one. Abraham obeyed God because his faith was anchored in the unshakable belief that God could even raise Isaac from the dead. Trusting God's promise above his own understanding, Abraham demonstrated a faith that placed resurrection power above fear and loss. His obedience revealed that his friendship with God mattered more to him than even the closest earthly relationships he held with his wife and son. By choosing faithfulness to God above all else, his actions testified that devotion to the divine outweighed every personal bond. To become God's friend, you must obey Him at all costs, because obedience is the truest evidence that you genuinely believe Him. Faith is not proven by words, emotions, or intentions, but by a willing heart that acts on God's commands even when it is difficult. Obedience declares trust, loyalty, and surrender, revealing a faith that is alive and real.

The story of King Saul in 1 Samuel tells the tragic tale of a man who did not obey God with all his heart. He listened to the voice of the people more than the voice of God and thought he could make up for his disobedience by offering up a burnt offering to God. Samuel confronted him and said, "Behold, to obey is better than sacrifice" (1 Sam. 15:22). Obedience means something to God, and you can never make up with sacrifice what you lose with disobedience. Saul's authority as king was stripped from him and he later committed suicide on the field of battle. He learned the hard way that, no matter what the cost, one must obey God rather than man. And when you do what God tells you to do, you then are in line to be considered God's friend. Jesus said in John 15:10, "I have kept My Father's commandments and abide in His love." Jesus maintained obedience at all costs and had a close relationship with the Father. You must follow His example and do the same.

| 23 |

"CROWNED WITH FAVOR"

God wants to be your friend and one thing almost all friends have in common is that they do favors for one another. Because you are God's friend, He wants you to bask in the sunshine of His favor. He said in Jer. 31:14 (NET), "I will provide the priests with abundant provisions. My people will be filled with the good things I provide." God longs for you to be a well-watered garden, flourishing, full of joy, always in blossom, living the good life. Jer. 32:40-42 says, "And I will make an everlasting covenant with them, that I will not turn away from doing them good; but I will put My fear in their hearts so that they will not depart from Me. Yes, I will rejoice over them to do them good, and I will assuredly plant them in this land, with all My heart and with all My soul. For thus says the Lord: Just as I have brought all this great calamity on this people, so I will bring on them all the good that I have promised them."

All things that pertain to life and godliness are yours so that you can experience the deepest joys and benefits of godly living. This is why Jesus came and the more you grow in the knowledge and love of God, the more His goodness will be increasingly experienced in your life. The Message Bible says in Acts 3:26, "But you are first in line: God, having raised up His Son, sent Him to bless you as you turn, one by one, from your evil ways." The Lord is good, He is merciful, kind, gracious, and very patient. Jesus came to give you a rich, full life and, because He died for you, you can live a good life. At His birth the angels proclaimed, "Glory to God in the highest, and on earth peace to men on whom His favor rests" (Luke 2:14 NIV). God's favor resting on man was the beginning of a new and awesome reality that was to change history forever. It is God's will for you to live the good life and He wants to amaze you with His favor.

The psalmist tells how the favor of God will be poured into the end-time church like no other generation in times past. Ps. 102:13 says, "You will arise and have mercy on Zion; for the time to favor her, yes, the set time, has come." The word "Zion" is symbolic of the church and the psalmist is saying that the set time to favor the church has come. It's in the mind and will of God and nothing can change it. When might this set time be? The psalmist says in vs. 16, "For the Lord shall build up Zion; He shall appear in glory." The Lord will build up His church, which you are a part of, and favor her just prior to His second coming. In other words, the set time is now! Is. 30:18 says, "Therefore the Lord will wait, that He may be gracious to you; And therefore He will be exalted, that He may have mercy on you. For the Lord is a God of justice; Blessed are all those who wait for Him."

The set time is now, and Paul says in Eph. 2:7 "that in the ages to come He might show the exceeding riches of His grace in His kindness toward us in Christ Jesus." If God has already been good to you then get ready because you haven't seen anything yet. Remember, before Jesus returns there will be a manifestation of the favor of God like no previous generation has ever seen. God has a set time to favor the church and that time is now! Yes, adversity will come but the favor of God will shine through the darkest clouds of trial and hardship. No matter what Satan tries to do, always confess the favor of God over your life and circumstances. Never forget, this is the season of God's favor. Ezek. 34:26 says, "I will make them and the places all around My hills a blessing; and I will cause showers to come down in their season; there shall be showers of blessing." Seek the showers of

God's blessings for it is His desire to pour forth into your life a torrential downpour.

Be joyful and overwhelmed with the goodness of God. Favor makes you achievers in the kingdom of God. It is the heavenly link to your success and will cause you to live a reigning life. David wrote in Ps. 5:11,12, "But let all those rejoice who put their trust in You; Let them shout for joy, because You defend them; Let those also who love Your name be joyful in You. For You, O Lord, will bless the righteous; With favor You will surround him as with a shield." The Amplified Bible says God "will crown you with favor." When God's favor comes into a person's life a zero becomes a hero. In the book of Esther the king chose her to be queen. In a single day she went from being a nobody to a somebody proving that one touch of God's favor is worth a lifetime of labor. With the favor of God operating in your life there is no way you can be defeated or overcome by the wiles of the enemy.

1 Peter 1:13 says, "Therefore gird up the loins of your mind, be sober, and rest your hope fully upon the grace that is to be brought to you at the revelation of Jesus Christ." You need to live each day anticipating more of God's favor in your life. When you align your thinking with God's thinking, your heart begins to desire what He desires, and your steps follow His wisdom instead of your own understanding. In that alignment, you open your life to levels of God's favor, blessing, and purpose far beyond anything you could have imagined. The Bible abounds with declarations of the goodness of God. Ps. 34:8-10 says, "Oh, taste and see that the Lord is good; Blessed is the man who trusts in Him! Oh, fear the Lord, you His saints! There is no want to those who fear Him. The young lions lack and suffer hunger; but those who seek the Lord shall not lack any good thing." God's goodness is available for your personal experience whenever you trust in Him.

Peter begins his second letter by saying, "Grace and peace be multiplied to you in the knowledge of God and of Jesus our Lord, as His divine power has given us all things that pertain to life and godliness, through the knowledge of Him Who called us to glory and virtue" (2 Peter 1:2,3). God's ability and His favor is available to you in multiplied measures. Peter is saying that the process for partaking of the showers of God's blessings simply requires you to grow in the knowledge of God. The Message Bible says, "Grace and peace to you many times over as you deepen in your experience with God and Jesus, our Master. Everything that goes into a life of pleasing God has been miraculously given to us by getting to know, personally and intimately, the One who invited us to God. The best invitation we ever received! We were also given absolutely terrific promises to pass on to you - your tickets to participation in the life of God after you turned your back on a world corrupted by lust."

God desires to bless you abundantly. This means you can have it all. Even Jesus said in John 10:10, "I have come that they may have and enjoy their life, and that they may have it more abundantly." The Message Bible says, "I came so they can have real and eternal life, more and better life than they ever dreamed of." David wrote in Ps. 31:19, "Oh, how great is Your goodness, which You have laid up for those who fear You, which You have prepared for those who trust in You in the presence of the sons of men!" The Message Bible says, "What a stack of blessing you have piled up for those who worship You, ready and waiting for all who run to You to escape an unkind world." Prov. 22:1 says, "A good name is to be chosen rather than great riches, loving favor rather than silver and gold." Favor is more valuable than silver and gold for it can do things money can't buy. Favor will bring you great achievements and great advancements more than you've ever known before.

Godly opportunities will come your way if you first make the choice to seek favor more than the uncertain riches of financial gain. The Lord said to Joshua, "This Book of the Lord shall not depart from your mouth, but you shall meditate in it day and night, that you may observe to do according to all that's written in it. For then you will make your way prosperous, and then you will have good success" (Josh. 1:8). It all goes back to knowing God in a personal, intimate way. Jesus also experienced an abundant measure of the favor of God. Luke 2:52 says, "And Jesus increased in wisdom and stature, and in favor with God and man." How did this come about? He studied the scriptures and was forever going about the Father's business (vs. 49). Luke 2:40 says, "And the Child grew and became strong in spirit, filled with wisdom; and the grace of God was upon Him."

Remember, Jesus came to earth as a man and relied fully on the Scriptures to guide His thoughts, decisions, and obedience to the Father just as much as you do. In the same way, God's Word is your anchor and authority, empowering you to stand firm, overcome temptation, and walk in victory. Luke 4:16 says, "So He came to Nazareth, where He had been brought up. And as His custom was, He went into the synagogue on the Sabbath day and stood up to read." It was His custom to do this and, as a result of His diligence, the grace and favor of God was upon Him. Notice also that not only did He grow in favor with God but also with men. Favor with God will automatically guarantee you favor with those you come in contact with. The word "favor" means 'friendly regard shown toward another especially by a superior; approving consideration or attention; partiality; leniency; popularity; in one's good graces; to one's advantage.'

Favor will put you into a social realm where you will receive special treatment from those around you. Esther 2:17 says, "The king loved Esther more than all the other women, and she obtained grace and favor in his sight more than all the virgins; so he set the royal crown upon her head and made her queen instead of Vashti." Humble yourself before the Lord and His grave and favor will exalt you. Like Esther, those who have God's favor are overshadowed by a divine plan that dictates their destiny, propels them into their God-given purpose, and causes all things to work together for their good. God gave Joseph favor in the sight of the keeper of the prison and he was placed over the whole prison. Favor gives you access to someone else's power. A young Jewish virgin named Mary was described as being "highly favored" and became the very mother of the Son of God. How amazing is that?

When you bask in the favor of God people will prefer to be around you more than others. You will receive recognition even when you seem like the least likely to receive it. 1 Sam. 16:22 says, "Then Saul sent to Jesse, saying, 'Please let David stand before me, for he has found favor in my sight.'" Like a spiritual magnet people will be drawn to you, resulting in promotion in whatever you put your hand to do. People will offer you their help, support, and assistance to help in whatever endeavor you are in. When the favor of God overflows in your life, when you taste and see that the Lord is good, battles will be won in which you won't even have to fight. The battle is the Lord's and you will experience greater victories in the midst of greater odds. Josh. 11:20 says, "For it was of the Lord to harden their hearts, that they should come against Israel in battle, that He might utterly destroy them, and that they might receive no mercy, but that He might destroy them, as the Lord had commanded Moses."

The greater the trial and the more impossible the battle looks, the easier the victory will come. Ps. 44:1-3 says, "We have heard our ears, O God, our fathers have told us, what deeds You did in their days, in days of old: How you drove out the nations with Your hand, but them You planted; How You afflicted the peoples, and cast them out. For they did not gain possession of the land by their own sword, nor did their own arm save them; But it was Your right hand, Your arm, and the light of Your countenance, because You favored them." Favor is a tool used to defeat the enemy. It drives out the barriers and the giants that are blocking your path to success. Favor will open doors for you and plant you in your own personal promised land. Favor is the doorway into the blessings of Canaan and supernatural provision. When you learn to tap into God's favor, you will have a tremendous advantage in everyday life. Doors will open for you that remain closed for others.

Like Joseph, you will receive preferential treatment that seems unusual to most people. However, for those living in the favor of God, it will be no less than what you will come to expect. It only takes one touch of God's favor to completely turn your situation around. Favor can turn adversity into victory, failure into success, and sickness into good health. One touch of God's favor can turn any situation around in an instant of time. This all happens when you discover the power of God's divine favor in your life. You've been crowned with favor so you can live with confidence and boldness knowing you're a child of the Most High God. The heart of God is to pour out His blessings on you. For sure, He wants to amaze you with His favor. Eph. 3:20 says, "Now unto Him Who is able to do exceedingly, abundantly above and beyond all that we could ask or think." Notice the words "above and beyond." That's the favor of God so get in agreement with Him and become more favor minded.

You will succeed more quickly with favor than you will without it. Don't be afraid to be bold and ask for what you really want, things you wouldn't normally ask for. You wear a robe of righteousness and a crown of favor is on your head. When you live the good life you have a right to receive preferential treatment. People will go out of their way to help you and God will step in and assist you and make your everyday life easier. Enlarge your vision and expect more of God's favor in your life. Favor is the difference between your present and your future. Make the decision today to operate in the unseen realm of God's divine favor. Get on the offensive and be favor-minded. Everyday speak favor over your life. Favor happens to those who believe and expect it to happen, so choose to believe! Choose to be favor-minded and declare it everyday of your life! God wants to provide you with favor and supernatural advantages. He wants to assist you and make your life easier so expect more of the favor of God.

In the parable of the sewer Jesus spoke of three levels in which people may experience the goodness of God. Speaking of seeds that are sown He said in Matt. 13:8, "But others fell on good ground and yielded a crop: some a hundredfold, some sixty, some thirty." There is a thirty-fold good life, a sixty-fold good life, and the ultimate hundred-fold good life. The Message Bible says, "Some fell on good earth, and produced a harvest beyond his wildest dreams." A careful study of the Word also reveals that there are three levels of relationships that you can have with God. Each of these three levels correspond to a level of the good life that you can experience in your everyday life. When you got born again you become a child of God and when you made the commitment to be used by God for His purpose you got promoted to being a servant of God. There are sons of God and there are servants of God. A friend of God is a combination of the two.

Some people are sons of God but not servants while others are servants but not sons. The truth be told, neither one of these relationships by themselves fulfill totally what God wants to accomplish and do in their lives. That distinction is reserved for the friends of God. The better you understand the characteristics of these three relationships, the better the opportunity for you to walk in the fullness of the good life. Believers who call themselves servants of God will give you the shirt off their back and do whatever needs to be done. They are always available to do works of service or whatever it takes to get the job done. The danger of being just a servant of God is that people run the risk of being so heavenly minded they're no earthly good. They're so busy serving God that they ignore the responsibilities they have toward their spouse and children. Many times they suffer burnout and some have tragically suffered an early death.

Why did this happen? Because they did not have a clear understanding of their rights and privileges as a son of God. On the other hand, there are those who have a clear understanding of sonship but won't lift a finger to serve God and help somebody else. These people are so earthly minded that they're no heavenly good. Those who are only sons of God will receive in their lives the blessing of having a nice car, home, job, and personal well-being. They're exercising their rights and privileges as a son which they are entitled to from the Word of God. Sadly, they have become so consumed with material blessings that advancing the Kingdom of God has taken a back seat in their lives. What was meant to be a blessing has quietly become a distraction, dulling their passion for eternal purpose. In order to experience everything that God has to offer there must be a balance between being a son and being a servant.

Some people give their lives completely for the sake of the gospel and don't receive anything in this life for it. The reason this happens is because they only saw themselves as servants and not sons. They didn't know they had rights and privileges as a son. They didn't know that "all these things would be added" to their lives (Matt. 6:33). They just knew they were supposed to serve God but if they knew of the blessings of sonship then they would have become a friend of God and had it all. However, even though they missed out on the temporary blessings in this life, they'll still receive eternal rewards in heaven which is the 60-fold blessing. On the other side of the coin is the person who partakes of the rights and privileges as a son but pushes aside the call to become a servant. This person will only receive the 30-fold blessing of temporal blessings and will have nothing to show for it in eternity.

In heaven the servants will live in mansions and sit on thrones, but a son will only get a palm branch to wave around. Remember, neither one of these positions by themselves will cause you to walk in God's perfect will for your life. But the person who has the knowledge of a son and walks in the light of what he knows, coupled together with the heart of a servant, will walk in the fullness of the hundred-fold blessing. He who walks in obedience to God will experience His blessings in this life - peace in the midst of trials, strength for each day, and favor that only heaven can provide. Every faithful step taken here echoes beyond the moment, storing up rewards that time can never erase. What God begins in the present, He completes in eternity, where the greatest rewards await those who trust Him fully. This is what happens to the friends of God. This is the good life. Never forget that God's best and ultimate blessing, His divine favor, is reserved for those believers whom He calls friends.

Jesus began His earthly ministry by proclaiming to the whole world that this was the Father's will. Luke 4:17-19 says, "And He was handed the book of the prophet Isaiah, And when He had opened the book, He found the place where it was written, 'The Spirit of the Lord is upon Me because He has anointed Me to preach the gospel to the poor. He has sent Me to heal the brokenhearted, to preach deliverance to the captives and recovery of sight to the blind, to set at liberty those who are oppressed, to preach the acceptable year of the Lord.'" Notice the phrase "the acceptable year of the Lord." The Message Bible says, "This is God's year to act!" and the Amplified translation says this is "the day when the free favors of God profusely abound." Jesus then closed the book and "began to say to them, 'Today this scripture is fulfilled in your hearing.'"

Jesus began to tell people two thousand years ago that God wanted to favor them with abundant blessings and He's saying the same thing to the church today. Believers are living in the day of the favor of God. Jesus was reading from Is. 61 and vs. 6,7 says, "But you shall be named the Priests of the Lord, men shall call you Servants of our God. You shall eat the riches of the Gentiles, and in their glory you shall boast. Instead of your shame you shall have double honor, and instead of confusion they shall rejoice in their portion. Therefore in their land they shall possess double; Everlasting joy shall be theirs." This is a description of the good life. Vs. 7 says restoration will come to you twofold. You'll get double for your trouble. Job 42:10 says, "And the

Lord restored Job's losses when he prayed for his friends. Indeed the Lord gave Job twice as much as he had before."

The favor of God brings restoration and prosperity to the level that others will recognize it and acknowledge that God provided it. Job lived the good life and was highly favored by God. He said in Job 10:12, "You have granted me life and favor, and Your care has preserved my spirit." What was it about this man named Job that made him the receiver of God's immeasurable blessings? Consider Job 1:1, "There was a man in the land of Uz, whose name was Job; and that man was blameless and upright, and one who feared God and shunned evil." Clearly he was a friend of God. Even God said "there is none like him on the earth" (Job 1:8). There is so much that you can learn from the life and character of Job that will shape and mold your life to the point that you become a friend of God. After the first assault of Satan on his life "Job arose and tore his robe and shaved his head, and he fell to the ground and worshiped" (Job 1:20).

His world was crumbling around him but still he had the heart to worship God. He then said in vs. 21, "Naked I came from my mother's womb, and naked shall I return there. The Lord gave, and the Lord has taken away; Blessed be the name of the Lord." Job had no idea what was going on behind the scenes and he wrongfully thought this destruction was coming from the hand of God. But he still held fast to his integrity (Job 2:3) and gave honor and praise to his God. Yes, Job had some reasonable complaints but God knew that in his heart was unshaken confidence. Job knew that "God does great things, and unsearchable, marvelous things without number. He gives rain on the earth, and sends water on the fields. He sets on high those who are lowly and those who mourn are lifted to safety" (Job 5:9-11). His friend Bildad said to him, "Though your beginning was small, yet your latter end would increase abundantly" (Job 8:7).

Job then answered and said, "He does great things past finding out, Yes, wonders without number" (Job 9:10). This is the favor of God!

What makes Job stand out is that even when he was not experiencing this favor his heart still clung to his God. He said in Job 13:15, "Though He slay me, yet will I trust Him." Is it any wonder that before and after this nine month trial he was radically blessed? Job had three friends who tried to comfort him but they weren't very successful with their efforts. In fact, Job says in Job 16:2, "Miserable comforters are you all." Notice, however, what Job went on to say, "I also could speak as you do, if your soul were in my soul's place. I could heap up words against you, and shake my head at you; But I will strengthen you with my mouth, and the comfort of my lips would relieve your grief." In the midst of his trials Job still had the desire to serve God by reaching out to bless his friends.

He was a son of God and this verse showed that he was also a servant of God thus making him a friend of God. This is why he was so abundantly blessed. This is why he lived the good life. Even though he was in a severe trial, Job knew better days were ahead. He said in Job 17:9, "Yet the righteous will hold to his way, and he who has clean hands will be stronger and stronger." He went on to say in Job 19:25,26, "For I know that my Redeemer lives, and He shall stand at last on the earth; and after my skin is destroyed, this I know, that in my flesh I shall see God." Do not forget Job 23:10-12, "But He knows the way that I take; when He has tested me, I shall come forth as gold. My foot has held fast to His steps; I have kept His way and not turned aside. I have not departed from the commandment of His lips; I have treasured the words of His mouth more than my necessary food." With an attitude like that, how could the man not be blessed?

Over and over again the book of Job shows why he was highly favored by God which caused him to live the good life. Job 29:14 says, "I put on righteousness, and it clothed me." This made him a son of God. His desire to be a servant of God is revealed in vs. 12,15,16, "Because I delivered the poor who cried out, and the fatherless and he who had no helper. I was eyes to the blind, and I was feet to the lame. I was a father to the poor." Job was known for helping people in trouble and standing up for those who were down on their luck. He spent his entire life being a blessing to others and received in return the ultimate favor of God. You can't live the good life without it. Job's friend Eliha said about the righteous, "If they obey and serve Him, they shall spend their days in prosperity, and their years in pleasures" (Job 36:11). The Message Bible says, "He never takes His eyes off the righteous; He honors them lavishly, promotes them endlessly." What more needs to be said?

The final verse in the book of Job says, "So Job died, old and full of days" (Job 42:17). This happened because he was a son and servant of God. This made him a friend of God and the receiver of the divine favor of God. Thus he lived the good life. Jabez also was a friend of God and this is evident in the prayer he prayed, "Oh God, that You would bless me indeed and expand my territory." To be "blessed indeed" is a blessing that comes on the sons of God. When Jabez prayed for God to expand his influence in the land he was openly declaring that he was a servant of God. This prayer reveals that Jabez was a friend of God and this is why God granted his request. Like Job, he was blessed with the favor of God, walking under His covering and provision. Because of that divine favor, he was able to live a good life marked by peace, purpose, and abundance. May you live all the days of your life following their example.

| 24 |

"LOVED AND HIGHLY FAVORED"

Like a stick dipped in honey, so is the favor of God in your life. The goodness of the Lord is breaking forth all over the world and His blessings will stick to you and will be a sweet rendering of how good He truly is. God's favor is to be experienced every day of your life, not just once in a great while. With God's favor you can expect incredible things to happen all the days of your life. When Moses came of age he walked away from the passing pleasures of sin in Egypt and chose instead to suffer hardship with the people of God. Heb. 11:26 says "for he looked to the reward" and with the favor of God in your life you can do the same thing. With confidence you'll have the same testimony as Nehemiah who said, "Because God heard my prayers and rested His hand of favor and love upon me, the king gave me everything I asked for!" (Neh. 2:8).

There is no greater experience in life than to have the favor of God present and in manifestation wherever you go. Every step you take will be a step of confidence because you know that behind every dark cloud is the silver lining of God's divine favor. All over the world people are talking about the darkness of sin that is covering this planet. Most of what's being said is indeed true but what needs to be emphasized even more is that those who walk in faith do not have to partake of the doom and gloom that is surely here. God prophesied way back in the Old Testament that in these last days believers can experience greater manifestations of His glory in their lives. Haggai 2:9 says, "'The glory of this latter temple shall be greater than the former,' says the Lord of hosts." The Message Bible says, "This temple is going to end up far better than it started out, a glorious beginning but an even more glorious finish: a place in which I will hand out wholeness and holiness."

The Bible teaches that the glory of God is the goodness of God. Moses asked God to show him His glory and the Lord responded, "I will make all My goodness pass before you" (Ex. 33:19). The glory of God is a manifestation of the goodness of God and Haggai says this goodness will increase here in the last days. Rejoice for you are a part of that generation that will experience the favor of God more than any generation since the dawn of time. Without restraint, God will open up the floodgates of His goodness and pour unspeakable blessings into your life. Stop talking about how bad the economy is but rather rejoice for the greatness of His favor that is coming upon you. Hosea 3:5 (NLT) says, "But afterward the people will return and devote themselves to the Lord their God and to David's descendant, their King. In the last days, they will tremble in awe of the Lord and of His goodness."

The Amplified Bible says "they will come trembling to the Lord and to His goodness and blessing in the last days." The prophet is saying that the favor of God will profusely abound in this last generation, so much so that there will be a clear and precise distinction between you and those who don't honor God. You've been set apart to experience and flow in the blessings and favor of God. Num. 6:24-26 says, "The Lord bless you and keep you; The Lord make His face shine upon you and be gracious to you; The Lord lift up His countenance upon you and give you peace." If you are born again then you have a God-given right to walk in divine favor every day of your life. It don't come automatically but if you'll believe it and receive it then for sure it can be yours. Dare to believe that God will cause you to prosper while others are struggling, that you will be protected when the wolves of calamity bring others down.

The favor of God is upon you, causing you to have an advantage that others do not have. God's face is shining down on you and this means you can rise up above your circumstances and become all God destined you to become. Your needs will be met, your health will be restored, and you'll go forth and fulfill that which you've been called to do. The favor of God can do for you what you could never do on your own. It can bring you blessings you didn't work for, promotions you didn't deserve, and houses you did not build. You are a child of the King and His hand of favor is upon you. Knowing this will cause you to pray bold prayers and dream big dreams. You'll expect good things to happen to you that may not happen to others. The favor of God will cause you to be the head and not the tail, above and not beneath. David knew this and he wrote in Ps. 41:11, "By this I know that You favor me, because my enemy does not triumph over me."

When others are upset and worried, you'll be at peace because you know there is a hedge of protection around you that the enemy cannot pass through. Yes, there will still be battles to be fought but you can be confident of victory every time because the favor of God is on your life. No matter what you're going through, the favor of God will put you on the victor's stand where the crown of victory will be placed upon your head. No longer do you have to fear and be troubled about what's going on in the world around you. No longer do you have to worry about the economy or your children's education. If God and His favor be for you, who or what can be against you? David knew the answer to that question and so should you. He said in Ps. 41:10,11 (MSG), "God, give grace, get me up on my feet. I'll show them a thing or two. Meanwhile, I'm sure You're on my side - no victory shouts yet from the enemy camp!"

Favor is a covenant blessing that belongs to you. Gal. 3:14 (NLT) says, "Through Christ Jesus, God has blessed the Gentiles with the same blessing He promised to Abraham, so that we who are believers might receive the promised Holy Spirit through faith." God told Abraham in Gen. 12:2, "I will make you a great nation; I will bless you and make your name great; And you shall be a blessing." The AMPC Bible says, "I will bless you with abundant increase of favors." The same blessing and favor that was on Abraham is on you also. Jesus died so that you could live in this favor so don't allow this special blessing to pass you by. Do not allow yourself to have a victim's mentality. Ps. 37:19 (NLT) says, "They will not be disgraced in hard times; even in famine they will have more than enough." As long as you stay connected to God, you will have access to His provision that will take you over the top of whatever situation you may be in.

God is a good God and through Jesus His favor is on you. No matter what comes against you, always believe that the favor of God will show up and turn your situation around. It is the favor of God that causes dreams to come true and desires to be fulfilled. It is the golden key that opens up the treasures of heaven and is the one blessing you should crave more than any other. The favor of God will cause the sun to stand still in the sky and the waters to be parted on your behalf. It will cause demons to shake and tremble when you walk into the room. It was the favor of God that brought Joseph from the pit to the palace in a single day and it's this same supernatural force that can be in operation in your life every single day. David wrote in Ps. 23:6, "Surely goodness and mercy shall follow me all the days of my life." The NLT says, "Surely your goodness and unfailing love will pursue me all the days of my life."

God wants to take you farther than you've ever gone before and David is saying that the favor of God will follow you and chase you down continually. Many people fear tomorrow and the giants they are now facing but the favor of God will cause you to run toward your giant with bold confidence knowing the victory is yours. Say out loud, "I am loved and highly favored." It matters not what your circumstances look like. David was highly favored but for years he ran away from King Saul who was trying to kill him. Joseph was also highly favored but he was thrown into prison for a crime he did not commit. Nobody was favored more than Jesus yet He was crucified and hung on a cross between two thieves. Stop looking at the pit you may now be in but instead look to the palace that God has created for you. Don't look at what you're going through but look to where you're going to. If God says you're highly favored, then you're highly favored.

Ps. 30:5 says, "For His anger is but for a moment, His favor is for life; Weeping may endure for a night, but joy comes in the morning." Remember, you're a child of the King and it's through Jesus that you have peace with God and access to His favor. Rom. 5:2 (AMPC) says, "Through Him also we have our access (entrance, introduction) by faith into this grace (state of God's favor) in which we firmly and safely stand. And let us rejoice and exult in our hope of experiencing and enjoying the glory of God." Grasp the fact that you are loved and highly favored by God. Cling to the knowledge that God wants to pour out His favor on you in greater ways than you could ever imagine. Rom. 8:31 says, "If God is for us, who can be against us?" You are a child of the King and are precious in His eyes. When you wake up in the morning, boldly thank God for who He is and for all the blessings He is about to pour into your life.

Declare openly that favor is on the way, that no matter what does or does not happen, God is working out everything for your good. Shout for joy and smile until your teeth sparkle in the noonday sun knowing that no weapon formed against you will prosper. God is on your side, and He knows you can't work hard enough to get everything you deserve. You need favor which is a gift from His mighty hand. Deut. 16:15 (NIV) says, "For the Lord your God will bless you in all your harvest and in all the work of your hands, and your joy will be complete." God did not create you to be average. He created you to come up higher and excel in everything you set out to do. Deut. 30:9 says,

"The Lord your God will make you abound in all the work of your hand, in the fruit of your body, in the increase of your livestock, and in the produce of your land for good. For the Lord will again rejoice over you for good as He rejoiced over your fathers."

The Message Bible says, "God, your God, will outdo Himself in making things go well for you: You'll have babies, get calves, grow crops, and enjoy an all-around good life. Yes, God will start enjoying you again, making things go well for you just as He enjoyed doing it for your ancestors." You are highly favored and you need to think like it, talk like it, and act like it. Favor is born in the womb of obedience so always do what God tells you to do. Obeying God will shorten the distance between you and the blessing He wants to bring into your life. You have a destiny to fulfill and a world to conquer and you need to believe and act like the royal blood of heaven is flowing in your veins. God is with you and if you're in the pit or the palace you can have the assurance that goodness is about to explode all around you. 1 Cor. 15:34 tells you to "Awake to righteousness." The word "awake" means 'to become aware; to become mentally and spiritually perceptive.'

Paul is saying to wake up and become aware that you have right standing with God. Along with this awareness comes the revelation that you also have favor with God. Ps. 5:12 says, "For You, O Lord, will bless the righteous; With favor You will surround him as with a shield." Walking in favor means you will no longer live a defeated lifestyle. You are not a survivor, you are more than a conqueror. Your cup isn't half empty, it's overflowing with the favor of God. There is a smile on your face and a bounce in your step. You are saved, redeemed, and highly favored and nobody can tell you different. No more do you moan and groan and no longer do you pray about what God told you to do six months ago. You have woken up to righteousness and with head held high you rise up in the favor of God and put the devil in his place. You will find God's favor when you do what He tells you to do for to do the will of God is the greatest achievement you will ever fulfill in your life.

1 John 5:14 says, "Now this is the confidence that we have in Him, that if we ask anything according to His will, He hears us." The favor of God rests upon those who walk in obedience to His will, not merely those who seek His blessings. Favor flows from surrender and faithfulness, for rebellion places the heart outside the purpose where His favor abides. The secret to success in life is discovering God's purpose for you and aligning your steps with His will. True fulfillment comes not from chasing your own plans, but from faithfully doing what God has called you to do, trusting Him with the results. The will of God is not always easy to follow, and often it requires sacrifice, trust, and courage beyond our comfort. Yet it is always the right path, perfectly aligned with His wisdom, purpose, and love for our lives. When we walk in obedience to His will, we step into His favor and experience blessings that far exceed what we could ever achieve on our own.

Read your Bible and you will learn what God's will is. Ps. 119:105 says, "Your word is a lamp to my feet and a light to my path." The Message Bible says, "By Your words I can see where I'm going; they throw a beam of light on my dark path. I've committed myself and I'll never turn back from living by Your righteous order." From God's Word comes wisdom and from wisdom comes favor. Prov. 8:33-35 says, "Hear instructions and be wise, and do not disdain it. Blessed is the man who listens to me, watching daily at my gates, waiting at the posts of my doors. For whoever finds me finds life and obtains favor from the Lord." God is merciful, gracious, and full of compassion and the longing of His heart is to bless you with an abundant increase of favors. When you asked Jesus into your heart, He gave you His righteousness and this is what qualifies you for divine favor. You are a child of the living God and He always loves to show favor where His children are concerned.

The favor of God will open doors that no man or devil can shut, doors that other people say are impossible to open. When God's hand is on your life, barriers fall, limitations break, and His purpose moves forward unhindered. Because the favor of God is shining down on you, you'll receive preferential treatment that will cause rules, regulations, laws, and policies to be changed and reversed to your advantage. You'll win victories in battles you won't even have to fight because the Lord will fight them for you. Ps. 44:3 says, "For they did not gain possession of the land by their own sword, nor did their own sword save them; But it was Your right hand, Your arm, and the light of Your countenance, because You favored them." The Message Bible says, "You gave it, smiling as You gave it, delighting as You gave it." God's favor is increasing here in the last days which means the best is yet to come. It's true, God oftentimes saves the best for last.

When Jesus turned water into wine the master of the feast said to the bridegroom, "Every man at the beginning sets out the good wine, and when the guests have well drunk, then that which is inferior; but you have kept the good wine until now" (John 2;10). Get your hopes up and enlarge your vision for the future. You are loved and highly favored and this means you'll be honored in the midst of your adversaries and everything the devil has stolen will be restored back to you many times over. You'll have increase in the midst of a bad economy and will receive recognition even when you seem like the least likely person to receive it. God is on your side and you are about to gain prominence in the world in which you live. There are gifts inside of you that God's favor will use to take you to the top of the mountain of success. You'll solve problems during a crisis that no other person can solve and this will bring promotion and increase into your life.

Wake up in the morning knowing that what's in your future will be greater than what was in your past. God said in Hab. 1:5, "Look among the nations and watch - Be utterly astounded! For I will work a work in your days which you would not believe, though it were told you." God is planning to amaze you with all the blessings He has planned for your future. Your responsibility is to turn away from those negative thoughts you've had in the past. Change your thinking for where the mind goes, the body will follow. Prov. 23:7 says, "For as he thinks in his heart, so is he." Begin to picture yourself as loved and highly favored by God. Imagine yourself as a winner who always receives the best in life. This is what you were predestined for so always set your mind on good things. Expect unprecedented favor to come to you for you attract what you expect. Prov. 23:18 (NIV) says, "There is surely a future hope for you, and your hope will not be cut off."

The Message Bible says, "Don't for a minute envy careless rebels; soak yourself in the fear of God. That's where your future lies. Then you won't be left with an armload of nothing." God favors the obedient, those who are righteous in His sight. When the devil attacks you, have the assurance that God will always promote you. Just release your faith and divine favor will invade your life. Believe that all things are possible and that you will walk in the blessings of God all the days of your life. God will multiply His favor in your life when you believe that the same favor that was on Jesus is also on you because of the work Jesus accomplished on the cross. You don't have to struggle to receive favor, just release it by speaking forth God's Word in faith. Confess out loud, "God's favor surrounds me like a shield. I have favor with God and man."

Believe that the favor of God is working on your behalf, causing doors to open and hearts to move in ways you could never orchestrate. People will go out of their way to bless you, often without even realizing that God is using them as instruments of His goodness. Believe that you'll be able to break through every barrier that is set on your path and that you'll be able to influence a great multitude of people. Ask God for favor with all your heart knowing that He can do amazing things in your life and bring you blessings that money could never buy. In the parable of the laborers Jesus told how the owner of a vineyard paid those who worked one hour the same wages as those who worked all day (Matt. 20:1-16). That was favor and deep inside of you must be the conviction and assurance that you've been marked with the same blessing. You've been marked for favor and knowing this will cause you to rise up and become great in the kingdom of God.

Paul had a revelation of this when he wrote in 1 Cor. 15:10 (NLT), "But whatever I am now, it is all because God poured out His special favor on me - and not without results. For I have worked harder than any of the other apostles; yet it was not I but God who was working through me by His grace." The more you understand and believe that you are loved and highly favored, the more that distinctive favor will be released into your life. Never in a hundred lifetimes could you work for and earn everything God wants to give you. When He breathed life into you, He marked you with greatness. He marked you for favor and blessing and this is why you can live a life that is free from fear, worry, and concern. You're in good hands with the favor of God. Psalm 91 is a psalm about the favor of God. Vs. 7 says, "A thousand may fall at your side, and ten thousand at your right hand: But it shall not come near you." Favor builds a hedge of protection around you that keeps you safe from all harm.

Stay in faith, for there is a shield of favor surrounding you covering your life, your family, your career, and your ministry. No matter what comes against you, God's favor goes before you, stands beside you, and protects all that He has entrusted to your hands. Vs. 10,11, "No evil shall befall you, nor shall any plague come near your dwelling; For He shall give His angels charge over you, to keep you in all your ways." That's favor. God said in vs. 14-16, "Because he has set his love upon Me, therefore I will deliver him; I will set him on high, because he has known My name. He shall call upon Me, and I will answer him; I will be with him in trouble. I will deliver him and honor him. With long life I will satisfy him and show him My salvation." Favor is part of the heritage you received when you got born again. You cannot earn favor for it is a gift from God, a gift that will cause you to be successful in life when normally you would fail.

1 Peter 2:9 says, "But you are a chosen generation, a royal priesthood, a holy nation, His own special people." The word "chosen" means 'marked for favor or special privilege'; the word "royal" means 'a person of royal blood, having status or power'; and "holy" means 'exalted or worthy, divine, sacred.' This is who God says you are. You've been chosen by God and marked with His divine favor. You are the apple of His eye and He created you with purpose and a destiny to fulfill. God has marked you to be blessed and this is your time and season to take possession of your inheritance. It's His divine favor that will cause you to fulfill your destiny, to walk through doors that otherwise would not be opened. As you walk in this favor, your spirit will be refreshed like a gentle spring rain, washing away weariness and renewing your strength. The grace of God will restore your soul, filling you with peace, hope, and a renewed passion for the journey ahead.

The fragrance of God is on you and the dynamic energy of His favor will cause you to bless nations. He'll take you places where you'll have maximum influence, places where people want to hear the good news you have to share with them. One of the biggest lies the devil will ever tell you is "it doesn't get any better than this." No, the best is yet to come. Incredible power is released when you believe that, giving you the advantage wherever you may go. As you rise up in faith, God will cause your life to shine as He takes you to a higher level in the fulfillment of your destiny. You are heavy with favor and there is nothing you can't do in the pursuit of your heavenly dream. It is your time to rise and shine for God is about to take you to places you've never been and cause you to do things you've never done. You are loved and highly favored and the set time for God to move in your life is right now.

It is in the season of overflow that dreams come to pass and it's the favor of God that takes you into that season. Dare to believe it and dare to act on it. What you think you can accomplish is nothing compared to what the favor of God can do. 1 Cor. 2:9 says, "Eye has not seen, nor ear heard, nor have entered into the heart of man the things which God has prepared for those who love Him." Now is the time for God to take you from the background into the foreground but you must believe that it will happen. Elizabeth told Mary, "Blessed is she who believed, for there will be a fulfillment of those things which were told her from the Lord" (Luke 1:45). With all your heart and soul believe that supernatural blessings have been ordained by God to come into your life. Believe what Paul said in 2 Cor. 1:20, "For all the promises of God in Him are Yes and in Him Amen, to the glory of God through us."

The Bible is filled with the promises of God to them that believe. He promised to never leave you or forsake you and to give you a way of escape when the burdens of life seem too hard to bear. He promised to keep you in perfect peace when your mind is stayed on Him and to supply all your need according to His riches in glory by Christ Jesus. He even said in Is. 55:11, "So shall My word be that goes forth from My mouth; It shall not return to Me void, but it shall accomplish what I please, and it shall prosper in the thing for which I sent it." The Message Bible says, "They'll do the work I sent them to do, they'll complete the assignment I gave them." The favor of God is on assignment to bring blessings into your life. God wants to use you to show the world how good He truly is. This desire of God is so great that 2 Chron. 16:9 says, "For the eyes of the Lord run to and fro throughout the whole earth, to show Himself strong on behalf of those whose heart is loyal to Him."

God is calling out to people that He can be good to. Will you answer the call? If so, then rise up and dare to believe that the favor of God will flow in your life. Believe that you'll stand out in a crowd and receive opportunities that others may not get. You are a child of the King - loved, chosen, and covered by His authority and care. Because you belong to Him, every good thing He has promised flows from His perfect wisdom and timing. Walk in confidence and trust, knowing He will withhold nothing that is truly good for your life. You've been crowned with favor and the Creator of the universe is breathing His life into you. You've been set apart so remind yourself that you've got a right to succeed when others fail, a right to prosper when others are going bankrupt, a right to flourish when others struggle. God knows how to give you the advantage, to cause you to be at the right place at the right time. It's called favor and it belongs to you.

| **25** |

"GOD'S AMAZING GRACE"

God's grace and His favor are so amazing yet very few people experience the goodness of God on a continual, daily basis. They walk around in fear and condemnation believing they've got to do something or perform some great task before God will be good to them. They were wounded and rejected by their natural father and wrongly believe that the Heavenly Father is the same way. These people know nothing about the heart of God for it is His ultimate desire to pour out and lavish on people extravagant quantities of His kindness and favor and power. You don't deserve this grace and you definitely can't earn it. What you can do is receive it and being made freely available is what makes God's grace so amazing. Eph. 2:8,9 says, "For by grace you have been saved through faith, and that not of yourselves; it is the gift of God, not of works, lest anyone should boast."

The Message Bible says, "Saving is all His idea, and all His work. All we do is trust Him enough to let Him do it. It's God's gift from start to finish! We don't play the major role. If we did, we'd probably go around bragging that we'd done the whole thing." There are nail prints in the hands and feet of Jesus and for that reason alone God is willing and anxious to be good to you. Get it settled once and for all that you will never be good enough to earn God's amazing grace on your own merit. Is. 64:6 says, "But we are all like an unclean thing, and all our righteousnesses are like filthy rags; We all fade as a leaf, and our iniquities, like the wind, have taken us away." You are saved and blessed not by what you have done, but by what Jesus did when He went to the cross on your behalf. Yes, God delights in the works of His people as long as they don't use their good deeds as a recipe for pride.

Remain humble for it is easy to get puffed up when you start talking about all the good things you've done for the Lord. If receiving praise from people is the motive for what you do, then praise from people is all you're going to get and even that won't last very long. Just remember that God gets all the glory and, when you acknowledge the fact that you are accepted by God not because of your works but in spite of them, you will put yourself in a position where God can pour His goodness and favor into your life. It is stunning how millions of people are not walking in the blessing and power that God's grace is making available to them. Paul tells what the problem is in 2 Cor. 6:1, "We then, as workers together with Him also plead with you not to receive the grace of God in vain." The people in this church were born again and Spirit-filled believers but here Paul is pleading with them because they had an incorrect understanding of what grace truly is.

Like most people today, they probably thought grace was something they could hide behind to cover-up for their disobedient lifestyle. They say, "Thank God for His grace. He loves me just the way I am." No, He doesn't. Yes, He loves you as a person but if you're living a sinful lifestyle, He does not love you just the way you are. He hates sin and so should you. People who use grace as a cover-up are running away from accepting the responsibility for their wrongful behavior and are thus receiving the grace of God in vain. They are abusing the true meaning of grace and perverting it to use for their own vile purposes. Paul was aware of what was happening and he pleaded with them to stop doing it. Don't tell other people you're saved if you're still practicing sin. The Bible says, "Examine yourselves as to whether you are in the faith. Prove yourselves" (2 Cor. 13:5). Paul's message to the Gentiles was "that they should repent, turn to God, and do works befitting repentance (Acts. 26:20).

The NIV says "they should repent and turn to God and demonstrate their repentance by their deeds." People today are not walking in the footsteps of Jesus because they're using grace as a cover-up instead of using its power to enable them to walk as He walked. 2 Cor. 7:1 says, "Therefore, having these promises, beloved, let us cleanse ourselves from all filthiness of the flesh and spirit, perfecting holiness in the fear of God." The grace of God is not a cover-up for sin but is the freely given power of God bestowed on you to make you stronger and more confident as you pursue the fulfillment of your destiny. Heb. 12:28,29 says, "Therefore, since we are receiving a kingdom which cannot be shaken, let us have grace, by which we may serve God acceptably with reverence and godly fear. For our God is a consuming fire." You were born to live an extraordinary life and it's only through God's amazing grace that this will come to pass.

The mistake many people make is they get so wrapped up in trying to define what grace is that they don't focus on the work that grace does. The standard definition most people come up with is that grace is unmerited favor and that is a partially true statement. Grace is definitely unmerited, it is undeserved, and it is unearned. People are happy with this definition and once they have it they go about their merry way giving no more thought to the subject of grace. They think they know what grace is and that's good enough for them. But what about God? Do these same people stop and consider what God's definition of grace is? No, they don't, for if they did their lives would be going in a different direction. God told Paul in 2 Cor. 12:9 (NIV), "My grace is sufficient for you, for My power is made perfect in weakness." Here in this verse God refers to His grace as His power. The Message Bible says, "My strength comes into its own in your weakness."

Peter said the same thing in 2 Peter 1:2,3, "Grace and peace be multiplied to you in the knowledge of God and of Jesus our Lord, as His divine power has given us all things that pertain to life and godliness." The grace of God is defined in the Bible as the divine power of God and most believers don't know that. They think grace and favor are one and the same thing but they're not. Grace is grace and favor is favor. You have been predestined to come to a place of greatness in Him and it takes the power of God to transform you into the person He wants you to become. This power is accessed through the supernatural grace of God. Strong's Concordance says grace "is a divine influence upon the heart, and its reflection in the life." With grace there is an outward reflection of what God is doing in the heart. The grace of God is not unmerited favor, it's unmerited power that gives you supernatural ability to build up the kingdom of God on the earth.

You can't do this with natural ability for Ps. 127:1 says, "Unless the Lord builds the house, they labor in vain who build it." The end is near and there is much work to do in the kingdom before the Lord's glorious return. Phil. 1:6 (NLT) says, "And I am certain that God, who began the good work within you, will continue His work until it is finally finished on the day when Christ Jesus returns." God is working in you and grace is needed to complete the work He desires to do in and through your life. This is why Heb. 4:16 says, "Let us therefore come boldly to the throne of grace, that we may obtain mercy and find grace to help in time of need." It takes faith to access the grace of God for you can't receive from Him anything unless you first believe. This is why it is so important that you understand what grace truly is so that you can believe correctly. It won't do you much good if you're believing for the wrong thing.

Once you know and understand what God says grace is, you can then use your faith as the channel that activates grace in your life. Rom. 5:2 says that through Jesus "we have access by faith into this grace in which we stand." The power of God's grace is there for the taking so believe for it right now. The kingdom of God is inside of you and you can impact your world through the power of God's grace. You have been called to come up higher and live in the power of the kingdom so that it will be on earth just as it is in heaven. Eph. 2:10 says, "For we are His workmanship, created in Christ Jesus for good works, which God prepared beforehand that we should walk in them." This is your calling and it's only through God's amazing grace that your destiny will be fulfilled. Paul said in 1 Cor. 15:10, "But by the grace of God I am what I am, and His grace toward me was not in vain; but I labored more abundantly than they all, yet not I, but the grace of God which was with me."

The Message Bible says, "It was God giving me the work to do, God giving me the energy to do it." Whatever God calls you to do, He will give you the grace to do it. When problems arise, proclaim the grace of God over them. The Lord said in Zech. 4:7, "Who are you, O great mountain? Before Zerubbabel you shall become a plain! And he shall bring forth the capstone with shouts of 'Grace, grace to it!'" Mountains of difficulty were in the way of his undertaking, but nothing is too hard for the grace of God. Whatever God calls you to do, there is a special grace for it over your life. When God gives you His grace, He gives you the fullness of who Jesus is. John 1:16 says, "And of His fullness we have all received, and grace for grace." The Message Bible says, "We all live of His generous bounty, gift after gift after gift." God will begin a good work in you and then He'll give you the fullness of Jesus to complete it. He initiates the call and furnishes the grace to fulfill it.

If the grace is not there then stop what you're doing and seek Him out because you are in the wrong call. Remember, there will be an outward reflection of what's done in the heart, something that can be seen and heard by those around you. Barnabas was sent to the churches in Antioch and Acts 11:23 says, "When he came and had seen the grace of God, he was glad, and encouraged them all that with purpose of heart they should continue with the Lord." Barnabas did not hear about this grace; he saw the empowerment that was reflected in their lives. He saw the power that gave them the ability to go beyond their own natural ability. Grace causes you to "be partakers of the divine nature" of Jesus (2 Peter 1:4). This means that God will give you the essential qualities and character of Jesus in full measure. That is power to the highest degree and 1 John 4:17 says, "As He is, so are we in this world."

If you are born again, Eph. 5:30 says, "For we are members of His body, of His flesh and of His bones." Paul is saying that you are the offspring of God. You are bone of His bone and flesh of His flesh. 1 John 3:2 says, "Beloved, now we are children of God." John also said, "He who says he abides in Him ought himself also to walk just as He walked" (1 John 2:6). It's the grace of God that allows you to do this. Acts 4:33 says, "And with great power the apostles gave witness to the resurrection of the Lord Jesus. And great grace was upon them all." God's great grace is God's great power. People who fall from grace are those who try to serve God with their own power and ability. The sons of Sceva tried to do this and the devil literally tore them to shreds (Acts 19:11-20). This is what happens when people don't know what grace truly is. Grace gives you the power to live like Jesus and to rule over your circumstances.

Rom. 5:17 says, "All who receive God's abundant grace and are freely put right with Him will rule in life through Christ." Most people are ruled by life but the grace of God causes you to rise above what's normal for others. You were created to do more than work your entire life for a paycheck that doesn't fulfill your needs and desires, retire at a ripe old age, and then die within five years because you no longer have anything to live for. You were created to flow in the power of God's amazing grace and to break out of the status quo and live an extraordinary life. You were created to touch the lives of people all over this world and be a powerful influence in their lives. You've got a destiny to fulfill and you must be aggressive in your pursuit of it. Paul said in Eph. 3:9,10 (MSG), "My task is to bring out in the open and make plain what God, who created all this in the first place, has been doing in secret and behind the scenes all along.

Through followers of Jesus like yourselves gathered in churches, this extraordinary plan of God is becoming known and talked about even among the angels!" Say out loud, "No more ordinary living for me." God's plan for your life goes beyond anything you could ever imagine, ask, or think. God wants you to turn your world upside down and He's given you the power of His grace to do it. Phil. 2:13 (NLT) says, "For God is working in you, giving you the desire and the power to do what pleases Him." Take hold of His grace, be overwhelmed by it, and then go out and do what you're supposed to do. You need to expand your horizons and start blazing paths of glory wherever you go. You are special and were made to be extraordinary so think outside the box and don't be confined to the limitations the world may try to put on you. Come up higher and let the grace of God take you places that most people only dream of.

Dan. 6:3 says, "Then this Daniel distinguished himself above the governors and satraps, because an excellent spirit was in him; and the king gave thought to setting him over the whole realm." The Message Bible says Daniel was "brimming with spirit and intelligence." Like Daniel, you also are called to be a light in the midst of a dark world. You've been called by God to go beyond the limitations that are normal on the earth today. It is the will of God for you to have a yearning on the inside of you to go higher and farther than where human effort and ability can take you. With the grace of God you can break through those barriers that will try to hold you back. The struggle is over when the grace of God flows in your life. You'll walk in His power, His anointing, authority, and ability. His promises will come to pass in your life and your prayers will be answered like you've never seen them answered before.

A lot of people pray for things they don't have because they forget something they already do have. Rom. 12:3 (MSG) says, "I'm speaking to you out of deep gratitude for all that God has given me, and especially as I have responsibilities in relation to you. Living then, as every one of you does, in pure grace, it's important that you not misinterpret yourselves as people who are bringing this goodness to God. No, God brings it all to you. The only accurate way to understand ourselves is by what God is and by what He does for us, not by what we are and what we do for Him." God wants you to walk in pure grace that is complete in and of itself. It is pure, it is free, and it is the mark of God's power and blessing in your life. You're not to walk in your own power and ability, you're to walk in God's power and ability. When you walk in pure grace you'll begin to reflect on how good God has already been to you.

David wrote in Ps. 103:2, "Bless the Lord, O my soul, and forget not all His benefits." Your gratitude, in turn, will release a dynamic faith in your inner man that, like a magnet, will bring to you everything that is missing in your life. The Christian life is not about the promises you make to God, it's about the promises He makes to you. The good news is that God keeps all His promises for "He is not a man that He should lie" (Num. 23:19). Paul says in 1 Thess. 5:24 (MSG), "The One who called you is completely dependable. If He said it, He'll do it." Paul closes out his letter to the Thessalonian church by saying, "The amazing grace of Jesus Christ be with you!" (vs.29). Grace that is pure and amazing is to believe that the nature of God is to bring to pass all that He has promised. As you go about the task of fulfilling your destiny, you can have the confidence that the grace of God will be with you every step of the way.

Ps. 138:8 (ESV) says, "The Lord will fulfill His purpose for me; Your steadfast love, O Lord, endures forever. Do not forsake the work of Your hands." The Message Bible says, "Finish what you started in me, God. Your love is eternal - don't quit on me now." People are always starting things that they're not able to finish but thoughtless action can never be associated with God. He knows the end from the beginning and when He gives you a destiny to fulfill, He will give you the grace and the power to complete the work He gives you to do. God is faithful and if you are endeavoring to fulfill the purpose for which He made you, then His abounding love and everlasting honor will bind Him to fulfill His part by giving you the grace you need. Grace is power and 1 Cor. 2:5 says "your faith should not be in the wisdom of men but in the power of God." Faith is the tidal wave of the inner man and, as it rises in your heart, the grace and power of God rise with it.

Walking in faith is when you let God be God. He is all powerful and your faith must rest in the grace and power of God. Grace believes that He is the author of your faith and the finisher of your faith (Heb. 12:2). God said in Jer. 1:12, "I am ready to perform My word." God always does what He says. He speaks His word and then watches over it to perform it. God will never require anything more from you other than to conform to what He is doing in your life. God loves you, He created you, and He sets you apart for His special purpose. You have a destiny to fulfill and destiny is what makes the difference between the ordinary and the extraordinary. It is a great honor and a brilliant privilege to work alongside Him here in the last days. It is a wonderful thing to see the plans and purposes of God being fulfilled in your life and this is why you must never cease to have faith in the power of God's amazing grace. In Him and in His grace "we live and move and have our being" (Acts 17:28).

The Message Bible says, "He doesn't play hide-and-seek with us! He's not remote; He's near. We live and move in Him, can't get away from Him!" Living an ordinary life is a pathetic way to live for God created you for so much more. He created you to be extraordinary and then gave you incredible power to become the person you were created to be. For years the believers of God have been tainted with the image of being a group of backward and passive people who have no idea who they are and what they're supposed to do. No more. You've been made in the image of God and His grace allows you to excel in life with power and energy that will not be denied. Creativity flows out of you and you'll be able to do things others say can't be done. You've got the mind of Christ and the grace of God that allows you to fulfill your destiny.

As you walk in the footsteps of Jesus you will quickly learn that He never was normal and never will be normal. Neither are you for you have been called to reflect His nature to those around you. You've been called to turn your world upside down and normal people can't do that. It takes real believers with real grace and real power to make a lasting impact on this world. God has no tolerance for counterfeit Christianity, for people who wear a cross around their neck but don't have Jesus in their heart. There is no such thing as a Christian who lies but there are liars who say they are Christian. Pastors who claim to be Christian but support same-sex marriages are hireling shepherds and moral cowards. These pastors are strangers in the kingdom of God and Jesus said in John 10:5, "Yet they will by no means follow a stranger, but will flee from him, for they do not know the voice of a stranger."

The problem in the church today is that its people have become normal just as the sinful world around them is normal. They have a form of godliness but deny its power (2 Tim. 3:5). The Message Bible says, "They'll make a show of religion, but behind the scenes they're animals. Stay clear of these people." God is telling you to turn away from what the world calls normal and live an extraordinary lifestyle. You're called to stand out in this sinful world and to be a shining light in the midst of all this darkness and gloom. It is time to walk away from those churches where the power of grace is not present and the truth of the gospel is not taught. Heb. 13:9 says, "Do not be carried about with various and strange doctrines. For it is good that the heart be established by grace." The Message Bible says, "The grace of God is the only good ground for life." God is saying to you that His amazing grace is sufficient for you to live an extraordinary life.

His grace is powerful and it is relentless. It is always pushing forward and allows you to do what you've been called to do. Where you are weak, God's grace makes you strong for His miracle-working power is made perfect in weakness. It shows itself to be most effective during times of personal weakness. Your weakness coupled together with God's power turns you into a force to be reckoned with. That's what grace is all about and is the reason why you need to make grace your way of life. Don't trust in your own ability but in the supernatural ability of grace. It's what turns you from a nobody into a somebody, from a zero into a hero. The grace of God is radical and it needs to be permanently established in your heart. It shouldn't be here one day and gone the next but be in manifestation every day of your life. Grace is a good thing and Philemon 6 (NLT) says you need to "understand and experience all the good things we have in Christ."

Grace is amazing only when you understand it and especially when you experience it. Stop trying to serve God with your own ability but allow His amazing grace to do it for you. Do not allow the grace of God to be wasted by doing nothing with it. There is nothing as sinful as wasting what God has so graciously given you. The most precious thing known to man is the grace of God. The more precious the thing being wasted, the more sinful the waste. God gave you His grace for a purpose and anytime the grace of God does not accomplish what God intended, the grace has been wasted. Do not allow this to happen in your life because it takes grace to make known the goodness of the Lord in this dying world. It takes grace for your light to shine in the darkness, for you to fulfill your destiny, so never take the grace of God in vain. Whatever you've been called to do, the fullness of God's grace has been provided for you to do it.

By the grace of God the children of Israel were gloriously delivered from the tyranny of Egypt but refused to rely on that grace to take them into the Promised Land. They wasted the grace of God and never did enter the land flowing with milk and honey. Do not neglect the opportunities God gives you to take advantage of His grace. In the parable of the wise and foolish virgins they were both provided the same opportunity. The foolish virgins were so busy doing other things that they neglected to get oil for their lamps. They wasted the opportunity that the grace of God had provided for them (Matt. 25:1-13). This is a serious matter. Heb. 10:29 (NIV) says, "How much more severely do you think someone deserves to be punished who has trampled the Son of God underfoot, who has treated as an unholy thing the blood of the covenant that sanctified them, and who has insulted the Spirit of grace?" Don't waste the grace of God but take full advantage of the situation you now find yourself in.

Paul made a point of saying that God's grace was not wasted on him and you need to be able to say the same thing. You've been filled with power from heaven and you've got to let this grace carry you, lead you, and empower you. If you don't use this power, then the grace of God is wasted and taken in vain. It's this power, this amazing grace, that puts God on display in your life. It's God's power working in you and through you that you're able to fulfill your destiny and show the world what He is truly like. It's your responsibility to make God look good and it's His grace that enables you to do that. 2 Cor. 6:1 (CJB) says, "As God's fellow-workers we also urge you not to receive His grace and then do nothing with it." Let every word you say and every action you take be flavored with grace. God's grace is always there, and you need to cherish it and put it to use in your life. Become like Paul who labored more than all the brethren. He fulfilled his destiny and, with the grace of God, so will you.

| **26** |

"AN ABUNDANCE OF GRACE"

The world had been turned upside down. Jesus had risen from the grave and ascended on high. Before doing so He made it clear to those who followed Him that they were to pick up the mantle and continue the mission to go out and make disciples of all men. In other words, they were sent to fulfill their destiny. No longer could they be mere spectators to the miracle-working power of Jesus but were commissioned to go into all the world and do even greater works than He did. The supernatural did not stop with Jesus and how amazed the disciples must have felt when they realized that soon this same Messiah would be living in them and working through them. A short time later those in the upper room were gloriously filled with the Holy Spirit and now the Lord's followers were taking the world by storm with a super-natural power never before seen since the dawn of time. Miracles galore were performed and souls were being added to the church daily.

The lame man at the gate of the temple called "Beautiful" was raised up and entered the temple walking, and leaping, and praising God (Acts 3:8). The whole city was shaken to its core and soon the religious Sanhedrin leaders "called them and commanded them not to speak at all nor teach in the name of Jesus" (Acts 4:18). Their threats were indeed spoken in vain as the disciples went to their own companions and raised their voice to God with one accord and asked for boldness and fearless confidence to continue preaching the message of the resurrected Savior. They prayed "'that signs and wonders may be done through the name of Your holy Servant Jesus.' And when they had prayed, the place where they were assembled together was shaken; and they were all filled with the Holy Spirit, and they spoke the word of God with boldness" (Acts 4:30,31).

What had been a small group of confused and frightened men just a few days prior to this were now fearless warriors thriving forward to fulfill the prophecy spoken by Jesus in Acts 1:8, "But you shall receive power when the Holy Spirit has come upon you; and you shall be witnesses to Me in Jerusalem, and in all Judea and Samaria, and to the end of the earth." When told to stop what they were doing they prayed to God for more boldness and more miracles. With much courage they pressed on with the great commission and their enthusiasm and joy carried them forward where in times past they would have run away and hid. The Message Bible says in Acts 2:43-47, "Everyone around was in awe - all those wonders and signs done through the apostles! And all the believers lived in a wonderful harmony, holding everything in common. They sold whatever they owned and pooled their resources so that each person's need was met.

They followed a daily discipline of worship in the Temple followed by meals at home, every meal a celebration, exuberant and joyful, as they praised God. People in general liked what they saw. Every day their number grew as God added those who were saved." Like Jesus, they also were turning their world upside down. Acts 4:33 states, "And with great power the apostles gave witness to the resurrection of the Lord Jesus. And great grace was upon them all." It takes great grace to accomplish what God wants you to do. Life is hard when you try to do it on your own without the grace of God in your life. Your talents and abilities are not enough to do all that God has called you to do. This is why Jesus said in Matt. 11:28, "Come to Me, all you who labor and are heavy laden, and I will give you rest." An invitation as sweet as this demands a fast and spontaneous acceptance. He wants you to do nothing else but come to Him for when you do He'll pour His grace into your life.

With grace what was once hard now becomes easy. Jesus continued in vs. 29,30, "Take My yoke upon you and learn from Me, for I am gentle and lowly in heart, and you will find rest for your souls. For My yoke is easy and My burden is light." The Message Bible says, "Are you tired? Worn out? Burned out on religion? Come to Me. Get away with Me and you'll recover your life. I'll show you how to take a real rest. Walk with Me and work with Me - watch how I do it. Learn the unforced rhythms of grace. I won't lay anything heavy or ill-fitting on you. Keep company with Me and you'll learn to live freely and lightly." The phenomenal grace of God is exceptional, outstanding, and unsurpassing. It is power not earned and means "to bend down, to stoop down in kindness" as in a superior reaching down to an inferior. You were saved by grace (Eph. 2:8) and you are to live by grace. With great grace you can do anything, be anything, and receive anything.

Great grace was upon those first century believers and since you are a part of this same church you must strive daily to walk in that same grace. Paul writes in Rom. 5:17, "Those who receive abundance of grace and of the gift of righteousness shall reign in life through the One, Jesus Christ." When Paul says an "abundance of grace" he is using a descriptive measure of grace just like Luke did in Acts 4:33 when he said "great grace" was upon them all. This means that grace can be increased and that you can have more grace than you're experiencing right now. About Jesus Luke 2:40 says, "And the Child grew and became strong in spirit, filled with wisdom; and the grace of God was upon Him." Vs. 52 goes on to say, "And Jesus increased in wisdom and stature, and in favor with God and man." The favor and grace that was on the life of Jesus increased and Peter says you are to "grow in the grace and knowledge of our Lord and Savior Jesus Christ" (2 Peter 3:18).

You can grow in grace if you choose to. God is the author and finisher of all that is good and you can receive an abundance of grace by getting to know Him more and more. All things that pertain to the kingdom of grace is in a state of readiness so that in a moment of time God can give help if your heart is prepared to receive it. James 4:6 says, "But He gives more grace. Therefore He says: 'God resists the proud but gives grace to the humble.'" To grow in grace you must grow in humility. Never take credit for what God does through you. Don't brag about your faith and how hard you work for God and how many hours you pray. It is the grace of God that gives you the ability and everything else you need to accomplish the opportunities you've been given. Gen. 6:8 says, "But Noah found grace in the eyes of the Lord." Grace made all the difference in his life and, like Noah, you also are in the ark of God's protection. You're safe and sound and you've found grace and favor in the eyes of the Lord.

The angel Gabriel said to the virgin Mary, "Rejoice, highly favored one, the Lord is with you; blessed are you among women!" (Luke 1:28). Mary was favored and blessed because the Lord was with her and not because of anything she had done on her own. She was chosen to be the mother of Jesus because the grace of God was on her life. Mary's humility was revealed in her response, "Behold the maidservant of the Lord! Let it be to me according to your word." The apostle John wrote, "And the Word became flesh and dwelt among us, and we beheld His glory, the glory as of the only begotten of the Father, full of grace and truth" (John 1:14). Grace is a big word and there are varying degrees of how much grace can be upon you. Great grace was upon the first century church and in Greek the word "great" means 'mega.' This was not a little grace. It was a big grace and it was upon them all.

John continues in vs. 16, "For out of His fullness (abundance) we have all received [all had a share and we were all supplied with] one grace after another and spiritual blessing upon spiritual blessing and even favor upon favor and gift [heaped] upon gift" (AMP). The Message Bible says, "We all live off His generous bounty, gift after gift after gift." This is a stacked grace, grace upon grace upon grace, layer upon layer. You can have so much grace upon you that what was once impossible is now possible. With an abundance of grace things that were once difficult now become effortless. With enough grace you can receive any miracle and overcome any struggle. You can be what you're supposed to be and do what you're supposed to do. With more grace you can run your race and finish your course. This is why Paul told Timothy to "be strong in the grace that is in Christ Jesus" (2 Tim. 2:1). The grace of God is the presence of God.

John 1:14 says that grace and glory go together and "glory" can be defined as 'the manifested presence of God.' A mark of His presence is that His goodness will be poured into your life and He will also give you rest and cause peace to abound in your life. The way of the wicked is hard but when you have peace you are not frantic or disturbed. You're in the eye of the hurricane, the favor zone, the safe harbor of God's comfort and protection. Acts 3:19 says "that times of refreshing may come from the presence of the Lord." The Message Bible says God will "pour out showers of blessing to refresh you." With an abundance of grace times of refreshing are always close at hand. God is always looking for opportunities to pour rich blessings into your life. He is willing and able to make all grace abound toward you. Always seek for higher and better things for God will bless you more abundantly when you become more ready to receive the blessing.

Being in the presence of the Lord makes these blessings more valuable for they are enhanced by the love you give to God in response to the love He gives to you. His presence will cause you to come up higher where the dark clouds of demonic oppression will never darken your Son-lit sky. Grace will abound in your life and the more grace that is upon you, the more peace you'll have. Put your trust in God for Is.

26:3,4 states, "You will keep him in perfect peace whose mind is stayed on You, because he trusts in You. Trust in the Lord forever, for in YAH, the Lord, is everlasting strength." David wrote in Ps. 5:11, "But let all those rejoice who put their trust in You; Let them ever shout for joy, because You defend them; Let those also who love Your name be joyful in You." You can't be in faith and be depressed. Faith always shouts and rejoices whereas doubt brings hardship and despair.

David tells you why to shout in vs. 12, "For You, O Lord, will bless the righteous; With favor You will surround him as with a shield." A shield of favor and grace is a spiritual force field that will surround you and protect you like it did Job. Satan said to God, "Have You not made a hedge around him, around his household, and around all that he has on every side?" (Job 1:10). Ps. 30:5 says, "His favor is for life" and vs. 7 states, "Lord, by Your favor You have made my mountain stand strong." The Message Bible says, "I'm God's favorite. He made me king of the mountain." Weakness of spirit causes you to stumble and fall but grace gives you strength, a spiritual backbone that will cause you to endure whatever the enemy brings against you. In His grace, there is life - abundant, sustaining, and powerful enough to re-new the weary soul. Even in the midst of distress, His grace makes you firm as a mountain, unshaken and standing strong through every storm.

Prov. 19:12 says the king's "favor is like dew on the grass." Dew can be light as a mist or it can be as if a heavy rain had fallen. In like manner there are various measures of grace. You can have little grace where you hardly notice it or so much grace that it's dripping off of you. Prov. 16:15 states, "In the light of the king's face is life, and his favor is like a cloud of the latter rain." A person who is highly favored walks in a greater degree of grace than others. In their life is grace upon grace upon grace. This is great grace and Heb. 4:16 says you can "come boldly to the throne of grace, that we may obtain mercy and find grace to help in time of need." God helps you with His grace and if you need more help, you'll need more grace. Ps. 119:57,58 says, "You are my portion, O Lord; I have said that I would keep Your words. I entreated Your favor with my whole heart; Be merciful to me according to Your word."

The Message Bible says, "Because You have satisfied me, God, I promise to do everything You say. I beg You from the bottom of my heart: smile, be gracious to me just as You promised." Ps. 89:17 says, "For You are the glory of their strength, and in Your favor our horn is exalted." The God's Word Bible states, "By Your favor You give us victory." The word "horn" is a symbol of power and the NLT says, "It pleases You to make us strong." You can initiate a grace increase and gain more favor by pleasing God. If you'll please Him more, you'll be favored more. Jesus said in John 8:29, "And He who sent Me is with Me. The Father has not left Me alone, for I always do those things that please Him." This is why Jesus walked in favor with God and man. The grace of God was on Him without measure and you can walk as Jesus walked and have the same grace He had. David wrote in Ps. 40:8, "I delight to do Your will, O my God, and Your law is within my heart."

God takes great joy in those who cheerfully do His will. Like David, an attitude of delightful desire should fill all your attempts to please God and when you do that even your enemies will be at peace with you (Prov. 16:7). Ps. 41:11 says, "By this I know that You are well pleased with me, because my enemy does not triumph over me." You win in life not by striving for applause, but by walking in obedience that pleases God. True success flows from His favor, because when God is pleased, He opens doors no man can shut and establishes the work of your hands. When you live for Him, His blessing, guidance, and victory follow you wherever you go. Your power of influence grows by pleasing God more and more. The Bible gives many accounts of people who also walked in the grace of God and man and a study of their lives will reveal how you also can walk in an abundance of grace.

The book of Esther is one such story and it is all about grace and favor. It is the theme of the entire book and tells how God raised a Jewish girl out of obscurity to become the queen of the most powerful empire in the world. An evil plot had been devised by Haman to annihilate all the Jews in the region and the book of Esther was written to show how the Jewish people were protected and preserved by the gracious hand of God. The name "Esther" is derived from the Persian word for 'star' and her courage and humility shined forth as she and her wise cousin Mordecai set out to counter the threat that had arisen against God's people. The story begins when King Ahasuerus provided a lavish banquet for the people of Shushan and proudly sought to make Queen Vashti's beauty a part of the program. The queen refused to come and "the king was furious, and his anger burned within him" (Esther 1:12).

When the queen refused to appear it was feared that the other women in the kingdom would become insolent if Vashti went unpunished. The king received counsel to depose her and seek another queen which he promptly did. From every province in the kingdom beautiful young virgins were brought to the citadel for a year of preparation to beautify themselves more than they already were and the one who pleased the king the most would be the new queen. Esther 2:13 says, "Thus prepared, each young woman went to the king, and she was given whatever she desired to take with her from the women's quarters to the king's palace." These women selfishly took whatever they wanted in hopes of gaining an unfair advantage over the others in this royal beauty contest. Not so with Esther. When the turn came for her to go in to the king "she requested nothing but what Hegai the king's eunuch, the custodian of the women, advised. And Esther obtained favor in the sight of all who saw her" (Esther 2:15).

Esther did not ask for special treatment nor did she feel entitled to receive it. Some people are always demanding things from other people but you can't be gracious to someone who thinks they deserve it.

God resists the proud but gives grace to the humble. Matt. 20:21 tells how the mother of Zebedee's sons came to Jesus asking for special treatment. "And He said to her, 'What do you wish?' She said to Him, 'Grant that these two sons of mine may sit, one on Your right hand and the other on the left, in Your kingdom.'" This is not how you get favor and an abundance of grace from God. This is pride and presumption and vs. 24 says, "And when the ten heard it, they were moved with indignation against the two brothers." When you expect nothing from other people and dispel the notion that they owe you something, you are then open to receive more grace from God. If people don't ask a lot from you, you just naturally want to do more for them.

Grace is not given to people who are always wanting something. Stop asking people for things with an attitude that they owe you and in faith ask God instead. Esther asked for no special treatment and Esther 2:17 says, "The king loved Esther more than all the other women, and she gained grace and favor in his sight more than all the virgins; so he set the royal crown upon her head and made her queen instead of Vashti." It was this same grace that allowed Esther to go into the inner court of the king unannounced and thus put an end to the plot to kill all the Jews in the region. All this happened because in humility Esther asked for no special treatment and thus gained an abundance of grace and favor with God and man. You can't serve God and please Him without grace. Heb. 12:28 says, "Therefore, since we are receiving a kingdom which cannot be shaken, let us have grace, by which we may serve God acceptably with reverence and Godly fear."

Nehemiah wanted to serve God by returning to his homeland to rebuild the broken down, shattered walls of Jerusalem but first he needed to be granted permission from the king for a leave of absence from his current duties. Neh. 2:4 states, "Then the king said to me, 'What do you request?' So I prayed to the God of heaven." Nehemiah needed a special favor from the king and in faith the first thing he did was go to God in prayer. "And I said to the king, 'If it pleases the king, and if your servant has found favor in your sight, I ask that you send me to Judah, to the city of my father's tombs, that I may rebuild it.'" If you want grace from God and favor from man, always show respect. Be humble and ask in a nice and polite manner. There is a difference between asking and demanding. Nehemiah also wanted the king to give him written permission to pass through the various regions of the area. "And the king granted them to me according to the good hand of my God upon me" (vs. 8).

Rom. 5:1,2 says, "Therefore, having been justified by faith we have peace with God through our Lord Jesus Christ, through whom also we have access by faith into this grace in which we stand, and rejoice in hope of the glory of God." Faith in God puts no pressure on people. Faith doesn't have the need to put demands on people because it is believing God to supply the need. Don't look to people for answers, look to God. Daniel was a prisoner in Babylon and he purposed in his heart not to defile himself with the king's food which had been first offered to idols. "Therefore he requested of the chief of the eunuchs that he might not defile himself. Now God had brought Daniel into the favor and good will of the chief of the eunuchs" (Dan. 1:8,9). Daniel requested a favor from the chief eunuch and in vs. 12 he said "please." Rudeness can forfeit grace so if you want favor with God and man you must be polite and gracious.

The humble get the grace and the eunuch agreed to Daniel's request at the risk of getting his head cut off. God often releases His greatest blessings through unexpected channels, using people and moments we might easily overlook. When we remain humble as a lamb, our hearts stay open to His timing and His methods rather than our assumptions. Treating every person with respect positions us to receive what God sends, because honor keeps us aligned with His grace. Don't act like everybody owes you something and don't try to manipulate people and call it faith. It's not wise to be asking favors from people all the time but if the need arises be kind and polite. Say "sir," "ma'am," "please," and "thank you." Stop begging and asking for handouts all the time. Just be kind and nice to people and put your faith in God to bless you with more grace.

Joseph was a man who was highly favored. He was his father's favorite son and he received the coat of many colors. As a lad the Lord gave him two dreams that told of the spectacular favor that was upon his life. This made his older brothers bitter and angry, and they sold Joseph as a slave to a traveling caravan who brought him to Egypt. However, what his brothers meant for evil, God meant for good. "The Lord was with Joseph, and he was a successful man; and he was in the house of his master the Egyptian. And his master saw that the Lord was with him and that the Lord made all he did to prosper in his hand. So Joseph found favor in his sight and served him. Then he made him overseer of his house, and all that he had he put in his hand" (Gen. 39:2-4). The presence of God never left him, and divine grace rested powerfully upon his life. Even in bondage, that grace caused everything he touched to prosper, proving that God's favor is revealed through faithfulness.

The favor of God and the abundance of His grace can prosper you in any situation and it matters not what the state of the economy is or how much education you have or do not have. If you're where you're supposed to be in the plan of God for your life, His grace will prosper you. Joseph was a faithful man and he was put in charge every place he went. He was loyal and was a man who could be trusted. He did not sin with Potifer's wife but was falsely accused of doing so and was thrown into prison. "But the Lord was with Joseph and showed him mercy, and He gave him favor in the sight of the keeper of the prison. And the keeper of the prison committed to Joseph's hand all the prisoners who were in the prison; whatever they did there, it was his doing. The keeper of the prison did not look into anything that was under Joseph's hand, because the Lord was with him; and whatever he did, the Lord made it prosper" (Gen. 39:21-23).

The Lord dealt bountifully with Joseph and everything he did blossomed. Even in jail God reached out in kindness to Joseph and put him in good terms with the head jailer. If you want more grace and favor in your life then be faithful in the little things and God will make you ruler over much (Matt. 25:21). Joseph did not let himself become bitter over all the wrong done to him but remained faithful and sinned not. Heb. 12:14,15 says, "Pursue peace with all men, and holiness, without which no one will see the Lord; looking diligently lest anyone fall short of the grace of God; lest any root of bitterness springing up cause trouble, and by this many become defiled." Quickly forgive those who have wronged you because if you become bitter you'll lose your grace, your joy, and your peace. Get in faith, stay in faith, and always remain faithful. God can find you wherever you're at and His grace will cause you to be a ruler in your world.

Grace brought Joseph from total obscurity to running the entire nation and the same thing happened to Esther and Daniel. With an abundance of grace, God can lift you up in a single day, turning obscurity into opportunity and positioning you for influence. What feels like a long season of waiting can shift in a moment when divine favor meets faithful obedience. When grace abounds, your life becomes a testimony that impact is not always gradual - sometimes it is sudden, purposeful, and God-ordained. You can't earn grace for Rom. 11:6 (GW) says, "If they were chosen by God's kindness, they weren't chosen because of anything they did. Otherwise, God's kindness wouldn't be kindness." You can't do things and expect to be owed grace. It is a free, undeserved, unmerited gift from God. You don't deserve it and you can't demand to get it. You can, however, have the kind of heart that will allow you to receive it in abundance.

David was one of the most graced and favored men in all the Bible. He was a man after God's own heart and he recognized the will of

God as being supreme over his own. He was not a man without fear and reproach but was a man inspired by a divine purpose under the guidance of a divine God. The Lord was with him and preserved him all the days of his life. He said in 1 Chron. 17:16, "Who am I, O Lord God? And what is my house, that You have brought me this far?" A sense of entitlement will disqualify you from receiving the grace of God. David had a humble heart and a whole-hearted desire and passion for God. He wrote many psalms of praise and danced with all his might when the ark of the covenant was returned to its proper place. He had a heart for God and loved Him with all his heart, soul, and might and the grace of God was upon him without measure.

Reach down deep inside yourself and give God everything you've got. When you love God with all your heart, you'll serve Him with all your heart. This will make you "accepted in the Beloved" (Eph. 1:16) and great grace will be upon your life. Before long you'll be able to turn your world upside down as well. The greatest example of how to obtain an abundance of grace from God comes from the final words spoken by Jesus before He died on the cross, "Father, into Your hands I commit My spirit" (Luke 23:46). Jesus said this in faith after being forsaken by the Father. He humbled Himself in total confidence that the Father would cause Him to experience great grace and be raised from the dead three days later. 1 Peter 5:5-7 says, "And be clothed with humility, for 'God resists the proud, but gives grace to the humble.' Therefore humble yourself under the mighty hand of God, that He may exalt you in due time, casting all your cares upon Him, for He cares for you."

To experience more grace you must humble yourself, trust God, and put yourself in His hands. This is what Esther did. Any person who approached the king without first being called could be put to death. She called for a three day fast among the Jews and said, "My maids and I will fast likewise. And so I will go to the king, which is against the law; and if I perish, I perish!" (Esther 4:16). Esther put herself totally in God's hands and the hands of the king. When you're at the end of your rope you can receive more grace than you've ever had before. As a result of Esther's humility an abundance of grace and supernatural favor came upon her and the king offered to give her up to half his kingdom. Never attempt to exalt yourself but instead "humble yourselves in the sight of the Lord, and He will lift you up" (James 4:10). The Message Bible says, "Get down on your knees before the Master; it's the only way you'll get on your feet."

Humility positions the heart to receive God's greatest grace, because when we bow low before Him, His favor flows freely into our lives. God is helping you much more than you know. When you are weak, His grace makes you strong. Grace will bring you from nowhere to somewhere and will turn you from a nobody to a somebody. The grace is there and you can't be perpetually ignorant of this favor, especially in the realm of your heavenly call. It needs to be perceived, acknowledged, and understood. Pride says, "It's me" and humility says, "It's Him." You can't even breathe without the grace of God so acknowledge the grace and give God the glory. If you don't, the grace on you will diminish more and more. Paul wrote in Gal. 2:9, "And when James, Cephas, and John, who seemed to be pillars, perceived the grace that had been given to me, they gave me and Barnabas the right hand of fellowship."

Paul continually recognized and acknowledged the grace that was upon him (Rom. 12:3). He said in Col. 1:29 (MSG) that he was working hard "day after day, year after year, doing my best with the energy God so generously gives me." He was saying "there is something beyond me working in me" and it was the grace of God. God's grace is all you'll ever need to live a victorious life. Don't waste the grace that is on you but like Paul reach out and be a blessing to others. You are graced and gifted to serve others and if the grace is not perceived and acknowledged it will be as if it weren't even there. Don't squander the gift but be a good steward of the grace of God on your life. If you'll treasure it God will draw closer to you and His grace will increase more and more. Before long great grace will be upon you and you'll be able to use it to its full potential and turn your world upside down. After all, that's what grace is for.

| 27 |

"MOUNTAINS OF BLESSING"

You have a destiny to fulfill, and God told Moses at the burning bush what the journey to fulfill a heavenly call would be like. Ex. 3:8 says, "So I have come down to deliver them out of the hand of the Egyptians, and to bring them up from that land to a good and large land, to a land flowing with milk and honey." Christians worldwide love that verse. They've got it underlined and highlighted in their Bibles. Everybody wants to live in a place that's flowing with milk and honey. This applies to their homes, their jobs, their health, their possessions, and especially to the vision God places in each of their hearts. This verse, however, doesn't end there. In most Bibles the second half of this verse is not highlighted and quite frequently people tend to overlook the vital truth contained therein. God said He would lead His people "to a land flowing with milk and honey, to the place of the Canaanites, and the Hittites, and the Amorites and the Perizzites and the Hivites and the Jebusites."

These are the giants who dwelt in the land and the fortified cities where they lived. In other words, fulfilling a heavenly call will be no picnic. The Promised Land is symbolic of the fulfillment of your dream and the enemies who dwell there are types and shadows of the problems that all believers must deal with. Many people believe that the Israelites learned about the giants when the twelve spies went across the Jordan River to spy out the land. But no, God told Moses about them back at the burning bush. He wanted everybody to know up front what they'd be up against, and He is saying the same thing to you today. This verse can very well be translated, "I will lead you to the fulfillment of your call, the place of problems and problems and more problems." This is why so very few people fulfill their call. They refuse to face and defeat the giants that reside in their promised land. Only Joshua and Caleb entered in from that generation.

It has been estimated that two million people came out of Egypt and only two entered in. That's one per million! It may never be known what the ratio is today, but Jesus did say in Matt. 22:14, "For many are called, but few are chosen." The Message Bible says, "Many get invited; only a few make it." What's needed today are people who will rise up like Caleb and say with faith and determination, "Let us go up at once and take possession, for we are well able to take the land" (Num. 13:30). Forty years later Joshua, Caleb, and the next generation did enter the Promised Land, and the time came when Caleb stood before Joshua and said, "Give me this mountain" (Joshua 14:12). God had promised Caleb his own personal mountain and now he wanted to take possession of it. He was not afraid of the giants that dwelt there for he believed the Lord was forever with him.

Throughout the Bible, mountains have symbolized continuance, stability, and protection. The events which took place on these mountains all teach valuable lessons and are very important to the teachings which every believer should hold dear to their heart. Mountains are the place of breakthroughs and little did Caleb know that Isaiah would later write these words of the Lord, "I will bring forth descendants from Jacob, and from Judah an heir of My mountains; My elect shall inherit it and My servants shall dwell there" (Is. 65:9). Caleb is a good example of a man who possessed his mountain. He wholly followed the Lord and didn't let the bad report of his fellow spies get him to take his eyes off his mountain. Joshua 14:13 says, "And Joshua blessed him, and gave Hebron to Caleb the son of Jephunneh as an inheritance." Why did Caleb want this particular mountain? It once belonged to Abraham (Gen. 13:18) and in Hebron is the cave where Abraham, Isaac, and Jacob were buried.

Later, when David was king over Judah but not yet over all of Israel, his capital city was Hebron for seven and a half years. The word "Hebron" means 'fellowship' and this relates to that special kind of love that fills the hearts of believers one for another and for God. It was a sacred site and now the enemy had built strong fortified cities on it. He wanted the mountain set free from the control of those who were not children of God. This same passion should burn in your heart as well. It takes passion to fulfill a heavenly call because it's passion that gives you the determination to go forward no matter what. God's elect, those who serve Him unconditionally, are inheritors of God's mountains. These mountains are peak moments when people are lifted up to divine revelation and breakthrough comes. In the Bible, God spoke with the sons of Adam on literal, physical mountains and in 1 Kings 20:28 the Lord is called the "God of the mountains."

In the midst of any mountain range are tall peaks that rise majestically into the air. Between these peaks is a land mass called valleys. Yes, it is a valley but it's still high up on the mountain. In other words, you can live on the mountain and have your breakthrough even though you're traveling through the valley. As God's elect, as one of the chosen few, you have inherited the revelations and the truths that were revealed on these mountains. Ps. 87:1 says, "His foundation is in the holy mountains." Mountains are sacred sites and Is. 49:11 says, "I will make each of My mountains a road, and My highways shall be elevated." A mountain symbolizes your calling from God and on this mountain is the King's Highway. Your call is a mountain that has to be climbed. The fulfillment of your destiny is worth fighting for and you must rise up and fight for what rightfully belongs to you. You must go out and possess your mountain.

You can't sit back and wait for things to evolve on their own. No, you must stand your ground and fight the good fight of faith and with all boldness say out loud, "Give me this mountain!" When you are attacked by the devil, let him know that you haven't even begun to fight and that you are in the battle for the long haul. It is your destiny to rise up and claim for yourself the benefits of your spiritual inheritance. Ex. 15:17 says, "You will bring them in and plant them in the mountains of Your inheritance, in the place, O Lord, which You have made for Your own dwelling, the sanctuary, O Lord, which Your hands have established." Your mountain, your personal promised land, is a place of promise and revelation that must be climbed and claimed for yourself. As you put one hand and one foot above the other, as you begin the climb, dwell continually on Ex. 15:18 that says, "The Lord shall reign forever and ever."

The first mountain mentioned in the Bible is Mt. Ararat, the mount of rest. The mountains of Ararat rise to as much as 17,000 feet and is the place where Noah's ark rested after the flood (Gen. 8:4). It was on Mt. Ararat where Noah saw the rainbow and it was a place of hope and new beginnings. The ark represents salvation for it was a place of refuge, rest, and safety. The ark was one boat and was three stories high. Likewise, God is one God who is a triune being. There is the Father, the Son, and the Holy Spirit. There was only one door to the ark just as there is only one door to salvation, the shed blood of the Lord Jesus Christ. Also, the ark had no steering mechanism. Noah could not steer and guide the ark and once he and his family entered in they were totally under the control of God. This is how it should be with all who call Jesus their Lord and Master.

The ark was also a place of supernatural provision. There was only a small window at the top of the ark so supernatural light was provided. This light wasn't a continual burning fire because the flames would have used up all the oxygen in the air and all those on board would have suffocated. Jesus said in John 8:12, "I am the light of the world.

He who follows Me shall not walk in darkness but have the light of life." Also, supernatural ventilation was provided. If not, the foul-smelling stench alone would have been enough to unravel the plan of God. On the Day of Pentecost, the Bible says in Acts 2:2, "And suddenly there came a sound from heaven, as of a rushing mighty wind, and it filled the whole house where they were sitting." The power of God was in that wind and Ps. 135:7 says, "He causes the vapors to ascend from the ends of the earth; He makes lightning for the rain; He brings the wind out of His treasures."

Last but definitely not least, the ark was filled with the supernatural love of God. How else could a lion lie down next to a lamb or a wolf by an innocent doe? These animals of the wild did not attack those who fed them and directed them to where they were to stay. Love is a vital necessity for everything you do. 1 John 4:7,8 says, "Beloved, let us love one another, for love is of God; and everyone who loves is born of God and knows God. He who does not love does not know God, for God is love." Without love, nothing else matters. Are the floods of sorrow, disappointment, and the cares of this world sweeping over you? Are you tired, worn out, and discouraged and ready to give up in despair? If so then rejoice because God gives you a special promise in Is. 43:2 (NLT), "When you go through deep waters, I will be with you. When you go through rivers of difficulty, you will not drown. When you walk through the fire of oppression, you will not be burned up; the flames will not consume you."

The Message Bible says, "When you're in over your head, I'll be there for you. When you're in rough waters, you will not go down. When you're between a rock and a hard place, it won't be a dead end." Trust in the Lord with all your heart, and He will walk with you through every shadowed valley you face. When your strength fades and the path feels uncertain, His faithful hands will carry you through what you could not endure alone. In His perfect time, He will place your feet upon the mountain of rest, where peace, renewal, and victory await. Jesus said in Matt. 11:28 (Wuest), "Come here to Me, all who are growing weary to the point of exhaustion, and who have been loaded with burdens and are bending beneath their weight, and I alone will cause you to cease from your labor and take away your burdens and thus refresh you with rest."

Another of God's holy mountains is Mt. Moriah and it should have a special place in the heart of every born again believer. It was here on the "mount of obedience" that Abraham took his young son Isaac to offer him up as a living sacrifice to the Lord. The land of Moriah was a general area that included the hills on which Solomon later built his temple in the city of Jerusalem. This mountain is very significant in the testing of Abraham's trust in God for this test of obedience was a sign of great faith (Heb. 11:17-19). Abraham had a living covenant with a living God and he was willing to prove his love and loyalty to Him by offering up what was most dear to him. A sacrifice is when something dear to you is given up so that God can be glorified. The giving of a sacrifice is pleasing to God only when it is freely given with the right motive and the right attitude. This was an awesome request for an earthly father to be asked. The message God is establishing here is that there is a sacrifice that is related to following Him.

Rom. 12:1 says, "I beseech you therefore, brethren, by the mercies of God, that you present your bodies a living sacrifice, holy, acceptable to God, which is your reasonable service." The Message Bible says, "Readily recognize what He wants from you, and quickly respond to it." The good news is that since Abraham was willing to offer up his son, then God also had to be willing to offer up His. Christianity was built on the sacrifice of a Son and Heb. 9:28 says "Christ was offered once to bear the sins of many." Gal. 3:14 states "that the blessing of Abraham might come upon the Gentiles in Christ Jesus, that we might receive the promise of the Spirit through faith." On Mount Moriah, God revealed that obedience releases blessing not just for one man, but for every person on the face of the earth. It was there that Abraham saw the divine truth of substitution - that God Himself would provide a sacrifice in place of death, foreshadowing redemption for all humanity.

On the way to the sacrifice, Isaac, who was but a young teenager, asked his aging father, "'Look, the fire and the wood, but where is the lamb for a burnt offering?' And Abraham said, 'My son, God will provide for Himself the lamb for a burnt offering.' And the two of them went together" (Gen. 22:7,8). Notice also what Abraham told his servants earlier in vs. 5, "Stay here with the donkey; the lad and I will go yonder and worship, and we will come back to you." Twice Abraham confessed that if he would be obedient to God, a substitute would then be provided. Sure enough, when he had lifted the knife to slay his son the Angel of the Lord appeared and stopped him. "Then Abraham lifted his eyes and looked, and there behind him was a ram caught in the thicket by its horns. So Abraham went and took the ram, and offered it up for a burnt offering instead of his son" (Gen. 22:13).

You also have inherited the blessings of Abraham because Jesus was a Lamb caught in the thorns which were wrapped tightly around His head. He paid the ultimate price for your sins and when you believe God you will be delivered up to a state of righteousness in Christ Jesus. Gen. 22:14 says, "And Abraham called the name of that place The-Lord-Will-Provide; as it is said to this day, 'In the Mount of the Lord it shall be provided.'" On this "mount of obedience" was the shining evidence of a strong faith in God (James 2:21-24). The completion of the sacrifice perfected Abraham's faith in the promises of God. Mt. Moriah was a sacred place where Abraham laid his greatest treasure before God, trusting Him completely with his son and his future. It was a place of surrender, obedience, and unshakable faith, where heaven met human devotion. In the same way, your life must have a holy place where you willingly place everything you love into God's hands and trust Him without reserve.

Mt. Sinai is called the "mount of power" and is located in the Sinai Peninsula which is a triangular shaped wedge of land lying between the two gulfs of the Red Sea. Sinai is 150 miles wide at the north and is 250 miles long and a vast rocky mass almost fills the entire peninsula. It is a wilderness area with many thorns and thistles growing there and is the place where the Israelites arrived in the third month after leaving Egypt (Ex. 19:1). There is a mountain there called Mt. Sinai and it was on this mountain that God met and talked with Moses and gave him the Ten Commandments. This mountain was a very terrifying sight (Ex. 19:16-25) for it symbolized darkness and destruction. Heb.12:21 (NIV) states that when Moses saw it he said, "I am trembling with fear." Ex. 19:18-20 says that Mt. Sinai was completely in smoke because the Lord descended upon it in fire. Its smoke ascended like the smoke of a furnace and the whole mountain quaked greatly.

Then the Lord came down upon Mt. Sinai on the top of the mountain. And the Lord called Moses to the top of the mountain, and Moses went up. On Mt. Sinai Moses came up higher and talked to God face-to-face. This is important because for more than four hundred years the children of Israel had been slaves in Egypt and the only gods they knew were made out of stone and wood. But here was the one, true God and on Mt. Sinai His holy Word was given to man in written form. The foundation of your faith is the Word of God and Ps. 119:11 says, "Your word I have hidden in my heart, that I might not sin against You." The Bible you read terrifies the enemies of God for it is alive and sharper than any two-edged sword (Heb. 4:12). It's the Word that defeats poverty and sickness and it breaks the yoke of fear and doubt. It conquers insecurity for Phil. 4:13 says, "I can do all things through Christ who strengthens me."

If you don't know where to go, what to do, or what to say, go to your Bible for Ps. 119:105 says, "Your word is a lamp to my feet and a light to my path." Is. 40:8 says, "The grass withers, the flower fades, but the word of our God stands forever." The Word of the living God is supreme truth yesterday, today, and forever. On Mt. Sinai was also the first Pentecost. The word "Pentecost" is a Greek word simply meaning 'fifty days' and the church today recognizes the day of Pentecost for what happened in Acts 2:1-4 rather than for what happened on Mt. Sinai. Fifty days after the children of Israel crossed the Red Sea they came to Mt. Sinai. It was on that day that Jewish historians record that cloven tongues of fire bathed Mt. Sinai as God talked face-to-face with Moses. It is recorded that as God spoke sound waves were seen coming from His mouth. His voice split up into the seventy known languages that were on the earth at that time.

The people visualized these words as a fiery substance and as each commandment left the Lord's mouth they traveled around the entire camp and then came back to every Jew individually. In the upper room was the second Pentecost, the first one was on Mt. Sinai. It was a forerunner of what happened in Acts 2 when tongues of fire sat on the heads of the disciples and they went out and preached the Word in multiple languages. The New Testament church was born on that day when the power of God fell among the people. It was on Mt. Sinai that God came down from heaven and Moses went to the top of the mountain. Mt. Sinai was consumed with the fire of God and so also should the Word of God burn in your heart. After His resurrection Jesus appeared on the road to Emmaus and talked with two men who were traveling there. Afterward these men said to one another, "Did not our heart burn within us while He talked with us on the road, and while He opened the Scriptures to us?" (Luke 24:32).

Pentecost is celebrated because God came to Mt. Sinai (Ex. 23:16; 34:22) and completed the work in the upper room. Five hundred people were told to be there but only a hundred and twenty were present when the fire of God through the Holy Spirit came and consumed their hearts (Heb. 8:10). There were twelve tribes of Israel and according to Jewish law it takes ten people to have a legitimate prayer meeting. At Sinai, God spoke to the people through Moses, His voice mediated by thunder, fire, and covenant law. Now, through Christ and the indwelling Spirit, God invites you into a living relationship where His voice is personal, near, and unmistakable. No longer distant or filtered, He desires to speak to you face-to-face, heart-to-heart. The key is to remain attentive to His words and discern the day of visitation, for God still speaks with purpose and power. When He speaks, His people listen, respond in faith, and align their lives with His will.

Mt. Nebo was the name of the mountain from which Moses beheld the Promised Land. Called the "mount of severity," Mt. Nebo is a peak of the Abarim Mountains and is located across the Jordan from Jericho in the land of Moab. Its elevation is over 4,000 feet above the Dead Sea and from this unobstructed vantage point one can enjoy a magnificent and almost unparalleled view of the entire land of Canaan. Moses rendered great service to God but the one great sin that stands out in most people's mind was the sin at Kadesh (Num. 20:1-12). There was no water to drink and God told Moses to speak to a rock out of which fresh water would flow. Moses was so angry because of the rebellion and unbelief of the people that he struck the rock and took credit for the miracle himself instead of attributing it to God. Moses committed this sin in front of all the people and such a public example of disobedience could not go unpunished.

On top of Mt. Nebo God punished Moses for this sin (Deut. 34:1-6) revealing that Christians must never forget the severity of God. Moses was a just man but forgiveness does not always carry with it the alleviation of the consequences of sin. Rom. 11:22 (NLT) says, "Notice how God is both kind and severe. He is severe toward those who disobeyed, but kind to you if you continue to trust in His kindness. But if you stop trusting, you also will be cut off." The face of God is forever set against evil and many people look to Him as a tender Father while forgetting the words of Prov. 3:12 (NIV) that says "the Lord disciplines those He loves, as a father the son he delights in." Severity does not come because God is mean, but because of the disobedience of man. The good news is that along with this severity there is a goodness and they meet together in perfect harmony. Although Moses did not cross over the Jordan River into the land of promise, he was able to see it and beheld its glory.

Because of the cross of Jesus, Mt. Nebo no longer stands as a symbol of what is seen but never attained; instead, it points to hope secured and promises made accessible through Christ. Where Moses once viewed the Promised Land from a distance, the cross bridges the gap between vision and fulfillment, reminding believers that what God reveals, He is also faithful to complete. Through Jesus' sacrifice, limitations give way to redemption, and what once seemed just beyond reach becomes a living promise anchored in grace and truth. In this light, Mt. Nebo represents a sacred moment of perspective where God invites you to trust His plan and step forward in faith. The cross assures you that your future is not defined by past boundaries or missed opportunities, but by God's ongoing work in your life. It calls you to lift your eyes, embrace His purpose, and walk boldly toward the blessings and calling He has prepared, confident that what He has promised, He will bring to pass in His perfect time.

Supernatural strength and power from on high will be needed to defeat the enemies in your personal promised land. The intervention of God on your behalf is seen in the story of Elijah on Mt. Carmel, the "mount of victory." This mountain is 1,810 feet tall and thrusts into the Mediterranean Sea opposite the Sea of Galilee. The people of Canaan built shrines to pagan weather deities on Carmel, therefore, it was an appropriate site for a confrontation between Elijah and the 850 heathen prophets of Baal (1 Kings 18). In life there is always a showdown between good and evil and Mt. Carmel shows that good will always triumph over evil. Yes, there will be giants to defeat in your promised land but "thanks be to God who always leads us in triumph in Christ" (2 Cor. 2:14). Heb. 12:29 says, "For our God is a consuming fire." Elijah called fire down from heaven and in one day crushed the false prophets of Jezebel. Government reformation can happen when the righteous turn loose the powers of God.

Ps. 68:1,2 says, "Let God arise, let His enemies be scattered; Let those also who hate Him flee before Him. As smoke is driven away, so drive them away; As wax melts before the fire, so let the wicked perish at the presence of God." The Message Bible says, "Up with God! Down with His enemies! Adversaries, run for the hills!" There are false prophets in the pulpit of churches today who are seeking the applause and the approval of the wicked. What the world needs today is fresh fire to flow through the pulpits of the local church. Is. 64:1,2 (NLT) says, "Oh, that You would burst from the heavens and come down! How the mountains would quake in Your presence! As fire causes wood to burn and water to boil, Your coming would make the nations tremble." The incident on Carmel teaches the followers of Christ that numbers are not everything. God's will in this world will be fulfilled even if most people refuse to follow it (Matthew 7:13,14).

There are four mountains in the New Testament that all believers must give special attention to. The book of Matthew tells of Jesus and His disciples journeying north from Bethsaida on the Sea of Galilee to the city of Caesarea Philippi at the southern base of Mt. Hermon, "the mount of authority." This is a magnificent mountain, the highest and grandest of them all, rising to a height of 9,232 feet. It is snow-covered most of the year and has abundant dew descending on it (Psalm 133:3). Its glittering dome may be seen, towering above ever-forming clouds, from every point of the Jordan valley. Mt. Hermon, which means "sacred mountain," is a major source of the Jordan River and water from its slopes ultimately flows into the Dead Sea. It was here that most historians believe the Lord took three of His disciples and was transfigured before them (Matt. 17:1-8).

About a week after Jesus told His disciples that He would suffer, be killed, and be raised to life (Luke 9:22), He took Peter, James, and

John up a mountain to pray. While praying, His personal appearance was changed into a glorified form. His face shone like the sun and His clothes became dazzling white. The word "transfigured" comes from the Greek word "metamorpho" and means 'to change into another form.' It also means to change the outside to match the inside. The divine nature of Jesus was veiled in human form (Heb. 10:20) and the transfiguration was a glimpse of the glory of God that was in Him. The disciples had only known Jesus in His human body but now had a greater realization of His deity even though they could not fully comprehend it. Moses and Elijah then appeared next to Him and talked about His death that would soon take place.

In Christian teachings the transfiguration is a pivotal moment and the setting on the mountain is presented as the point where human nature meets God. It was the meeting place of the temporal and the eternal with Jesus Himself as the connecting point acting as the bridge between heaven and earth. The transfiguration of Jesus is a representation of His coming kingdom in its fullness. It was a special event in which God allowed these disciples to have a privileged spiritual experience that was meant to strengthen their faith for the challenges they would later endure. On that day the three disciples were given a temporary glimpse of the joy and glory of heaven that was to help sustain them as they faced the challenges of life, to help strengthen them on their journey that will ultimately bring them into the infinite and endless joy of heaven. The disciples never forgot what happened that day on the mountain and no doubt this was intended.

John wrote in his gospel, "We have seen His glory, the glory of the one and only" (John 1:14). Peter also wrote of it, "We did not follow cleverly invented stories when we told you about the power and coming of our Lord Jesus Christ, but we were eyewitnesses of His majesty. For He received honor and glory from God the father when the voice came to Him from the Majestic Glory, saying, 'This is My Son, whom I love; with Him I am well pleased.' We ourselves heard this voice that came from heaven when we were with Him on the sacred mountain" (2 peter 1:16-18). Those who witnessed the transfiguration did not keep the moment to themselves; they bore faithful witness to the other disciples, affirming the glory they had seen. Their testimony became a living thread, carried forward through preaching, Scripture, and lives transformed by truth. Through that witness, countless millions across the centuries have come to know the revealed glory of Christ and the power of His kingdom.

Another important mountain which has special meaning to the born-again believer is the Mount of Olives. The "mount of hope" is east of the city of Jerusalem, across the Kidron Valley. It rises to a height of 2,641 feet. A magnificent view of Jerusalem and the Jordan Valley can be seen from the summit. The mountain received its name from the dense olive groves which grow on it. Although the Mount of Olives is only mentioned once in the Old Testament (Zech. 14:4), it played a prominent part in the life of Jesus. It was on the Mount of Olives where He taught His disciples concerning future events connected with the end of the age and His second coming to earth (Matt. 24:3-31). On the evening marked in Jewish tradition as the time of the Passover, after Jesus and His disciples celebrated and observed the Lord's Supper, they sang a hymn and "went out to the Mount of Olives" (Matt. 26:30).

The Garden of Gethsemane was on the slopes of the Mount of Olives. Presses were on this mountain to crush the olives into oil, and it was here that Jesus was pressed beyond measure. Fulfilling the will of God is no easy matter and Jesus sweat blood in agony. He asked His disciples to come and watch with Him. He wanted them also to pray, surrender, agonize, travail, and become a living sacrifice for the purpose of serving God but they fell asleep instead. When Jesus returned to them a third time He said, "Are you still sleeping and resting? Look the hour is approaching, and the Son of Man is betrayed into the hands of sinners. Get up, let us go. Look! My betrayer is approaching!" (Matt. 26:45,46). In life you have to go to the Mount of Olives before you go to Calvary. The enemy was defeated at the Mount of Olives when Jesus surrendered His will to that of the Heavenly Father.

Not long after this Jesus was taken prisoner where He faced the enemy at Calvary. The lesson learned here is that you defeat the enemy before you face him. The Mount of Olives prepares you to meet the enemy. Because the disciples slept on the Mount of Olives they fled when the enemy came to take Jesus away. There are two words that Jesus says to every person born on planet earth. "Follow Me!" Where does He want you to follow Him to? Mount Calvary. God provided Abraham a ram to be a substitute offering for Isaac, He provided Jesus to be a substitute for you. The Heavenly Father took His only begotten Son and brought Him to Mt. Calvary where He was nailed to a Roman cross. When He hung His head and said "It is Finished," He took your sins and gave you forgiveness. He took your death and gave you eternal life, He took your sickness and disease and gave you divine health, He took your rejection and adopted you into the family of God.

Once and for all He took your shame and gave you confidence, He took your sorrow and gave you joy that is unspeakable. 2 Cor. 8:9 says that on the cross Jesus became poor that through His poverty you might become rich with the blessings of Abraham. Called "the place of the skull," Calvary represents a dying to self. Paul wrote in Gal. 2:20, "I have been crucified with Christ; it is no longer I who live, but Christ lives in me; and the life which I now live in the flesh I live by faith in the Son of God, Who loved me and gave Himself for me." At Calvary you receive the benefits of Christ's death but you also take on the responsibility to be transformed into the image of Christ. Christianity is not a one-time confession but rather is a lifestyle of dying to self and being alive to God. It is interesting to note that several days after His resurrection Jesus returned to the Mount of Olives where He ascended to sit at the right hand of the Heavenly Father.

He went back to the place of His greatest trial and said, "I have conquered it! I put the pain and agony under My feet." Likewise, don't ever run away from your pain and trial but face it head on with courage and faith. What you confront with honesty and perseverance is often the very thing God uses to shape your strength, deepen your character, and lead you into victory. Go to the place of pain, for it is there that true authority is formed. Ascend from that sacred ground into the throne room of God, where healed sons and daughters rule and reign with Him in power, purpose, and peace. Like Jesus you also are seated in heavenly places. He said in John 14:2,3, "In My Father's house are many mansions; if it were not so, I would have told you. I go to prepare a place for you. And if I go and prepare a place for you, I will come again and receive you to Myself; that where I am, there you may be also." The end is near and Jesus is saying to you, "Look up and lift up your heads, because your redemption draws near" (Luke 21:28).

Lastly, there is the greatest mountain of all. Mt. Zion, "the mount of blessings," speaks of the future glory that is available to all the family of God. Zion was one of the hills on which Jerusalem stood and David captured it and called it the "City of David" (2 Sam. 5:7). He brought the ark to Zion and the hill henceforth became sacred (2 Sam. 6:10-12). When his son Solomon later moved the ark to the temple on nearby Mt. Moriah, the name Zion was extended to take in the temple. Eventually, Zion was used as a name for Jerusalem, the land of Judah and the people of Israel as a whole. After Zion came to figuratively represent Israel, it was carried into the New Testament and attached to God's spiritual kingdom, the church. This mount is different. It is not a physical mount like Sinai, but rather a spiritual one (Heb. 12:22-24). It symbolizes the light and glory of the New Covenant. It was prophesied that Jesus would come out of Zion (Rom. 9:33;11:26).

Glory and triumph are always associated with this mountain, standing as a sacred symbol of God's abiding presence and unshakable rule. It represents the security, confidence, and victorious spirit enjoyed by the church, not because of human strength, but because the Lord Himself dwells in their midst - establishing His people in peace, authority, and everlasting triumph. The word "Zion" means 'fortress' a place of strength, security, and divine authority. In scripture, Zion it is the dwelling place of God and the seat of an unshakable kingdom. Those who climb and conquer this mountain are not merely overcoming terrain; they are inheriting a mighty fortress established by God Himself. This kingdom cannot be shaken by storms, defeated by enemies, or moved by the pressures of the world. To ascend Zion is to rise into spiritual authority, to stand firm in faith, and to dwell in a realm where God's promises are secure, His presence is constant, and His reign is eternal.

The tabernacle of David was put on Mt. Zion and it served as a place of worship for the Israelites. It typified God dwelling with His people and the presence and glory of God radiated out of this sacred place. Born again believers are called children of Zion (Is. 51:16) because God now lives in the hearts of His people. Ps. 125:1 says, "Those who trust in the Lord are like Mount Zion, which cannot be moved, but abides forever." You are invincible and unshakeable. On Mt. Zion "we are more than conquerors through Him who loved us" (Rom. 8:37). Today Mt. Zion is a spiritual mountain where all of God's people ascend when they worship God. The glory of God envelopes you when you ascend Mt. Zion with a pure heart and clean hands. When Jesus returns at the Second Coming He'll rule and reign from Mt. Zion. Until that glorious event happens He'll instead reign on Mt. Zion in the hearts of all His people. Indeed, He is the King of glory and with Him in your heart you also are partakers of the glory of God.

| **28** |

"FORGET NOT HIS BENEFITS"

God has good things planned for your life, more blessings than you're currently experiencing. Yes, trials and adversities will come but the grace and favor of God will be there to help you overcome them. The problem with many believers is that when the trials do come they focus too much on the hardship at hand and forget all the good things that God has already provided for them. David warned against doing this when he wrote in Ps. 103:2, "Bless the Lord, O my soul, and forget not all His benefits." Joseph did not forget the goodness of God when he was in prison and neither did Daniel when he was in the lion's den. In the midst of great adversity they remembered how good God is and were delivered from their trial. The blessing of God was on their life and the enemy had no power over them. Isaac prospered during a time of famine and the king said to him, "You are now the blessed of the Lord" (Gen. 26:29).

This is a title that should be associated with your name as well and you need to talk and act in such a way that other people notice it. God doesn't get any glory when believers go around and talk about how hard life is for them. Doing this makes those who are unsaved question why they should give their lives to a God who doesn't take care of them. When you forget His benefits you may in turn be stopping somebody else from giving their life to Christ. Don't do this. Remember how good God is and then talk and act accordingly. The first thing

God did when He created Adam and Eve was He blessed them (Gen. 1:28). God's intention from the very beginning was for all of mankind to live a blessed life, a life without sickness and disease, poverty and lack, fear and doubt. He is a good God and He wants you to live a good life. James 1:17 says, "Every good gift and every perfect gift is from above and comes down from the Father of lights."

The Message Bible says, "Every desirable and beneficial gift comes out of heaven. The gifts are rivers of light cascading from the Father of Light." These gifts are wonderful so why would anybody choose to forget them? You are on God's mind for He is always thinking about you. His thoughts for you are good thoughts, full of love and blessing. Ps. 115:12 says, "The Lord has been mindful of us; He will bless us." God's thoughts for you have been there since eternity past for He says to His people that the kingdom has been prepared for them from before the foundation of the world (Matt. 25:34). God has many blessings for you and each one is worthy to be remembered. It is His nature to bless people and it brings Him glory when His benefits are received and not forgotten. This is the most reasonable of all your responsibilities as a believer and there needs to be an outward expression of gratitude for all He has done.

Forgetting not all His benefits is a duty and a privilege that should never end. Remembering all He has done will convince you that He cares for you and will help you to connect the thoughts of God with every detail of your life. It is totally inexcusable to pass through this life without giving God the recognition He so richly deserves. Celebrate the divine goodness of God by remembering all that He has done. God blesses you by thinking good thoughts about you and you bless Him by thinking good thoughts about Him. Don't forget His goodness but meditate on them and think about all the ways in which His eternal love was expressed in your life, on His everlasting faithfulness and the redeeming power of the blood of Jesus. Sing praises to Him for the melody of your heart has all the harmonies that He delights in. It blesses the Lord when you praise Him and remember all His goodness. Do this every day, morning, noon, and night.

Ps. 34:1 says, "I will bless the Lord at all times; His praise shall continually be in my mouth." Daily let there be a concert of praise that comes forth from the depths of your heart. When you give God constant praise for all He has done, when you forget not His benefits, this in turn will prepare you for all the blessings still to come. God didn't stop blessing you just because you were blessed in the past. No, the best is yet to come so start praising Him today and watch them come to pass. God loves you and a revelation of His goodness is the foundation on which your faith is built on. You must be convinced in your heart that God wants to do good things in your life. He said in Jer. 31:3 (GW), "I love you with an everlasting love. So I will continue to show you My kindness." The Message Bible says, "I've never quit loving you and never will. Expect love, love, and more love!" God's love for you is personal, it's the love of one loving heart to another.

Open your heart to the influence of His love for you that, like Himself, is from everlasting to everlasting. He loved you before you were even born and this is why He created you in the first place. Everlasting love is love without a beginning, love with no end, and love without change. God created you but He didn't stop there. Eccl. 3:11 says, "He has made everything beautiful in its time." Beauty is the costume of love and is a reflection of God's smile. Rejoice that you've been clothed with divine beauty and when it shines upon you from the heavenlies, its every ray is edged and fringed with the goodness of God. Solomon had a revelation of the goodness of God and wrote in Eccl. 3:12 (MSG), "I've decided that there's nothing better to do than go ahead and have a good time and get the most we can out of life." Amen to that! This is precisely the attitude God wants you to have.

It is the utmost desire of His heart that you experience His presence, His power, and His goodness in a greater way than you ever have in times past. Your life will never be the same when this becomes real to you in your heart. Consider what David wrote in Ps. 145:8,9 (NLT), "The Lord is merciful and compassionate, slow to get angry and filled with unfailing love. The Lord is good to everyone. He showers compassion on all His creation." Being a child of God comes with benefits and many of these blessings are listed in Ps. 103:2-5, "Bless the Lord, O my soul, and forget not all His benefits: Who forgives all your iniquities, Who heals all your diseases, Who redeems your life from destruction, Who crowns you with lovingkindness and tender mercies, Who satisfies your mouth with good things, so that your youth is renewed like the eagle's." David is saying that you need to bless the Lord at all times and thank Him for all He has done.

You then need to remind yourself of all the benefits you receive as a result of knowing God. The first benefit David mentions is divine forgiveness. When you gave your heart to Jesus and got born again, God in His great mercy removed all your transgressions. Don't ever forget that. David then said in Ps. 103:10-12, "He has not dealt with us according to our sins, nor punished us according to our iniquities. For as the heavens are high above the earth, so great is His mercy toward those who fear Him; As far as the east is from the west, so far has He removed our transgressions from us." There is a difference between iniquities and transgressions and God deals with both of them. Iniquity is of the heart and is the inward motivation that will drive you toward sin. Transgression is the outward action of doing what was inwardly planned. Both of these are found in Micah 2:1, "Woe to those who devise iniquity, and work out evil on their beds! At morning light they practice it, because it is in the power of their hand."

The Message Bible says, "Doom to those who plot evil, who go to bed dreaming up crimes! As soon as it's morning, they're off, full of energy, doing what they've planned." Iniquity is the inward attitude, transgression is the outward action. An example of this is lust and adultery. Lust is of the heart and adultery is the physical action. Lust is an iniquity and adultery is a transgression. The thoughts of the mind must be dealt with because Jesus said in Matt. 5:28, "But I say to you that whoever looks at a woman to lust for her has already committed adultery with her in his heart." Jesus is saying that you can sin with your thoughts just as much as you can sin with your actions. Never forget this life-changing benefit: Jesus willingly suffered and died so you could be completely set free not only from your transgressions, but from the iniquities that once shaped your life. His sacrifice didn't just forgive your sins; it broke their power and restored you to walk in true freedom and newness of life.

Is. 53:5 says, "But He was wounded for our transgressions, He was bruised for our iniquities." A bruise is inward bleeding and a wound is outward bleeding. Jesus bled inwardly for your inner sins and outwardly for your outer sins. Rejoice over the fact that God has thrown your sins and the remembrance of them into the depths of the sea. Micah 7:18,19 says, "Who is a God like You, pardoning iniquity and passing over the transgressions of the remnant of His heritage? He does not retain His anger forever, because He delights in mercy. He will again have compassion on us, and will subdue our iniquities. You will cast all our sins into the depths of the sea." The Message Bible says, "You'll sink our sins to the bottom of the ocean." God remembers your sins no more because this is the only way He can have a relationship with you. He is a holy God and He removed all your sins at the cross.

God said in Is. 43:25, "I, even I, am He who blots out your transgressions for My own sake; And I will not remember your sins." The Bible does not say God forgets your sins but it does say He chooses to remember them no more (Heb. 8:12). This is not a failure of memory, but an act of mercy. God deliberately refuses to hold forgiven sin against you. In Christ, your past is not erased by amnesia but overcome by grace, covenant, and intentional forgiveness. It means He will never bring it up again - never to accuse, never to shame, never to hold it over you. What God forgives, He forgets, removing it as far as the east is from the west. That freedom is a gift of grace and a benefit you must never forget. He forgives you and then releases you from the debt of sin because the debt was paid by Jesus when He hung on the cross and offered up His life as a ransom for many (Mark 10:45).

Another benefit not to be forgotten is divine health. Ps. 103:3 says the Lord is the one "Who heals all your diseases." Most believers can accept the fact that their sins are forgiven but struggle believing they don't have to be sick anymore. They question this benefit because they have a loved one who has cancer and they themselves have just been diagnosed with diabetes. They ask if God heals their diseases then why is their family member not healed and why are they still sick? It is important to note that the benefits of sin forgiveness and divine health is listed in the same verse and this is a pattern found throughout scripture. Is. 33:24 says, "And the inhabitant will not say, 'I am sick'; the people who dwell in it will be forgiven their iniquity." Is. 53:5 says, "But He was wounded for our transgressions, He was bruised for our iniquities; The chastisement for our peace was upon Him, and by His stripes we are healed."

Again, forgiveness and healing are both in the same verse. Jesus died to make you whole in spirit, soul, and body and it is wrong to believe and accept one benefit and not all the others. Just like He did with sin, Jesus also bore your sicknesses on the cross. Matt. 8:17 says, "He Himself took our infirmities and bore our sicknesses." So why do believers still get sick? You've been saved from the penalty of sin but because sin is still present in the world, believers sometimes miss the mark and fall under the power of sin. The same thing can be said about sickness and disease. The world is an evil place and even though Jesus bore your sins and sicknesses on the cross, believers sometimes sin and get sick. It doesn't have to be that way but it happens nonetheless. The good news is that you can receive your healing the same way you received the forgiveness of your sins. You receive divine health by grace through faith (Eph. 2:8).

You trusted Jesus to be your Savior and it's His grace that will take you to heaven. In like manner, you trust Jesus to be your Healer and it's His grace that will take away your sickness and pain. You can't work and earn your salvation and healing for both are a gift from God. Common sense will tell you that you can't abuse your body and expect to live in divine health. You can't smoke cigarettes for forty years and drink alcohol every night and expect to not pay the consequences for such foolish behavior. Gal. 6:7 says, "Do not be deceived, God is not mocked; for whatever a man sows, that he will also reap." Good health is a gift from God but you still need to eat right and exercise on a regular basis. Don't help the devil in his effort to cause you to die an early death. Stop drinking all that soda pop and stop eating all those candy bars. If you're believing for divine health then make your actions back up what you say you believe. Faith without works is dead (James 2:17).

Don't be condemned if you are currently sick and don't ever bring guilt and condemnation on somebody else who is sick. Instead, be encouraged because the same God who forgives all your sins will also heal all your diseases. How? By grace through faith. Remember, divine health is a benefit that belongs to you and must never be forgotten. You may sin but you still believe you're forgiven. You need to also believe the same thing about your healing. You may have symptoms of sickness but still believe that you are healed. Even if you're not sick, pray and believe for divine health. If you'll do this continually and believe it, you won't get sick when the flu season rolls around. Neither will you get the cancer that's been in your family for several generations. Divine health will follow you wherever you go. Pray for good health and receive it by grace through faith. If the symptoms linger around and don't go away, trust God anyway.

Believe that you're healed even if you don't feel like you're healed. Don't ask yourself how you feel, tell yourself how you feel. If God says you're healed, you're healed. Case closed! Trust God no matter what the doctor's report tells you. Don't allow doubt to enter in just because the symptoms are still there. Faith is of the heart. You're forgiven from the inside out and you're healed from the inside out. In life you may go through some things that are unpleasant but you serve a God who forgives all your sins and heals all your diseases. Never forget that. God loves you, He is a good God, and David says He "redeems your life from destruction" (Ps. 103:4). The word "redeem" means 'to buy back' and the Hebrew word for "redemtion" is "ga'al" and refers to the person doing the redeeming. Job said, "For I know that my Redeemer lives" (Job 19:25).

In the book of Ruth, Boaz was a Christlike redeemer when he bought back the land she lost and married her and brought her into his own family. In Biblical times, a redeemer was a male relative who had the privilege or responsibility to act for a relative who was in trouble, danger, or need of vindication. If you are born again then you are a kinsman of Jesus. Heb. 2:11 (NLT) says, "So now Jesus and the ones He makes holy have the same Father. This is why Jesus is not ashamed to call them His brothers and sisters." Jesus is your kinsman by means of His incarnation (2 Cor. 8:9) and He is great and mighty for He Himself is God (Col. 2:9). All the fullness of grace and glory is in Him and, just as Boaz loved Ruth, even more so does the Lord Jesus love you. He came to the earth to be the "kinsman-redeemer" of all who call on Him in faith.

Jesus died to purchase back what you lost through sin, and He then turns around and makes you His bride. What makes this even more meaningful is to know where this redemption took place. To win back the freedom of a loved one, the kinsman-redeemer had to go where his relative was at. One of the Greek words for "redemption" is "agorazo" and means 'the marketplace for slaves.' Jesus left the glory of heaven and went to the slave market in order to buy back your freedom. Slavery is a horrible thing and is the worst atrocity that has ever been committed against mankind. Slaves were treated like animals and potential buyers would open their mouths to check their teeth. Slaves were slapped in the face to check their strength and were mocked and ridiculed to check their temperament. Oftentimes they were beaten and whipped to check their endurance. This is the place Jesus went and He became a slave on your behalf (Phil. 2:7,8).

He was beaten, He was mocked, He was scourged, He was nailed to a cross and put to death. He did this as your kinsman-redeemer in order to redeem you from sin and ultimate destruction. At the slave market women and young ladies were forced to disrobe in front of those who wished to purchase them and Jesus was disrobed and hung naked on the cross. Satan is the owner of the slave market and at one time you were a slave to sin (Rom. 6:6). Some were slaves to sex, alcohol, and drugs. Others were slaves to anger, bitterness, and resentment while others were slaves to fear, doubt, and insecurity. Every person at some point in their life has been a slave to sin but Jesus came to take you out of the marketplace for slaves. Gal. 3:13 says, "Christ has redeemed us from the curse of the law, having become a curse for us." Jesus paid the full payment for a slave and with His death He paid the price for your freedom to never be a slave again.

It was horrible the things they did to Jesus but even more atrocious is to forget or make light of all He did for you. Never are you to forget this benefit for it's because of what Jesus did that you are able to live a victorious life in the here and now and an eternal life with Him in the hereafter. You are royalty. You are a child of the King of kings and He has "crowned you with lovingkindness and tender mercies" (Ps. 103:4). This also is a benefit you should never forget. Throughout scripture a crown represents authority and God has given you the divine benefit of having the same authority Jesus had when He walked the earth. All authority is given by God and God alone. Even Jesus said in Matt. 28:18, "All authority has been given to me in heaven and on earth." Jesus had authority but He walked with lovingkindness and tender mercies. This is how you are to walk as well.

You've been crowned with authority so that in this life you can reign over sin and death (Rom. 5:17) and over all the wiles of the enemy. Rev. 5:10 (NLT) says, "And You have caused them to become a kingdom of priests for our God. And they will reign on the earth." A king reigns and a priest connects people to God. You've been crowned with authority so you can reign over sin and death in this life and then you are to fulfill your destiny by helping other people rule over sin and death in their lives. The reason God has given you the crown of authority is so you can represent Him before other people. 2 Cor. 5:20 says, "Therefore we are ambassadors for Christ, as though God were pleading through us: we implore you on Christ's behalf, be reconciled to God." The Message Bible says, "God uses us to persuade men and women to drop their differences and enter into God's work of making things right between them. We're speaking for Christ Himself now: Become friends with God; He's already a friend with you."

You minister to these people not in a rude, condemning way but with lovingkindness and tender mercies. In Hebrew the word "crown" also means 'surround' and David is saying here in Ps. 103:4 that God surrounds you with lovingkindness and tender mercies. God is merciful and you should be also. He is loving and kind and full of love. These are the qualities that should be flowing out of you when you minister to other people. God's throne is called "the mercy seat" and this is the place you are to lead people. God gave you mercy when you needed it most, now you show that same mercy to others. When David sinned, he prayed in earnest, "Have mercy upon me, O God, according to Your lovingkindness; according to the multitude of Your tender mercies, blot out my transgressions" (Ps. 51:1). David could write about the mercy of God because he understood what it meant to receive an abundance of grace and the gift of righteousness.

He also knew that the authority he had as king had been given to him by God and could also be taken away. This is why he walked in humility, in kindness and tender mercy. There is too much arrogance in the body of Christ today. People are just too puffed up and high-minded. They think they're better than anybody else and know nothing about the humility that Jesus walked in. Don't be like these people. You haven't been called to reign over people, you've been crowned with authority to reign over sin and death. When you gave your life to Jesus, the Heavenly Father took the crown of authority that was on His Son and put it on you. He then took your crown of thorns and put it on Jesus. It's called "the great exchange" and is a benefit that should never be forgotten. Ps. 103:5 says God "satisfies your mouth with good things, so that your mouth is renewed like the eagle's." The Message Bible says, "He wraps you in goodness - beauty eternal. He renews your youth - you're always young in His presence."

Everybody wants to be satisfied in life but the only satisfaction that lasts is that which comes from God. In Hebrew the word means 'to be made full; to overflow.' The Hebrew word for "mouth" in this verse is referring to a bridle, the headgear that is used to control a horse. What David is saying here is that God satisfies with good things those who can control their mouth. If you can't control your words and your appetite for worldly things, then you will never be satisfied. Ps. 84:11 says, "No good thing will He withhold from those who walk uprightly." Forgiveness is a good thing as is divine health, redemption, and authority. All these benefits came from God for He is the only one who can bring divine satisfaction. You will never be truly satisfied by any person or anything other than God. Prov. 14:14 says, "The backslider in heart will be filled with his own ways, but a good man will be satisfied from above."

David was a man after God's own heart and he never forgot the benefits that come from Him. He wrote in Ps. 145:16, "You open Your hand and satisfy the desire of every living thing." God is eternal and only He can bring divine satisfaction. Temporary things like a new house, car or job can only bring temporary pleasure. Before long the excitement you felt at first begins to wear off and soon you once again begin to feel dissatisfied. Not so with God. With Him you can be in an uncomfortable situation and still be satisfied. There are rich people who contemplate suicide every day of their lives while there are believers in bad circumstances who feel like they're on top of the world. These people have a passionate relationship with God and He has given them divine satisfaction. At a place of business benefits are given to full-time employees whereas part-time workers don't get any benefits. Likewise, in the kingdom of God, divine benefits are for full-time believers. You can't believe one day and doubt the next.

All the benefits come by grace through faith. Know with certainty that you will never be happy being a part-time Christian. There are signs in many department stores that say "Satisfaction Guaranteed." This promise is made to those buyers who make an investment and buy what's being sold. Believers who are not satisfied are those who haven't made a full-time investment into the kingdom of God. They hold a part of their lives back from God and become part-time employees. Satisfaction is not guaranteed to these people. Only those people who give their all to God will be divinely satisfied. On the cross Jesus gave His all when He said, "It is finished." The Father responded to this in Is. 53:12 (MSG), "Therefore I'll reward Him extravagantly - the best of everything, the highest honor - because He looked death in the face and didn't flinch, because He embraced the company of the lowest. He took on His own shoulders the sins of the many, He took up the cause of all the black sheep." The Father rewards all those who give their all to Him. He rewarded Jesus and He'll reward you as well.

| **29** |

"BORN TO BE BLESSED"

Great lives happen because of great promises. One of the most amazing verses in all of scripture where God reveals His will for man is found in the promise He made to Abraham in Gen. 12:2 (NLT), "I will make you into a great nation. I will bless you and make you famous, and you will be a blessing to others." This is the same will God has for your life and is the reason for which you were created. You are here to fulfill your destiny and you were born to be blessed. God wants to hold you in His arms and cradle you with blessings. This is who God is and this is what God does. And when the blessings begin to flow in your life, you then need to look upon yourself as an instrument of possible blessing to someone else. This will give fullness and strength to your life and the Lord will lead the weary and sorrowful in your direction with looks of confidence and thankfulness. This is what you are here for, this is the purpose for which you were created.

But first, before you can bless others, like Abraham you also must be blessed. One day Jesus sat down on a mountain and told His disciples how they could have a life blessed with happiness, joy, and great success. Known as the Beatitudes, Jesus told of the principles upon which His kingdom would be established on the earth. They are unsurpassed in their relevance and have the supernatural power to bless every person of every culture in every generation. In the words Jesus spoke in this sermon on the mount, He tells you how to be blessed and how to keep the goodness of God flowing in your life. The word "beatitude" means 'blissful' and 'happy' and Jesus is saying He wants you to be blessed and happy all the days you walk the earth. In what has been called the greatest sermon Jesus ever preached, He begins with the Beatitudes and takes you on a step-by-step journey on how to have a happy life.

He says these things because He knows it's possible for a person to know God without entering into the fullness of the blessed life. Many do not know that it is God's will for them to be blessed and this is why they have to accept the guidance He gives and to surrender their will to His. You are a child of the living God and all things are possible to them that believe. Let faith explode in your inner man and believe God wants to bless your life and He wants to do it right now. Confess out loud what you believe for there is a miracle in your mouth waiting to be spoken into existence. When you latch onto the divine principles taught by Jesus, you can begin to anticipate that He is going to give you a blessed life and allow you to come up higher to the very presence of God. He wants to give you the joy of having a victorious life. He wants you to walk in health and prosperity, to have authority and power, and to be a positive influence in the world in which you live.

When you're blessed, you can have what the Bible says you can have and you can do what the Bible says you can do. It will happen because the power of God is in your life working on your behalf. You were born to be blessed because God is your Heavenly Father and He chose to bless you with blessings that will flow out of you, blessings that there shall not be room enough to contain them all. You were born to be blessed and you shall be a blessing. That is your destiny. The Greek word for "blessed" is "mararios" and is defined as 'the state of one who has become a partaker of God; to experience the fullness of God.' This word can also be translated as 'happy' but the way most people define happiness is not found in the Bible. People wrongly believe that they can only be happy if and when they experience some good luck or a favorable circumstance happens to them.

This is totally opposite of what Jesus taught for He said things like "Blessed are those who mourn" and "Blessed are those who are persecuted." The Beatitudes teach us that true happiness is not found in what we possess, achieve, or experience outwardly, but in who we are becoming inwardly. Jesus reveals that blessing flows from a heart shaped by humility, mercy, purity, and faith, regardless of external conditions. Lasting joy is born when our inner attitude aligns with God's values, not when our circumstances align with our preferences. The Greek word "Makarios" refers to the believer in Christ who is satisfied and secure in the midst of life's hardships because of the indwelling fullness of the Spirit of God. 1 Peter 4:14 says, "If you are reproached for the name of Christ, blessed are you, for the Spirit of glory and of God rests upon you." Those who are blessed are able to rejoice and celebrate in spite of their circumstances.

Jesus begins the Beatitudes by saying, "Blessed are the poor in spirit, for theirs is the kingdom of heaven" (Matt. 5:3). This is a divine pronouncement of truth. Jesus is saying that those who are poor in spirit can immediately partake of the kingdom of heaven right here and right now. He says this because this is where your journey with God begins. The only way that you will go to heaven is to realize that your spirit is completely bankrupt in the eyes of God. You can never be good enough or do enough good works to earn your way into heaven. You just can't get there on your own merit no matter how hard you try. Self-righteousness is the greatest enemy to happiness you'll ever have. It's rooted in pride and this was the original sin. Lucifer became prideful in heaven because of his beauty and later told Adam and Eve they could become like God if they would eat of the forbidden fruit. The problem with that is they were made in the image of God and were already like Him.

They were originally poor in spirit but lost it all when works of self-righteousness entered in. The greatest deception in life is to think you need nothing when the truth is you need everything. In Rev. 3:17 (MSG) Jesus condemned the church of Laodicea when He said, "You brag, 'I'm rich, I've got it made, I need nothing from anyone,' oblivious that in fact you're a pitiful, blind beggar, threadbare and homeless." King James says these people are "wretched, miserable, poor, blind, and naked." These words were not spoken to a group of unsaved sinners but to a church filled with born again believers. Because they had become self-righteous, Jesus said in vs. 16, "So then, because you are lukewarm, and neither cold nor hot, I will spew you out of My mouth." Indeed, the ultimate deception is to think you have everything when in fact you have nothing. This is why you need to become poor in spirit and believe that you are nothing without Christ.

Eph. 2:8,9 says, "For by grace you have been saved through faith, and that not of yourselves; it is the gift of God, not of works, lest anyone should boast." When you become poor in spirit, when Jesus becomes your everything, you will be blessed because now the kingdom of heaven is yours. The kingdom of heaven belongs to those who seek in Christ the sufficiency they do not find in themselves. It takes a humble person to admit they're poor in spirit but in the kingdom of God humility and greatness always go together. James 4:10 says, "Humble yourselves in the sight of the Lord, and He will lift you up." God will lift you up by giving you the kingdom of heaven and, when you possess God's kingdom, you possess all things. The kingdom of heaven includes planet Earth and when you become poor in spirit and get born again, there is nothing you can't have and nothing you can't own. The universe and all its glory belong to God and you are an heir to all that He has created.

Rom. 8:17 says the children of God are 'heirs of God and joint heirs with Christ." This means that what Jesus Christ gets, you get also. Ps. 24:1 (NLT) says, "The earth is the Lord's, and everything in it. The world and all its people belong to Him." When you surrendered your life to Jesus, you were not merely forgiven - you were adopted. God did not make you a servant standing at a distance; He made you a son or daughter brought fully into His family. Through Christ, you inherited the wealth of heaven's grace, the power of His Spirit, and the majesty of His eternal kingdom. What belongs to the Father is now made available to you - not as something earned, but as something lovingly given. Your identity changed, your authority shifted, and your future was secured. You now live from inheritance, not lack; from sonship, not striving; and from kingdom purpose, not earthly limitation.

When you realize that you are poor in spirit, you will mourn and repent for the life you once led. The good news is found in Matt. 5:4 where Jesus said, "Blessed are those who mourn, for they shall be comforted." All mourners are not blessed because not everybody has the same attitude about sin. Most people don't regret what they did, they only regret getting caught for doing it. A sexual sin was happening in the Corinthian church and nothing was being done about it. Paul reprimanded these people and wrote in 1 Cor. 5:2 (NLT), "You are so proud of yourselves, but you should be mourning in sorrow and shame. And you should remove this man from your fellowship." Never boast about your sin but have the same attitude as Isaiah who said, "Woe is me, for I am undone!" (Is. 6:5). The Message Bible says, "Doom! It's Doomsday! I'm as good as dead!" It is one thing to be spiritually poor, it is another to grieve and mourn over it.

Jesus is talking here about those who mourn the loss of their innocence, their righteousness, and their self-respect. It is the sorrow of a heart that is truly repentant before God. The world has become a free-for-all when it comes to sin. People sin at will and go so far as to protest to have laws passed that give them the legal right to commit the same sins that brought about the destruction of Sodom and Gomorrah. Worse than all that is this same attitude about sin has made its way into the local church. Born again believers don't seem to know right from wrong anymore and their hearts no longer feel sorrow when they do sin. For many, habitual sin has quietly become a way of life, dulling conviction and normalizing what once troubled the conscience. As a result, the outward evidence of transformation has grown so faint that there is little visible distinction between those who claim salvation and those who do not.

It is time for the children of God to break free from the bondage of sin and James 4:7-10 tells you what to do, "Therefore submit to God. Resist the devil and he will flee from you. Draw near to God and He will draw near to you. Cleanse your hands, you sinners; and purify your hearts, you double-minded. Lament and mourn and weep! Let your laughter be turned to mourning and your joy to gloom. Humble yourselves in the sight of the Lord and He will lift you up." When you humble yourself and mourn for your sin, the Lord will lift you up and bring comfort into your life. Just remember, there can be no comfort where there is no grief. David said in Ps. 34:18, "The Lord is near to the brokenhearted, and saves those who are crushed in spirit." People with broken hearts think God is far away from them when in truth He is as close as He ever has been. When in sorrow, look for the heart and hand of God for He is truly near.

He said in Is. 57:15 (NLT), "I live in the high and holy place with those whose spirits are contrite and humble. I restore the crushed spirit of the humble and revive the courage of those with repentant hearts." He also said in Joel 2:12, "Turn to Me with all your heart, with fasting, with weeping, and with mourning." When humble tears flow from a heart that is sorrowful, the good Lord will wipe those tears away and will draw you in and hold you close to His bosom. Ps. 30:5 says, "Weeping may endure for a night, but joy comes in the morning." Your tears may fall to the earth but a heart that is mournful will reach the heart of God. The blessings of the Beatitudes are for those who are realistic about their sinfulness, who are repentant of their sin, and who are responsive to God in His righteousness. Mourning because you are poor in spirit will produce in you a meekness that will give you strength that is under control.

Matt. 5:5 says, "Blessed are the meek, for they shall inherit the earth." The word "meek" comes from the Greek word "praus" and is always translated 'gentle.' A person's strength should always be in their gentleness. 1 Peter 3:4 says a gentle and quiet spirit is very precious in the sight of the Lord. In classical Greek, the word was used to describe a wild animal that has been tamed and is completely submissive and obedient to its master. Prov. 16:32 says, "He who is slow to anger is better than the mighty, and he who rules his spirit than he who takes a city." It is a word that is also used to describe a soothing medicine, a mild or soft word, a gentle voice or a gentle breeze. The person who is meek is strong because they are under the control of the Spirit of God. They are gentle, meek, and mild but exercise self-control which makes them strong as a lion in the kingdom of God.

Meekness is not weakness nor does it use its power for selfish purposes. Meekness is controlled strength that is completely surrendered to God's will and control. Gentleness is a fruit of the Spirit (Gal. 5:23) which means the strength and softness of the spirit of meekness is ultimately the spirit of Christ Himself. Jesus said in Matt. 11:29, "I am gentle and lowly in heart." Meekness always bows its knees at the throne of God and like Jesus you also should say, "Not my will, but Yours be done." The Greek word "praus" describes a person whose temper is always under complete control. Eph. 4:26 says, "Be angry, and do not sin." The meek person knows when to be angry and when not to be angry. Righteous anger is controlled and carefully directed and is not a careless and wild venting of emotions that does more harm than good. A meek person will control their anger and will never allow their anger to control them.

Since a meek person is not self-centered, their anger is not about that which happens to them but is rather a righteous anger at what is wrongly done to others. Jesus said the meek and only the meek will inherit the earth. David writes in Ps. 37:11 (NIV), "But the meek will inherit the land and enjoy peace and prosperity." A person who is truly meek is always satisfied in spite of their circumstances. God is your Provider and He will use your meekness to bring you health, prosperity, comfort, and safety. He will give you all things that pertain to life and godliness (2 Peter 1:3) and He will give you richly all things to enjoy (1 Tim. 6:17). The earth and all its fullness will be given to those who are strong enough to be gentle. The meek will find more pleasure in simple things than evil-doers in all their wealth. They're blessed by the beauty of the setting sun, the laughter of children, the melody of chirping birds, the fragrance of budding flowers, and the peace and tranquility of being in the presence of God.

The person who is meek gets the best out of life, both in the here and now and in the hereafter. Soon and very soon there will be a new heaven and a new earth (Rev. 21:1) where the meek will forever be with the Lord. A person who is meek will mourn over their sin and will seek to become like Jesus in every area of their life. If you will do that then you will be blessed because Jesus said in Matt. 5:6, "Blessed are those who hunger and thirst for righteousness, for they will be filled." The ICB says, "Those who want to do right more than anything else are happy. God will fully satisfy them." All people naturally want to be happy but most don't know what to do to be that way. The Lord tells them in Lev. 20:26 (MSG), "Live holy lives before Me because I, God, am holy. I have distinguished you from the nations to be My very own." The distinctive character of every true Christian is that they desire holiness "without which no one will see the Lord" (Heb. 12:14).

A hunger to be like Jesus is a blessed hunger and in the midst of this spiritual craving all fleshly desires die out. True godliness is found in the things you desire. David wrote in Ps. 191:20 (NLT), "I am always overwhelmed with a desire for Your regulations." The Message Bible says, "My soul is starved and hungry, ravenous! - insatiable for Your nourishing commands." You were born to be blessed and it will happen when all your desires are continually for the things of God. What you desire reveals what's in your heart and the spiritual appetite Jesus calls for is the desire to be like Him. When you hunger and thirst for righteousness there will be a desperation in your heart that will not be satisfied with a shallow knowledge of God or a minimal improvement in moral conduct. No, the call to holiness is radical and David went on to say, "I opened my mouth and panted, for I longed for Your commandments" (Ps. 11:131).

Does this describe you? Is your life marked by a deep, burning desire to truly know God, to walk in joyful obedience to His Word, and to reflect His heart more each day? This holy longing is the evidence of a soul being drawn closer to Him, shaped daily into His likeness. Is your heart panting to be conformed to the image of Jesus, longing not just to believe in Him, but to become like Him? If so, then rejoice for your hunger will be satisfied and you will know the fullness of all He has promised to bless you with. True transformation is born from surrender, where your desires are reshaped and your character is refined through daily obedience and faith. When Christ becomes the measure of your life, your heart will learn to hunger for holiness more than comfort. You will be filled and will keep on being filled with the goodness of God. Luke 1:53 says, "He has filled the hungry with good things, and the rich He has sent away empty."

Jesus then said in Matt. 6:7, "Blessed are the merciful, for they shall obtain mercy." God has been merciful to you and now you are being merciful to others. When you do that, God will cause you to come up to a higher level of living where you can literally experience heaven on earth. Those who are merciful are actively compassionate to others in thought, word, and deed. The Greek word "eleemon" means 'to give help to the wretched, to relieve the miserable.' Mercy gives help and attention to those in misery and does something to alleviate the distress. Being merciful is important for it shows that you are becoming more and more like the Lord. When the fountain of your heart is full of mercy you will feel sorrow over someone else's bad situation and will try to do something about it. Feeling sorry for somebody by itself is not mercy for mercy always moves from feelings to action.

James 2:15,16 says, "If a brother or sister is naked and destitute of daily food, and one of you says to them, 'Depart in peace, be warmed and filled,' but you do not give them the things which are needed for the body, what does it profit?" Nowhere do you imitate God more than in showing mercy to someone else. Mercy reflects the very heart of God - His willingness to extend compassion and offer grace where it is undeserved. When you choose mercy, you step beyond instinct and self-interest and align yourself with divine character. Mercy listens before condemning, restores instead of discarding, and heals rather than wounds. It sees people not merely as they are, but as they can become through love and patience. In moments when you forgive instead of retaliating, help instead of ignoring, and show kindness instead of harshness, you become a living reflection of God's nature. Mercy is strength guided by love, and through it, God's presence is made visible in everyday human relationships.

The good Samaritan showed mercy when he stopped to help the Jewish man who had been beaten and stripped by robbers (Luke 10:30-37). Mercy stops and stoops toward one who has nothing to offer the giver and has never shown favor to the one giving the mercy. Mercy is love in action and when you show mercy to the poor, the wretched, and the guilty it shows that you are like God. The good news is that what you make happen for others, God will make happen for you. Mercy is the manifestation of the righteousness of Christ in the child of God that opens a life to the blessings of God. Ps. 18:25 says, "With the merciful You will show Yourself merciful." Those who are merciful will receive God's mercy. What Jesus is saying in this Beatitude is that as God pours out His rich mercies on you, you will respond by showing mercy to others which in turn causes you to receive more mercy from God. You will have more than you had at the beginning and that is called a blessed life.

When you begin to be merciful to other people, you will then be pure in heart. Matt. 7:8 says, "Blessed are the pure in heart, for they shall see God." The Greek word for "pure" is "katharos" and means 'to be clean and unmixed; without blemish; spotless.' The pure in heart are those who walk with integrity, remaining true in their thoughts, motives, and actions. Their hearts are not divided between truth and compromise but fully aligned with what is right and pleasing to God. They exhibit single mindedness, undivided devotion, and a spirit that is incorruptible. They have a heart that is unmixed in its devotion and motivation. When a person gets born again, God does more than wash away their sins and make them His children. He also puts within them a new heart that wants to focus wholly on Him. Jer. 32:39 (NLT) says, "And I will give them one heart and one purpose: to worship Me forever, for their own good and for the good of all their descendants."

The problem in the church today is that in this wild and hectic world very few believers are capable of the spiritual attention this Beatitude calls for. They want to serve the Lord and follow the world at the same time. They are double-minded and unstable in all their ways" (James 1:8). Focusing on God with singleness of heart is one of the biggest challenges for modern day believers. Yet, because the end is so near, this is the one thing that needs to be done more than anything else. Double-mindedness has always been one of the great plagues of the church and this is why you need to wake up each morning and totally surrender your life to Him. David wrote in Ps. 63:1, "O God, You are my God; Early will I seek You; My soul thirsts for You; My flesh longs for You in a dry and thirsty land where there is no water." The Message Bible says, "God - you're my God! I can't get enough of You!"

These are the words of a man who was pure in heart. David was a man after God's own heart and you should be also.

It was David who wrote, "Create in me a clean heart, O God, and renew a steadfast spirit within me" (Ps. 51:10). God is more interested in what you are on the inside than what you do for Him on the outside. He said in 1 Sam. 16:7, "For the Lord does not see as man sees; for man looks at the outward appearance, but the Lord looks at the heart." If people do good things without a pure heart then what they do is virtually worthless. A pure heart is to be the control center for all things that pertain to your life. Prov. 4:23 (GW) says, "Guard your heart more than anything else, because the source of your life flows from it." God wants you to be pure in heart because your heart is the root of all your actions. From your heart comes your motives, desires, and emotions. Jesus said the pure in heart shall see God because He will reveal Himself to those who obey, and only the pure in heart obey. It is only those with a pure heart who will experience the reality of His presence within.

You should be motivated to stop being so busy, recognizing that constant distraction can quietly erode the purity of your heart. God reserves intimate knowledge and deep fellowship with Him for those who guard their inner life and make space for His presence. When you slow down and choose purity over busyness, you open yourself to a closer, clearer walk with Him. With a pure heart, you dwell in the presence of God, where His peace, truth, and love continually surround you. Purity of heart opens the way for deeper intimacy with Him, allowing your life to reflect His light in every moment. You'll realize He is there beside you and you'll hear His voice. You'll enjoy greater intimacy with Him than you could have ever imagined. You will also see Him at work in your circumstances. Your needs will be met and all your problems will be solved. You'll be blessed on the inside as well as on the outside.

When you are merciful to other people out of a pure heart, you'll begin to help them make peace with God and with those around them. This will cause you to be abundantly blessed for Jesus said in Matt. 5:9, "Blessed are the peacemakers, for they shall be called sons of God." The first thing you need to understand is that without God, there is no peace. He is the author of peace (1 Cor. 14;33) and Jesus is called the Prince of Peace (Is. 9:6). Man simply can not produce peace on his own. Almost four billion people have died as the result of war and in all recorded history there has only been 268 years where there has been no war someplace on the planet. Clearly mankind is in need of a peacemaker but first it will help to know what peace is. Most people think peace is the absence of conflict but the Bible describes peace as the presence of righteousness. With Jesus in your heart you can be in the midst of turmoil and still have peace. Jesus is righteousness and peace comes from His presence in your life.

Peace is knowing Jesus and allowing Him to direct your steps. If you have no peace in a certain area of your life, you need to bring Jesus into that situation. Who are the peacemakers? Paul said in 2 Cor. 5:18, "Now all things are of God, who has reconciled us to Himself through Jesus Christ, and has given us the ministry of reconciliation." The word "reconcile" means to 'restore friendly relations between; cause to coexist in harmony; make or show to be compatible; to make peace.' Paul is saying that the peacemakers are those who have made peace with God. If you're born again and have made peace with God, you have been given the responsibility in the kingdom to be a peacemaker. 2 Cor. 5:20 says, "Therefore we are ambassadors for Christ, as though God were pleading through us: we implore you on Christ's behalf, be reconciled to God." You are an appointed representative of the God of peace and you have been called to be a peacemaker.

A person will never come to a knowledge of salvation without the intervention of a peacemaker. You will be blessed as you go out into the world to seek and to save those who are lost. Is. 52:7 says, "How beautiful upon the mountains are the feet of him who brings good news, who proclaim salvation, who says to Zion, 'Your God reigns!'" A peacemaker is a person who brings Jesus into a situation. James 3:18 says, "Now the fruit of righteousness is sown in peace by those who make peace." With Jesus on the scene, people in conflict will turn toward each other and embrace one another in spite of their differences. A peacemaker will help bind or join together that which is broken or divided. Peacemakers manifest themselves as sons of God for they are engaged in the very work that the God of peace is doing. Their primary goal is not to avoid conflict but rather to resolve conflict. Jesus is saying blessed are those who work for and do the things that make for peace.

The way of the peacemaker is not a retreat into silence or avoidance, but an intentional, active engagement in the sacred work of restoration. True peacemaking steps into the tension, listens with humility, speaks with wisdom, and labors patiently to mend what has been torn apart. It recognizes that unity rarely happens by accident; it must be pursued with courage, compassion, and perseverance. Rather than choosing sides or withdrawing for self-preservation, the peacemaker seeks common ground, confronts injustice with love, and builds bridges where walls once stood. It is hard enough to keep the peace; it is even more difficult to bring peace where it is not. This is why peacemakers have to be aggressive in what they're doing and not take the weak-kneed approach. Nobody said this was easy but those who have the courage to do it will receive a special blessing of being called the sons of God.

When you come up higher and decide to fulfill your destiny at all costs, you can count on the fact that you will be persecuted. This is why Jesus said in Matt. 5:10, "Blessed are those who are persecuted for righteousness' sake, for theirs is the kingdom of heaven." The Message Bible says, "You're blessed when your commitment to God provokes persecution. The persecution drives you deeper into the kingdom." That is indeed good news for Jesus went on to say in vs. 12, "Rejoice and be exceedingly glad, for great is your reward in heaven, for so they persecuted the prophets who were before you." Jesus is saying you're in good company when you get persecuted for being and doing right. Just stop and consider what they did to Him. Paul said in Phil. 3:10 (NLT), "I want to know Christ and experience the mighty power that raised Him from the dead. I want to suffer with Him, sharing in His death."

Peter wrote, "Dear friends, don't be surprised at the fiery trials you are going through, as if something strange were happening to you. Instead, be very glad for these trials make you partners with Christ in His suffering" (1 Peter 4:12,13 NLT). It is important for new believers to grasp the reality of persecution early so they don't get discouraged when it does happen. They can't be disillusioned by thinking those who show mercy to others and are pure in heart will be welcomed with open arms. The truth of the matter is that those who walk the straight and narrow way will be persecuted by those who walk the broad and crooked way that leads to destruction. Jesus is the light of the world and His light shining in and through you will expose the evil nature of their words and actions. You will be persecuted for this because "men loved darkness rather than light" (John 3:19). If you're not currently being persecuted for His Name's sake then you probably soon will be if you truly belong to Him.

Jesus said it would happen so get ready for it. He also said in John 16:33, "These things I have spoken to you, that in Me you may have peace. In the world you will have tribulation; but be of good cheer, I have overcome the world." Just remember the truth that you are blessed even when you don't feel blessed. Jesus said you are so stand on the truth of what He said. Those who are poor in spirit and those who are persecuted have the same blessing. Jesus said "for theirs is the kingdom of heaven." This blessing is in the present tense for all kingdom citizens have already entered into the Lord's kingdom. Jesus prayed, "Your kingdom come, Your will be done on earth, as it is in heaven" (Matt. 6:10). All the blessings of heaven can be experienced right now by those who are citizens of the kingdom. The only difference is that they will be higher and more pure and glorious in the ages to come.

The kingdom of heaven becomes present in your life when your will bows in humble surrender before the King of kings and Lord of lords. As self is dethroned and Christ is exalted, His authority, peace, and righteousness begin to rule your heart. Where He reigns, heaven's order, power, and purpose are made manifest on earth. Only those who cast off self-will and self-reliance make room for God's rule in their lives. In surrender, pride gives way to trust, and independence is replaced with humble obedience. True citizenship in God's kingdom begins where self ends and faith fully yields to His will. The kingdom is given to be entered into and the persecution you experience as a child of God will only make your continual possession of His kingdom more vivid and more joyous. Persecution gives you hope for a better future and thus becomes infinitely sweet and blessed. When people revile and say all kinds of evil things against you, leap for joy for yours is the kingdom of heaven.

| 30 |

"TO LIVE IS CHRIST"

There is a verse in the Bible that is so radical that if you could grasp its full meaning it would change your life forever. Most people skim over this portion of scripture without latching onto the importance of what's being said. Don't let this happen to you. With an open mind and a heart that is attentive read carefully the words of 1 John 4:17, "As He is, so are we in this world." Was your heart captivated by what you just read? Are you enraptured by what God is saying to you right now? The Message Bible says, "Our standing in the world is identical with Christ's." If you are born again, then positionally speaking you are right now "as He is." This means that you are so closely identified with Christ as members of His body that your position in this world is like His exalted position in heaven. This means that the Father will deal with you just as He deals with His own beloved Son. In other words, what Jesus gets, you get also. If that don't make you jump and shout then nothing will.

There are few things that will have deeper significance to you than the statement that says as Jesus is, so are you in this world. Jesus is the Son of God and so are you. As Jesus is loved by the Heavenly Father with an everlasting and unchangeable love, so are you loved with the same kind of love. Jesus pleased the Father in everything He did, so can you please the Father in everything you do. Jesus walked in divine health and so can you. All His needs were met and so also can all your needs be met. Jesus was blessed abundantly by the Father and then there was the ultimate blessing of all blessings. Jesus said in Rev. 1:18, "I am He who lives, and was dead, and behold, I am alive forevermore." Just as Jesus was raised from the dead and lives forevermore, so also have you won the victory over death, hell, and the grave and will live in the presence of God for all eternity.

The only hope you have of ever going to heaven is in the fact that Jesus died for your sins and arose from the dead three days later. And because you are as He is, you also will be raised up to life eternal. Paul wrote in 1 Cor. 15:57, "But thanks be to God, who gives us the victory through our Lord Jesus Christ." This is a popular verse that believers quote during times of trial and hardship. Indeed, it is a good verse and should be quoted often. However, there is a primary application of what Paul is saying God gives you the victory over here in this chapter. The entire chapter is talking about the resurrection of the dead. Consider vs. 20-22 (NLT), "But in fact, Christ has been raised from the dead. He is the first of a great harvest of all who have died. So you see, just as death came into the world through a man, now the resurrection from the dead has begun through another man. Just as everyone dies because we all belong to Adam, everyone who belongs to Christ will be given new life."

Vs. 54,55 (NLT) goes on to say, "Then, when our dying bodies have been transformed into bodies that will never die, this scripture will be fulfilled: 'Death is swallowed up in victory. O death, where is your victory? O death, where is your sting?'" It is then that Paul writes vs. 57 (NLT), "But thank God! He gives us victory over sin and death through our Lord Jesus Christ." Death is not your friend. It is an enemy and Paul says in vs. 25,26, "For He must reign till He has put all enemies under His feet. The last enemy that will be destroyed is death." Man was created to live forever and it's only because of sin that death is in the world. The good news is that soon and very soon God's original plan for man will be fulfilled. Death will be done away with and all of God's people will live forevermore in glorious splendor. People won't die, animals won't die, and the grass, trees, and flowers won't die.

Vs. 42-44 says, "So also is the resurrection of the dead. The body is sown in corruption, it is raised in incorruption. It is sown in dishonor, it is raised in glory. It is sown in weakness, it is raised in power. It is sown a natural body, it is raised a spiritual body." Remember, what Jesus gets, you get also. Phil. 3:21 (NLT) says, "He will take our weak mortal bodies and change them into glorious bodies like His own, using the same power with which He will bring everything under His control." The Message Bible says, "He'll make us beautiful and whole with the same powerful skill by which He is putting everything as it should be, under and around Him." Believers have the assurance that their sins are forgiven because of the Lord's death on the cross and they have the assurance of the glorification of their bodies because of His resurrection. It is the empty tomb that makes possible the future transformation Paul is describing.

Because you are "as He is," you will be given the same type of glorified body Jesus had when He stepped triumphantly out of that tomb. He was not limited by time or space for He could appear one moment in Jerusalem and the next in Galilee. His body was not restricted by the physical realm for He was able to walk through walls when all other means of entrance were sealed. Jesus ate food even though His glorified body was not dependent on food. Most of all, your new body will permit you to be completely who God created you to be and this will allow you to enjoy perfect fellowship with Him forever. Imagine being like Jesus for all eternity. 1 John 3:2 (NLT) says, "Dear friends, we are already God's children, but He has not yet shown us what we will be like when Christ appears. But we do know that we will be like Him, for we will see Him as He really is."

In all of recorded history, there has nothing been written that is as majestic and awe-inspiring as 1 John 3:2. To be told in the Bible that you will one day be like Jesus should leave you standing in wonder and amazement. You need to take this one verse and meditate on it day after day after day. Don't read it only one time and forget about it five minutes later. No, read it until it becomes a part of you, until it's all you ever think about. Doing so will be an enriching experience for you for it will take you up to the highest realms of glory and never bring you back to mediocre thinking. What's more, John is saying that you are a child of God right now, not just in the future when you go to heaven. This alone should transform your thinking and radically impact your life each and every day. You must fight to keep from forgetting that you are now God's beloved child so that you might conduct yourself in a manner worthy of the children of the King.

As wonderful as being a child of God is today, your future with Him will be even more extraordinary. Rejoice that you are now a child of God but what 1 John 3:2 is telling you is that the best is yet to come. 1 Cor. 2:9 says, "Eye has not seen, nor ear heard, nor have entered into the heart of man the things which God has prepared for those who love Him." Take advantage of the eternal life you already have but with joy unspeakable look forward to what's about to happen. Rom. 8:18,19 (MSG) says, "That's why I don't think there's any comparison between the present hard times and the coming good times. The created world itself can hardly wait for what's coming next." The glories of the new heaven and the new earth are beyond human imagination for they are being prepared for you by Jesus Himself (John 14:2,3). No more will there be any limitations that are currently being imposed on you in this physical world.

For all eternity all the desires of your heart will be fulfilled but, still, that is not the greatest blessing of heaven. The ultimate blessing is that Jesus will be there and to see Him as He is will be the greatest experience of your eternal existence. 1 Cor. 15:51-53 (NLT) says, "But let me reveal to you a wonderful secret. We will not all die, but we will all be transformed! It will happen in a moment, in the blink of an eye, when the last trumpet is blown. For when the trumpet sounds, those who have died will be raised to live forever. And we who are living will also be transformed. For our dying bodies must be transformed into bodies that will never die; our mortal bodies must be transformed into immortal bodies." Soon and very soon God is going to give you a glorified body that can once and for all keep up with your recreated spirit. It is then that Paul says "death is swallowed up in victory."

The Message Bible says, "Death swallowed by triumphant Life! Who got the last word, oh, Death? Oh, Death, who's afraid of you now?" Thank God today for He has given you the victory over death through the Lord Jesus Christ. No longer does the fear of death have to keep you in bondage all the days of your life. The truth is, you will never live a free life here on the earth until you are no longer afraid to die. Why fear something that is the doorway to living in the physical presence of God forevermore? Let's face it, everybody dies. Even at the rapture people will die to the way they currently live. David calls death "the way of the earth" (1 Kings 2:2). Somewhere in the world two people die every second. That averages out to 120 every minute, 7200 every hour, over 172,000 every day, and over 63 million every year. Death is a common occurrence yet most people are afraid to think about it or talk about it.

They're in bondage because deep in their heart they know they haven't lived in such a way that death would be gain to them. Their fear and dread will warp their life and stop them from doing what they've been called to do. Freeing people from the fear of death is the reason Jesus came to the earth. Heb. 2:14,15 (NLT) says, "Because God's children are human beings - made of flesh and blood - the Son also became flesh and blood. For only as a human being could He die, and only by dying could He break the power of the devil, who had the power of death. Only in this way could He set free all who have lived their lives as slaves to the fear of dying." You are not ready and fit to live until you are ready and unafraid to die. When you're not afraid to die, you will come up higher and receive supernatural boldness, courage, and confidence to live life at the highest level.

The curtain of fear no longer surrounds you and you'll have the backbone to do whatever God tells you to do. You'll have the daring determination to fulfill your destiny no matter what roadblocks the enemy may try to put across your path. You're standing on the promise found in Ps. 91:16, "With long life I will satisfy him, and show him My salvation." You need to understand that your attitude about death determines how you live your life and will affect every decision you make. Those who are afraid to fly are not afraid of airplanes, they're afraid of dying in a plane crash. People aren't afraid of heights, they're afraid of falling and dying. The fear of death is holding them in bondage for they believe dying is the worst thing that could happen to them. Not so for the born again believer. Paul said it best in Phil. 1:21, "For to me, to live is Christ, and to die is gain."

Paul had been saved for thirty years when He made this glorious declaration of his passion for Christ. After all this time and everything he had gone through, Paul was still hopelessly addicted to the presence of Jesus in his life. The GWT says, "Christ means everything to me in this life, and when I die I'll have even more." This was the key verse in this epistle and should be the key verse in your life as well. You have a purpose for living and that purpose is to glorify God and live for Him. Every aspect of your life must be centered around the Lord Jesus Christ. Paul said in Col. 1:9,10 (NLT), "We ask God to give you complete knowledge of His will and to give you spiritual wisdom and understanding. Then the way you live will always honor and please the Lord, and your lives will produce every kind of good fruit. All the while, you will grow as you learn to know God better and better."

The Lord needs to be the essence of all your life and you need to grow daily in your experience with Him so that He becomes your all in all. You need to live in such a way that you have no conception of life apart from Him. When you're not afraid to die you are free to focus on things that really matter. You'll be consumed with doing God's will and living totally for Him. Paul was absorbed in his living for Christ, and this is why he could say with all confidence "to die is gain." The world sees death as the end of all things and the loss of all for which one has lived. Nothing could be farther from the truth for the born-again believer. Paul is saying that if you'll live your life wholly and fully devoted to the Lord then death is the entrance to gain, not the exit from living. Also, the more fully your life is devoted to Jesus and the fulfillment of your destiny, the greater your gain will be in heaven.

When you pass on to the other side you will live a life of freedom and abundance with the joyous experience of being completely like Christ. Paul knew that death is not a defeat to the born-again believer but is in fact a graduation to the realm of glory. In heaven you'll have a perfect, eternal, and glorious union with Christ unhindered by the world, the flesh, and the devil. Paul knew that at the moment of his death he would be in the presence of Christ and that would truly be gain for him. The word "gain" means to get more of the same thing so if to live is Christ, then to die would be to get more of Him. Your thoughts and opinions should change when you realize that death doesn't take you to a cemetery but to a sanctuary. The word "gain" is also a monetary term that means to make a profit on an investment. Paul invested his life in serving the Lord and when he passed on to the other side he exchanged the burden of earthly life for the eternal joy of heaven.

The question to be asked is what are you living for? Most people live for fortune and fame and work themselves into an early grace. Many live for an early retirement so they can play golf, travel, tend to a garden, watch TV, and grow old together with all their friends. For these people, for sure, death will be the loss of all things. But for those who live for Jesus, in death they will gain a release from suffering and sin, a reward for service rendered unto the Lord, and a happy reunion with Jesus and all other saints in heaven. Life is what you are alive to. The thing that excites you is the thing that is life to you. In Paul's case, Christ was his life. Jesus excited him and made his life worth living. For him, to live is Christ, to die is gain. How about you? Some people hold on so tightly to this present life and are in such fear of letting go of what they have that they become slaves to their mortality. They don't realize that all the things they lived for will not remain after their death.

All their possessions will be given to others, and their fame will soon be forgotten. They died and had nothing to show for the life they lived. What a tragedy. Paul, on the other hand, lived for Christ and he didn't fear dying because he knew death was the vehicle that would take him home to be in the presence of God forevermore. Paul saw death as the door to eternal life thus freeing him to live with purpose, meaning, and commitment to the cause of Christ. Because he was ready to die, he was able to really live. He lived for Christ and was confident of his eternal destination. Life is passing by faster than people can grasp onto it. James asks, "For what is your life? It is even a vapor that appears for a little time and then vanishes away" (James 4:14). Doesn't it seem like only yesterday you were a young child and now here you are an adult getting older and older by the day? David wrote, "Man is like a breath; His days are like a passing shadow" (Ps. 144:4).

What's being said here is if you're not living for Christ today that the swift current of time passing by may not give you the opportunity to do so. Solomon understood this when he wrote in Eccl. 1:2 says, "Life is fleeting, like a passing mist. It is like trying to catch hold of a breath; All vanishes like a vapor; Everything is a great vanity." You need to realize that if your destiny is not being fulfilled then vanity is all there is to life. You have to stop being so consumed with the affairs of this world that you forget to remember God and His purpose for creating you in the first place. Your life matters to Him and you need to make right choices or else life for you will be meaningless. Come up higher and live for Jesus for to live is Christ, to die is gain. Be aware that those who wait until tomorrow usually die today and then it will be too late. There is no lasting good in the world today and a person's stay here is too brief for them to reap any real advantage from all their hard toil.

Without Jesus all satisfaction vanishes and gets replaced with discouragement, despair, and disappointment. The mind of man craves for something permanent and progressive and this is found only when one actually pursues the fulfillment of their destiny. Only a life devoted to pleasing God can remove the sorrow and perplexity that comes with only seeking worldly pleasures. Solomon asks, "What profit has a man from all his labor in which he toils under the sun?" (Eccl. 1:3). Everything is temporal and no person or pursuit in and of itself will bring lasting satisfaction. It will be without substance, value, permanence, or significance. Solomon is trying to shock you out of complacency and get you to realize that life only has meaning, stability, and durability when it is devoted to Christ. The truth be told, percentage-wise very few people will fully live for Christ and fulfill their heavenly call. Good help is just too hard to find. It's true in the natural world and especially true in the kingdom of God.

Matt. 9:35-38 says, "And Jesus went about all the cities and villages, teaching in their synagogues, preaching the gospel of the kingdom and healing every sickness and every disease among the people. But when he saw the multitudes He was moved with compassion for them because they were weary and scattered like sheep having no shepherd. Then He said to His disciples, 'The harvest truly is plentiful but the laborers are few. Therefore pray the Lord of the harvest to send out laborers into His harvest.'" Jesus said "the laborers are few." Since the beginning of time this has been a stark reality and an intense search has always had to be made to find "a worker who does not need to be ashamed" (2 Tim. 2:15). God said in Ezek. 22:30, "So I sought for a man among them who would make a wall and stand in the gap before

Me on behalf of the land that I should not destroy it; but I found no one."

To live for Christ and be a servant of the Lord takes diligence, sacrifice, and a willingness to lay down one's own plans and desires in order to fulfill the will of the Master. In truth, the majority of believers don't have what it takes to be a servant of God and are content to step back and let others take on the responsibility of doing the work of the ministry. For these people the requirements of living for Christ are too high for it comes with a price they are unwilling to pay. Jesus said to the rich young ruler, "If you want to be perfect, go, sell what you have and give to the poor, and you will have treasure in heaven; and come follow Me." When the young man heard that saying he went away sorrowful for he had great possessions" (Matt. 19:21,22). Indeed, good help is hard to find. Paul gives a detailed yet unlikely description of the person God takes delight in using to fulfill His will and purpose on earth.

1 Cor. 1:26-28 says, "For you see your calling, brethren, that not many wise according to the flesh, not many mighty, not many noble are called. But God has chosen the foolish things of the world to put to shame the things that are mighty; and the base things of the world and the things which are despised God has chosen." The Message Bible puts it this way, "Take a good look, friends, at who you were when you got called into this life. I don't see many of 'the brightest and the best' among you, not many influential, not many from high society families. Isn't it obvious that God deliberately chose men and women that the culture overlooks and exploits and abuses, chose these 'nobodies' to expose the hollow pretensions of the 'somebodies'?" According to Paul, God delights in choosing people who are not highly educated or gifted with special insight and enlightenment according to worldly standards.

Rarely does He call those who are from the high class of society but instead chooses those from a normal, average background. Elisha was a farmer while Moses and David were both shepherds. Of the twelve disciples, one was a tax collector, another a thief, and several were smelly fishermen. God uses people the world will never recognize. Movie stars, big name athletes, stockbrokers, bankers, and those of high prestige and royalty are almost never called to be used by God. Instead, God calls those who are considered insignificant and despised by the world. Is. 53:3 says that even Jesus was "despised and rejected by men." Whom the world rejects and throws away, God does not discard - He redeems and repurposes. What others overlook or label as broken, God chooses as evidence of His grace and power. In His hands, the rejected become the called, and the forgotten become vessels of lasting impact.

A better and more detailed rendering of what Paul is saying to the Corinthian church is this, "For you see your calling, brothers, how not many of you were especially bright, educated, or enlightened according to the world's standards. Not many of you were impressive. Not many of you came from high-ranking families or from the upper crust of society. Instead, God selected people who are idiots in the world's view; yet God is using them to utterly confound those who seem smart in the world's eyes. God has picked out people who are laughable; yet through them, He is confounding those who think they are high and mighty. Low-class, second-rate, common, average. These are the ones God has chosen." The word "chosen" is a compound of two Greek words which literally means "Out! I say!" God says you are to separate yourself and come out from the world.

When you do that, you will become "a chosen generation, a royal priesthood, a holy nation, His own special people, that you may proclaim the praises of Him Who called you out of darkness into His marvelous light" (1 Peter 2:9). Many people pull away from the privilege of serving God because in and of themselves they do not feel qualified to do so. For the most part, these people are correct in their thinking. They are not qualified and this is the exact reason God called them. Paul writes in 2 Cor. 3:5,6, "Not that we are sufficient of ourselves to think of anything as being from ourselves, but our sufficiency is from God Who also made us sufficient as ministers of the new covenant." Those who are qualified run the risk of taking credit for what God does through them thus robbing God of all the glory. This is a dangerous thing to do for Jesus said in John 15:5, "I am the vine, you are the branches. He who abides in Me, and I in him, bears much fruit for without Me you can do nothing."

This being so, a servant of God must therefore be teachable and have a hunger to fulfill the will of God. Prov. 16:26 says that the laborer's appetite works for him and his hunger drives him on. Jesus said in Matt. 5:6, "Blessed are those who hunger and thirst for righteousness for they will be filled." A lazy and self-satisfied person will rarely be motivated to work but a person who is hungry for the things of God will be motivated to seek a course of action that will help fulfill and meet the need. David revealed that he had a servant's heart when he wrote in Ps. 25:4,5, "Show me Your ways, O Lord; Teach me Your paths. Lead me in Your truth and teach me for You are the God of my salvation; On You I wait all the day." Solomon also testified that good help is hard to find when he wrote, "Most men will proclaim their own goodness, but who can find a faithful man?" (Prov. 20:6).

To be a servant of God one must die to self and put aside their personal agendas and choose to live a life for a cause much more noble than their own self interests. Without much outside motivation a faithful person keeps moving forward each day driven by their mission and the Word of God in their heart. They do not grow weary in doing well as they perform the same righteous tasks day in and day out. A faithful person will never give up as they look for opportunities to serve and witness because of their love for Jesus and the Word of God. God is looking for a few good men and women, those who are faithful and willing to do whatever it takes to get the job done. In Matt. 20:16 Jesus concluded the parable of the laborers by making what could be considered a shocking statement. He said, "For many are called but few chosen." A careful study will reveal that, in truth, all believers are called to be laborers for God (Rom. 8:30). You get chosen only if and when you respond to the call that is on your life.

To do this, you must first and foremost have a willing heart and a surrendered mind, always ready to obey the voice of the Lord. True obedience flows from a posture of humility, where trust in His direction outweighs personal desire and fear. In Judges 4 God used the prophetess Deborah and the warrior Barak to defeat the army of the Canaanites. Afterward they sang a song of victory which began with these words, "When leaders lead in Israel, when the people willingly offer themselves, bless the Lord." Simply put, God chooses those who are ready and willing to work for Him, hearts fully surrendered to His purpose. He calls men and women who will answer without hesitation, even when obedience demands sacrifice and unwavering faith. True calling is proven not by comfort, but by a steadfast commitment to follow Him no matter the cost. Those who do can rightfully be called "the chosen few." For them, to live is Christ, to die is gain.

SUMMARY

The journey of coming up higher is not a destination reached in a single moment - it is a lifelong invitation to walk in ever-deepening relationship with the Triune God. Throughout this book, we have explored the truth that abundant life is not a future promise alone, nor a reward reserved for a select few, but the natural outflow of intimacy with the Father, union with the Son, and daily dependence upon the Holy Spirit.

God has never called His people to live beneath their redemptive potential. From creation to redemption, His purpose has remained consistent: that humanity would reflect His glory, walk in His authority, and flourish according to His design. The abundant life Jesus promised is not accidental - it is intentional, relational, and rooted in alignment with heaven.

To come up higher is to reject a shallow, distant faith and embrace a life of closeness with God. It is choosing relationship over routine, transformation over information, and obedience over convenience. As believers learn to abide in Christ, listen to the Spirit, and trust the Father's heart, abundance ceases to be something pursued and becomes something produced.

This higher life is not defined by the absence of challenges, but by the presence of God in the midst of them. It is marked by peace that steadies the soul, wisdom that guides decisions, strength that endures trials, and fruitfulness that glorifies God. Success, in its truest sense, is not measured by worldly acclaim, but by faithful stewardship of what God has entrusted to us and faithful fulfillment of His purpose through our lives.

You were created to succeed not through self-reliance, but through divine partnership. When your life is aligned with the Triune God, success becomes the natural expression of obedience, faith, and intimacy. The Father establishes your identity, the Son secures your victory, and the Holy Spirit empowers your daily walk. Together, they invite you to live above limitation and beneath heaven's open door.

As you close this book, the invitation remains. God is still calling you upward—into deeper relationship, greater trust, and fuller expression of the abundant life He designed for you. The climb is not burdensome when walked with Him, and the view from higher ground reveals a life shaped not by fear or failure, but by faith, purpose, and divine success.

The call is clear. The way is open. The invitation stands. Come up higher.